Ethnicity and Territory
in the Former Soviet Union

THE CASS SERIES IN REGIONAL AND FEDERAL STUDIES
ISSN 1363-5670
General Editor: John Loughlin

This series brings together some of the foremost academics and theorists to examine the timely subject of regional and federal issues, which since the mid-1980s have become key questions in political analysis and practice all over the world.

The Political Economy of Regionalism
edited by Michael Keating and John Loughlin

The Regional Dimension of the European Union:
Towards a Third Level in Europe?
edited by Charlie Jeffery

Remaking the Union: Devolution and British Politics in the 1990s
edited by Howard Elcock and Michael Keating

Paradiplomacy in Action: The Foreign Relations of Subnational Governments
edited by Francisco Aldecoa and Michael Keating

The Federalization of Spain *by Luis Moreno*

Ethnicity and Territory in the Former Soviet Union: Regions in Conflict
edited by James Hughes and Gwendolyn Sasse

Local Power, Territory and Institutions in European Metropolitan Regions
edited by Bernard Jouve and Christian Lefèvre

ETHNICITY AND TERRITORY IN THE FORMER SOVIET UNION: REGIONS IN CONFLICT

Edited by

JAMES HUGHES
and
GWENDOLYN SASSE

FRANK CASS
LONDON • PORTLAND, OR.

First published in 2002 in Great Britain by
FRANK CASS PUBLISHERS
2 Park Square, Milton Park, Abingdon, Oxon, OX14 4RN

and in the United States of America by
FRANK CASS PUBLISHERS
270 Madison Ave,
New York NY 10016

Transferred to Digital Printing 2005

Website http://www.frankcass.com

Copyright ©2002 Frank Cass & Co. Ltd.

British Library Cataloguing in Publication Data

Ethnicity and territory in the former Soviet Union :
regions in conflict. – (The Cass series in regional and
federal studies)
1. Ethnicity – Former Soviet republics 2. Territory, National
– Former Soviet republics 3. Former Soviet republics –
Politics and government
I. Hughes, James, 1959– II. Sasse, Gwendolyn
320. 1'2'0947
            ISBN 0 7146 5226 1 (cloth)
            ISBN 0 7146 8210 1 (paper)
            ISSN 1363-5670

Library of Congress Cataloging-in-Publication Data:

Ethnicity and territory in the former Soviet Union : regions in conflict.
/edited by James Hughes and Gwendolyn Sasse.
    p. cm. – (The Cass series in regional and federal studies, ISSN
1363-5670)
Includes bibliographical references and index.
ISBN 0-7146-5226-1 (cloth). – ISBN 0-7146-8210-1 (pbk.)
1. Ethnic conflict – Former Soviet republics. 2. Ethnic
conflict – Former Soviet republics – Case studies. 3. Former Soviet
republics – Ethnic relations. 4. Post-communism – Former Soviet
republics. 5. Democractization – Former Soviet republics. I. Hughes,
James, 1959– . II,. Sasse, Gwendolyn, 1972– . III. Series.
    DK33.E8364 2001
    305. 8'00947 – dc21   2001004679

This group of studies first appeared in a Special Issue of *Regional & Federal Studies*
(ISSN 1359-7566), Vol.11, No.3 (Autumn 2001), published by Frank Cass and Co. Ltd.

Contents

List of Maps

ETHNIC AND REGIONAL CHALLENGES IN THE FSU

Russian Federation

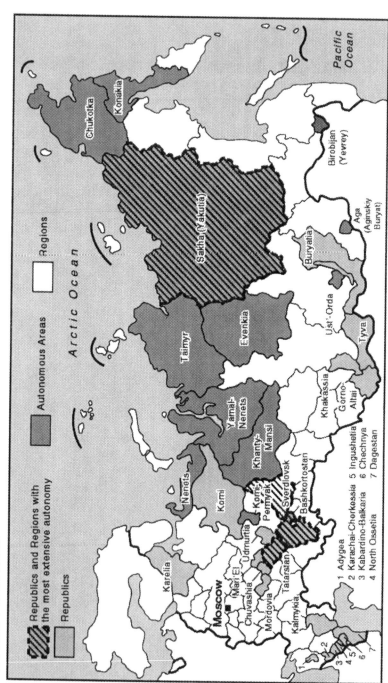

Republics and Regions with the most extensive autonomy

Republics

Autonomous Areas

Regions

Pacific Ocean

Arctic Ocean

Chukotka
Konakia
Birobijan (Yevrey)
Sakha (Yakutia)
Buryatia
Aga (Aginsky Buryat)
Taimyr
Evenkia
Ust'-Orda
Tyva
Yamal-Nenets
Khakassia
Gorno-Altai
Khanty-Mansi
Komi-Permyak
Sverdlovsk
Bashkortostan
Nenets
Komi
Karelia
Udmurtia
Tatarstan
Kalmykia
Moscow
Mari El
Chuvashia
Mordvia

1 Adygea
2 Karachai-Cherkessia
3 Kabardino-Balkaria
4 North Ossetia
5 Ingushetia
6 Chechnya
7 Dagestan

Ukraine

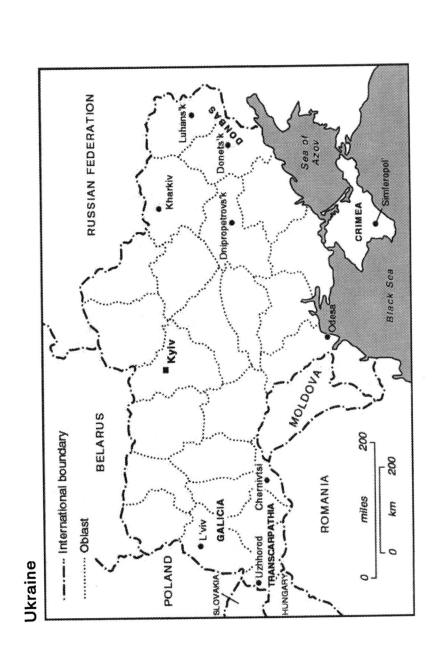

International boundary
Oblast

POLAND

SLOVAKIA

Uzhhorod
TRANSCARPATHIA

HUNGARY

L'viv
GALICIA

Chernivtsi

BELARUS

Kyiv

MOLDOVA

ROMANIA

RUSSIAN FEDERATION

Kharkiv

Luhans'k
DONBAS

Donets'k

Dnipropetrovs'k

Odesa

Sea of Azov

CRIMEA

Simferopol'

Black Sea

0   miles   200

0   km   200

Moldova

Caucasus

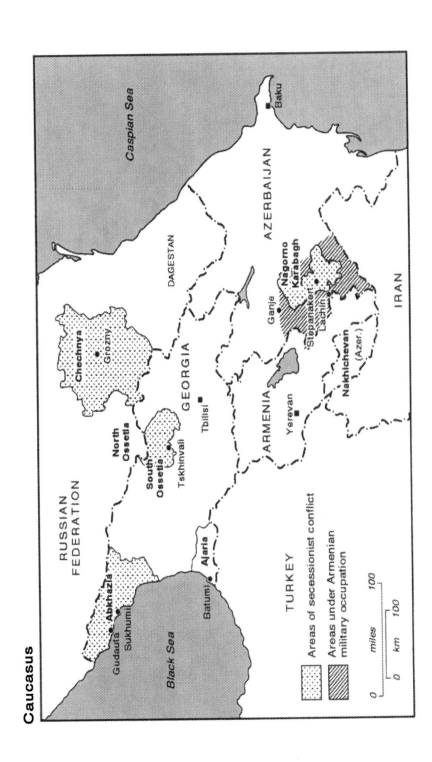

Caspian Sea

Baku

AZERBAIJAN

DAGESTAN

Chechnya

Grozny

Nagorno
Karabagh

Ganje

Stepanakert
Lachin

North
Ossetia

GEORGIA

South
Ossetia

Tskhinvali

Tbilisi

ARMENIA

Nakhichevan
(Azer.)

IRAN

Yerevan

RUSSIAN
FEDERATION

Abkhazia

Gudauta
Sukhumi

Ajaria

Batumi

Black Sea

TURKEY

Areas of secessionist conflict

Areas under Armenian
military occupation

0   miles   100

0   km   100

Central Asia

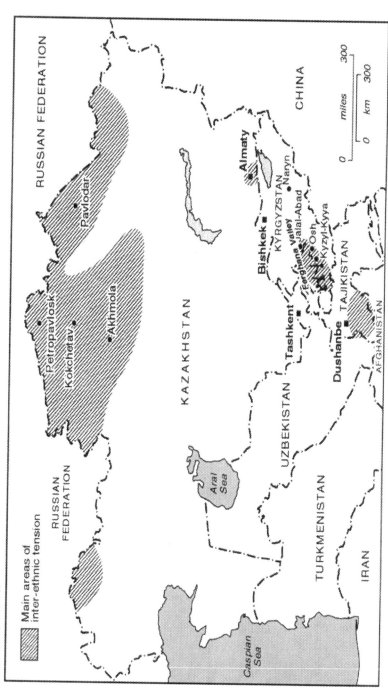

List of Post-Soviet Conflicts

VIOLENT CONFLICTS

Cases	Initiation	Resolution Status	International[1] Mediation
Azerbaijan/Nag.-Karabakh/Armenia	02/1988–	Ceasefire	Russia/OSCE
Moldova/Transdnistria	09/1991–	Ceasefire	Russia/Ukraine/ OSCE/HCNM
Russia/Chechnya	12/1994–08/1996 10/1999–	Ceasefire and treaty Conflict	OSCE/HCNM OSCE[2]
Georgia/Abkhazia	04/1989	Ceasefire	Russia/CIS/UN/ OSCE/HCNM
Georgia/South Ossetia	01/1991	Settlement	Russia/OSCE
North Ossetia/Ingushetia	01/1991	Control regime	Russia
Tajikistan	05/1992–04/1999	Settlement	Russia/CIS/ OSCE/HCNM
Uzbekistan/Ferghana Valley	06/1989	Control regime	No

NON-VIOLENT CONFLICTS

Cases	Initiation Status	Resolution	International Mediation
Ukraine/Crimea	1990	Constitutional autonomy	OSCE
Russia/Tatarstan	03/1990	Treaty autonomy	None
Russia/Bashkortostan	03/1990	Treaty autonomy	None
Moldova/Gagauzia	09/1991	Constitutional autonomy	HCNM
Northern Kazakhstan	01/1992	Control regime	OSCE/HCNM
Georgia/Ajaria	01/1991	Constitutional autonomy	None
Estonia/Slavic Minority	N/A	Ethnic democracy	OSCE/HCNM/EU
Latvia/Slavic Minority	N/A	Ethnic democracy	OSCE/HCNM/EU

1 For details of the role of the OSCE and the High Commissioner for National Minorities in the FSU see Walter A. Kemp, *The OSCE in a New Context: European Security towards the Twenty-First Century*, London: Royal Institute of International Affairs, 1996.

2 An OSCE Assistance Group was established in Chechnya in 1995, based in Grozny. There was an OSCE 'presence' at the Khasavyurt truce talks. OSCE personnel were evacuated to Moscow in 1998. The Assistance Group reopened in Grozny in June 2001.

Comparing Regional and Ethnic Conflicts in Post-Soviet Transition States

JAMES HUGHES and GWENDOLYN SASSE

The rapid retreat of communism from Eastern Europe in the late 1980s and early 1990s was closely chased by an upsurge of violent upheavals that are almost universally referred to as 'ethnic' or 'nationalist' conflicts. One of the most common observations on the conflicts that arose from the collapse of communism is that they are an echo of earlier struggles. This view is shared across the spectrum of thinkers on nationalism, from Modernists to Marxists, and to those who favour a primordialist account of the origins of nationalism. For a Modernist liberal like Ernest Gellner Soviet communism was an 'intervening' force that 'defeated' nationalism so long as it captured and controlled the state. In this sense, communism had been a deep freeze for nationalism, and its demise had thawed conflicts whose outcome, even within his own schema, was difficult to predict (Gellner, 1997: 86). Similarly, the Modernist Marxist, Eric Hobsbawm, argued that 'fear and coercion kept the USSR together' and helped to prevent ethnic and communal tensions from degenerating into mutual violence. The nationalist disintegration of the USSR, according to Hobsbawm, was more a 'consequence' of the breakdown of the regime in Moscow than a 'cause' of it (Hobsbawm, 1990: 168). Primordialist-inspired understandings of conflicts are generally the provenance of parties to the conflict, though the crude stereotyping of 'ancient hatreds' is often widely disseminated by policy-makers and journalists interested in the promotion of specific global or regional security frameworks.[1]

We do not propose to challenge the notion that many potential nationalist, ethnic and regional conflicts in the Former Soviet Union were kept dormant under communism. As Ian Lustick has demonstrated, suppression or control is a remarkably effective means of conflict regulation in deeply divided societies (Lustick, 1979 and 1993). Furthermore, the control regime of the USSR cynically manipulated nationalisms by the use of quasi-federal institutional devices, in particular the theoretical right of union republics to secession and pseudo-cultural rights. This helped not only to secure internal stability, but also to project an external image of the Soviet Union as a model of a multinational state for anti-colonial movements in the Third World. The hollow Soviet claim to be the 'sentinel for self-determination', as Walker Connor phrased it, began with Lenin and Stalin and continued through the Khrushchev and Brezhnev eras (Connor, 1984: 53).

It is undeniable that the end of the Soviet regime released conflict potential. Many of the Soviet successor states have fought ethnic and regional wars with each other or within themselves as part of their nation- and state-building projects. Such conflicts are not so surprising since previous cases of end of empire led to similar conflicts, with battle lines drawn along ethnic and regional fissures. We do contest, however, the widely held notion that the contemporary conflicts in the Former Soviet Union (FSU) can be primarily explained as resurgent unfinished business from past nationalist or ethnic conflicts. We do not deny that the momentum for the half-tied knots of history to be undone or completed is a significant factor in the origins of some conflicts, perhaps most obviously in Nagorno-Karabakh and Abkhazia. We should not overlook, however, the critically important contingent factors, in particular, the political-institutional changes and adjustments to Soviet legacies made as part of the transition, in the causation and prolongation of the conflicts. Furthermore, the 'unfinished business' explanation does not account for the fact that some expected conflicts have not happened, others have been amenable to management by strategies of accommodation, while a few have degenerated into violence for which solutions are as yet elusive. In our view, the non-conflict cases are as important as those where conflict has occurred. One can be easily seduced into complacency by the routine passivity of certain conflicts. The routine, however, is generally a product of structured behaviour, and consequently how non-conflicts have been routinized may yield guidance as to the structures and codes of conduct which may work in the management of post-Soviet conflicts.

We explore regionalism and ethnic conflict in the FSU from a comparative perspective by examining the factors that account for the causation or prevention of conflict. The cases investigated here allow us to evaluate whether the successor states to the USSR exhibit common trends and differences in their responses to the challenges of state-building in ethnically and regionally divided societies. One of our recurring themes is how ethnic and regional conflicts impact critically on other aspects of post-communist transition, such as constitutional design, economic reforms and nation and state-building. To clearly identify the conceptual parameters of the dynamics of conflict and conflict-regulation, we begin by applying the principal theoretical propositions of the significant literatures on ethnic conflict, regionalism and transition to the analysis of post-Soviet conflicts.

ETHNICITY, TERRITORY AND CONFLICT RESOLUTION

Ernest Gellner argued that there was no 'third way' for cultural pluralism between the assimilatory and the nationalizing state (Gellner, 1997). For this lack of sensitivity to the political mechanisms, constitutional architectures and the role of political engineers in the 'thwarting' and managing of nationalist conflicts, he has been rightly criticized (O'Leary, 1998). By now there is a significant body of writing in political science and political philosophy which holds that societies that are deeply riven by ethnic and national divisions can be stabilized by political strategies of regulation. Surveying the range of solutions available O'Leary identified two main instruments: an institutionalist approach that focuses on constitutional and instititutional design with a preference for consociational devices, federalism, or autonomy arrangements; and a 'group-differentiated rights' approach (O'Leary, 2001). Federalism is often the key structural or institutional stabilizing mechanism prescribed for ethnically divided states, though it is not without significant problems as studies of post-colonial federations, such as India and Nigeria, demonstrate (Horowitz, 1985: 601–28). Our analysis of post-Soviet conflicts focuses on the former approach. It is concerned not only with how institutions *per se* affect state stability by preventing or promoting conflict, or the efficacy of new power-sharing devices during transition, or indeed whether the state under consideration is a democracy or non-democracy. Rather, it focuses on the institutional foundations of the state-building process itself, democratic or otherwise, which is, in the main, inherited from the Soviet ethno-federal state architecture. This legacy, which has been termed 'institutionalized multinationality' by Brubaker, is presented in many studies as the key contributory factor in the ethnification of politics and the 'ethno-constitutional' crises during the fall of the Soviet Union (Brubaker, 1996; Roeder, 1999: 867). We argue that the Soviet institutional legacy for managing ethnicity and how it was dissassembled or reassembled as part of state-building after the fall of the Soviet Union, is a crucial structural factor in the causation of post-Soviet conflicts. Since it was the combination of control and quasi-federal institutional constraints that had managed historical antagonisms in the Soviet Union, it was inevitable that the end of this control regime would refocus attention on the institutional dimension of the Soviet settlement of the nationalities question.

Studies of ethnic conflicts, whether multiple or single-case studies, generally fall within one of two schools. Primordialists view ethnicity as an innate category, and explain ethnic conflict as a struggle for hegemony between competing claims of identity based principally on common language, shared history, and appropriated territory. Modernists, on the other hand, emphasize that nationalism is an artifice of modernity that is in flux – constantly being constructed and reshaped. Ethnic and regional conflicts are almost universally fought in the name of emotionally charged identity issues such as ethnicity, language, territory and historically conditioned memories and rights. Modernists focus on the role of elites in instrumentally mobilizing the population along ethnic lines for specific political goals, where ethnicity is primarily a label used for political advantage. Thus, ethnic conflict is not inherently different from other types of political activity and likewise should be amenable to political bargaining and incentives (Lake and Rothchild, 1998: 5–6).

A contested territorial issue that is tied to a sovereignty claim is usually at the root of an ethnic and regional conflict. If competing claims are not prevented, regulated or managed by political control or institutional compromise, the resulting discontent can develop into radicalized zero-sum conflicts that eradicate or marginalize the space for political compromise. Such competing claims may be mobilized by ethno-historical mythologies as well as by socio-economic grievances. They may be essentially domestically driven (endogenous), or they may involve the interference of significant external (exogenous) factors and agencies. Brubaker has encapsulated this interconnection by his notion of the 'triadic nexus' between 'nationalizing state', 'national minority', and 'homeland state'(Brubaker, 1996: 23–54; 55–76). Brubaker's notion depicts national minorities as the key state- and nation-building issue, and assumes a degree of political mobilization on the part of these minorities. The latter assumption is problematic in itself, since there are many cases in the FSU where political mobilizations by minorities have been extremely weak. Nevertheless, the major weakness in this explanation is that it fails to address the often overarching influence of great powers or international organizations in the management of ethnic and regional conflicts (discussed below). Sometimes wider diasporas also may have a significant impact on the nation- and state-building process of a homeland state.

There are several elaborate taxonomies which attempt to classify ethnic conflicts and, if appropriate, the means of conflict-regulation employed in order to come to a finite set of strategies. The categories appear to be ever expanding. McGarry and O'Leary identified eight 'end or mend' strategies for the regulation of ethno-national differences (McGarry and O'Leary, 1993: 1–40).[2] Heraclides details as many as 50 (Heraclides, 1997: 495–8). A taxonomy or classification system does not explain, however, the causes of particular conflicts and why certain strategies are chosen in any given case at any given time. There is also a tendency to employ vague correlations such as: 'the greater the discrimination – the more likely is organised action' (post-Soviet states offer several counter examples to this claim, for example, the Russian/Russophone-speaking minorities in Estonia, Latvia and Northern Kazakhstan) or 'the more strongly a person identifies with a group the more likely is action' (Gurr and Harff, 1994: 83–4). Both theory and evidence are still lagging behind political developments, for as Carment and James have stated: 'Agreement exists that some combination of economic, political and psychological factors can explain ethnic conflict. Consensus, however, ends at that point' (Carment and James, 1997: 2).

Studies by Horowitz, Rothchild, Nordlinger and others observe that elites may be motivated to play the ethnic card as part of their power-accumulating or profit-maximizing agenda.[3] They also stress the importance of cross-cutting cleavages within supposedly united ethnic groups for the management of politicized ethnicity (Horowitz, 1985; Rothchild, 1981; Nordlinger, 1972). This emphasis may be theoretically sound, but in practice cross-cutting cleavages are less likely to generate the modified behaviour sought if a line of cleavage related to the national, ethnic or regional divisions is the dominant one. Similarly, Esman differentiates between ethnic conflicts that are characterized by *internal divisions* within groups (such as class, occupation, ideology, kinship-lineage), those that are driven by *stratification* between ethnic groups (a dominant versus subordinate relationship), and those that involve conflicts between *segmented* ethnic groups (essentially parallel power and status systems) (Esman, 1994: 20). Predicting the scale and intensity of ethnic mobilization seems to have no general rule. Elite-led rather than mass mobilization tends to moderate conflict potential, whereas mass ethnic mobilization may radicalize situations and act as a constraint on elites, limiting their policy and decisional calculus.

Inter-ethnic competition is widely seen as a trigger for conflict along ethnic or regional lines. This is a rather ambiguous term, however, and can involve perceptions related to elite and mass reactions to real or imagined discrimination, or threats to existing privileged status. While the arguments used in a particular ethnic conflict are nearly always couched within a discourse of identity, victimization and discrimination, the list of motivations is often much longer and more complex. The situational context and historical memories can determine which of the ethnic markers become most politically salient, but the key to the conflicts and also to conflict regulation is the rational and instrumental aspect of ethnicity. Ethnic conflict, then, is a political problem requiring a political solution within an institutional context. Formal institutions are critical, observed Horowitz, because they 'structure incentives for political behaviour' (1985: 601). This point was reinforced by O'Leary who noted that 'the political regime within which national minorities operate, rather than their material or cultural grievances, may best explain their predispositions to be secessionists, federalists, or consociationalists' (O'Leary, 1997: 217). In post-Soviet states, where the content of identity is highly uncertain and under construction as part of the simultaneity dilemma of nation- and state-building and transition processes, institutional design for managing potential conflicts is even more necessary.

One solution to the dilemma of multi-ethnicity in a democratizing state is the de-ethnification of politics, that is, the removal of ethnicity from politics. This is a central pillar of liberal thinking on the political management of multi-ethnicity. Gellner, as we noted earlier, offered us two solutions from European history: assimilation and ethnic-cleansing. In a recent survey of democracy and nationalism Snyder dismissed the promotion of institutionalized power-sharing, and asymmetric federal arrangements in particular, as undermining of democracy (Snyder, 2000: 40). This seems to us to be a rather impracticable prescription for poly-ethnic states undergoing a regime transition. It is not simply the significance of the correlation with democratization indicated by Snyder that matters, but rather as Horowitz explains: '[T]imes of transition are often times of ethnic tension. When it looks as though the shape of the polity is being settled once and for all, apprehensions are likely to grow' (Horowitz, 1985: 190). Times of transition are also interludes of opportunity. A secessionist aspiration, for example, may be revived or invigorated by the preoccupation of the centre with the trials of transition, as the cases of Nagorno-Karabakh and Chechnya suggest.

Comparative experience indicates that policies of ethnic inclusion can be structured through consociational power-sharing or other accommodative institutional mechanisms (Lijphart, 1977). Kymlicka's propositions on multiculturalism offer a range of institutional responses for guaranteeing group-specific rights (Kymlicka, 1995).[4] Incentives, whether distributive, structural or both, as a means of conflict-management, in particular the use of power-sharing consociational and multicultural institutional designs, have become a key issue for policy-makers and political scientists. Horowitz defined these elements as follows: 'Distributive policies aim to change the ethnic balance of economic opportunities and rewards. Structural techniques aim to change the political framework in which ethnic conflict occur.' (Horowitz, 1985: 596). Others argue that political accommodations may well be dependent on 'deliberate strategies of interethnic generosity' (Hislope, 1998: 140–41).

The debates on divided societies tend to focus on ethnic cleavages, although *per definitionem* the term 'divided societies' covers a whole range of different cleavages which may vary in strength and political significance or cross-cut one another. A key question to ask is: what are the main politically significant or *salient* cleavages, and to what degree do they cause fragmentation? Do the different cleavages cross-cut and, therefore, counterbalance each other, or do they coincide in a mutually reinforcing manner and intensify political mobilization? How strong is the countervailing effect of an overarching identity or loyalty to the state? Following Lijphart, cross-cutting cleavages and overlapping membership in different groups are now widely regarded as the key mechanism for moderating political attitudes and actions and minimalizing the ethnic factor in politics, which may be cemented through institutionalized political parties (Lijphart, 1977). As we observed above, the moderating effect of cross-cutting cleavages on ethno-political allegiances is subject to certain qualifications, for example the extent to which they cut across rather than coincide with each other, the differential intensity of the cleavages and the overall socio-economic context. Cross-cutting cleavages of an equal intensity can simply lead to the formation of antagonistic groups and a further segregation of society. Arguably, the kind of regionalized multi-ethnicity that exists in the FSU is such a variant of cross-cutting ethnic allegiances.

The most generally applied framework for explaining trends in territorial politics is the Lipset and Rokkan model of how cleavage structures are translated into voter alignments and party systems. Derived from their study of West European history, they distinguished between four types of cleavages: centre–periphery (cultural issues), state–church (ideological), land–industry (economic), worker–owner (class). Their argument that West European democratization evolved from a process whereby these cleavages were 'frozen' in a party system at the outset of the democratization process is not clearly relevant to the post-Soviet states where cleavages are less clear-cut and party systems are weak or non-existent (Lipset and Rokkan, 1967: 1–64). Although the Lipset-Rokkan model assumes rational actors, their historical account does not explain how elites mobilized cleavages for their own purposes and who these actors are. Their study, and Rokkan's other work on regions, is more concerned with elaborating structural variation than with explaining the political phenomenon of regionalism. For example, they say little of the nature of the resources at stake and the motivations and strategic choices made by the political and economic actors involved.

The Comparative Politics literature on regions resembles in many ways the literature on ethnic conflict in that it is driven by attempts to classify different types of regions, such as political, economic, administrative and cultural regions. As pointed out by Rokkan and Urwin in their study on West European regionalism, peripheral politicization results from an incongruity between cultural, economic and political roles – an incongruity which has existed as long as there have been states. Despite the distinctions between different types of regions, scholars of regionalism such as Rokkan, Urwin and Keating tend to concentrate their analysis on regions in which the ethnic cleavage is the predominant one. Their studies of regionalism are dominated by cases of nationalism, such as Catalonia, the Basque Country and Scotland (Rokkan and Urwin, 1983; Keating, 1988; Keating, 1998). Thus, the literature on regionalism tends to conflate regionalism with nationalism within existing states. This trend is reflected in the literature on post-Soviet conflicts, where regional mobilization based on patterns of settlement and the economic policies of the Soviet era have often been subsumed under the generic label of 'ethnic conflict'. Notwithstanding the inconsistencies in all of the above-mentioned approaches, their shared emphasis on elite mobilization concurs with a central fixture of transitology – the other school of important theories, approaches and models relevant to post-Soviet ethnic and regional conflicts.

ETHNICITY, 'STATENESS' AND DEMOCRATIZATION

Perhaps the most common feature of theories of nationalism, ethnic conflict regulation and transition to democracy is that they employ the same level of analysis. These key approaches take the nation-state as the main unit of analysis and, thereby, tend to limit their focus to central elites and institutions. Since national and democratic state-building are viewed as state-level processes, those factors which lie outside this level of analysis, such as regions, tend to be downplayed, if not excluded altogether. Drawing on liberal democratic theory, transitology assumes that ethnicity – or multi-ethnicity to be precise – is destabilizing, especially where there is a territorialization of difference. The 'ethnification' of transition politics is seen as an almost insoluble problem with 'strong causes and weak cures' (Offe, 1996: 50–81). A comparison with Central and Eastern Europe confirms the trend that democratization and transition in general have been most successful in those countries that are most homogeneous and have few or no serious ethnic cleavages, such as Hungary, Poland, the Czech Republic and Slovenia. It is not coincidental that these are states which 'benefited' most from the homogenizing ethnic and racial policies of Hitler, Stalin and Tito.

Transitologists emphasize in the first instance that the zero-condition for transitions is, as Rustow observed, 'national unity', by which he meant that the 'overwhelming majority' of the population concurs on national identity (Rustow, 1970: 351). Multi-ethnicity, particularly when territorialized, is widely seen as an impediment to democracy builders. This pessimistic view originated with one of the founding fathers of liberalism, John Stuart Mill, who asserted that democracy in an ethnically diverse state was 'next to impossible' (Mill, 1861 [1974]: 389–90).[5] Democracy is inherently incompatible with multinationality or poly-ethnicity, it is argued, precisely because the integrity of the state will be threatened by secession (Barry, 1989: 38). This pessimism has been imprinted on a generation of political scientists by Dahl who believed that in societies with high levels of 'sub-cultural pluralism': 'the price of polyarchy may be a breakup of the country. And the price of territorial unity may be a hegemonic regime' (Dahl, 1971: 121). Similarly, multi-ethnicity was rationalized by Rabushka and Shepsle as creating an inexorable logic for ethnic competition and 'outbidding' in plural societies leading to polarization, democratic breakdown and secession (Rabushka and Shepsle, 1972). A cornerstone of democratic theory today is Dahl's observation that: 'The criteria of the democratic process presuppose the rightfulness of the unit itself' (Dahl, 1989: 207). The logic is that states must assimilate or break up: 'If the community is so radically divided that a single citizenship is impossible, then its territory too must be divided' (Walzer, 1983: 62). Linz and Stepan have paraphrased this liberal tradition as the 'stateness' question, suggesting that agreements about 'stateness' are logically prior to the creation of democratic institutions and that democracy and the nation-state form complimentary logics. When post-communist states have been captured by a hegemonic ethnic group, Linz and Stepan argue, they are prone to exclusivist 'nationalizing' policies, rather than assimilation. Such policies may result in homogenization, but they are more likely to instigate and nurture inter-ethnic rivalries leading to conflicts which may obstruct democratization (Linz and Stepan, 1996). Given the multi-ethnic complexity of many post-Soviet states, the inherent pessimism of liberal democratic theory clearly does not bode well for the prospects of successful democratic state-building, and in some respects could be taken as an agenda for forced assimilation or mass expulsions. There is no question that the likelihood of a commitment problem will be greater among a territorialized ethnic minority in a newly democratizing state, and that this creates a voice or exit option in terms of secession-potential. Linz and Stepan single out two institutional means as having a stabilizing effect: consociationalism and 'electoral sequencing'. Consociationalism is a complex political system with a limited record of stabilizing ongoing conflicts (Lijphart, 1977; Horowitz, 1985; O'Leary and McGarry, 1993). Moreover, one of the inherent dilemmas of consociational solutions to ethnic conflicts is that greater segmental autonomy may entrench undemocratic sub-national elites in power (Lustick, 1979). On the other hand, Linz and Stepan compare Spain, Yugoslavia and the USSR to claim that a state-level solution of better 'electoral sequencing', whereby the first democratic and legitimating 'founding elections' are conducted at the statewide level rather than at the regional or local level, may be an important factor in warding off ethno-political mobilization (Linz and Stepan, 1992).[6]

The second essential condition for transitologists is the importance of elite pacts at the central state level during transition (Rustow, 1970; Higley and Burton, 1989). For transitologists, the key decision for elites in a transition state is whether, as Linz put it, to make democracy 'the only game in town', while democracy itself is widely seen as being 'crafted' or built 'from scratch' (Di Palma, 1990; Fish, 1995 and 1999), and a contingent outcome of actor 'games' (Przeworski, 1992). Inter-ethnic issues or regional diversity in elite bargaining strategies simply do not figure in such analyses. Clearly, we need to take a broader account of the elite factor since how ethnic differences become conflictual or are accommodated largely depends not only on how elites interact during transition but also *which* ones. If as part of the overall post-Soviet constitution-making process an elite pact is inter-ethnic and links centre and periphery, it is reasonable to assume that it is more likely that there will be a strategy of accommodation, whether in the maximalist form of a power-sharing agreement or some form of institutionalized autonomy, or a more minimalist partial elite cooption. Conversely, we can assume that the absence or weakness of an ethnic or regional dimension to the elite pact is likely to inflate the potential for a destabilizing political mobilization along these cleavage lines.

Third, transitology attaches great significance to basic constitutional engineering during a transition and, in particular, emphasizes their stabilizing or destabilizing properties, depending on whether a state opts for a presidential, mixed or parliamentary system. Linz has nurtured the perception that the compromises born of parliamentarism create a better environment for a politically stable democratic transition. In contrast, presidentialism has certain 'perils' that should make it the least preferred institutional option for democracy-builders, the main dangers being that it tends to polarize society, engender authoritarian temptations, foster the personalization of power and retard institutional development. Moreover, the rigidity of presidential terms, it is argued, tends to make such systems less flexible in managing political crises, giving them a predisposition to fall into all-out regime crisis in emergencies. Most transitologists accept that presidential systems are the 'least conducive' to stable democracy in transition states (Linz, 1990 and 1994). A more refined version of this thesis holds that it is the 'presidential-premier' system that is most unstable of all (Shugart and Carey, 1992), and that is precisely the institutional configuration that predominates in the FSU (Shugart, 1996).

Linz's thesis is patently derived from transition experiences in the ethnically homogenous states of Latin America, and, therefore, of questionable validity in poly-ethnic conflictual societies. Following this line of argument, Horowitz used a case study of Nigeria to demonstrate that instability in ethnically divided societies results more from the use of a Westminster-type plurality electoral system, rather than presidentialism *per se*, which can in practice be an institutional unifier and guarantor of inter-ethnic peace. For Horowitz, Linz had drawn an 'unfounded dichotomy' between presidential and parliamentary systems 'divorced from the electoral and other governmental institutions in which they operate' (Horowitz, 1990). Horowitz offers a strong critique but his solution is still rather narrowly defined, focusing specifically on how the configuration of the electoral system for presidents can be a useful device for managing territorial and ethnic challenges if it maximizes accommodation by promoting inclusion rather than exclusion in divided societies. It leaves open the question of whether a presidential or parliamentary system is the most effective form of constitutional engineering in an ethnically divided society.

The state-centred analytical focus of transitology exercises a levelling effect on diverse state institutional legacies and structures, and also deflects analysis from the interaction between state and sub-state dimensions in shaping transition outcomes. Furthermore, the analysis of conflicts over institutional designs in transition is concentrated on two inter-related dimensions: the choice between presidentialism or parliamentarism, and the engineering of electoral and party systems. By such a narrow focus, transition theorists have neglected the other key dimensions highlighted by the Horowitz critique, namely, the role of other governmental institutions. In recent work, Stepan has admitted the failure of transitology to address the role of state institutions in the management of multi-ethnicity, arguing that federalism can be a key stabilizing device in multi-ethnic states undergoing democratization (Stepan, 1999). In practice, then, the capacity of a new regime to manage ethnic and territorial challenges during a transition will be largely determined by the extent to which a state has a homogenous or heterogeneous society, how it is constitutionally equipped, whether the state is unitary or federal in its structure, and whether a consensus can be forged among elites and key groups to accept the designs.

THE INTERNATIONAL DIMENSION IN POST-SOVIET CONFLICTS

The study of the international relations dimension of ethnic and regional conflicts has now moved beyond the realist assumption of the state as the sole actor in the international arena, and the focus of attention has switched mainly to the role of supra-national organizations or inter-regional blocs and networks. Only very recently has this discipline begun to incorporate ethnic groups as one of the range of possible non-state actors. Concurrently, the study of ethnic conflict and conflict-regulation has begun to place more emphasis on the internationalization of conflict. States and international organizations outside the conflict zone, however, are still mainly seen normatively as 'mediators' and 'arbiters' promoting or imposing a settlement, rather than pursuing self-interest. In this respect, it is a serious flaw in transitology that it has systematically neglected the role of the international dimension. The studies by Whitehead and Schmitter of the international dimension of democratization have given us some basic analytical tools, such as 'control', 'contagion', 'consent' and 'conditionality' (Whitehead, 1996: 3–25; Schmitter, 1996). We can re-appropriate these tools for the post-Soviet context and evaluate them in terms of templates for centralizing or regionalizing tendencies, demonstration effects, and incentives for conflict-management. Often they are tied to bilateral inter-state dependencies or membership in international organizations, such as the Council of Europe and the EU. Whitehead's and Schmitter's studies, however, offer us a narrow conception of the 'international dimension' by limiting it to the impact of Western democracies on transition countries.

Post-Soviet conflicts are a significant contribution to the 30 or so wars, most of them internal, that were ongoing globally by the mid-1990s. Whether the Cold War was a condenser of certain types of conflicts, literally taking the steam out of them, is debatable. For most analysts, the Cold War led to a stabilized Soviet hegemony over Eastern Europe as part of the international system that allowed it to consolidate a strong control regime that insulated it against ethnopolitical movements. Certainly, we can say that the Cold War had no such effect in Western Europe where prolonged nationalist conflicts occurred in Northern Ireland and the Basque Country. By the end of the Cold War many analysts were deprived of one of their most widely employed labels of convenience for national and ethnic conflicts: the ideological conflict between East and West. From around 1990–91 the causes of conflicts in most parts of the world underwent a redefinition. The disintegration of the Soviet Union and, in particular, Yugoslavia (FRY) realized the worst possible scenario for potential post-communist conflicts. For the first time since the Second

World War, waves of genocidal massacres and mass population expulsions occurred in Europe. This caused many analysts to view the rise of ethnic and regional conflicts in Eastern Europe and the FSU as the continuation of a global trend for such conflicts to move from the developing to the developed world, rather than being a *sui generis* regional phenomenon specific to the post-communist countries (Gurr and Harff, 1994: 13).

Of the 300 or so politically active ethnic and religious groups in the twentieth century Gurr singles out the European ethnic warfare of the early 1990s as the culmination of a long-term trend that began in the 1950s and reached its peak shortly after the end of the Cold War (Gurr, 2000: 53). According to Gurr, 'initiations' of 'ethnopolitical' protests and 'rebellions' in the FSU peaked in 1992 (Gurr, 1996). Following Gurr, Rubin has argued that the lack of new 'initiations' of conflict since 1992 equates to a 'stabilization of the post-Soviet space' (sic) which is accounted for by three factors: state-building, Russian influence and processes of internationalization (Rubin, 1998: 166–8). Post-crisis stability is important to recognize, but it should not deflect us from understanding the nature of the conflicts and the nature of the stability, as conflicts may simply be frozen. A focus on the absence of new occurrences of conflict in the FSU does not explain why the conflicts arose and what mechanisms are used in conflict management and resolution. In fact Gurr and Rubin, like most analysts, subsume a wide range of different types of post-Soviet conflict, whether political, economic, or social, religious and regional under the generic label 'ethnic conflict', thus creating a ubiquitous negative association with state-building in the successor states (Walker, 1996: 3).

The politicization of ethnicity and mobilization for conflict that followed the collapse of the FSU has also added weight to the argument that the late twentieth century saw a fundamental shift in the nature of conflicts away from *inter-state* conflicts within the international order to *intra-state* conflicts (Carment and James, 1997: 2). By the mid-1990s while we see a return to the policy of non-recognition of secession in the international order (Kosovo and East Timor excepted), we also see a shift towards a much more interventionist approach by a plethora of international organizations and multilateral organizations (UN, OSCE, NATO, EU, PACE) in the domestic affairs of 'sovereign' states which is primarily geared to managing the increase in intra-state conflict. This new interventionism is justified partly by the ideology of 'global governance' and partly by the political rhetoric of 'ethical foreign policy' among certain Western governments. The weakening of Russia as a Great Power has also created space for rival powers to expand their influence in post-

Soviet states, from the NATO/EU double enlargement eastward, to the increasing role of the USA, Turkey, Iran and Afghanistan in the South Caucasus and Central Asia. The international influences on regional and ethnic conflicts in the FSU are clearly significant and yet the interaction between the external and internal dimensions of these conflicts is poorly theorized and explained.

We extend the concept of international dimension to include not only the relationship between external and internal dynamics of conflicts, but also the interdependencies between the post-Soviet states and the impact they have on each other. In the FSU the issue of interdependence reverberates in both the links between regional and ethnic conflicts across the FSU and the way in which violent conflicts – in particular those of Nagorno-Karabakh, Abkhazia and Chechnya – and attempts at conflict-management, as in Crimea and Tatarstan, have shaped the perceptions of the elites and masses throughout the post-Soviet states. The involvement of the OSCE in all of the violent and some of the potential conflicts in the FSU provided an additional linkage between individual cases and decision-makers in conflict regions throughout the post-Soviet space. In fact, the OSCE initiatives also assume the comparability of post-Soviet conflict dynamics and promote a common bundle of resolution strategies. OSCE involvement has raised elite and public awareness of the causes of conflicts, the role of external agents and the feasibility of the institutional solutions recommended by the OSCE.

Horowitz's study of post-colonial Africa described how the international dimension of secessionist movements can lead to 'reciprocal secessionism'. Sequences of separatism in one state can have a demonstration effect that propels separatism into action elsewhere where it did not previously exist (Horowitz, 1985: 279–81). This could be a model for explaining the demonstration and contagion effects of post-Soviet conflicts within the former Soviet space. Carment and James define the central issue as 'the conduct of states external to a conflict and the implications of internal changes (most notably democratization) for outside intervention' (Carment and James, 1997: 3). This is a useful initial template for understanding the foreign policies of Russia and the West, in particular the USA, in post-Soviet conflicts, though it sidelines the vital economic interests that are often at stake. The role of transnational linkages between ethnic groups and their diasporas can sometimes be as salient a factor as the impact of international factors on ethnic and regional conflict in general (Carment and James, 1997: 254). What is still missing from these approaches is the impact that transition countries have on each other. In fact, we argue that the interdependent nature of post-communist transitions and post-Soviet conflicts is a sufficiently distinguishing feature to make them a specific type of conflict category.

SECESSION AND RECOGNITION

If the main goal of nationalist movements is to establish an independent nation-state, then nationalist secessionism is the most extreme challenge to the territorial integrity of an existing state. Secession may also, of course, aim to (re-)unify with another state that is seen as an ethnic kin-state or nationalist 'homeland' state. Secession, consequently, is a claim that is generally legitimated by the act of 'national' self-determination. The most basic characteristic of secession is that it is a political act perpetrated against an existing state and ultimately reshapes, however marginally, the existing international order. In this sense, it is essentially an international act, as it depends critically on recognition which is itself determined by the international climate of prevailing interests and norms. Secession may result in the international recognition or partial recognition of a new state, or in non-recognition but *de facto* independence. The right to self-determination today is almost universally applauded in theory, but is highly circumscribed in international practice. The principle of national self-determination was imbued with a qualified moral status in international relations after the First World War by the Wilsonian principles of 'government by consent' for certain national groups in Europe.[7] The First World War marked a shift to nationalism as the major mobilizing political force in the international political system and, as a consequence, and in a hitherto unprecedented way, the Great Powers acted collectively to manage nationalism over a huge territorial expanse in Central and Eastern Europe through the vaguely defined and selectively enforced Wilsonian principles of self-determination. In the process new nation-states were manufactured where none had previously existed, as in Czechoslovakia and Yugoslavia. Great Power intervention, arbitration and 'hegemonic control' also followed the defeat of Germany in 1945, when Europe was carved up into spheres of influence at Yalta. In a crude attempt at homogenization the Great Powers presided over the forced mass transfers of ethnic populations, mainly Germans, while in the Soviet Union there were mass deportations of Chechens, Crimean Tatars and other 'suspect' ethnic groups.

The principle of self determination was extended to non-Europeans by the universalist claims of the UN Charter of 1945, where Articles 1(2) and 55 enshrined the 'principle' (not the 'right') of 'self determination of peoples'. Adopted just as the era of decolonization was accelerating, Chapters XI and XII of the charter stipulated that colonial powers should promote 'self-government' of 'territories', not ethnic groups, thus reaffirming the norm for colonial administrative demarcations to become the basis for new states (Halperin *et al.*, 1992: 20). The shift from principle to enforceable right in international law came in 1976 with the entry into force of two international covenants agreed in 1966: the International Covenant on Civil and Political Rights and the International Covenant on Economic, Social, and Cultural Rights. The first article of both covenants declared, 'All peoples have the right of self-determination'. The binding legal effect, however, was accompanied by a number of ambiguities, most importantly over defining 'peoples', which created conceptual incoherence (Lapidoth, 1997:19–23)

Historically, the 'morality' of secession has rarely been an uncontested claim (Buchanan, 1991). Although strictly limited and geographically confined in practice, in the Twentieth Century there were three concentrated periods of self-determination, all of which fell after periods of extreme chaos in the international order: after the First and Second World Wars, and after the Cold War. It is the latter period which we may characterize as the era of 'post-communist self-determination'. The stability of borders was the guiding logic of the CSCE balance of power in Europe established at Helsinki in 1975. Consequently, the key pillars of international norms in Europe during the height of the Cold War were, first, the inviolability of recognized state borders, and second, the demarcation of zones where states had conditional sovereignty dependent upon the interests of Superpowers and Great Powers. The greatest tests for the principle of self-determination came after the Second World War in the post-colonial new states in Africa and Asia. Decolonization embedded the doctrine of *uti possidetis juris* in the creation and maintenance of new states, which held that the established colonial status quo with respect to borders was to be preserved at all costs, and any unilateral redrawing of the boundaries of states by secession was to be strongly discouraged (Shaw, 1996). Exceptionally, disputed territories were given an indeterminate status. Until the war in Kosovo these territories were overwhelmingly outside Europe, or on its periphery.[8]

The recognition of secession in international practice falls into five principal categories (Kingsbury, 1992: 487):

(1) Mandated territories, trust territories, and territories created as non-self governing units under Chapter XI of the UN Charter;
(2) Distinct political-geographical entities subject to carence de souverainete (the only possible example being Bangladesh);
(3) Territories in respect of which self-determination is applied by the mutual agreement of the parties involved;
(4) Highest level constituent units of a federal state which has been, or is in the process of being, dissolved by agreement among all (or at least most) of the constituent units. The precedent for the practice

of *uti posseditis* was set by the decolonization of Latin America, when the internal colonial boundaries of the Spanish empire became, by mutual consent, the international boundaries of the successor states (though they were subsequently reconfigured by war). This precedent was generally followed in the decolonization of Africa and Asia after 1945. In advising on the secessions from FRY the Badinter Judicial Commission for the EU in late 1991 and early 1992 recognized this principle as a 'pre-emptive' element of customary international law when empires or federal states dissolve. We should note, however, that the EU itself did not follow the Badinter recommendations on recognizing secessions but was driven by Germany-led unilateral recognitions (Kumar, 1997: 49–50; Woodward, 1995: 199–222);

(5) Formerly independent territories that are joined to another state which reassert their independence with at least the tacit consent of the established state, especially where incorporation into the other state was illegal or of dubious legality. The problem with the latter category, of course, is that the international order can tolerate illegal occupations over the long term, as the cases of East Timor and Northern Cyprus demonstrate.

During the collapse of the Soviet Union Western international practice on the recognition of secession lacked a consistent rationale. As we observed at the outset, most of the violent and potential post-Soviet conflicts have involved secession. Until late 1991 Western states, in particular the EC and USA, adopted a policy of extreme caution and non-recognition in their foreign policy reasoning on secession in the Soviet Union.[9] This policy of caution was overturned dramatically in the second half of 1991 in FRY, leading to, as noted above, unilateral recognition of the secession of Slovenia by Germany in December 1991. Claims of sovereign independent statehood by many of the USSR's constituent union republics went unrecognized until the August Coup of 1991 and the physical disintegration of Soviet governance structures. In contrast, a good case can be made that the EC recognition of Slovenia prompted the disintegration of FRY (Woodward, 1995). The conflicts that arose from the collapse of the USSR became hinged on the two conflicting principles: recognition of state territorial integrity versus self-determination. In fact, post-communist state- and nation-building has been informed by a conceptual delusion that is a *sine qua non* for recognition in the international system – the idea of the nation-state – despite the fact that the homogenous 'nation-state', as envisaged by liberal democratic theory, is to a large degree fictional. Only very few states fit this ideal type. Most states have to continuously engage in the accommodation of ethnic or regional diversity within their boundaries. Many states have had learning curves that lasted decades, if not centuries, to manage competing ethnic and regional claims by regionalization, autonomization, and other forms of self-government, including some West European states, such as Spain, Italy, and the United Kingdom.

The *de facto* collapse of the Soviet Union in late 1991 led Western states to follow the *uti possidetis* doctrine established in previous decolonizations. In practice, the right to recognition as a new 'state' was tied to the highest level of administration immediately below the state. In the FSU, as in many of the cases of decolonization in Africa and Asia, *uti possidetis* legitimated an artificial pattern of state territoriality which had been defined by the colonizing power. Such administrative demarcations were often arbitrary, and generally deliberately designed irrespective of ethnic and other cleavages. While Leninist and Stalinist 'planned' bounding of ethnicity in the Soviet Union was not characterized by the kind of colonial 'scramble' for territory that occurred in Africa, its outcome was often just as crude, creating administrative units without regard to history, ethnicity or geography. In the East European communist federations it was the constituent union republic administrative entities that gained recognition as new states in the period 1991–92. The new 'successor states' were soon confronted with similar secessionist demands from within their own boundaries, as a kind of nested doll 'matryoshka' nationalism kept shifting the challenge inwards and downwards to the sub-state level. Whether secessionist governments were democratically mandated or not, in the interests of international order Western states froze the recognition process and no new secessions were recognized apart from the 15 union republics of the former USSR.[10]

This policy of recognition by Western states was justified by the need to maintain stability in the post-Soviet space and conformed with previous international norms. In the collapse of the USSR the rationale for accepting the union republics as incubators for new states is questionable. Leaving aside the obvious issue of the 'administrative' nature of most union republic boundaries, and the generally 'titular' nature of their ethnic definition, let us concentrate on the 'legal' reasoning (which was also applied to FRY). Recognition of union republics was based on their right of secesson under the Soviet constitution, most lately that of 1977. Accordingly, only the union republics were founding constituent 'members' of the USSR. Thus, they were the only administrative tier that approximated to 'states-in-the-making'. This ignores key developments in the USSR federal system in the late perestroika period. Gorbachev supposedly once claimed that '*perestroika ne perekroika*' (reconstruction is not a restitching). What he meant by this was that his reforms did not entail a reassembly of the ethno-territorial patchwork of the USSR. In fact, this was precisely the policy that he drifted into during 1989–90. The groundwork for the refederalization of the USSR was laid by Gorbachev's new treaty-based (*dogovornyi*) constitutional arrangement for power-sharing between the federal centre in Moscow and the constituent units of the federation. A generous interpretation is that his goal was to renegotiate with the union republics the Union Treaty of 1922 on which the USSR was founded (Hough: 1997, 379). A crucial landmark in his policy, however, was the 'Law on the Division of Powers between the USSR and the Subjects of the Federation' passed by the USSR Congress of People's Deputies on 26 April 1990 which radically altered the federal arrangement of the Soviet Union. Previous to this law the principal constitutional distinction between union republic and autonomous republic was that the former was technically 'sovereign' and had the right to secede whereas the latter did not. The new law eradicated this distinction and treated both types of federal unit as 'subjects of the federation'. By equalizing the status of union republics and autonomous republics, and making both equally subordinate to the federal government, Gorbachev may have hoped to deter secessionism by the union republics and strengthen his leverage on them to negotiate a new Union Treaty. Gorbachev had introduced an institutional mechanism for the mutually assured destruction of the territorial fabric of the Soviet Union. Once this law was passed, a secessionist union republic exercising its constitutional right to 'sovereignty' and secession (though there was no clearly defined legal means of so doing) could be faced by similar secessionist demands from an autonomous republic (if it contained one).

There can be little doubt that the law, which coincided with the creation of a more powerful Soviet presidency, was a manoeuvre by Gorbachev aimed at the one union republic that was in the vanguard of the moves to decentralize the Soviet Union – Boris Yeltsin's Russian government – which contained the largest number of autonomous republics.[11] After the passage of this law, the language of 'delimiting powers', 'power-sharing', 'sovereignty' and 'secession' became the common currency of the political discourse over refederalization, whether of the Soviet Union, Russia, or other union republics with autonomous units or territorialized minorities. This new federal arrangement was reiterated in the New Union Treaty of June 1991, though its passage into law was pre-empted by the failed August 1991 coup. The concepts embodied in the new Gorbachevian federalism strengthened the claims of secessionists across the Soviet Union, from Crimea to Nagorno-Karabakh and Abkhazia, and in Tatarstan and Bashkortostan in Russia.

Gorbachev's tactic backfired badly, for rather than bringing Yeltsin and the other leaders of union republics to heel, it incited them to intensify the 'war of sovereignties' against the centre. In the course of 1990–91 Yeltsin mobilized Russian nationalism and accelerated Russia's disassociation from the USSR, in the process turning Gorbachev's April 1990 law on its head by appealing to Russia's ethnic republics to 'take as much sovereignty as you can stomach' during a visit to the Tatarstan capital, Kazan, in August 1990. This was a message that horrified nationalist leaders in other union republics with autonomous units, who feared an empowerment of the federal structures and favoured nationalizing state-building projects. Given this context of extreme instability and a rapidly weakening central authority, it is not surprising that once protected minorities which enjoyed a measure of institutionalized self-government in the Soviet system feared the resurgent nationalism of titular groups in the union republics. It was this clash between two radically different concepts of state-building in a multi-ethnic environment, federalization versus nationalizing state, that sparked many of the post-Soviet conflicts.

STATE-BUILDING AND 'SUBVERSIVE' INSTITUTIONS

Logically, we should begin our analysis of post-Soviet conflicts and non-conflicts with those institutions for managing ethnicity and regional issues which were already in place when the USSR collapsed. While Soviet federalism was little more than a sham, the ethno-territorial institutional edifice provided the basis for political mobilization once the Communist Party's monopoly of power and will for coercion disintegrated. Bunce, following Brubaker's earlier account, has argued from a neo-institutionalist perspective that the collapse of communist federations into ethnic conflicts is indicative of the 'subversive' nature of their institutionalization of territorialized identities (Brubaker, 1996; Bunce, 1999). By focussing on how ethnic identities were constructed and territorialized in communist federations, how potential conflicts were controlled and mediated by communist parties, state and other institutions, and how the discourses of nationalism were directed and controlled, Brubaker and Bunce identify four main underlying elements in the rise of conflict:

(1) the arbitrary drawing of boundaries and redistribution of territory and resources over time;
(2) patterns of communist-era population settlement and 'settler colonialism' by the hegemonic population (Russian-speaking settlers, mainly Slavs);

(3) problems arising from the territorial rehabilitation of displaced peoples and back-migration;
(4) problems arising from institutionalized multinationality.

When the overarching supranational political entity – the Soviet Union – disintegrated, the default mechanism and starting-point for reconstructing elites and political identities, according to Brubaker and Bunce, was the inherent, if hollowed out, institutional autonomization. The disempowered formal ethno-territorial institutions of the Soviet system were empowered by a sudden transfer of elites and political capital from the collapsing Communist Party during the breakdown phase of communism. Since the ethno-federal institutional structure was one of the key interlocking mechanisms for integrating national and sub-national level politics (the other being the CPSU), what was the fate of these institutional legacies of the Soviet era once the state-building projects of the successor states began?

Post-Soviet states have been confronted with the immediacy and simultaneity of two contradictory challenges: they are engaged in a process of nation- and state-building and consolidating the new central 'national' authority, while concurrently grappling with challenges to the centre posed by 'sub-national' ethnic or regional political mobilization and demands for autonomy or secession. Moreover, due to the nature of the post-communist transition process, where state assets are being redistributed and appropriated by elites through pseudo 'privatization' schemes, the political and economic incentives involved in the struggle for power are immense. Such conditions significantly raise the stakes in conflict potential. Issues of self-determination and autonomy may be raised instrumentally by territorialized elites as a response to the central state being captured by a rival elite network or networks. There may be a substantive 'ethnic' content to inter-elite or mass struggles, or this element may be instrumentally employed in conflicts as part of a mobilizing strategy. Consequently, it is important to consider how ethnic and regional conflicts may also be part of a struggle between elites to 'short-circuit transition processes, to forestall change, and to re-impose authoritarian rule under the guise of 'limited democratization' (Walker, 1996: 11).

Since the collapse of the Soviet Union in the late 1980s, there have been eight violent ethnic and regional conflicts in the FSU and eight significant potential conflicts that have not erupted into violence (see list of Post-Soviet Conflicts). We define conflicts here by their sustained violent nature, as opposed to sporadic episodes of rioting.

With the sole exception of the civil war in Tajikistan, the post-Soviet cases of violent conflict have involved attempted secession. Additionally, there have been cases of potential conflicts that have not degenerated into violence, though on the whole these cases have involved either demands for greater autonomy short of secession, and thus more readily negotiable, or the imposition of a strong control regime. Consequently, understanding why potential conflicts do not occur, in our view, is as important as explaining those that do lead to violence since they offer alternative strategies for the management of conflict potential.

Existing academic studies of post-Soviet conflicts generally fall into three main categories of explanation. First, there is a rather disparate body of descriptive studies of ethnic and regional conflicts, which while being empirically rich lacks a broader engagement with comparative theory (Forsberg, 1995; Drobizheva, 1996; Arbatov, 1998). Second, there is by now a vast literature on post-Soviet nation-building which rests on the assumption that ethnicity and, in particular, the question of the Russian diaspora scattered across the FSU are the key factors in post-Soviet conflicts (Szporluk, 1994; Kolsto, 1995; Melvin, 1995; Chinn and Kaiser, 1996; Bremmer and Taras, 1997; Laitin, 1998; Smith *et al.*, 1998). Third, there are those studies which are informed by theory, whether theories of nationalism and ethnic conflict regulation, or theories of democratic transition, or more rarely a combination of the three (Brubaker, 1996; Linz and Stepan, 1996; Bunce, 1999).

Previous studies of post-Soviet conflicts have not, in our view, established the appropriate balance between comparison and generalization on the one hand, and rigorous empirical study on the other. Van Evera, for example, emphasizes the role of weak states in the link between nationalism and war using a 'danger scale' that expresses the likelihood of nationalism turning violent on the basis of three types of factors: structural (arising from the geographic and demographic arrangement of a nation), political-environmental (arising from the past or present conduct of a people's neighbours) and perceptual (arising from the nationalist movement's self-image and images of others). He concludes that Eastern Europe and the FSU are danger zones characterized by a rising tide of nationalism and violence, yet offers little empirical evidence to ground his hypothesis (Van Evera, 1994: 34). Similarly, surveying the obvious in several centuries of state-building, Snyder views the dynamics of the historical process of democratization as the main cause of ethnic conflict (Snyder, 2000).[12] In a sketch of post-communist conflicts, he surmises that they are a product of Soviet-era ethno-federalism and regional autonomy, without any elaboration of this point (Snyder, 2000: 40). Comparative studies are sometimes characterized by a lack of regional knowledge which gives rise to serious factual errors. A recent article by Carment and James, for example, confuses the Soviet Union and

Russia, stating: 'Antagonisms within Russia proper – i.e. Tatarstan, North and South Ossetia, Donbass and the Crimea and the Trans-Dniester region – are ongoing'(Carment and James, 2000: 190). One of the few studies that draws on the three literatures discussed above is that of Roeder (1999: 854–84). Roeder's argument about post-communist state- and nation-building reiterates the doubts inherent in liberal-democratic theory about the sustainability of democracy in ethnically divided societies and about the efficacy of institutional mechanisms for managing ethnicity. Roeder criticizes the promotion of power-sharing as aggravating the ethnification of politics through a polarization of preferences, which ultimately undermines the consensus for democracy. Power-sharing institutions are considered less important for conflict management than demographic and cultural factors. One of these key factors is a quantifiable dimension – the size of the ethnic minority relative to the core nation; the other, however, is an unquantifiable one – the cultural distance between the core nation and the minority (Roeder, 1999: 873–76). Cultural proximity, however, is no panacea for national or ethnic tensions, as the uneasy relations between Russia and Ukraine demonstrate. Most importantly, Roeder's argument appears to be shaped by the notion of 'democracy from scratch'. This neglects the fact that an institutional architecture, and in many cases a multi-ethnic society, were already *in situ* when the USSR collapsed and successor states began their state-building projects, and it dismisses the capacity of institutions *per se* to be an effective means of democratic conflict-resolution. In contrast, our approach emphasizes the critical role of institutions both for the initiation of conflict and for how states may stabilize, manage or even prevent conflict. Roeder assumes that most successor states have experienced conflicts amidst democratization. If this were so, then his conclusion, that a stable democracy cannot triumph in countries that have not solved their 'nation-ness problems', would be valid. For most post-Soviet states, however, a focus on the question of the 'survival of democracy' is premature and tells us little, if anything, about state-building and conflict-management in states that are very much unconsolidated democracies, and with many being strongly authoritarian and sultanistic in character.

It is crucial to remember that we are dealing with new states which suffered a severe debilitation of their institutional capacity as a result of Gorbachev's disastrous mismanagement of reform, the collapse of the USSR, and the strains of transition. By 1991 many of the successor states were in a steadily accelerating spiral into anarchy. In such conditions, how was the Soviet institutional legacy decommissioned, and to what extent and with what effects was it re-engineered or re-tooled to manage issues of autonomy and centralization? What was the relationship between the handling of the institutional legacy and the descent into conflict and anarchy? These are some of the questions that will be explored in the case studies to follow. Our aim is to distinguish better between causal factors and contributing background conditions by focussing on the role of institutions. If we can identify better the institutional issues at the root of many of the post-Soviet conflicts, then the relative importance of the structural and contingent factors can be reassessed. In particular, we may find that supposedly 'ethnic' conflicts are, in fact, more complex and driven not only by ethnicized political issues but also socio-economic, regional, external and other issues.

The contributors to this volume offer a variety of different analyses and interpretations of post-Soviet conflicts, but collectively they pivot their case studies on four key sets of questions: (1) what are the causes of post-Soviet conflicts, and how unique or comparable are these conflicts when measured against the explanations suggested by comparative politics theory?; (2) to what extent are the post-Soviet conflicts ethnic or regional in nature, and what do they tell us about the ethnic and regional dimensions of post-Soviet transition?; (3) what is the relationship between conflict-management or conflict-prevention and the wider challenge of post-communist institutional engineering, given that some conflicts appear to be intractable while others have been resolved or stabilized?; and (4) how does the interaction between domestic and international factors shape the dynamics of post-Soviet ethnic and regional conflicts?

The above questions capture important aspects of the broad use of the terms 'institution' and 'institutionalization' central to our comparative analysis: the formal and informal nature of institutions, the dynamics between the institutional framework and those operating within it, the question of institutional design, institutional hierarchies and the implications of institutional change – whether the de-institutionalization of Soviet legacies occurred by 'nationalizing' and state-building successor states, and the mode of their reassembly, or their revamping into a new form. Our approach to ethnic and regional conflicts in the FSU is, consequently, informed by a focus on the key role of institutions. In particular, we are concerned as a group with the use of formal and informal institutionalized autonomy as a key device for the management of regional and ethnic challenges, since the political dynamics generated by the granting, denial, withdrawal or prospect of attaining of autonomy appears to underpin many post-Soviet conflicts. Autonomy is increasingly viewed, both internationally and by many of the key actors in post-Soviet conflicts, as the key to conflict resolution. It comes, however, at a price for the parties to conflicts, by diluting or even derailing nationalizing projects and by constraining secessionism. This is why its realization is so problematic.

What kind of institutions are we concerned with? The predominant behaviouralist school in political science was challenged in the 1980s by a renewed emphasis on the role of institutions – broadly defined – and their central role for mediation and aggregation between structural factors on the one hand and individuals and interest groups on the other hand. Institutions raise issues of inclusion and exclusion, of representation, mediation, efficiency and transaction costs. The economic historian Douglass North, in an attempt to integrate institutional analysis, economics and economic history, defined institutions as 'any form of constraint that human beings devise to shape human interaction' (North, 1990: 4). Importantly, his general definition includes both 'formal constraints – such as rules that human beings devise – and informal constraints – such as conventions and codes of behaviour'. Another useful definition of 'institution', focusing on the political process, has been suggested by O'Donnell: 'Institutions are regularized patterns of interaction that are known, practiced, and regularly accepted (if not normatively approved) by social agents who expect to continue interacting under the rules and norms formally or informally embodied in those patterns. ...Some political institutions are formal organizations belonging to the constitutional network of a polyarchy... Others, such as fair elections, have an intermittent organizational embodiment but are no less indispensable.' According to O'Donnell, institutions are key elements in the political process because they perform a range of vital functions: they incorporate and exclude, they shape the probability of distribution of outcomes, they aggregate the action and organization of agents, induce patterns of representation, stabilize agents/representatives and their expectations, and they lengthen the time-horizon of actors (O'Donnell, 1996: 96–8). According to these definitions, autonomy can be both a formal or informal institution, that is, fixed by constitutional or legal rules or an informal practice, thus incorporating both *de jure* and *de facto* notions of autonomy. Furthermore, our emphasis on institutions includes both formal rules of the game and the actors involved in playing the game. Institutions, consequently, in addition to structuring the incentives also act as constraints on behaviour.

The contributions to the volume can be broadly divided into case studies where conflicts did not occur because of strategies of accommodation and case studies of conflicts which arose for a variety of historical and contingent reasons. Institutional mechanisms, most importantly different kinds of asymmetric federalism and autonomy arrangements, have emerged as the single most important strategy of regional conflict-prevention and inter-ethnic and regional accommodation in the FSU. If we understand this as embracing formal and informal institutional mechanisms, then our task is to explain why in some places elites reached a settlement on a new institutional architecture for power-sharing through peaceful negotiation and other cases ended in violent conflict.

Crimea is, perhaps, the case of a conflict that did not occur *par excellence*. Gwendolyn Sasse traces the process of integration of Crimea into post-Soviet Ukraine as one of the key tests of its state- and nation-building. She observes that the Russian secessionist movement that mobilized in Crimea in the early 1990s was not simply a response to perceived Ukrainian nationalizing policies in Kyiv and in the region, but also was impelled by the economic concerns of the regional elite. As Crimea was one of the most 'Sovietized' regions in the whole of the former USSR both in terms of popular attitudes and economic structure (it was heavily dependent on Soviet tourism and MIC industries), Crimea was severely affected by the economic crisis of the early transition years. As Sasse explains, Ukraine's ethnic and linguistic bifurcation between Ukrainophones and Russophones is extremely fuzzy. More importantly, Ukraine is a 'regional state' composed of distinct regions which have never before been united within one independent state. Consequently, the 'new' Ukraine has had to face several territorial challenges from its 'new' regions, rather than clear-cut ethnic challenges, since gaining independence in 1991. Transcarpathia, the Donbas region and, above all, Crimea emerged as potential conflict areas in the immediate aftermath of the Soviet collapse. In fact, fears of forced Ukrainization and economic decline did not result in significant ethno-political mobilization in Transcarpathia, the Donbas and other East Ukrainian regions. Only in Crimea, where there were complex historical, multi-ethnic, linguistic, socio-economic and international factors at play, was there a serious ethno-regional challenge to Ukrainian state-building. Sasse demonstrates how the Crimean challenge was defused by a constitution-making process which locked national and regional elites into the same bargaining arena from 1990 to 1998 and resulted in a special autonomy status for Crimea in the Ukrainian constitution. Moreover, the process of resolving the Crimean issue fostered a more generic civic definition of the Ukrainian state, though it detracted from progress on economic reform.

Another example of a constitutionally embedded accommodation strategy is analysed by Steven Roper who compares the different policies pursued by the Moldovan government in managing the demands of Transdnistria and Gagauzia. The Gagauz, a territorially concentrated Turkish-speaking Christian people, declared an independent republic in 1989, but Moldova did not perceive it as a threat to its territorial integrity and embarked on a negotiation process to accommodate it within the new state. The Gagauz were not only highly Russified and Sovietized, but also largely agricultural and economically dependent on Moldova – factors which appear to have eased the accommodation. The result was a limited but constitutionalized autonomy arrangement agreed in 1995. In contrast, although similar factors prevailed in Transdnistria, which is the Russified, Sovietized and highly industrialized eastern part of the country on the River Dnistr bordering Ukraine, an accommodation proved impossible to negotiate. In this case, the overwhelmingly Russophone regional population felt threatened by the nationalizing policies pursued by Moldova's post-independence governments, in particular the privileging of the Romanian language. It was feared that the promotion of Romanian would be a first step towards unification with Romania. While the linguistic concerns of the ethnic Russian and Sovietized population of Transdnistria were a salient factor behind the outbreak of conflict, inter-elite centre–periphery economic competition was also a significant factor. The Transdnistrian regional elite favoured *de facto* secession in order to resist any political and economic takeover by rival Moldovan elites based in the capital Chisinau. As Roper explains, the Transdnistria conflict had a crippling effect on Moldova's transition politics, forcing the resignation of the government in 1994 and causing a serious neglect of socio-economic issues. Consequently, the early parliamentary elections of 1994 saw a shift in Moldova's emerging party system away from ethno-political mobilization to politics based on more pragmatic and cross-cutting socio-economic issues and cleavages. This culminated in the return of former communists to power in the 2001 elections. The shift away from ethno-nationalism has assisted the move to an accommodation of Transdnistrian separatism on the Moldovan side, but this has been met by an impenetrable radicalization on the Transdnistrian side that has so far prevented a resolution of the conflict.

Accommodation strategies may also be parallel or co-constitutional arrangements. The asymmetric federalism of the bilateral treaties between the Russian Federation and Tatarstan and Bashkortostan are examples of this type. The chapter by James Hughes shows how developments within the Russian Federation set a precedent for preserving and empowering the asymmetric federal institutional arrangements inherited from the Soviet Union. When confronted by secessionist movements, the Russian Federation experimented with extra-constitutional power-sharing bilateral treaties to defuse conflicts, most notably with Tatarstan and Bashkortostan in 1994. A crucial role in the institutional accommodation of separatism in Russia was played by the emergence of a strong presidential patrimonial system under Boris Yeltsin. Thus, in Russia formal and informal institutional processes of elite bargaining and accommodation were intertwined, at least during the initial period in the immediate aftermath of the Soviet collapse. It was precisely, however, this interconnection of informal rules, institutional flexibility and the personalization of the bargaining process that prevented an accommodation of what proved to be Russia's most serious secessionist challenge, Chechnya, due to irreconcilable personal animosities between Yeltsin and Chechen leader Dzhokhar Dudaev. The bloody military conflict in 1994–96, leading to the Russian defeat and forced withdrawal from Chechnya, was a national humiliation for Russia that intensified inter-ethnic hatred and made politically stable relations between Russian and Chechnya a near impossibility. Russia's launch of a second war in the autumn of 1999 was, in essence, an instrumentalization of the conflict with Chechnya to bolster Putin's domestic popularity and chances of succession in the run-up to the post-Yeltsin regime alternance. The protracted, bitter and bloody nature of the conflict in Chechnya has radicalized positions on both sides and makes a political solution along the lines of the Tatarstan model remote in the immediate future.

Constitutional referents are fundamental to the conflicts in Georgia. Monica Duffy Toft maps the historical background to the conflicts, tracing them to the foundation years of the Soviet Union. In the 1920s Abkhazia was a Soviet SSR alongside Georgia before being downgraded to a subordinate ASSR in 1935 under Stalin. Similarly, attempts to unite North and South Ossetia after the Bolshevik revolution failed and South Ossetia became an Autonomous Oblast' within Georgia in 1922. The democratization reforms of Gorbachev led to renewed claims for constitutional changes which culminated in 1989–90 during the war of sovereignties between the USSR government and the union republics. The contagion effect of separatism by the union republics was strongly felt in particular in those union republics with teritorialized autonomous units, such as Russia and Georgia. The conflicts in Abkhazia and South Ossetia were exacerbated by the concerns of national minorities at the rise of Georgian nationalism and the nationalizing policies pursued by Georgia's nationalist president Zviad Gamzakhurdia and continued by his successor Eduard Shevardnadze. South Ossetia and Abkhazia followed the 'parade of sovereignties' initiated by Yeltsin and the autonomous republics of Russia from summer 1990, declaring themselves 'Soviet republics'. South Ossetia demanded reunification with its northern part in Russia, while the Abkhaz wanted built-in institutional and electoral guarantees against domination from the ethnic Georgian majority in Abkhazia. The wave of separatism provoked a backlash from the nationalist dominated Georgian parliament which voted to unilaterally abolish South Ossetia's autonomy status in December 1990. The conflict in Abkhazia was sparked later when Shevardnadze sent a military force into the republic in August 1992. In contrast, the territorial challenge from Ajaria came from a group who defined themselves as 'Georgians with a different religion'. Ajaria's authoritarian leader, Aslan Abashidze, built close patrimonial ties with the controlling networks at the political centre in Georgia, and successfully negotiated a *modus vivendi* and *de facto* greater autonomy by not questioning the Georgian state- and nation-building process. Such demands were much more easily accommodated within a nationalizing Georgian state than those of Abkhazia and South Ossetia, though Ajaria's autonomy status was not constitutionally entrenched.[13]

Soviet history also resonates in another Caucasian conflict, as Razmik Panossian demonstrates in his study of Nagorno-Karabakh. This conflict has its roots in the politics of Soviet boundary-making in the 1920s and 1930s, which gave the Karabakh Armenians the status of an ASSR within Azerbaijan in 1923 and failed to unite them with their Armenian homeland in subsequent bouts of boundary redrawing. This settlement was potentially explosive given the historical ethnic and religious enmity between Turks and Armenians, but was successfully constrained by the Soviet control regime. The Artsakh (the Armenian name for Karabakh) secessionist movement of 1988 was one of the first ethno-political mobilizations to emerge from Gorbachev's liberalization and led to the imposition of direct rule by the Soviet government in 1989. All-out military conflict erupted after the end of the Soviet Union in 1991 and continued to 1994. The initial drive for secession originated within the region itself and while the Soviet Union still existed, and in fact before the democratizing aspects of perestroika were fully implemented. One of the distinctive features of the Nagorno-Karabakh conflict, compared with those in other parts of the FSU, is that it was not triggered by the post-Soviet nationalizing policies of a hegemonic ethnic group, the so-called 'titular nationality' of a union republic. The Artsakh secessionist movement was an internally produced nationalist irredentism that quickly rallied mass popular support from Armenia *propre* and its influential diaspora in North America. In the case of Nagorno-Karabakh the de-institutionalization of Soviet administrative structures came from below, rather than from above from an Azerbaijani nationalizing state. In fact, Armenian secessionism intensified a reactive nationalist mobilization within Azerbaijan.

Kyrgyzstan, Kazakhstan and Uzbekistan offer additional evidence for the impact of type of regime on the management of conflict potential. As Neil Melvin demonstrates, Central Asia has emerged as a distinct sub-set of post-Soviet states, characterized by quasi-dynastic authoritarianism and a preference for informal rules and patrimonialism arrangements. These regimes have, in effect, re-affirmed the control regime of the Soviet era in the management of regional, ethnic and religious diversity, but some have had more success than others. The main trends in state- and nation-building are for centralization and coercion. In Kyrgyzstan, ethnic clashes involving the Uzbek population in the south of the country had already erupted prior to the breakdown of the USSR in the Osh region in 1990. In the period following independence Kyrgyzstan was regarded as the 'democratic island' in Central Asia. During the public debate on how to develop its democracy in the early 1990s the idea of a federation or confederation of the north and the south of the country was raised. President Askar Akaev's rise, however, symbolized the victory of the north over the more Sovietized south, and led to a steady erosion of the nascent democracy in preference for centralized authoritarianism. In Kazakhstan, the early post-Soviet years of 1991–95 were characterized by the containment of a potential ethno-regional challenge from the Russophone north of Kazakhstan by a twin strategy of control, by suppression of Russophone political movements and Kazakhization of administration and security, and the accommodation of Russophone elites by cooption, particularly in the economy. President Nursultan Nazarbaev's authoritarian rule took a gradualist approach to 'nationalizing policies'. In 1995 he implemented a significant territorial restructuring to disaggregate the Russophone northern regions and further centralize control. The lack of mobilization in the north demonstrates the fragmented nature of the Russian community and its 'Sovietness' rather than ethnic Russian identity. Consequently, the preferred option for Russians became 'exit' by emigration to the Russian Federation and not 'voice' in a steadily repressive and neo-traditional Kazakhized regime. Uzbekistan is another control regime, where the inherited regional networks of the Soviet era have been reconfigured by the centralizing rule of President Islam Karimov. For example, the Autonomous Republic of Karakalpakstan, inherited from the Soviet era, continues to exist under the post-Soviet constitution of Uzbekistan. Despite the socio-economic and environmental catastrophe caused in the region by the erosion of the Aral Sea, Karakalpakstan is strictly subordinated by the repressive control regime of Karimov. The violent inter-ethnic clashes in the Ferghana Valley from 1989 demonstrate the importance of territorial disputes among the three states that intersect it (Uzbekistan, Kyrgyzistan and Kazakhstan). Home to a highly intermingled multi-ethnic population, the valley has seen the emergence of a vibrant Islamic mobilization which is largely the product of extreme socio-economic deprivation and demographic problems. Melvin's perspective demonstrates the potential fragility of the highly centralized presidential regimes of the region over managing the complex issues in the Ferghana Valley, which is widely recognized to be one of the prospective flashpoints for violent conflict in the FSU. To strengthen the comparative aspect of our study the analysis of ethnic and regional conflicts is not tied exclusively to emerging post-Soviet democracies, or to formal institutional trends, but aims to be as inclusive as possible by incorporating authoritarian and quasi-dynastic regimes in Central Asia and the Caucasus. In the latter cases, informal institutional devices are more evident in the management of multi-ethnicity through informal cooption and reward structures, though this is not to overlook the fact that patrimonial relations are a strong inherited feature in the politics of the whole FSU. While elite and mass ethnic and regional grievances over historical and contingent factors may be closely intertwined in both rhetoric and actual practice, the case studies which follow aim to clarify the relative balance of significance between these elements and the role of institutions in order to identify the primary factors of causation and the driving forces behind the range of post-Soviet conflicts.

ACKNOWLEDGEMENTS

The authors gratefully acknowledge the comments on earlier drafts of this paper of their fellow contributors at the panels on Ethnic Conflict in the FSU at the Political Studies Association annual conference, LSE, April 1999, of their colleagues Brendan O'Leary, Dominic Lieven and Jennifer Jackson-Preece, and of the participants at the ECPR Joint Sessions workshop on Political Transformation in the Soviet Successor States, Grenoble, April 2001.

NOTES

1. A recent article on conflicts in the Caucasus in *The Economist* illustrates this stereotyping very well. A hotchpotch of misreporting of facts and the roles of external actors, such as Russia, USA or Europe, in stabilizing the region, it presents a crude table of the sterotypical characteristics of the parties to the various conflicts. See 'The Caucasus: Where Worlds Collide', *The Economist*, 19 August 2000, pp.19–23.
2. They distinguish between eight different forms of macro-political conflict-regulation in two categories: *Methods for eliminating differences* (genocide, forced mass-population transfers, partition and/or secession [self-determination], integration and/or assimilation), and *Methods for managing differences* (hegemonic control, arbitration [third-party intervention], cantonization and/or federalization, consociationalism or power-sharing).
3. This instrumental interpretation of ethnicity is informed by rational choice theories. There is an expanding literature on ethnicity and rational choice, but for the purposes of this volume the mere acknowledgement that pragmatic choices can underpin ethno-political mobilization will suffice.
4. These are: (1) self-government rights, e.g. devolution of power, federalization, balance between centralization and decentralization; (2) poly-ethnic rights, e.g. the permission to express cultural particularities without fear of discrimination or prejudice; and (3) special representation rights, e.g. a certain number of seats in the legislature reserved for a specific group.
5. Mill's full observation was: 'Free institutions are next to impossible in a country made up of different nationalities. Among a people without fellow-feeling, especially if they read and speak different languages, the united public opinion, necessary to the working of representative government, cannot exist.'

6. Their argument is that the temporal sequence of founding elections is crucial for state cohesion: 'If in multi-national polities the first elections are regional, ...there will be strong incentives for political contestation to focus on antistate ethnic issues.'
7. Wilson's own Secretary of State, Robert Lansing, insisted that the principle should be applied to 'certain races' only. In creating new states, the Great Powers at Versailles neither respected ethnic self-determination considerations in Europe (as the cases of Germany and Hungary all too clearly demonstrated) or in Germany's colonies, nor indeed in their own domains (Halperin et al., 16–19).
8. Conflicts leading to indeterminate status for territories include those between Israel and Palestine and neighbouring Arab states, India and Pakistan over Kashmir, Greece and Turkey over Northern Cyprus, Taiwan, and Northern Ireland.
9. Most infamously in the 'Chicken Kiev' speech of US President George Bush on 1 August 1991, when he told Ukrainian leaders that 'Freedom is not the same as independence', New York Times, 2 August 1991.
10. It remains to be seen how the latest test case for this policy of recognition, Kosovo, will be resolved, but as of April 2001 the territory is militarily occupied by a NATO and Russian force and has an indeterminate status.
11. This appears to be common in state break-ups: the centre argues that peripheries within the secessionist unit should also have the right of secession. Examples include the promotion by UK elites of the 'Ulster Question' leading to the partition of Ireland in 1921, and the Canadian federalists' encouragement of Inuit claims in Quebec.
12. Snyder describes the link between democratization and conflict as follows: 'As more people begin to play a larger role in politics, ethnic conflict within a country becomes more likely, as does international aggression justified by national ideas' (p.27). He also includes the prospects of incomplete democratization: 'Democratization gives rise to nationalism because it serves the interests of powerful groups within the nation who seek to harness popular energies to the tasks of war and economic development without surrendering real political authority to the average citizen' (p.36).
13. Article 1 of the Georgian Constitution of 1995 specifically claims sovereignty over the 'Autonomous Soviet Socialist Republic of Abkhazia, and the former Autonomous District of South Ossetia', but it does not mention the Autonomous Region of Ajaria. Other articles such as 4, 55, 67, 89, treat Ajaria as having the same or similar status as Abkhazia. See: http://www.parliament.ge/GOVERNANCE.

REFERENCES

Arbatov, Alexei (ed.) (1977), *Managing Conflict in the Former Soviet Union: Russian and American Perspectives*. Cambridge, Mass.: MIT Press.

Barry, Brian (1989), *Democracy, Power and Justice: Essays in Political Theory*. Oxford: Clarendon.

Bremmer, Ian and Ray Taras (eds) (1997), *New States, New Politics: Building the Post-Soviet Nations*. Cambridge: Cambridge University Press.

Brubaker, Rogers (1996), *Nationalism Reframed: Nationhood and the National Question in the New Europe*. Cambridge: Cambridge University Press.

Buchanan, Allen (1991), *Secession: The Morality of Political Divorce from Fort Sumtner to Lithuania and Quebec*. Boulder: Westview Press.

Bunce, Valerie (1995), 'Should Transitologists Be Grounded?', *Slavic Review*, Vol.54, No.1 (Spring), pp. 111–27; (1995) 'Paper Curtains and Paper Tigers', *Slavic Review*, Vol.54, No.4 (Winter), pp. 979–87; (1995) 'Comparing East and South', *Journal of Democracy*, Vol.6, No.3 (July), pp.87–100; (1999) *Subversive Institutions. The Design and the Destruction of Socialism and the State*. Cambridge: Cambridge University Press.

Carment, David and Patrick James (1997), 'Ethnic Conflict at the International Level: An Appraisal of Theories and Evidence', in D. Carment and P. James (eds), *Wars in the Midst of Peace. The International Politics of International Conflict*, Pittsburgh: University of Pittsburgh Press; (2000) 'Explaining Third-Party Intervention in Ethnic Conflict: Theory and Evidence', *Nations and Nationalism*, Vol.6, No.2 (2000), pp.173–202.

Chinn, Jeff and Robert Kaiser (1996), *Russians as the New Minority. Ethnicity and Nationalism in the Soviet Successor States.* Boulder: Westview Press.

Connor, Walker (1984), *The National Question in Marxist-Leninist Theory and Strategy.* Princeton: Princeton University Press.

Dahl, Robert (1971), *Polyarchy: Participation and Opposition,* Yale: Yale University Press, New Haven and London; (1989) *Democracy and its Critics.* New Haven: Yale University Press.

Di Palma, Guiseppe (1990), *To Craft Democracies: An Essay on Democratic Transitions.* Berkeley: University of California Press.

Leokadia Drobizheva *et al.* (eds) (1996), *Ethnic Conflict in the Post-Soviet World: Case Studies and Analysis.* Armonk: M.E. Sharpe.

The Economist (2000), 'The Caucasus: Where Worlds Collide', 19 August, pp.19–23.

Esman, Milton J. (1994), *Ethnic Politics.* Ithaca: Cornell University Press.

Fish, M. Steven (1995), *Democracy from Scratch: Opposition and Regime in the New Russian Revolution.* Princeton, N.J: Princeton University Press; (1999) 'Postcommunist Subversion: Social Science and Democratization in East Europe and Eurasia', *Slavic Review,* Vol.58 (Winter 1999), pp.794–823.

Forsberg, Tuomas (ed.) (1995) *Contested Territory: Border Disputes at the Edge of the Former Soviet Union.* Aldershot: Edward Elgar.

Gellner, Ernest (1997), *Nationalism.* London: Weidenfeld & Nicholson.

Gurr, Ted Robert and Barbara Harff (1994), *Ethnic Conflict in World Politics.* Boulder: Westview Press.

Gurr, Ted Robert (2000), 'Ethnic Warfare on the Wane', *Foreign Affairs,* Vol.79, No.3, pp.52–64.

Halperin, Morton H., David J. Scheffer, with Patricia L. Small (1992), *Self-Determination in the New World Order.* Washington D.C.: Carnegie Endowment for International Peace.

Heraclides, Alexis (1997), 'Ethnicity, Secessionist Conflict and the International Society: Towards a Normative Paradigm Shift', *Nations and Nationalism,* Vol.3, No.4, pp.493–520.

Higley, John and Michael G. Burton (1989), 'The Elite Variable in Democratic Transitions and Breakdowns', *American Sociological Review,* Vol.54, No.1 (February), pp.17–32.

Hislope, Robert (1998), 'Ethnic Conflict and the "Generosity Moment"', *Journal of Democracy,* Vol.9, No.1, pp.140–53.

Hobsbawm, Eric (1990), *Nations and Nationalism Since 1780: Programme, Myth and Reality.* Cambridge, Cambridge University Press.

Horowitz, Donald L. (1985), *Ethnic Groups in Conflict.* Berkeley: California University Press; (1990) 'Comparing Democratic Systems', *Journal of Democracy,* Vol.1, No.4 (Fall), pp.73–9.

Hough, Jerry (1997), *Democratization and Revolution in the USSR.* Washington D.C.: The Brookings Institution.

Keating, Michael (1988), *State and Regional Nationalism: Territorial Politics and the European State.* New York: Harvester; (1998) *The New Regionalism in Western Europe: Territorial Restructuring and Political Change.* Northampton, Mass.: Edward Elgar.

Kemp, Walter A. (1996), *The OSCE in a New Context: European Security towards the Twenty-First Century.* London: Royal Institute of International Affairs, Discussion Paper 64.

Kingsbury, Benedict (1992), 'Claims by Non-state Actors in International Law', *Cornell International Law Journal,* Vol.25, No.3, p.487.

Kolsto, Pal (1995), *Russians in the Former Soviet Republics.* London: Hurst & Co.

Kumar, Radha (1997), *Divide and Fall? Bosnia in the Annals of Partition.* London: Verso.

Kymlicka, Will (1995), *Multicultural Citizenship: A Liberal Theory of Minority Rights.* Oxford: Clarendon Press.

Laitin, David (1998), *Identity in Formation: The Russian-Speaking Population in the Near Abroad.* Ithaca: Cornell University Press.

Lake, David A. and Donald Rothchild (eds) (1998), *The International Spread of Ethnic Conflict: Fear, Diffusion, and Escalation.* Princeton: Princeton University Press.

Lapidoth, Ruth (1997), *Autonomy: Flexible Solutions to Ethnic Conflict.* Washington, D.C.: United States Institute of Peace Research.

Lieven, Dominic (2000), *Empire: The Russian Empire and Its Rivals*. London: John Murray.

Lijphart, Arend (1977), *Democracy in Plural Societies: A Comparative Exploration*. New Haven: Yale University Press.

Linz, Juan (1990), 'The Perils of Presidentialism', *The Journal of Democracy*, Vol.1, No.1 (Winter), pp.51–69; (1994) 'Presidential or Parliamentary Democracy: Does It Make a Difference?', in J. Linz and A. Valenzuela (eds), *The Failure of Presidential Democracy, Comparative Perspectives, Vol.1*. Baltimore: Johns Hopkins University Press, pp.3–87.

Linz, Juan J. and Alfred Stepan (1996), *Problems of Democratic Consolidation: Southern Europe, South America, and Post-Communist Europe*. Baltimore: John Hopkins University Press; (1992) 'Political Identities and Electoral Sequences: Spain, the Soviet Union and Yugoslavia', *Daedalus*, Vol.121, No.2, pp.123–39.

Lipset, Seymour and Stein Rokkan (1967), 'Cleavage Structures, Party Systems, and Voter Alignments: An Introduction', in S. Lipset and S. Rokkan (eds), *Party Systems and Voter Alignments. Cross-National Perspectives*. New York: Free Press, pp.1–64.

Lustick, Ian (1979), 'Stability in Deeply Divided Societies', *World Politics*, Vol.31, No.3, pp.325–44; (1993) *Unsettled States, Disputed Lands: Britain and Ireland, France and Algeria, Israel and the West Bank-Gaza*. Ithaca: Cornell University Press.

Melvin, Neil (1995), *Russians Beyond Russia: The Politics of National Identity*. London: The Royal Institute of International Affairs/Pinter.

Mill, John Stuart (1861), *Considerations on Representative Government*. Oxford University Press, Oxford [1974].

Nordlinger, Eric A. (1972), *Conflict-Regulation in Divided Societies*. Cambridge, Mass.: Center for International Affairs, Harvard University.

North, Douglass C. (1990), *Institutions, Institutional Change and Economic Performance*. Cambridge: Cambridge University Press.

Offe, Claus (1996), *Varieties of Transition: The East European and East German Experience*. Cambridge: Polity Press.

O'Donnell, Guillermo (1996), 'Delegative Democracy', in Larry Diamond and Marc F. Plattner (eds), *The Global Resurgence of Democracy*. Baltimore: John Hopkins University Press, pp.94–108.

O'Leary, Brendan and John McGarry (eds) (1993), *The Politics of Ethnic Conflict Regulation*. London: Routledge.

O'Leary, Brendan (1997), 'On the Nature of Nationalism: An Appraisal of Ernest Gellner's Writings on Nationalism', *British Journal of Political Science*, Vol.27, No.2, pp.191–222; (1998) 'Ernest Gellner's Diagnoses of Nationalism: A Critical Overview, or, What Is Living and What Is Dead in Ernest Gellner's Philosophy of Nationalism', in John A. Hall (ed), *The State of the Nation: Ernest Gellner and the Theory of Nationalism*. Cambridge, Cambridge University Press, pp.40–90; (2001) 'Nationalism and Ethnicity: Research Agendas on Theories of Their Sources and Their Regulation', in Daniel Chirot and Martin E.P. Seligman (eds), *Ethnopolitical Warfare: Causes, Consequences and Possible Solutions*. Washington D.C.: American Psychological Association, pp.37–48.

Przeworski, Adam (1992), 'The Games of Transition', in Scott Mainwaring, Guillermo O'Donnell and J. Samuel Valenzuela (eds), *Issues in Democratic Consolidation*. Notre Dame: Indiana University Press, pp.105–52.

Rabushka, Alvin and Kenneth Shepsle (1972), *Politics in Plural Societies: A Theory of Democratic Instability*. Columbus, Ohio: Merrill.

Roeder, Philip G. (1999), 'Peoples and States after 1989: The Political Costs of Incomplete National Revolutions', *Slavic Review*, Vol.58, No.4 (Winter), pp.854–84.

Rokkan, Stein and Derek W. Urwin (1983), *Economy, Territory, Identity: Politics of West European Peripheries*. London: Sage.

Rothchild, Joseph (1981), *Ethnopolitics: A Conceptual Framework*. New York: Columbia University Press.

Rubin, Barnett (1998), 'Conclusion: Managing Normal Instability', in B. Rubin and J. Snyder (eds), *Post-Soviet Political Order: Conflict and State Building*. London: Routledge, pp.166–8.

Rustow, Dankwart (1970), 'Transitions to Democracy: Toward a Dynamic Model', *Comparative Politics*, Vol.2, No.3 (October), pp.337–63.

Schmitter, Philippe and Terry Lynn Karl (1994) 'The Conceptual Travels of Transitologists and Consolidologists: How Far to the East Should They Go?', *Slavic Review*, Vol.53, No.2, pp.173–85; (1995) 'From and Iron Curtain to a Paper Curtain: Grounding Transitologists or Students of Communism?', *Slavic Review*, Vol.54, No.4, pp.965–87.

Schmitter, Philippe (1996), 'The Influence of the International Context upon the Choice of National Institutions and Policies in Neo-Democracies', in Laurence Whitehead (ed.), *The International Dimensions of Democratization: Europe and the Americas*. Oxford: Oxford University Press, pp.26–54.

Shaw, Malcolm (1996), 'The Heritage of States: The Principle of Uti Possidetis Juris Today', *British Yearbook of International Law*, Vol.67, pp.75–154.

Shugart, Matthew and John M. Carey (1992), *Presidents and Assemblies: Constitutional Design and Electoral Dynamics*. Cambridge: Cambridge University Press.

Shugart, Matthew (1996), 'Executive–legislative Relations in Post-Communist Europe', *Transition*, December 1996, pp.6–11.

Smith, Graham, Vivien Law, Andrew Wilson, Annette Bohr and Edward Allworth, (1998), *Nation-Building in the Post-Soviet Borderlands: The Politics of National Identities*. Cambridge: Cambridge University Press.

Snyder, Jack (1998), 'Introduction: Reconstructing Politics amidst the Wreckage of Empire', in Barnet Rubin and Jack Snyder (eds), *Post-Soviet Political Order: Conflict and State Building*. London: Routledge, pp.1–13; (2000) *From Voting to Violence: Democratization and Nationalist Conflict*. New York: W.W. Norton & Co.

Stepan, A (1999), 'Federalism and Democracy: Beyond the US Model', *Journal of Democracy*, Vol.10, No.4, pp.19–34

Szporluk, Roman (ed.) (1994), *National Identity and Ethnicity in Russia and the New States of Eurasia*. Armonk: M.E. Sharpe.

Van Evera, Stephen (1994), 'Hypotheses on Nationalism and War', *International Security*, Vol.18, No.4 (Spring), pp.5–39.

Walker, Lee (1996), 'Nationalism and Ethnic Conflict in the Post-Soviet Transition', in Leokadia Drobizheva *et al.* (eds), *Ethnic Conflict in the Post-Soviet World. Case Studies and Analysis*. Armonk, NY: M.E. Sharpe, pp.3–13.

Walzer, Michael (1983), *Spheres of Justice: A Defence of Pluralism and Equality*. Oxford: Blackwell.

Whitehead, Laurence (ed.) (1996), *The International Dimensions of Democratization: Europe and the Americas*. Oxford: Oxford University Press.

Woodward, Susan (1995), *Balkan Tragedy: Chaos and Dissolution after the Cold War*. Washington, D.C.: The Brookings Institution.

Managing Secession Potential in the Russian Federation

JAMES HUGHES

The survival of the Russian Federation for a decade after the fall of communism is an exceptional case in post-communist transitions since all the other federal communist states have collapsed. The Soviet Union dissolved suddenly and chaotically, Czechoslovakia had a peacefully negotiated disassociation, and Yugoslavia was ruptured by civil war. This pattern suggests that the combination of multi-ethnicity, federal state, and democratizing transition is a highly unstable compound. Democratization of communist-type federations is generally seen as conducive to state collapse because of the institutional territorialization of ethnicity, what Brubaker terms 'institutionalized multinationality' (Brubaker, 1996: 26). This institutional feature is seen as exercising a 'subversive' corroding effect on central authority which in certain conditions may be the catalyst for a break-up of the state (Bunce, 1999). Such conclusive statements about the poor viability of communist era federations generally exclude the non-collapse of the Russian Federation from their analysis. The survival of Russia as a federal state seems all the more unusual given that it exhibits many of the characteristics that contributed to the collapse of the Soviet Union: its huge size, territorialized ethnicity in complex administrative divisions, together with the general dysfunction and weakening of the state during political and economic transition.

THE STUDY OF RUSSIA'S FEDERAL TRANSITION

Studies of transition by and large have neglected the role of federalism in the ethnic and territorial dimensions of democratization – a neglect that is compounded significantly when both dimensions coincide in a federal transition, as they have done in Russia. Recent studies of post-Soviet Russian federalism, particularly by scholars in the USA, are strongly influenced by those theories of federalism which, as indicated in the introduction to this volume, draw on the pessimism of liberal democratic theory and are negative about the prospects for stability in plural societies. Consequently, such works are generally dismissive of the prospects for a stable refederalization in Russia. This view gained momentum during the 1990s when new institutional designs were developed in Russia which refashioned the territorially defined asymmetric federalism inherited from the Soviet era by selectively empowering it. This process of asymmetric refederalization culminated in a largely non-transparent process of bilateral treaty-making between the federal presidency of Boris Yeltsin and many of the executives of republics and regions in the period 1994–98. By the summer of 1998, 46 of the 89 'subjects' (constituent units) of the federation, including all republics, had negotiated bilateral treaties, the last being signed with Moscow City in May 1998. As only a small number of these treaties provided for a significant devolution of powers, the refederalization of Russia was territory specific, with the most significant power-sharing agreements being concluded with the key 'ethnic' republics of the federation, Tatarstan, Bashkortostan and Sakha. The salience of the 'ethnic' factor in the power-sharing geometry of Russia's refederalization led to a perception among many scholars, both Russian and Western, that the process would strengthen separatist and secessionist threats to the territorial integrity of the state.

For some the principle of asymmetric federalism is inherently destabilizing because it created a two-tier federation with a few key 'ethnic' republics enjoying a privileged constitutional position and revenue-enhancing economic concessions compared with the majority of regions which are overwhelmingly Russian populated (Dmitrieva, 1993; Busygina, 1994; Slider, 1994; Lapidus and Teague, 1995; Umnova, 1996; Aklaev, 1999). Asymmetric federalism was also viewed as creating a potential deluge of instability caused by a downward spiral of 'ethnic' deviance. Since the rebellious sub-national elites that mobilized an 'ethnic revival' were 'rewarded', coopted and bought off by the centre through bilateral treaties, their demands were likely to steadily expand and create a crisis of control (Treisman, 1996 and 1999). Economists have applied the 'fiscal federalism' approach derived from the experience of advanced capitalist federal states such as the USA, Canada and Germany, despite the absence of fiscal transparency, and the unreliability of published budgetary data in Russia (Wallich, 1992, 1994, 1997; Bahl and Wallich, 1995).

The 'federal bargaining' approach of William Riker has been widely employed by US political scientists to analyse Russian federalism. Based on the study of the federal system in the USA, this model stresses the critical importance of political parties as agents for making the process work. In the absence of the mediating presence of strong political parties, it is argued, the 'bargaining game' of Russian federalism is unworkable (Ordeshook, 1995). Of course, 'bidding games' over power, authority and status, like those propagated by Russia's refederalization in the 1990s, are merely the stuff of politics. All federations are asymmetric as regards the political influence and socio-economic power of constitutent units

(Duchacek, 1970). The issue is whether built-in constitutional or institutional asymmetries are an exceptionally destabilizing factor. Some have argued that asymmetric federalism fostered an anarchic 'scramble for benefits', which by 1998 in Russia had fed into a logic for a 'beggar-thy-neighbour "race to the bottom"' that threatened its territorial integrity (Solnick, 1996, 1998, 2000). If Russia's asymmetric federalism has selectively peripheralized power, however, and it is characterized by weak parties, and yet it is a stable state in the sense that it is not in a process of disintegration, then Riker's theory of federalism is evidently flawed.

While some scholars de-ethnify the study of Russian federalism, concentrating on its impact on notions of democracy and state capacity (Stepan, 2000), others associate asymmetric federalism with a dangerous 'ethnification' of Russian politics that was seen as an obstacle to the building of a harmonizing 'civic' national identity (Smith, 1998 and 1999). Such arguments underpinned a general scholarly consensus by the second half of the 1990s that Russian federalism was *sui generis*, unlike any federal form found in the West, and unlikely to be stable (DeBardeleben, 1997: 48–50; Alexseev, 1999: 13). In sum, the critique of asymmetric federalism contains morally grounded (all citizens and constitutent units should be equal) and practical (without transparent 'standard rules of the game' federal coordination and stability was impossible) components. Such views ignore the growing literature on the importance of 'group-specific rights' and consociational-type institutionalized power-sharing as foundations for stable democracy in multi-ethnic settings (Kymlicka, 1993; O'Leary, 2001).

There is a tendency to confuse Russia's asymmetric federalism based on power-sharing treaties with 'foralistic federalism'.[1] In particular, there is uncertainty as to whether 'foralistic federalism' is stabilizing or destabilizing, and of where appropriate comparative examples can be found. An influential Russian study demonstrates this erroneous tendency to interpret 'foral federalism' as highly destabilizing, citing the Canada–Quebec, Germany–Bavaria (sic), and India–Punjab cases as evidence of the 'damage' (*sic*) caused by this type of 'treaty-federalism', claiming that it inevitably leads to the 'break up of the federation' (Umnova, 1996: 80–82).[2] In contrast, positive comparisons are made with Spain, where the division of powers between centre and 'autonomies' was institutionalized by a series of bilateral agreements (Chinarikhina, 1996: 20–25; Solnick, 1998: 61). Again, this is an inappropriate comparison as there are substantive differences. The creation of the Spanish 'state of autonomies' through power-sharing agreements was a transparent process ratified by parliament, approved by regional referenda, and the texts entrenched bodily as addenda to the 1978 constitution in the form of the

Autonomy Statutes. This means that Spain is governed by a single constitution. Spain is a decentralized state with segmental autonomies, not a federal state. It does not have federal integrative territorial institutions, but rather has a loose institutional framework which encourages competitive bargaining for further decentralization through party strategies and negotiations (Colomer, 1998). In Russia, in contrast, as we shall see below, the 1992 Federal Treaty was overwritten by the 1993 Constitution, and the Constitutional Court has only recently made a judgement (the Komi case of February 1998), confirming this. The bilateral power-sharing treaties differ in that they exist as para-constitutional texts and in some cases federal–republic relations are regulated by both the Federal Constitution and the republic's constitution (in the case of Tatarstan and Bashkortostan for example). This constitutes a major jurisdictional obstacle for a federal process of judicial review. Thus, one of the paradoxes of Russia's federal development is that there is a relatively transparent judicial process about a non-transparent treaty process.

EXPLAINING FEDERAL STABILITY

The approach taken here differs from the above-mentioned studies by arguing that the asymmetric refederalization of post-Soviet Russia was stabilizing for the state. As a positive feature of institution-building during transition, asymmetric federalism has acted as an institutional counterweight to centuries of ethnic Russian hegemonic control and the policies of Russification, coercion and centralization that accompanied it. Furthermore, as the introduction to this volume explains, comparative experience of conflict regulation in multi-ethnic societies suggests that such institutional arrangements are part of the repertoire of creative and flexible solutions employed for managing secession potential and conflicting rights. The institutional engineering of a refederalization of Russia was critical to its non-collapse and, moreover, this refederalization was undoubtedly shaped by other institutional choices made as part of Russia's broader attempt at transition to democracy after 1991. In particular, refederalization was correlated with the rise of a strong presidency under Boris Yeltsin.

The fundamental measure of political stability in any state is the maintenance of its territorial integrity, and in a federal state this is generally understood as the management of 'secession potential' (Lemco, 1991). By this measure the Russian Federation has been very successful. While there are nominally 21 'ethnic' republics out of a total of 89 federal subjects in Russia, since independence in 1991 there has been only one significant secessionist conflict, that in Chechnya. Chechnya is a protracted conflict, which has resulted in two costly wars in 1994–96 and 1999 to the present. It is also very much a 'deviant' case in Russia's federal transition since secession-potential and conflicts have either been non-existent or successfully managed in the 20 other 'ethnic' republics, some of which also strenuously asserted demands for 'sovereignty' against the federal government after 1991.

According to conventional accounts a supposed 'ethnic' revival, or *matryoshka* nationalism, intensified in Russia from 1990. The demands for 'sovereignty' from Russia's regions and republics were magnified by contagion effects from the revolutions in Eastern Europe and the 'war of sovereignties' in the USSR in 1989–90, when separatism escalated in key union republics, including Russia itself. Obviously, time has revealed the 'ethnic' revival account of a potential disintegration of Russia as flawed, since non-compliance with federal state-building and secession potential has been a serious challenge in just two republics: Tatarstan and Chechnya. Obviously, to argue that the limited scale of secession potential was a factor in the non-collapse of Russia would be to present a circular logic. Nevertheless, the question remains why, in a state with 39 significant ethnic minorities and 21 ethnically designated constituent units, has secession potential been vigorously and consistently asserted by just two, and violently by only one. Furthermore, why did the federal government take such a radically differentiated policy approach to the management of these two cases? In the case of Tatarstan, the federal government initiated a bargaining process, with negotiations proceeding for three years and including the direct involvement of the president, which led to an institutionalized settlement in a bilateral treaty where a wide lattitude of autonomy was conceded to Tatarstan. In the case of Chechnya, no serious negotiations were held under Yeltsin, who refused to engage directly with the Chechen leadership and preferred a disastrous policy of coercion in 1994–96. This pattern has been repeated under Putin since late 1999.

STRUCTURAL CONSTRAINTS ON SECESSION POTENTIAL

Secession potential in Russia has been softened by five types of structural constraints. Four of the constraints were internal features of the Russian state: demographic composition, resource interdependencies, spatial location, and historical assimilation. The fifth was an external constraint: the non-recognition of secession by the international system (this factor will not be discussed here since it is analysed in detail in the introduction to this volume).

Demographic Composition

One of the most potent conditions for separatism is the presence of a territorially concentrated and dissatisfied minority group. Although Russia's titular ethnic republics account for 29 per cent of the territory of the federation, this spatial significance is not matched by demographic presence. An important force for territorial cohesion in Russia is the high level and spatial spread of Russian ethnic homogeneity across almost all the federal units. At the time of the 1989 census Russians constituted a bare majority (50.78 per cent) of the USSR's 286.7 million population. In contrast, in the RSFSR (renamed the Russian Federation in January 1992) ethnic Russians were an overwhelming majority (81.5 per cent) of the 147 million population. The multi-ethnic demographic complexity of Russia was clear from the 1989 census which identified 101 ethnic groups in the state, and this is probably an underestimate. Although many ethnic groups numbered less than 5,000, the census revealed that there were 39 major ethnic groups numbering more than 100,000. One would imagine that this significant number of diverse minorities would greatly complicate federal nationalities policy and constitute strong secession potential, particular given the standard accounts of the effects of 'institutionalized multinationality'. This demographic structure, however, was subject to a crucial moderating factor. It is not simple numerical superiority as a proportion of the total demographic balance of the Russian Federation that makes ethnic Russian homogeneity a limiting constraint on secession potential, but the spread and strength of the ethnic Russian population throughout the vast majority of the 89 federal subjects. According to the Soviet census of 1989, the then RSFSR contained 31 subjects with a titular ethnic designation (16 Autonomous Soviet Socialist Republics, 5 Autonomous Oblasts [regions], and 10 Autonomous Okrugs [districts]).[3] Only four of these ethnically designated units (North Ossetia-Alania, Tuva, Checheno-Ingushetia, and Chuvashia), all of them autonomous republics, had an absolute majority of the titular ethnic group. In three autonomous republics (Tatarstan, Kabardino-Balkar and Kalmykia) the titular ethnic group enjoyed a simple majority. In the remaining autonomous republics ethnic Russians were an absolute majority or the majority group.[4] In fact, the largest ethnic minority group in Russia, the Tatars (6.64 million), are a minority within their titular ethnic homeland of Tatarstan (Tatars are only 48 per cent of the population, Russians 43 per cent) and have a large diaspora population dispersed across the federation but mainly concentrated in the large urban centres of European Russia.

The spatial spread of ethnic Russians is not a recent phenomenon but occurred as a historically gradual development linked to Russian imperial expansion from the mid-sixteenth century, and the Tsarist and Soviet modernization policies from the late nineteenth century onward. While the spread and strength of ethnic Russian homogeneity is an important factor, it is not a sufficient explanation. It is not unusual, after all, for cases of national and ethnic conflicts to arise where a titular homeland group feels threatened, discriminated against, or 'swamped' by local majorities of settler-colonists.

Resource interdependencies

In the context of the early transition period of the early 1990s only four ethnic republics were among the most economically important units of the federation, enjoying significant natural resource endowments or being major industrial areas, while the others were heavily dependent on federal transfers from the centre. In the early 1990s Tatarstan accounted for around one quarter of Russia's oil output and was a major industrial manufacturing region, Bashkortostan was a key oil refining and transit region, Sakha-Yakutia produced almost 100 per cent of Russia's diamonds, while Chechnya's importance owed less to its small oil output and more to its refining capacity and strategic straddling of the main Baku-Novorossisk oil pipeline linking Russia to the energy resources of the Caspian Basin. Outwardly, these resource endowments may indicate a capacity for economic independence from the centre, or at least much less dependency on it. There were other constraining factors, however, on such capacity, principally the spatial location of these republics (discussed below). The question of 'ethnic' separatism and secession potential, nevertheless, cannot be fully understood in isolation from the political economy of transition and how distributive issues and the intra-elite struggles to control economic assets affected secessionism and refederalization.

The demand for 'sovereignty' was pursued vigorously in many republics and regions, but only those with significant economic assets had the leverage to bargain seriously with the federal government. Consequently, secession potential was propelled by political economy distributive issues (principally resentment at the lack of federal revenue sharing and the weakness of local control over local resources), although the primacy of the issues of decentralization and autonomy in economic matters was often coated with an 'ethnic' veneer of political rhetoric about 'sovereignty'. The widespread use of the term 'ethnic separatism' in studies of Russian federalism blurs many of the nuances of federal relations. Apart from Chechnya and Tatarstan, there is little evidence for an 'ethnic' mobilization against Russia from the republics as there were no mass nationalist demonstrations and no significant inter-ethnic violence against Russian settler populations. When the 16 autonomous republics of the RSFSR joined the union republics in the so-called 'parade of sovereignties', beginning with North Ossetia in July 1990, all but two (Checheno-Ingushetia and Tatarstan) affirmed their sovereignty with the proviso that it was 'within the RSFSR'.

The role of cross-cutting cleavages in republics is also much understated. For example, it is clear that a significant part of Tatarstan's large Russian minority supported its declaration of sovereignty in the April 1992 referendum and has consistently exhibited strong electoral support for its autonomy. This seems to indicate an embryonic 'Tatarstani' identity (Hanauer, 1996: 82). The Bashkirs have been more politically hostile to the presence of the large Tatar population (around 30 per cent) in Bashkortostan than they are with mobilizing against Russians. For example, Baskortostan's 1998 language law recognized only Bashkir and Russian as official languages, excluding Tatar.

The general trend in post-Soviet Russia was for a high degree of elite continuity, as the former communist party nomenklatura adapted to the new conditions, retained its grip on political-administrative power and exercized enormous influence over economic development during the transition. The ethnic elites in the key republics mentioned above did not diverge from this trend, being deeply acculturated with Soviet values through the nomenklatura system. Not surprisingly, these elites are more concerned with the consolidation of their networks of local control and distributive issues, than with the assertion of ethnic demands per se (McAuley: 1997). This is not to underestimate the accumulating anecdotal evidence for an 'ethnification' of power vertically and horizontally in republics through nationalizing policies to promote, for example, 'Tatarization', or 'Bashkirization'. Nationalizing policies in Tatarstan, for example, have a strong cultural dimension (mosque building, rewriting of textbooks, Latinization of the Tatar alphabet, censorship). No quantitative studies of such processes exist, however, though we can reasonably assume that such discriminatory trends would over time accentuate the ethno-national cleavage within republics and lead to inter-ethnic conflict. In the first decade of post-Soviet transition in Russia they have not done so. Only in Chechnya was there something akin to an 'ethnic' conflict, though this is only part of the explanation for its causation. As we shall discuss later, Chechnya is a deviant case in post-Soviet Russia.

Spatial Location

Geography has an immensely important impact on the capacity of a federal unit to assert secession potential. Generally, the more peripheral a unit the greater is the capacity for secession potential, and the more difficult it is to control. If the location of such a unit places it at or near an international frontier, this increases the likelihood that it will be influenced by external forces, or linked to other states, thus strengthening secession potential. Likewise, if the location of a unit places it close to the core of the federal state, and encircles it with loyalist units, then the capacity to achieve its secession potential is severely constrained. Of the republics with strong secession potential, only the geography of Chechnya spatially favours its assertion of independence, as only it is located on an international frontier, with Georgia, though it is a former internal boundary of the USSR. Since the start of the latest Russian military intervention in Chechnya in September 1999 Russia has increasingly pressurized Georgia's jurisdiction over this border. Of the others Tatarstan and Bashkortostan are landlocked by ethnic Russian regions in the heart of European Russia, while Sakha (Yakutia) is peripheralized and effectively landlocked in Siberia. The precedents are stacked against states with this kind of geography becoming independent, as the only other states wholly landlocked within other states are the Vatican and Lesotho.[5] Furthermore, the advantages of significant natural resource endowments in such republics is counterbalanced by their geography, which renders them dependent on Russia for refining, processing and transhipping their resources.

Historical Assimilation

When assessing the issue of secession potential in the Russian federation it is important to note the proviso that here we are contending with radically different historical traditions of statehood compared with secessionist cases in other postcommunist states, or indeed in the USSR. Neither Tatarstan nor Chechnya, nor indeed any other Russian region or republic have had recent historical experience of independent statehood for any significant period.[6] Secessionism is acutely weak in the only republic with a prolonged experienced of quasi-independence, Tuva, which was an independent semi-protectorate of the USSR between 1921 and 1944.

While it is also true that many of the former Soviet union republics, such as Ukraine, Moldova, Belarus, and the five Central Asian states, have weak or non-existent state traditions, and many of them were opposed to the break-up of the USSR, these new states have a combination of advantages that Russia's secessionist republics do not have, such as international recognition and a geography which gives them an effective capacity to assert their independence. Moreover, in conditions of weak statehood tradition, nationalizing states are required to invest a great deal of institutional capacity in the construction of a new national identity. Recognition as part of the international community of states obviously helps to embed this, a factor that was absent in Chechnya and Tatarstan.

Historical mythologies are fundamental to the idea of statehood, and the weaker the provenance of a state, the stronger its nationalizing project tends to be. In stretching political mythologies to construct and solidify ethnic and regional identities into a new variant of nationalism, the Tatars mythologize the Kazan Khanate, which was annexed and destroyed by Ivan the Terrible in 1552. The Chechens, however, in their contemporary struggle against Russia, have mobilized more around ethno-religious myths of the nineteenth century and islamicist resistance to Russian imperial conquest. It is significant that the contemporary Tatar political elite has been much more attuned to the negotiation of an institutional basis for their status, whereas the Chechen elite tends to view its conflict with Russia as a more fundamentalist ethno-cultural struggle. This is not to impute, in some form of historicism, that longevity of colonial subordination reduces ethnonationalism (there are many counter examples), or that brevity strengthens secessionist tendencies.

Unlike many other empires, as the Russian state expanded from the late sixteenth century, the distinction between the Russian *core* and its contiguous imperial *periphery* became blurred. The conflation of core and periphery in the making of Russian identity makes for a very distinctive problem of settler colonialism in Russia. Proponents of a 'civic' federalism in Russia are concerned with how to combine genuine group autonomy with individual liberties (Smith, 1998). The difficulty is that ethnic Russians perceive their identity as being congruent with the current territorial boundaries of the whole Russian Federation. Russian views of federal construction tend to be polarized into either hegemonic or assimilationist camps. Hostility toward minorities is cloaked by arguments for federal symmetry and the equalization of status of federal units, a position often encouraged by attempts to propagate the United States model of federalism.[7] Western ideal types of 'ethnic' and 'civic' nationalism are used to associate asymmetric federalism with a dangerous 'ethnification' of Russian politics that is counterposed to the cultivation of a harmonizing 'civic' national identity (Tishkov, 1997; Tolz, 1998). To forge such a 'civic' identity it is suggested that the federation be reconfigured into ten or twelve super regions, largely defined by 'economic' criteria (a dream of Soviet-era planners), and eliminating the 'ethnic' marker altogether. 'Civic' also tends to infer the eradication of the constitutional recognition of citizens of the Russian Federation as a 'multi-national people' (*mnogonatsional'nyi narod*), and the inculcation of a new state identity of 'civic Russian' (*rossiiskii* or *rossiianin*). For non-ethnic Russians, however, these terms have an acquisitive 'belonging to' or 'demi-Russian' connotation.

Thus, the proponents of a 'civic' Russianess share a common trait with the radical Russian ethnocrats, whether it is Zhirinovsky on the extreme nationalist right, the centrist Luzhkov, or the communist Zyuganov. It is the view that multi-ethnic bargaining is somehow illegitimate, an appeasement, and a betrayal of the Russian 'nation'. The problem is that such a restructured, more symmetrical federation would go against the grain of 70 years of Soviet nationalities policy, and therein lies its danger. Symmetric federalism in Russia would inevitably unravel the particular legacies of historical assimilation inherited from Soviet 'institutionalized multinationality'. It would mean a concentrated Russian domination of minorities, a politics of exclusion, and potentially more, not less, political instability since it would most likely be accompanied by a strong control regime for the management of multi-ethnicity.

REDESIGNING ASYMMETRIC FEDERALISM

Despite his failure to refederalize the Soviet Union, many of the elements of Gorbachev's policy were retained in the attempt to refederalize Russia. The question of the status of the autonomous republics (mostly located within Russia) acquired great salience after Gorbachev equalized their status with that of the union republics in March 1990 (Hough, 1997). In particular, the language of the 'New Union Treaty' process established a verbal currency for the political discourse of Russia's post-Soviet refederalization after 1991, with terms such as 'delimiting powers', 'power-sharing' and 'sovereignty' becoming pervasive. The refederalization involved a difficult policy learning curve and a passage through three federal institutional designs.

Design 1: Ethnified Asymmetric Federalism
The first phase of refederalization in Russia began even while the Soviet Union still existed. In 1990–91 the Rumiantsev Constitutional Commission of the Russian parliament proposed to abolish the asymmetric framework inherited from the nominal Soviet federal structure by erasing the distinction between republics and regions and creating about 50 new *zemli* (lands) with equal status and without ethnic labels along the lines of the German *Länder* (though without their extensive powers). This configuration would have created, in effect, a state structure conducive to ethnic Russian hegemonic control. This option was blocked by vigorous protests from the ethnic republics and, consequently, the Federal Treaty agreed between president, parliament and the governments of the regions and republics and signed in March 1992 not only reaffirmed the ethnified asymmetric institutional architecture of the federation, but empowered it in

such a way as to make it the defining feature of the new federal system (*Federativnyi Dogovor*, 1992). The Federal Treaty was a triadic agreement composed of three separate treaties: the first, with titular 'ethnic' republics, the second with overwhelmingly Russian populated krais (territories) and oblasts, and the third with the titular 'ethnic' autonomous oblasts and okrugs. The treaty was supported by a broad institutional consensus in Russian politics in the immediate aftermath of the August Coup and the collapse of the USSR in December 1991. We should remember, however, that the treaty was ratified at a time when there was an uneasy balance of power between president and parliament. Consequently, greater segmental autonomy for the titular ethnic republics was conceded in the context of a fragmentation of power at the centre, where neither president or parliament could afford to alienate the potential support of the republics. Assuming they engaged in collective action to defend their segmental autonomies, the republics were potentially a powerful force in both chambers of the Russian parliament.

The treaty empowered Russia's asymmetric federalism, not so much from the terminology, which recognized the 20 constituent republics existing at that time as 'sovereign republics within the Russian Federation', since this was a replication of Soviet jargon, but from the effective and specific segmental autonomies that were granted to the republics compared with the 68 regions. They were given the right to adopt their own constitutions, whereas regions could only have charters, and they were conceded wide autonomy over their internal budgets, foreign trade, and, most importantly for budgetary independence, they were given powers of ownership and use of natural resources and land (article III, clause 3). In secret addenda three republics (Bashkortostan, Komi, and Karelia) were ceded even more power (Slider, 1994: 247–8). Four of the five titular ethnic autonomous oblasts were raised to the status of 'republic', while the other ethnically denominated okrugs were given equal status with the krais and oblasts, thus ending their administrative subordination to overwhelmingly ethnic Russian regional governments. Only Tatarstan and Checheno-Ingushetia refused to sign the Federal Treaty, holding out for the prospect of even more concessions and as a symbolic assertion of their sovereignty from Russia. The Federal Treaty, in essence, recycled the 'institutionalized multinationality' of the Soviet era, while empowering it in such a way that the unequal status of the two main groups of federal units was copperfastened and made much more meaningful. The *republics* were now treated as empowered autonomous units within the federation, while the *regions* were effectively dealt with as administrative units under the vertical power of a unitary state.

Design 2: De-ethnified Symmetric Federalism

The second phase of federal state-building lasted from March 1992 to the October crisis of 1993. In this period no overarching 'elite settlement' or consensus on the nature of the Russian federal state and its constitution could be reached between the centre and the republics and regions. Some leaderships in the ethnic Russian regions, incensed by the consensus at the federal centre for the 'ethnic' privileging of the republics, reacted by intensifying a populist regionalism. For example, the eight so-called 'inter-regional associations', or lobbying blocs of regions, formed in Russia in 1990–91 largely on the basis of planning regions, became an institutional platform for regionalism. The most politically significant challenges came from the regions with significant natural resource endowments, and in particular those regions from which Russia earns most of its export revenues: the Urals, Siberia and the Far East. As with regionalism elsewhere, for example in Western Canada and Northern Italy, challenges to the state from the overwhelming majority of units in the Russian Federation have been mobilized around economic distributive issues rather than the outright assertion of secession. In Russia, however, collective action by regional organizations was disrupted by clashes of interests between the member regions, leading to intra-regional conflicts and multiple opportunities for the federal government to exploit the divisions (Hughes, 1994).

The Constitutional Assembly, of dubious legitimacy, convoked by Yeltsin in July 1993 failed to break the deadlock over the federal architecture. Inevitably, given ethnic Russian hegemony in the state, the Constitutional Assembly was overwhelmingly dominated by ethnic Russians. The gathering marked, nevertheless, a watershed for an outpouring of aggressive ethnic nationalist Russophilism among the Russian political elites, which was largely coordinated by Yeltsin's representative Sergei Shakhrai. Hostility toward the ethnic republics was evident in the agenda-setting and discussions, which focused on the equalization of the status of all federal units to the exclusion of all other options. Chechnya refused to send a delegation, and although Tatarstan initially attended it withdrew its delegation early in the proceedings. The constitutional impasse over refederalization was only broken as a result of developments in the other major constitutional logjam in Russia's transition, the president versus parliament conflict. The latter conflict had intensified during 1992 to reach a crisis point in late September–early October 1993, when Yeltsin used the military to forcibly dissolve parliament. Freed from political constraints and flush with his success, Yeltsin imposed strong presidential rule on Russia and pushed through a new constitution ratified by a falsified referendum conducted in December 1993 (White, Rose, and McAllister, 1997: 98–101, 126–9).[8]

The new constitution closely followed the proposal for an equalization of status which had been favoured by the regional representatives in the Constitutional Assembly. Overriding the demands of the republics the text of the Federal Treaty was not incorporated into the new constitution, thus ending their short-lived segmental autonomy. The 1993 Constitution polarized the Russian Federation along an ethnic cleavage as, according to the heavily falsified and much underestimating official reports, seven ethnic republics returned majority votes against the new constitution (unofficial estimates suggest even more). The leadership of Tatarstan advocated a boycott and, when only 13.4 per cent of those eligible actually voted, declared the referendum invalid. Chechnya refused to participate. The highest vote against was 79 per cent in the Republic of Dagestan.

In principle, the provisions of the Federal Treaty are contained in article 11 of the 1993 constitution, however, only in so far as they conform with other articles in the new constitution. Most pointedly, references to the 'sovereign' status of republics contained in the Federal Treaty were dropped and both republics and regions have equal status as subjects of the federation (articles 5 and 65). Significantly, one of the key segmental autonomies made exclusively to the republics and enshrined in the Federal Treaty, the ownership of land and natural resources on their territory, was replaced in the constitution by joint jurisdiction (article 72) for all subjects with the federal government (*Konstitutsiia Rossiiskoi Federatsii*, 1995). It took more than four years for Russia's nascent process of judicial review to establish the precedence of the 1993 constitution over the Federal Treaty in a February 1998 decision of the Russian Constitutional Court in a case brought by Komi Republic.

Design 3: Partial Asymmetric Federalism

Article 11 of the 1993 Russian Constitution states that the division of powers between the federal government and the subjects may be regulated by 'treaties' in addition to the constitution, although no mechanism for treaty-making is specified. Whatever the uncertainties of the 1993 constitution in this respect, the serious budgetary impact of an escalating tax war between Moscow and key republics in the course of 1993, when federal taxes were withheld by Chechnya, Tatarstan, Bashkortostan, and Sakha, forced the presidential administration into a new phase of federal design. The strong presidential rule of Yeltsin not only secured the 'equalizing' and centralizing clauses in the federal relations sections of the 1993 constitution, and the abrogation of the Federal Treaty, but also allowed him to negotiate with the leaders of the most important ethnic republics in the search for an accommodation. To manage the long-running problem of contested sovereignty between Russia and Tatarstan and other key republics, Yeltsin aimed to coopt these key republican leaders into his presidentialist patrimonial system. To achieve this goal Yeltsin promoted a new type of federal architecture based on a highly selective system of partial asymmetric federalism. Power-sharing treaties were signed with the key resource rich republics, beginning in February 1994 with Tatarstan, and followed by Bashkortostan and Sakha (Yakutia). The treaties had a limited institutional basis of support within the Russian political system, since parliament was excluded from the process, and they were essentially executive agreements between the Yeltsin presidency and the presidents of the republics. The limited consensus of the bilateral treaties between the Russian president and the presidents of Tatarstan, Bashkortostan and Sakha stood in sharp contrast to the Federal Treaty of 1992 which was agreed by Yeltsin, the speaker of parliament, Ruslan Khasbulatov (and was ratified by the Russian parliament), and involved all regions and republics of the federation (with the sole exception of Chechnya). In fact, the bilateral treaty process began even as the new 'equalizing' constitution was being drafted, as in late 1993 a number of power-sharing agreements in non-controversial policy areas were signed by Yeltsin and Tatarstan president Mintimer Shaimiev.

THE FAVOURED FEW: BILATERAL POWER-SHARING TREATIES

The key autonomies and power-sharing arrangements for Tatarstan were detailed in a treaty codicile of 12 'cooperation agreements' on major policy areas (economic cooperation, production and transportation of oil, property, customs, environment, higher education, foreign trade, budget, defence, law and order, military organization). These were time limited for a term of five years, after which they were to be reviewed and renegotiated if necessary. The cooperation agreements were initially secret but have been subsequently published (*Rossiskaia Gazeta*, 18 February 1994; Guboglo, 1997: 416–38).[9] It is significant that the most prolonged negotiations involved policy domains that touched most on the sovereignty issue (law and order, budget, banking credit and foreign currency, foreign economic relations, and defence). Both presidents placed the treaty in the context of building a post-Soviet federation that guaranteed the republic's 'sovereignty' while preserving the territorial integrity of the Russian Federation. Yeltsin was also determined that the preferential treatment of Tatarstan would not be a 'model' for an overhaul of federal relations (*Segodnia*, 31 May 1994).

The selective asymmetric federalism was subsequently extended in a series of power-sharing treaties in 1994–95 with other republics. The treaties, however, institutionalized a partial asymmetry that was exceptionally hierarchical. Those treaties of a core group of resource-rich republics on which the centre is economically heavily dependent, first and foremost Tatarstan, Bashkortostan, and Sakha (Yakutia), were conceded an even deeper form of segmental autonomy than had been given in the federal treaty of 1992. The power-sharing contained in the treaties generally fall into five main policy domains: legal, economic, cultural, foreign economic relations, and security. If ethnic conflicts generally contest two key issue dimensions: effective and symbolic recognition of status, and material distribution (Offe, 1996: 55–7), then these core treaties address both dimensions. With regard to the first dimension, they are embued with symbolic language, variations in which are an indication of important differences in the power-sharing arrangements. Thus, it was not only differences in power-sharing that distinguished the core treaties with Tatarstan, Bashkortostan, and Sakha (Yakutia), but also their language of recognition of a special status for these republics. In general, treaties with other republics simply reproduce the formulaic language of article 72 of the 1993 Constitution, often verbatim, which broadly delimits powers in favour of the federal government. In fact, as the bilateral treaty process was extended in a formulaic manner to all republics, and more widely to Russia's regions, a presidential decree of 12 March 1996 established a standardized format and a specific vocabulary for them (*Sobranie zakonodatel'stva Rossiiskoi Federatisii*, 1996: 12, 1058).

An important feature of the partial asymmetric federalism is that areas specified by the treaties as being of joint authority or equal status also often constitute a significant loss of power for the federal government. Shaimiev illustrated this point in a speech at Harvard University in October 1994, when he observed that the equalization of language status for Tatar and Russian in Tatarstan was a 'win' for the Tatar language since it would be 'upgraded' to an official language (*Suverennyi Tatarstan*, 1997: 51). Tatarstan was conceded the widest degree of autonomy, placing it at the top of the bilateral treaty hierarchy. In effect, the treaty with Tatarstan established a co-sovereignty arrangement with Russia. The first sections declare that Tatarstan is a 'State' that is *united with* the Russian Federation' [my italics], on the basis of both the Russian and Tatarstan constitutions and the treaty itself (differences over interpretations were to be resolved by a special conciliation commission). Consequently, the treaty was clearly viewed as having a paraconstitutional status in regulating Russia–Tatarstan relations. There are clauses in the Constitution of Tatarstan of November 1992 which declare its laws to be 'supreme' (article 59), proclaim it to be 'a sovereign state, a subject of international law *associated to* the Russian Federation' (article 61), reserve for itself the right to conduct foreign relations, hold exclusive ownership of natural resources, and restrict military service of its citizens to its own territorial jurisdiction (*Konstitutsii respublik*, 1996). Such constitutional provisions are obviously in flagrant disagreement with the 1993 Russian federal constitution.

Such clauses are not easily reconcilable with the sovereignty of the Russian Federation over its whole territory, and indeed, many Russians, and particularly Yeltsin's political opposition in the Duma and in the regions, consistently criticized this and the other treaties as a threat to Russia's territorial integrity. In contrast, Tatarstan's leaders saw the treaty as an institutional buffer between the Russian and Tatarstan constitutions and as a protective device against Russian hegemonic control (Khakimov, 1996). After Tatarstan, treaties with other republics offered much less generous power-sharing concessions, although the economic leverage of Bashkortostan and Sakha meant they could also extract considerable powers. The Bashkortostan treaty describes it as 'a sovereign state within the Russian Federation' (article 1), and accords its constitution 'equal status' with that of Russia in the regulation of joint relations (article 2). The treaty with Sakha describes it as a state 'conforming to the Constitution of the Russian Federation *and* [my italics] the Constitution of the Republic of Sakha (Yakutia) within the Russian Federation'. Russian sovereignty is technically compromised by the constitution of Sakha, which claims among other things jurisdiction over its airspace and continental shelf (article 5).

The key treaties with Tatarstan, Bashkortostan, and Sakha (Yakutia), conceded them enormous economic privileges: ownership or use of natural resources and land, wide autonomy in budgetary and tax powers with enhanced revenue-sharing with the federal government, and the right to engage directly in foreign economic relations. The privileges evoked the common response to privileging policies in conditions of inter-ethnic competition: antagonism and intense pressure from disgruntled elites in ethnic Russian regions for equal treatment, inclusion in or the abrogation of the process. Whereas the treaties with the republics were, in essence, only tangentially linked with the democratization process in Russia, the extension of the treaties to Russia's regions is directly related to it. Once Yeltsin allowed the shift to elected rather than appointed governors, some mechanism had to be devised to contain democratic mandates for regionalism, which in part reflects a trend toward a form of 'delegative democracy' in Russia (O'Donnell, 1994). In the autumn of 1993 the regional governor who was among the most fervent advocates of regional 'sovereignty', Eduard Rossel in Sverdlovsk (Yeltsin's home region), made a mockery of the ethnic republics' special status under the Federal Treaty of 1992 by adopting a regional 'constitution' and declaring a 'republic' (*Vash Vybor*, 5, 1993: 10). Although dismissed by Yeltsin in October 1993, Rossel returned to power as one of the first elected governors in Russia's transition to democracy in August 1995. By the time the election of regional governors began in autumn 1995, all republics barring Chechnya had signed bilateral treaties with the Federal government and the process moved to the regions.

The first regional treaties were signed with Kaliningrad, Sverdlovsk, Orenburg, and Krasnodar in January 1996. As with the ethnic republics, the language of the regional treaties is indicative of a hierarchy of status and power-sharing. Sverdlovsk, in particular, achieved *de facto* 'republic' status by winning substantial economic privileges, though time limited to five years as with the republics (Guboglo, 1997: 652 passim). A demonstration of linguistic symbolism of the Sverdlovsk treaty is that it is the only treaty with a region where President Yeltsin and Governor Rossel were signatories on behalf of their respective 'governments'. A further 24 treaties with regions were concluded in time for the first round of the presidential election in June 1996. If this was a calculated strategy by Yelstin to woo the support of regional elites for his re-election campaign it largely failed. In the first round of voting only half the regions with treaties gave a majority vote for Yeltsin, illustrating the fact that for many regions the treaties were largely symbolic and politically irrelevant. Yeltsin lost in most of the republics, the notable exception being Tatarstan where the voting was heavily rigged in favour of Yeltsin (Chinarikhina, 1996: 24).

Partial asymmetric federalism was as deeply unpopular as was the ethnified asymmetric federalism of the Federal Treaty among the hegemonic ethnic Russian political class across the whole political spectrum from the communists and nationalists to the social democrats and liberals. The key treaties clearly involved a massive loss of revenue for the federal government and were a source of considerable resentment among Russian elites, particularly as they hindered a common federal fiscal policy and regional strategy. Russian parliamentarians were incensed in particular by the fact that the treaties created legislative no-go areas, while the representatives of the republics could vote on legislation that did not affect them.[10]

After Yeltsin's re-election in July 1996 there began a period of retrenchment against further power-sharing. Attempts to recentralize power were made by economic liberals such as Head of the Presidential Administration Anatoly Chubais, who fancifully argued that the key treaties distorted compliance with the tight fiscal targets set by the IMF. Chubais recruited Vladimir Putin, a former KGB officer and Deputy Mayor of St Petersburg who had a reputation for toughness, into the presidential administration to oversee relations with the regions and republics, and to ensure compliance with the vertical command line from the presidential administration. Chubais embarked on a test confrontation with one of the key resource-rich republics Sakha (Yakutia). The 1994 treaty with Sakha institutionalized a prior informal agreement between Yeltsin and Sakha president Mikhail Nikolaev, which granted the republic the right to keep 25 per cent of the profits from its diamond sales (*Rossiiskaia federatsiia*, 3, 1995: 22–3). The Yeltsin-Nikolaev agreement was an immense revenue enhancing device for Sakha given that the republic accounts for over 80 per cent of known diamond reserves and over 99 per cent of Russia's diamond output, while Russia accounts for about one quarter of global production. Chubais unilaterally reneged on the treaty with Sakha in summer 1996 in an attempt to compel the republic to deliver its diamonds to the state monopoly producer, Alrosa, under less preferential terms. Sakhan leaders spoke of an economic 'blockade' from the centre to force them to comply. These efforts proved short-lived, however, and after the forced resignation of Chubais over a corruption scandal in autumn 1996, Yeltsin's administration re-established a cooperative relationship with Sakha, though on the basis of changes to the diamond deal that favoured the centre. The drive to roll back power-sharing with republics resurfaced in spring 1998 under the government headed by economic liberal Sergei Kirienko, when he attempted and failed to renegotiate the treaty with Tatarstan. Under Primakov's tenure as prime minister from in 1998–99 no new treaties were signed, for even as foreign minister he had been a vehement opponent, regarding them as a dilution of Russian sovereignty and too much of an encouragement to sub-national foreign policy-making. For example between December 1991 and October 1998 Tatarstan signed 50 treaties, agreements and protocols with foreign states without the sanction of the Russian foreign ministry.[11] This pattern of federal government attempts to renege on the treaties continued under Putin's premiership from August 1999, and once in power as acting president from January 2000 Putin used the powers of the office to implement a radical restructuring and recentralization of Russian Federalism.

PRESIDENTIAL FEDERALISM: ACCOMMODATION AND CONFLICT

The Role of Yeltsin

The development of a post-Soviet federal institutional architecture in Russia was closely interlinked with the emergence of strong presidential rule under Yeltsin, to such an extent that we could refer to it as a type of 'presidential federalism'. As observed in the introduction to this volume studies of democratization almost universally associate strong presidential rule with a Latin American model of a dangerous personalization of power and a destabilizing, consensus-averting, zero-sum politics that it tends to inject into the body politic (Linz: 1990 and 1994). The discordant note in this conventional wisdom was sounded by Donald Horowitz, who demonstrated how presidential rule in deeply divided societies, such as in West Africa, can be a stabilizing force (Horowitz, 1990). The combination of multi-ethnic diversity, institutional debilitation and rampant corruption in the Russian state has more parallels with the weak states of post-colonial Africa, than it does with the overwhelmingly homogenous states of Latin America. In such conditions, as Horowitz emphasizes, presidentialism may be the only institutional bond to avert disintegration into ethnic conflict. If our focus is central politics and institutions there is much evidence of Yeltsin's reluctance to compromise and preference for unilateral action and confrontation. To a large degree it was Yeltsin's uncompromising 'winner takes all' approach to reform in Russia that caused the October 1993 crisis with parliament (Colton: 1995; Shevtsova; 1999). In contrast, Yeltsin's impact on the management of Russia's multi-ethnic diversity has been on the whole a crucial stabilizing factor, with the notable exception of Chechnya.

The impact of Yeltsin on Russia's federal development began with his efforts to thwart Gorbachev's New Union Treaty. Yeltsin was one of the leading advocates for the break-up of the USSR, and as Chairman of the RSFSR parliament in 1990–91 he stirred up the ethnic republics of Russia to join the 'parade of sovereignties' of the union republics. The drive to undermine Gorbachev's power was encapsulated in his appeal to Russia's ethnic republics to 'take as much sovereignty as you can stomach' during a visit to Tatarstan's capital, Kazan, in August 1990. Although all of the then existing autonomous republics, except for Chechnya and Tatarstan, declared themselves sovereign 'within the RSFSR', in his attempts to destroy the Soviet Union Yeltsin incited centrifugal pressures and legitimized secessionist tendencies within the Russian Federation itself.

Yeltsin used his great personal authority to pragmatically build pacifying patrimonial relations with the leaders of the ethnic republics throughout his tenure as Chairman of the RSFSR parliament and then as Russian president in 1990–91. He played an instrumental role in securing the ratification of the Federal Treaty of 1992, which empowered the ethnified asymmetric federalism inherited from the USSR. During the conflict of dual authority between the president and parliament in 1992–33, Yeltsin appears to have shifted his position and began to push for an equalization of status option for Russian federalism. This is evident from the role of his key minister and adviser on nationality and regional affairs, Sergei Shakhrai, in orchestrating the Constitutional Assembly of July 1993, and the proposal for an ex-officio upper house of parliament, the Federation Council, composed of regional and republic leaderships, proposed to them at Petrozavodsk in August 1993. The irony is that Yeltsin's forced dissolution of parliament in October 1993 was a decisive step in the aversion of a parliamentary republic, which most likely would have eradicated the segmental autonomy of the republics and restored ethnic Russian hegemony over them. That outcome may well have led to conflict with the most recalcitrant republics, Chechnya and Tatarstan, and perhaps with Bashkortostan also. While enforcing the adoption of equality of status in the new constitution, Yeltsin astutely led the attempts to reach an accommodation with the key republics of Tatarstan, Bashkortostan and Sakha. He employed his extensive decree powers under the constitution to bypass the new nationalist and communist dominated parliament elected in December 1993, and to implement a federal design of partial asymmetry based on bilateral power-sharing treaties. Yeltsin's role was instrumental to the process in the face of strong opposition from many of his key advisers on federal questions.[12] Yeltsin's pragmatic approach continued throughout the 1990s, as even as late as 1999 he attempted to entice leaders of key republics and regions into sacking Prosecutor General Yuri Skuratov (then investigating Yeltsin's role in Kremlin corruption) by promising: 'We will give you more independence than set down in the bilateral agreements we have signed. Let us gradually revise these agreements.'[13]

Thus, the presidential personalization of power, so widely viewed as destabilizing in a transition to democracy, was central to establishing a rapport with the leaders of the ethnic republics and eased the treaty-making process. To a great extent it replicated the traditional patrimonialism of the Soviet nomenklatura system. It was precisely these characteristics that were absent from Yeltsin's management of the secession crisis with Chechnya. As the secessionist republic *par excellence* one would have expected Chechnya to be the priority for the president in his search for an institutional accommodation. In fact, Chechnya was excluded from the bilateral power-sharing treaty process, and instead Yeltsin and a 'war party' within his administration presided over a long-running dirty campaign of military subterfuge to undermine Chechen President Dzhokhar Dudaev (Dunlop, 1998). The explanation of why Chechnya was excluded from the partial asymmetry of the power-sharing treaty process is complex and involves historical, politically contingent, political economy and personal factors (Hughes, 2001). Certainly, there were Russian sensitivities to a potential threat to its influence in the Caspian Basin from an independent and hostile Chechnya, but economic distributive issues were a characteristic feature of many conflicts between the federal government and other republics and were stabilized by treaties. When the treaty with Tatarstan was signed Yeltsin's chief negotiator, Sergei Shakhrai, stated that a similar agreement would most likely be the basis of a solution for the Chechnya crisis.[14] A power-sharing treaty offered the best prospect for a peaceful resolution to the conflict and would have averted the war of 1994–96, and possibly prevented that beginning in late 1999, both of which rank alongside Bosnia as the most bloody conflicts of the post-communist era.[15]

History provides part of the explanation for the conflict in Chechnya. Chechen nationalism, unlike that of Tatarstan and other republics, was mobilized around a much more recently ingrained and bitter historical memory of Russian imperialism, notably the genocidal deportation of 1944. Historical grievances against Russia, profoundly embedded in Chechen society, were a significant constraint on Dudaev's room for compromise. The main obstacle, however, to an accommodation between Russia and Chechnya was the 'personalization' of the clash between Yeltsin and Dudaev (Tishkov, 1997). We should not minimize, moreover, the extent of mutual 'ethnic' hatred contributing to this 'deep-seated personal animus' between Yeltsin and his key advisers on the one hand, and Dudaev on the other (Dunlop, 1998: 215–19; Lieven, 1998: 76).[16]

The personalization of the conflict was evidently immensely important to its drift into war. Perhaps the main stumbling block, however, was not so much the 'ethnic' rivalry factor, but the fact that Dudaev, unlike Shaimiev and the leaders of the other republics, was not a former member of the party nomenklatura. As a former military officer, by training and temperament he was very much an outsider to the tightly closed patrimonial networks of the party nomenklatura. The clash of personalities and egos so often referred to as the source of the conflict lay in this insider–outsider dynamic. Dudaev lacked the personal skills for integrating with an executive federalism constructed around Yeltsin's new patrimonialism, and Yeltsin was too arrogant to engage with Dudaev at an appropriate level of respect. Consequently, Yeltsin never entered negotiations with Dudaev, and left the task to Shakhrai. That Yeltsin personally was central to the continuation of the conflict is indicated by the fact that the war was pursued even after the removal from office of the key ministers who formed the so-called 'party of war' (Grachev, Shakhrai, Yerin, Soskovets, Yegorov et al.) by summer 1996.

Much as Yeltsin personally contributed to the cause of the first war, he was also instrumental in bringing it to a swift conclusion. With Dudaev killed by Russian forces, and Yeltsin facing a difficult re-election campaign in spring 1996, he instructed key subordinates, at first Prime Minister Viktor Chernomyrdin, and later his Security Council chief, Aleksandr Lebed, to negotiate a settlement. The importance of the new federalism in shaping the behaviour of Russia's elites was evident in the way that Tatarstan president Shaimiev acted to mediate between Russia and Chechnya.[17] The Khasavyurt Agreement of August 1996, followed by a power-sharing treaty in May 1997, led to a Russian military withdrawal and the end of its effective sovereignty over Chechnya. In its place a special status of 'association' between the Russian Federation and Chechnya was established, where a final decision on the status of Chechnya was postponed for 'up to' five years, while it remained part of a 'common economic space' with the Russian Federation. In practice Chechnya was left in limbo, cut off from Russia, and without significant external support; the new president Aslan Maskhadov attempted, with great difficulty given the radicalization and Islamicization of Chechen field commanders, to rule it as a *de facto* independent state. This was most obviously demonstrated by the introduction of *Shariiat* law in Chechnya in early 1999 in complete indifference to the Russian Constitution.

The Role of Putin

The highly patrimonial presidential federalism that had developed under Yeltsin was built on an extremely narrow institutional consensus and imprecision of meaning, being the outcome of non-transparent executive agreements between the president and heads of the republics and regions. Consequently, they were vulnerable to unravelling after a presidential alternance in Russia. Parliament passed a federal law on power-sharing treaties in June 1999 which stipulated that all of the existing treaties must be revised to comply with the Russian constitution by 2002.[18] While it was unlikely that Yeltsin would comply with this law, the shift to a more centralizing policy began when Vladimir Putin became prime minister in August 1999. Putin had been deeply involved in the failed drive by Chubais to nullify the treaties and recentralize power in summer 1996. His intent to rebuild a strong central state in Russia became clear almost immediately on taking office when in September 1999 he took a leading role in the new war to re-establish Russian control in Chechnya. As acting president from 31 December 1999, and as elected president from March 2000, Putin used recentralization as a key platform in his credo to reverse the 'weakening of state power' that had occurred under Yeltsin.[19] Putin viewed the treaties as contributing to the legal chaos in the country whereby thousands of legal acts at all levels of power contradicted the federal constitution and federal law.[20] His answer was to enact a 'dictatorship of law', though the precise meaning of this term was left vague, by a range of devices, from institutional reform, negotiation, the Constitutional Court, and in the case of Chechnya, coercion.

After his election as president Putin implemented a package of significant institutional reforms to Russia's federal architecture the goal of which was to strengthen the 'executive vertical' in order to 'cement Russian statehood'. In May 2000, he initiated a territorial-administrative reconfiguration of the federation by stealth, by dividing the subjects into seven new federal districts, each headed by a presidential plenipotentiary representative, commonly referred to as 'governor-generals' after the Tsarist military governors of the provinces.[21] The new heads of the federal districts have ultimate authority for economic coordination and security in their areas. The control factor is evident from the strong military-security bias in the appointments; two of the new presidential representatives were former commanders in the 1994–96 Chechen war, and two others were former senior officials in the internal security apparatus. The reform suggests that Putin has opted for a simplistic military-bureaucratic solution to the complex problems of centre–regional and federal relations in Russia.

Putin's next step was to radically restructure the upper house of parliament, the Federation Council, to end the situation whereby it is composed of ex-officio republican and regional executives (presidents or governors), and heads of assemblies. Exploiting his enhanced authority from the successful (at that stage) military operation in Chechnya, and his victory in the presidential election, he easily pushed a new federal law through the parliament in August 2000, which removed the governors and replaced them with representatives nominated by the governors and approved by a republic's or region's legislative assembly for a four-year term. The law also gave the president the power to remove and replace governors for repeated violations of federal law. The reform deprived the governors of their most important forum for organizing collective action against the centre. Putin created a new State Council as an alternative consultative forum for the regional and republican leaders, but it meets in plenary session only four times a year. While its seven-member presidium meets monthly, its composition and agenda are decided by Putin. These are clearly substantially weaker bodies than the former Federation Council.

In the late 1990s, Russian prime ministers and leading officials had tried without success to modify the bilateral power-sharing treaties with the most powerful republics, Tatarstan, Bashkortostan, and Sakha. Federal fiscal flows (including non-budgetary funds) are distorted by the exceptions contained in the key treaties, thus constraining any federal policies of regional wealth redistribution or development. By 1998 only 26 of the 89 regions and republics were net 'donors' to the federal budget and the rest were dependent on federal transfers (EastWest Institute, 1999). Putin exploited his new authority as president to renegotiate the treaties. He also had the advantage of a period of weakness of key republican leaders like Shaimiev, whose credibility had been damaged by their involvement in the Fatherland-All Russia movement, formed to fight Putin's Unity Bloc in the Duma elections of 1999, and which had performed badly. Putin evidently felt institutionally constrained by the treaties, since he did not unilaterally revoke them and had to engage in negotiations with the republics to reverse some concessions. From March 2000 Putin focused on the economic aspects of the treaties, forcing Tatarstan to relinquish back to the federal government some of the fiscal privileges that had been allocated by the 1994 treaty. Tatarstan, which contributed about $350 million in 2000, is already one of the key donors to the federal budget, but the centre wanted even more. It was now to return the same proportions of tax revenue to the federal budget as other regions, though Putin accepted a symbolic face-saving formula for Shaimiev whereby the revenues would stay in Kazan at the regional branch of the federal treasury and would be spent on federal projects in Tatarstan. Afterwards, Putin visited Bashkortostan and agreed similar forfeits of fiscal exceptions with President Rakhimov. In 1999, for example, Bashkortostan was the only subject that did not transfer income tax revenues to the centre. The treaty revisions, therefore, strengthen the federal treasury and give the federal government greater control over tax collection in these wealthy resource-rich republics. In principle, this should make for improved coordination of federal economic policy and a more equitable regional development policy. Putin appears to want to erode the partial asymmetry further, and perhaps remove it altogether and impose a symmetric federal system.[22] Shaimiev, in contrast, recently observed that wtihout the power-sharing treaty the relations between Tatarstan and Russia have no defined constitutional basis, since Tatarstan did not sign the Federal Treaty of 1992, or ratify the 1993 Russian constitution.[23]

Putin used another avenue of attack on the treaties, judicial activism by the Constitutional Court. In a landmark test case on the status of the power-sharing treaties, in June 2000 the Constitutional Court struck down Bashkortostan's electoral law.[24] Bashkortostan argued unsuccessfully that its constitution was protected by exceptions contained in its power-sharing treaty. The case established the important *de jure* precedent that the constitutions of republics must comply with the federal constitution. Subsequently, Sakha amended its constitution to comply with the court's ruling in August 2000. It remains uncertain how this process of judicial review of the treaties will be given effect, as in November 2000 Bashkortostan's parliament approved a new law to bring the republic's constitution into conformity with the federal constitution, but concurrently included *verbatim* the text of the 1994 power-sharing treaty in its new constitution, a *de facto* non-compliance.

In the space of one year, Putin has radically transformed the nature of Russian federalism, by an ambitious programme of measures to recentralize power. The power of the leaders of republics and regions has been seriously weakened, both institutionally and politically. Some of the important concessions made by Yeltsin to the key republics in the power-sharing treaties, principally in the fiscal domain, have been reversed. Chechnya has been reoccupied militarily, though how this problem is to be managed politically remains one of the greatest challenges facing Russian federalism. While, with some justification, Putin can claim to have restructured executive power in the Russian state in a more 'constitutionally united' system, the partial asymmetric federalism has been modified, not eradicated.[25]

CONCLUSION

Weak secession potential in the Russian Federation during its transition to democracy has been mainly a result of, I have suggested, *structural limitations* and *institutional experimentation* with federal designs to accommodate ethnic and territorial diversity. The small number of effective cases of secession potential made this task less complicated and more manageable. The institutional experimentation was founded on a recycling and empowerment of the inherited asymmetric federal architecture of Soviet 'institutionalized multinationality'. Rather than being a 'subversive' flaw for federal state-building, this path-dependent institutional legacy was an advantage in refederalization, and was crucial for the defusing of serious secession potential in Tatarstan and the lesser variants in Bashkortostan and Sakha (Yakutia). This refederalization evolved quickly over time through three major phases before settling on a system of partial asymmetry based on a hierarchy of bilateral treaties between the federal government and the republics and regions to institutionalize varying degrees of autonomy.

The bilateral power-sharing treaty process can be viewed as destabilizing for Russia's federal transition for several reasons. The treaties were a product of a relatively limited institutional consensus, reflecting executive interests and based on executive agreements at the federal and republic or regional level, and excluding participation by or consultation with the Russian parliament. Since they have an imprecise paraconstitutional status (though judicial review by the Constitutional Court is redefining their status *within* the 1993 constitution), and were the outcome of executive agreements (president-to-president in the case of republics, president-to-governors in the case of regions), the treaties were vulnerable to unravelling once there was an alternance in the presidency. This is, in fact, what has happened under Putin's presidency. Second, notwithstanding the spatial constraints on secession potential, the treaties have been regarded with almost unanimous hostility by the Russian political elites, and Russian and Western scholars. On the part of the former, the hostility reflects concerns at the weakening of ethnic Russian hegemony by power-sharing, while the latter equate asymmetric federalism with a weakening of state capacity and the promotion of administrative confusion. The most common criticisms are that the treaties institutionalize ethnic privileging, disrupt the process of civic nation-building, undermine the constitutional and administrative coherence of the federation, dilute economic reform and contribute to disequilibria in economic wealth distribution and regional development, and even threaten the territorial integrity of the state by encouraging secessionism, as in Chechnya.

In the event, only Chechnya fought to secede from the Russian Federation, and yet it was the only republic with which there was a failure to achieve an institutional accommodation. Furthermore, problems of weak federal control, difficulties with embedding democratic practice, rule compliance, order, economic reform and state administrative coherence exist in Russia irrespective of the status of the subject, or whether it has a power-sharing treaty or not. Asymmetry may also have led to some disparities in federal revenue distribution in favour of ethnic republics, but this pales compared with the immense disparity of wealth concentrated in Moscow by ethnic Russian elites during the economic transition.

Partial asymmetric federalism has had important stabilizing effects on the management of federal relations with the key ethnic republics:

First, by decentralizing power over a wide range of policy domains the treaties have been important institutional counterweights to the powerful residues of a centralizing unitarist state tradition in Russia, which has historically practised ethnic control, assimilation and oppression against its national minorities.

Second, the treaties have engineered a new institutional structure for the accommodation of Russia's multi-ethnic society. The process by which these new institutional arrangements were crafted is as important as their functional operation. The negotiation, bargaining and compromise that accompanied the institutional engineering of a treaty framework was a critical element in the construction of the federal process in politics itself. The negotiations before the treaties were signed were lengthy and complex (lasting three years in the case of Tatarstan), and this bargaining has continued over their operation and interpretation (the Tatarstan treaty was renewed by mutual agreement in 1999). The process has by its very nature helped to regularize federalism as a political, if not constitutional, process of institutionalized bargaining. Evaluating the impact of the treaties, once adopted, on federal relations is a more complicated task given the non-transparency of the cooperation agreements covering key policy domains and the secrecy surrounding the reconciliation of differences. The fact that the process of negotiation has continued under Putin, however, is indicative of the enduring significance of the treaties and their power-sharing provisions. Consequently, asymmetric federalism performs the crucial functions of promoting political stability and institutionalizing elite bargaining, factors that were so damaging for democratic consolidation by their very absence in central politics.

Third, a lack of transparency, leading to an information deficit, is an intrinsic part of the bilateral power-sharing treaty process. Secrecy may lead to bidding games, but it also gives the centre the flexibility to negotiate on a case-by-case basis and is a useful instrument for breaking up potential regional and republican coalitions. Secrecy also serves the interests of those key republics and regions (like Tatarstan, Bashkortostan, Sakha and Sverdlovsk) that have the most leverage and can extract the most concessions.

Fourth, the successful management of separatist and regionalist challenges by Russia's asymmetric federalism is an attractive alternative conflict resolution mechanism to the 'Bosnian' model of segregation in 'ethnic' enclaves. The Russian experience of federal transition may even have had a beneficial contagion effect as, for example, the institutionalization of Crimean autonomy in the Ukrainian constitution of 1996 was influenced by the Tatarstan model. In recent years, the debate in Georgia over Abkhazia and South Ossetia, and in Moldova over Transdnistria, has shifted in support of asymmetric federal type solutions.

Finally, fragmentation of state authority, for example in foreign policy, is a sign of modernization and democratization. Such 'perforations' in national sovereignty have been the trend in advanced industrial democracies since the 1960s, primarily in those with federal systems, as local and regional actors play an increasingly significant role in the 'marbled diplomacy' of international relations (Duchacek, 1990; Strange, 1995).

A focus on new institutional designs exclusively would be a wholly insufficient explanation for any development during transition given the crucial role played by the political actors and elites who inhabit the key institutions. The success and failure of refederalization as a management strategy for secession potential in Russia has also critically depended upon the rise of a strong presidency. Yeltsin and Putin pursued similarly ambivalent policies, preferring negotiation and accommodation with Tatarstan and other republics, and reserving a coercive strategy for Chechnya. The failure of refederalization in Chechnya was largely an 'actor' problem, which was exacerbated by a lack of institutional mechanisms for managing the conflict and embittered by historical enmities. This 'actor' failure was evident in both the 1994–96 war and the renewed war from late 1999, although the latter conflict was marked by a radicalization that was a by-product of the first war. The process of federal institutional experimentation has continued under Yeltsin's successor, Putin, though now with stronger centralizing tendencies. Consequently, the benefits and limitations of the interaction of presidentialism and federalism during Russia's transition – what in essence was a kind of executive federalism – are evident in the contrast between the two most important cases of success and failure in the management of secession potential, Tatarstan and Chechnya. Post-Soviet federal development in Russia, the war in Chechnya apart, is confirmation of the view that where there is a territorialization and politicization of ethnicity, a strong presidency can promote stability by imposing institutional mechanisms to accommodate and manage ethnic and regional challenges. In the absence of strong presidentialism, federal power-sharing would have been blocked by an ethnocracy based on an ethnic-Russian dominated parliament. This type of parliamentarism would have made little difference to the pattern of conflict with Chechnya. It is doubtful whether any alternative institutional arrangement to asymmetric federalism would work as well in managing Russia's ethnically and territorially divided society.

NOTES

1. The term originated with the Spanish *fueros* of the Middle Ages, whereby the state gave certain localities preferential or exceptional powers enshrined in a charter or treaty. The term 'federalism' itself, however, is derived from the Latin *foedus* meaning 'treaty'. See Elazar, 1987: 59.
2. The author is a legal specialist and Chief Consultant to the Russian Constitutional Court, and the book is an official text for the Ministry of Justice.
3. For the ethno-demographic structure see *SSSR v tsifrakh v 1989g.*, 23–5; *Argumenty i fakty*, 13 March 1991, p.1. The Federal Treaty of February 1992 recognized 20 ethnically designated 'republics', 16 of which were inherited from the autonomous republics of the RSFSR (Bashkortostan, Buriatia, Checheno-Ingushetia, Chuvashia, Dagestan, Kabardin-Balkar, Kalmykia, Karelia, Komi, Marii El, Mordovia, North Ossetia-Alania, Sakha (Yakutia), Tatarstan, Tuva, Udmurtia), and four were upgraded from autonomous oblasts of the RSFSR (Adygeia, Altai, Karachai-Cherkess, Khakassia). See *Federativnyi Dogovor: Dokumenty, Kommentarii*, Moskva, Izdatel'stvo 'Respublika', 1992.
4. By 1994 the Russian population in these 11 republics was as follows: Karelia (73.6%), Buriatia (69.9%), Adygeia (67.9%), Mordova (60.8%), Altai (60.4%), Urdmutia (58.9%),

Komi (57.7%), Sakha (Yakutia) (50.3%), Marii El (47.5%), Karachai-Cherkess (42.4%), Bashkortostan (39.3%). See *Narody Rossii, Entsiklopediia, Bol'shaia Rossiiskaia Entsiklopediia*, Moscow, 1994: 433–5.

5. Lesotho, a British 'protectorate' until independence in 1966, is landlocked by South Africa, and effectively reverted to that status after a South African military intervention in September 1998.
6. The Russian Far East was briefly an independent republic in 1919–22.
7. In 1993–95 I participated in several Russo-American conferences on federalism held in Novosibirsk under the auspices of the USAID programme and attended by leading specialists on federalism from Russia and the USA. I was alone in proposing an asymmetric federal model for Russia.
8. The result of the constitutional referendum was almost certainly falsified by the Yeltsin administration. It legally required a 50% turnout of registered voters, which almost certainly did not occur. It is even doubted that the referendum secured the majority of votes.
9. The treaty and its codiciles have been published on the official website of the Republic of Tatarstan: http://www.tatar.ru/00000038.html.
10. This problem is termed the 'West Lothian' question in the UK. It involves a jurisdictional problem when a Scottish Parliament has exclusive spheres of policy competence independent of the Westminster Parliament, yet Scottish representatives continue to legislate at Westminster in areas that will not affect Scotland. Author's interview with Anatolii Sychev, then head of the Federation Council's Committee on Federal Affairs and Regional Policy, Novosibirsk, August 1997.
11. For a list of the agreements see: http://www.tatar.ru/00000078.html. See also Paul Goble, 'Diplomacy Within Russia', *Radio Free Europe/Radio Liberty*, 20 July 1998.
12. Author's conversations with a senior presidential adviser on nationalities and regional policy (member of the presidential council) in Russia in 1994–96. Sergei Shakhrai, deputy prime minister for nationalities and regional policy, was the chief negotiator, although he had been a keen advocate of equalized status at the Constitutional Assembly.
13. Russian Public TV, 20 April 1999.
14. *Segodnya* 17 February 1994.
15. Estimates of casualties in 1994–96 vary from a low of 4,379 military dead and in excess of 20,000 civilian dead, with no accounting of wounded (Lieven, 1998: 108), to a high of 80,000 dead and 240,000 wounded, announced by General Alexandr Lebed in *Izvestiia*, 4 September 1996. In the current war, officially Russia admits to just over 3,000 military killed, but unofficially estimates are at least double this, and no-one knows the scale of Chechen military and civilian casualties.
16. Lieven suggests that Yeltsin's two key advisers on federal questions, Sergei Shakhrai (a Terek Cossack), and Ramazan Abdulatipov (a Dagestani Avar) were driven by ethnic hatred of Chechens.
17. See *Rossiiskaia Gazeta*, 5 March 1996.
18. *Parlamentskaia gazeta*, 30 June 1999.
19. Putin's statement was published on the Russian government website as 'Russia at the Turn of the Millennium' on 31 December 1999.
20. At a conference on federalism in Moscow in January 1998, Justice Minister Sergei Stepashin stated that one-third of the 16,000 regional laws examined by the Justice Ministry since summer 1995 violated federal legislation. *Radio Free Europe/Radio Liberty Research Report*, 20 January 1998.
21. The districts are: Central, North West, North Caucasus, Volga, Urals, Siberia, and Far East.
22. In late June 2001 Putin established a special presidential commission under Deputy Head of the Presidential Administration, Dmitri Kozak, to examine the whole question of power-sharing treaties with a view to their complete removal. *Kommersant-Daily*, 27 June 2001.
23. *Izvestiia*, 1 June 2001.
24. The law required candidates for the Bashkortostan presidency to be bilingual, effectively

disqualifying four out of five Bashkortostani citizens since Bashkortostan is only 20% ethnic Bashkir (ethnic Russians account for 40% and Tatars almost 30%).
25. Putin's speech to the State Council on 22 November 2000: http://www.president.kremlin .ru/ events/105.html.

REFERENCES

Aklaev, Airat R. (1999), *Democratization and Ethnic Peace: Patterns of Ethnopolitical Crisis and Management in Post-Soviet Settings*. Aldershot: Ashgate.
Alexeev, Mikhail A. (ed.) (1999), *Center–Periphery Conflict in Post-Soviet Russia: A Federation Imperiled*. London: Macmillan.
Argumenty i fakty, 13 March 1991, p.1.
Bahl, Roy and Christine I. Wallich (1995), 'Intergovernmental Fiscal Relations in the Russian Federation', in Richard M. Bird, Robert D. Ebel, Christine I. Wallich (eds), *Decentralization of the Socialist State*. Washington D.C.: The World Bank.
Bahry, Donna (1987), *Outside Moscow: Power, Politics, and Budgetary Policy in the Soviet Republics*. New York: Columbia University Press.
Brubaker, Rogers (1996), *Nationalism Reframed: Nationhood and the National Question in the New Europe*. Cambridge: Cambridge University Press.
Bunce, Valerie (1999), *Subversive Institutions: The Design and the Destruction of Socialism and the State*. Cambridge: Cambridge University Press.
Busygina, Irina (1994), 'Regional'noe izmerenie politicheskogo krisisa v rossii', *MEMO*, Vol.5, pp.5–17.
Chinarikhina, Galina (1996), 'Dogovor kak sposob razgranicheniya polnomochii i predmetov vedeniya mezhdu subektami federativnykh otnoshenii v Rossii', *Vlast*, Vol.9, pp.20–25.
Colomer, Josep M. (1998), 'The Spanish 'State of Autonomies': Non-Institutional Federalism', *West European Politics*, Vol.21, No.4, October, pp.40–52.
Colton, Timothy (1995), 'Boris Yeltsin, Russia's All-Thumbs Democrat', in Colton T. and Tucker R. (eds), *Patterns in Post-Soviet Leadership*. Boulder: Westview, pp.49–74.
Joan DeBardeleben and Larry Black (eds), *Beyond the Monolith: The Emergence of Regionalism in Post-Soviet Russia*. Washington D.C.: The Woodrow Wilson Center Press, pp.35–56.
Dmitrieva, Olga (1993), 'Politicheskie igri vokrug budzheta', *Moskovskie novosti*, Vol.28, pp.8–9.
Duchacek, Ivo (1970), *Comparative Federalism: The Territorial Dimension of Politics*. New York: Holt, Rinehart & Winston; (1990) 'Perforated Sovereignties: Towards a Typology of New Actors in International Relations', pp.1–33, in H.J. Michelmann and P. Soldatos (eds), *Federalism and International Relations: The Role of Subnational Units*. Oxford: Clarendon Press.
Dunlop, John B. (1998), *Russia Confronts Chechnya: Roots of a Separatist Conflict*. Cambridge: Cambridge University Press.
EastWest Institute (1999), *Federal Budget and the Regions: Analyzing Fiscal Flows*. Moscow: Dialogue-MSU.
Elazar, Daniel J. (1987), *Exploring Federalism*. London: University of Alabama Press.
Federativnyi Dogovor: Dokumenty, Kommentarii (1992), Moskva: Izdatel'stvo 'Respublika'.
Guboglo, M.N. (ed.) (1997), *Federalizm vlasti i vlast' federalizma*. Moscow: IntelTekh.
Hanauer, Laurence (1996), 'Tatarstan and the Prospects for Federalism in Russia: A Commentary', *Security Dialogue*, Vol.27, No.1, pp.81–6.
Hough, Jerry (1997), *Democratization and Revolution in the USSR, 1985–1991*. Washington D.C.: Brookings Institution Press.
Hughes, James (1994), 'Regionalism in Russia: The Rise and Fall of Siberian Agreement', *Europe–Asia Studies*, Vol.46, No.7, pp.1133–62; (1996) 'Russia's Federalization: Bilateral Treaties Add to Confusion', *Transition*, Vol.2, No.19 (20 September), pp.39–43; (2001) 'Chechnya: Understanding the Causes of a Protracted Post-Soviet Conflict', *Civil Wars*,

Vol.4, No.3 (Autumn).

Khakimov, Raphael S. (1996), 'Prospects of Federalism in Russia: A View from Tatarstan', *Security Dialogue*, Vol.27, No.1, pp.71–6.

Konstitutsii respublik v sostave Rossiiskoi Federatsii (1996), Moscow: Izvestiya, Vols 1–2.

Konstitutsiia Rossiiskoi Federatsii (1995), Moscow: Nauchnoe Izdatel'stvo.

Kymlicka, Will (1993), *Multicultural Citizenship*. Oxford: Oxford University Press.

Lapidus, Gail W. and Elizabeth W. Teague (1995), 'Nationalism, Regionalism, and Federalism: Center–Periphery Relations in Post-Communist Russia', in Gail Lapidus (ed.), *Russia's Troubled Transition*. Cambridge: Cambridge University Press.

Lemco, Jonathan (1991), *Political Stability in Federal Governments*. New York: Praeger.

Lieven, Anatol (1998), *Chechnya: Tombstone of Russian Power*. London: Yale University Press.

Linz, Juan (1990), 'The Perils of Presidentialism', *The Journal of Democracy*, Vol.1, No.1 (Winter), pp.51–69; (1994) 'Presidential or Parliamentary Democracy: Does it Make a Difference?' in J.J. Linz and A. Valenzuela (eds), *The Failure of Presidential Democracy: Comparative Perspectives, Vol.I*. Baltimore: Johns Hopkins University Press.

Lustick, Ian (1979), 'Stability in Deeply Divided Societies: Consociationalism or Control', *World Politics*, Vol.31, pp.325–44.

McAuley, Mary (1997), *Russia's Politics of Uncertainty*. Cambridge: Cambridge University Press.

O'Donnell, Guillermo (1994), 'Delegative Democracy', *Journal of Democracy*, Vol.5, No.1 (January), pp.55–69.

O'Leary, Brendan (2001), 'Nationalism and Ethnicity: Research Agendas on Theories of Their Sources and Their Regulation', in Daniel Chirot and Martin E.P. Seligman (eds), *Ethnopolitical Warfare: Causes, Consequences and Possible Solutions*. Washington D.C.: American Psychological Association, pp.37–48.

Offe, Claus (1996), *Varieties of Transition: The East European and East German Experience*. Cambridge: Polity Press.

Ordeshook, Peter (1995), 'Reexamining Russia: Institutions and Incentives', *Journal of Democracy*, Vol.6, No.2 (April), pp.46–60.

Sharlet, Robert (1994), 'The Prospects for Federalism in Russian Constitutional Politics', *Publius: The Journal of Federalism*, Vol.24 (Spring), pp.115–27.

Slider, Darrell (1994), 'Federalism, Discord, and Accommodation: Intergovernmental Relations in Post-Soviet Russia', in T. Friedgut and J. Hahn (eds), *Local Power and Post-Soviet Politics*. Armonk: M.E Sharpe, pp.239–69.

Smith, Graham (1998), 'Russia, Multiculturalism and Federal Justice', *Europe–Asia Studies*, Vol.50, No.8 (December), pp.1393–412; (1999) *The Post-Soviet States: Mapping the Politics of Transition*. London: Arnold.

SSSR v tsifrakh v 1989g (1990), Moscow: *Finansy i statistika*, pp.23–5.

Solnick, Steven (1996), 'The Political Economy of Russian Federalism: A Framework for Analysis', *Problems of Post-Communism* (November/December), pp.13–25; (1998) 'Will Russia Survive? Center and Periphery in the Russian Federation', in Barnett Rubin and Jack Snyder (eds), *Post-Soviet Political Order: Conflict and State-Building*. London: Routledge, pp.58–80; (2000) 'Is the Center Too Weak or Too Strong in the Russian Federation', in Valerie Sperling (ed.), *Building the Russian State: Institutional Crisis and the Quest for Democratic Governance*. Boulder, Colorado: Westview Press.

Stepan, Alfred (2000), 'Russian Federalism in Comparative Perspective', *Post-Soviet Affairs*, Vol.16, No.2, pp.133–76.

Strange, Susan (1995), 'The Defective State', *Daedalus*, Vol.124, No.2 (Spring), pp.55–74.

Suverennyi Tatarstan (1997), Moscow: insan.

Tishkov, Valery (1997), *Ethnicity, Nationalism and Conflict In and After the Soviet Union: The Mind Aflame*. London, Sage.

Tolz, Vera (1998), 'Forging the Nation: National Identity and Nation Building in Post-Communist Russia', *Europe–Asia Studies*, Vol.50, No.6 (September), pp.993–1022.

Treisman, Daniel (1996), 'The Politics of Intergovernmental Transfers in Post-Soviet Russia', *British Journal of Political Science*, Vol.26, pp.299–335; (1999) *After the Deluge:*

Regional Crises and Political Consolidation in Russia. Michigan: University of Michigan Press.

Umnova, Irina A. (1996), *Konstitutsionnye osnovy sovremennogo Rossiiskogo Federalizma.* Moscow: Delo.

Wallich, Christine I. (1992), *Fiscal Decentralization, Intergovernmental Relations in Russia, Studies of Economies in Transformation, Paper Number 6,* Washington D.C.: The World Bank; (1994) (ed.), *Russia and the Challenge of Fiscal Federalism,* Washington D.C.: The World Bank; (1997) 'Reforming Intergovernmental Relations, Russia and The Challenge of Fiscal federalism', in B. Kamininski (ed.), *Economic Transition in Russia and the New States of Eurasia,* London: M.E. Sharpe, pp.252–76.

White, Stephen, Richard Rose and Ian McAllister (1997), *How Russia Votes.* Chatham, N.J.: Chatham House Publishers.

The 'New' Ukraine: A State of Regions

GWENDOLYN SASSE

The Ukrainian state that emerged from the Soviet Union in 1991 is a historical novelty. While Ukraine's current borders go back to 1954, the year of Crimea's transfer from the RFSFR to the Ukrainian SSR, an independent political entity had never existed within these territorial boundaries prior to 1991. 'Ukraina' translates as 'borderland' and encapsulates a key feature of modern Ukraine: its history as a space between the Habsburg, Russian, Ottoman and Soviet empires. Ukrainian nation-building is 'an undertaking to transform the peripheries of several nations...into a sovereign entity able to communicate directly with the larger world' (Szporluk, 1997: 86). Internationally, this historical development links Ukraine to Central and Eastern Europe, Russia and the Black Sea region. All four empires left their cultural mark on Ukraine, and the Soviet period, in particular, accounts for a complex institutional and socio-economic legacy. Domestically, the disparities between the different territorial components – their ethnic, linguistic, religious and socio-economic cleavages, historical memories and different political and foreign policy orientations – make Ukraine's single most important characteristic its construction as a state of regions. This emphasis on regional differences neither calls Ukraine's territorial integrity into question nor does it preclude the prospect of successful post-Soviet transition and state- and nation-building. It simply highlights the fact that the regional factor was bound to shape Ukraine's post-Soviet political and economic development.

In the aftermath of the Soviet collapse the potential for conflict in Ukraine hinged on questions about the feasibility of an independent Ukraine and its territorial integrity. Ukraine's possible disintegration along an east–west territorial divide appeared to be the predominant internal challenge. Russia's hesitant recognition of independent Ukraine and Ukraine's economic dependence on Russia led Western academics and policy-makers to focus on the potential for instability in Ukraine (Rumer, 1994; Larrabee, 1994). The east–west divide figured prominently in Western accounts of post-Soviet Ukraine and was often tied to speculations about a break-up of Ukraine and its security implications for Europe (Holdar, 1995). Additionally, Crimea emerged as a potential violent flashpoint. Comparisons with the wars in former Yugoslavia were frequently invoked around 1994 (Kuzio, 1994a/1994b; Meek, 1994). *The Economist* went furthest, depicting a 'long-running, acrimonious, possibly bloody, and conceivably nuclear dispute' over Crimea (*The Economist*, 17 July 1993). Ukraine's national security concept of 1997 also defined regional separatist tendencies as one of the key potential threats. Regional diversity has arguably been the predominant feature of Ukraine's transition and state- and nation-building process. However, as I will argue here, it has also been a key to Ukraine's political stability, although its stabilizing role is generally overlooked.

This contribution will begin by mapping Ukraine's experience with regionalization and decentralization. It will then analyze the regional challenges in post-Soviet Ukraine. The main focus will be on the politicization of Ukraine's regional diversity, most notably in Zakarpattya, the Donbas and Crimea, the latter being the greatest ethno-regional challenge to post-Soviet Ukraine. The 'new' Ukraine is one of the best examples of the contradictory challenge inherent in post-Soviet state-building: strengthening central state capacity within an institutionalized state unit inherited from the Soviet period, while simultaneously engaging with sub-national demands for more autonomy. Kyiv perceived a unitary state as the best guarantor of the centre's control over both a diverse polity and transition strategies. However, as a result of a protracted struggle between regional and national elites the unitary Ukrainian state, as defined in the constitution of June 1996, is perforated by an asymmetric institutional autonomy arrangement in Crimea. Thus, the inherent tension between centralization and decentralization was inscribed in the constitution. Moreover, Ukraine's political institutions, its socio-economic profile, and its administrative structures are permeated by distinct regional characteristics.

THE CONSTRUCTION OF A REGIONALIZED STATE

The ethnic cleavage between Ukrainians and Russians is often portrayed as the key to post-Soviet politics in Ukraine. This simplification rests on several problematic assumptions: first, the 'Russian factor' tends to be projected backwards into Ukrainian history when, in fact, historically the Polish dimension of the Ukrainian nation-building project was equally important. Second, the binary opposition between ethnic Russians and Ukrainians implies clear-cut ethno-political mobilization, although the ethno-sociological and political boundaries between these two groups are extremely blurred (Bremmer, 1994). Third, the juxtaposition of ethnic Russians and Ukrainians – according to the Soviet census of 1989 72.7% and 22.1% – ignores the considerable number of ethnic Ukrainians who regard Russian as their mother tongue (33–34%), let alone the many bilinguals. The emphasis on language has given rise to the equally problematic notions of 'Russophones' and 'Ukrainophones' which suggest that language is the predominant factor in Ukrainian politics and consists of two mutually exclusive categories. Fourth, an overemphasis on the ethno-linguistic cleavages tends to obscure the political significance of regions *per se* and has effectively delayed a systematic analysis of the role of the regional factor in Ukrainian politics.

The territorial patchwork of Ukraine is the product of a long historical process. 'The various regions that make up modern Ukraine have moved in and out of Ukrainian history at different times, but have never really interacted together as an ensemble... There are therefore serious difficulties in imagining Ukrainian history either as a temporal or a geographical continuum' (Wilson, 1997: 25). This lack of a historical continuum even stirred a debate about whether Ukraine 'has a history' (von Hagen *et al.*, 1995). The recognition that all 'national' histories are tainted and that the comprehensive study of diverse empires, nations and regions is ultimately more important than historical linearity or value judgements about the validity of a certain claim to nation- and statehood underpinned this debate.

Until the middle of the seventeenth century almost all Ukrainians lived in the Polish-Lithuanian Commonwealth which extended beyond the river Dnipro eastward. After 1667, parts of this territory – Poltava, Chernihiv and Kyiv – came under the jurisdiction of the Russian tsar. The territory west of the Dnipro stayed within the Polish-Lithuanian Commonwealth until 1793–95, although the 'Polish factor' remained significant until after the Russian revolution of 1917 (Szporluk, 1997: 87). The concept of a modern Ukrainian nation goes back to the late eighteenth century, but in its current boundaries, the Ukrainian state and, in particular, its western border, is by and large a Soviet construct. Ukraine's Soviet past, consequently, is part of the fabric of the state itself. Unlike historical memory in the Baltic states, Ukraine's post-Soviet rewriting of history had to tread carefully and selectively in addressing its post-imperial legacies. As discussed in the introduction to this volume, the internationally recognized principle of territorial integrity imbued the Soviet-era boundaries with new legitimacy.

Today's regions of L'viv, Ternopil' and Ivano-Frankivs'k had belonged to Poland from the fourteenth century onwards. From 1772 to 1918 this region, known as eastern Galicia, was part of the Habsburg empire. After a brief spell of independence as the 'West Ukrainian People's Republic' (ZUNR) in 1918–19 the region came under the rule of the new Poland and, after Poland's destruction, under Soviet rule. In September 1939 Western Ukraine, comprising Galicia and Volhynia, was annexed by the Soviet Union and integrated into the Ukrainian SSR on the basis of the

Molotov-Ribbentrop pact. Galicia was briefly occupied by Germany before becoming Soviet again in 1944. Northern Bukovina, the northern part of the former Hapsburg province of Bukovina, including the administrative and cultural centre Chernivtsi, belonged to Romania in the period 1918–40 before it was annexed by the Soviets in 1940.[1] The region was incorporated into the Soviet Union only in 1944 after a brief interim period during which Romania regained control. For centuries Zakarpattya had been part of Hungary before it was incorporated into Czechoslovakia in 1919 as part of the territorial changes after the First World War. From 1939 to 1944 the region became Hungarian once more before being annexed to the Soviet Union in 1945 and, thus, effectively ruled by Moscow for the first time in its entire history. The majority population of Zakarpattya, the Rusyns, were subsequently categorized as 'Ukrainians'.

Today Western Ukraine is generally seen as the heartland of Ukrainian national identity and the home of the Ukrainian national movement. Historically, however, the idea of a separate Ukrainian nation was first articulated in the eastern part of today's Ukraine (Szporluk, 1997: 89). Repressive Russian imperial policies forced the national ideas into exile: they found their primary outlet in the Habsburg controlled Western Ukraine where it thrived on the confrontation with Polish nationalism. Thus, the concept of a separate Ukrainian nation travelled across the territory of today's Ukrainian state and embodied two different, equally important and regionalized struggles of self-determination: the struggle against both Russian and Polish dominance.

The transfer of the Crimean peninsula from the jurisdiction of the RSFSR to the Ukrainian SSR in 1954 completed the map of modern Ukraine.[2] Since its annexation in 1783 the peninsula had been under Russian rule. Prior to the Russian conquest, Crimea was part of the Crimean Tatar Khanate, which had split off from the Golden Horde and continued to exist as a protectorate of the Ottoman empire from 1475 onwards. After a brief phase of different autonomy experiments after the 1917 revolution, Crimea became an ASSR within the RSFSR which existed until 1945.[3] After the large-scale deportation of the Crimean Tatars under Stalin in 1944, Crimea's status was downgraded to that of an ordinary region. The issue of Crimean autonomy was only revived in the late Gorbachev era and resulted in a regional referendum as early as January 1991. This referendum effectively paved the way for a new ASSR within the Ukrainian SSR and, thus, left Ukraine with a still undefined but existing asymmetric institutional set-up when the Soviet Union collapsed in late 1991 and the majority of voters in all the regions of the Ukrainian SSR voted for independence.[4] This choice, underscored by hopes for economic prosperity, did not immediately bring about an integrated state identity or a clear concept of the Ukrainian nation, but it marked the beginning of a political commitment to one. Initially, Ukraine's state- and nation-building process was interpreted as an elite choice between an ethnic Ukrainian identity and a civic identity open to all national groups residing in Ukraine (Liber, 1998: 189). In reality, Ukraine's regional diversity, reinforced by the presence of a large Russian minority, a considerable degree of russification of Ukrainians and economic dependence on neighbouring Russia, meant that the constituency for an exclusivist, homogenizing nation-state building project was small.

Upon independence Ukraine consisted officially of 24 regions (*oblasti*), an as yet weakly defined Autonomous Republic in Crimea plus two cities of republican jurisdiction (Kyiv and Sevastopol'). From the outset, the status of Crimea and Sevastopol' emerged as key issues both in domestic and international politics. While the first changes to Crimea's status had already been introduced in the late Soviet period, Sevastopol' had officially enjoyed federal status alongside Leningrad and Moscow since 1948, following a special resolution of the Supreme Soviet of the RSFSR. Since that time, however, Sevastopol' had maintained an ambiguous position in Soviet decision-making. As archival evidence proves, Soviet economic planning often included Sevastopol' in the Crimean and Ukrainian budgets, and Sevastopol' was a constituency of the Ukrainian SSR in Soviet elections.[5]

In addition to clear challenges arising from the inherited Soviet institutional architecture, such as the status of Crimea and Sevastopol', post-Soviet Ukraine has had to grapple with a range of structural legacies at the regional level, such as a pronounced south-east vs north-west socio-economic cleavage and ethno-linguistic (and to a somewhat lesser extent religious) settlement patterns. There is a widespread tendency to equate Ukraine's regional diversity with ethnicity. Szporluk aptly described the imprecise nature of this measure: 'Some of these people are Soviet in the morning, Russian in the afternoon and Ukrainian in the evening – the order may change' (Szporluk, 1998: 317). Some authors have argued that 'linguistic patterns...demonstrate regional difference best' (Wilson, 1997: 23–4). Language use has often been equated with the ethnic cleavage between Russians and Ukrainians. In fact, language is an inexact proxy for both regional and ethnic cleavages. The use of the Russian and Ukrainian languages is not mutually exclusive and not necessarily tied to ethnic identity, but often depends on an individual's social context or their generation (Arel, 1996; Jackson, 1998: 107–110). Moreover, an overemphasis on language locks the whole discussion about Ukraine's regional diversity into the discussion about national identity and ethnicity, while neglecting socio-economic cleavages or regional political interests. Ukraine's complex religious cleavages (Uniate Church, Ukrainian

Orthodox Church–Moscow Patriarchy, Ukrainian Orthodox Church–Kyiv Patriarchy, Ukrainian Autocephalous Orthodox Church) are often associated with ethno-linguistic categories, in particular when narrowed down to the juxtaposition of Greek Catholic Uniate vs. Orthodox believers. Religious affiliations reflect some historical and political divides, but by itself religion is neither a key political faultline nor a clear-cut ethnic marker, as for example the high number of parishes of the Ukrainian Orthodox Church–Moscow Patriarchy in central and western Ukraine demonstrates (Wilson, 1997: 91). Few studies have challenged the thesis that ethnicity is the decisive element in self-identification in Ukrainian politics more generally. Eastern Ukraine, in particular, is a good case-study to illustrate that socio-economic cleavages have been more important than ethnic criteria (Nemyria, 1999: 80–83).

The economic regionalization of post-Soviet Ukraine does not coincide exactly with the main historical divisions outlined above. Nevertheless, the western and central regions are mostly agriculturally oriented (with some pockets of light industry, manufacturing and mining), whereas the eastern regions represent the industrial base of the country (coal-mining, metallurgy, machine-building, chemical industry). The eastern regions are the most densely populated regions of Ukraine, a fact that translates directly into electoral weight. The regions of Donets'k, Luhans'k and Kharkiv were already the most industrialized regions in the pre-Soviet period. Under Soviet rule the Donbas enjoyed numerous privileges; officials from the region also routinely moved up the Soviet career ladder in Moscow.

The fact that the southern and eastern regions of Ukraine are still characterized by higher wages and lower official unemployment in comparison with western, northern and central regions is an indicator for the lack of structural reform of the Soviet-era economy in Ukraine.[6] The higher wage arrears and higher living costs in the east and south counterbalance this trend to some extent, but on the whole living standards are still considered to be higher in the previously privileged, highly sovietized areas. While the eastern and southern regions show a greater distribution of small and medium-size enterprises than western regions – usually considered a motor of economic growth – privatization is most advanced in western regions (in addition to the capital Kyiv). As early as April 1991 the legal basis for Free Economic Zones (FEZ) was established (*UCIPR Research Update*, 2000). The rationale behind these zones was to attract foreign investment and to turn them into a model of economic and infrastructure development (*Holos Ukrainy*, 19 September 2000). According to the data provided by the Cabinet of Ministers in September 2000, however, the 11 zones operational in Ukraine have only met 23% of their investment targets and created and saved less than half the jobs envisaged (*UCIPR Research*

Update, 2000). There are special economic zones in Crimea, Zakarpattiia, the *regions* of Volyn', Chernihiv, Donets'k, Luhans'k, Mykolaiv and Kyiv, as well as in Kharkiv and Shostka. At present, the zones make for a set of unconnected islands characterized by special tax regimes. At this point the future of Ukraine's FEZ seems uncertain, in particular as the IMF pushes for their abolition. Regardless of their effectiveness varying and their overall impact on Ukraine's economy being unclear, the fact that they were set up by normal legislative procedures that require a parliamentary consensus is a tacit recognition of Ukraine's *de facto* economic regionalization.

The regions (*oblasti*) of the Ukrainian SSR were set up as administrative structures and were not concomitant with historically evolved cultural or functional regions, which often cut across two or more Soviet regions (for example, Galicia, Novorossiya, Donbas). Nevertheless, the region as the key administrative legacy at the sub-national level quickly emerged as a shorthand to denote a Ukrainian 'region' in the post-Soviet period, and the two terms are often used interchangeably. Administrative, political, historical, socio-economic and cultural definitions of regions are used alongside each other without clear distinctions. Scholars have put forward a range of different delimitations, varying from two to 11 regions. These distinctions are based, for example, on the historical divide between the 'Right Bank' and 'Left Bank' along the river Dnipro (Khmelko and Wilson, 1998), five historical regions (former Habsburg regions in the far west, Western Volhynia, Right Bank, Left Bank, former Ottoman lands) vs. the economic division between two regions, the south-east and the centre-north (Birch, 2000: 1018–20), four regions based on the results of the 1994 parliamentary elections (Arel and Wilson, 1994; Khmelko and Wilson, 1998), five regions (West, Centre-West, Centre-East, East, South) based on large-scale Ukrainian sociological surveys (*Hromads'ka Dumka Ukrainy*)[7] or 11 geographical/ geopolitical regions (Nemiria, 1999: 74–5). Thus, while the significance of regional cleavages in Ukraine has increasingly been acknowledged, there is as yet little agreement on what constitutes a region. In transition countries the existence of strong regional identities is often interpreted as a sign of weak state capacity. Some simplistically view them as 'an indicator of an incomplete identity in transition' (Kuzio, 1996: 603–4). This approach turns regional differences into a transitional phenomenon, and reveals a bias for nation-state-building as a homogenizing and assimilatory process, while underestimating the potential for the coexistence of multiple identities in modern societies.

Article 132 of the 1996 Ukrainian constitution refers to both centralization and decentralization of power. Decentralization is primarily interpreted as local self-government. The Soviet-era regions became the territorial administrative unit at the meso-level, and their lack of historical legitimacy has pushed the issue of autonomization further into the background. In fact, the powers of Soviet-era regions vis-à-vis the centre were reduced to a minimum: power rests, first and foremost, with the centre and, second, with local self-governing bodies, while the regions are simply subordinate administrative 'transmission belts'. The constitution of 1996 subsumes regional self-government under 'local self-government'. The heads of the regional and district administrations are appointed by the president himself. Only the Law on Local Self-Government in Ukraine (1997) stipulated that the assemblies at the region and raion levels were to be directly elected.

As discussed in the introductory essay, the term 'regionalism' is essentially a political term, describing a degree of mobilization around regional cleavages rather than simply the existence of regional diversity. Public opinion polls in Ukraine have continuously highlighted a link between the place of residence and issue polarization (Hesli, 1995; Hesli et al., 1998; Kubicek, 2000), but the sheer existence of spatial characteristics should not be equated with the political phenomenon of regionalism.[8] The discussion about regionalism in Ukraine is highly politicized: it was generally perceived of as a means of legitimizing regions as independent political actors which would ultimately undermine the centre's control and Ukraine's territorial integrity. The politicization of the term 'region' is also due to the grossly simplified portrait of Ukraine as a culturally 'cleft country' (Huntington, 1996: 165).

Studies of Ukraine's early post-Soviet elections, in particular the parliamentary and presidential elections of 1994, tended to confirm the east–west divide (Arel and Wilson, 1994; Bojcun, 1995; Birch, 1998). In 1994 over half of the Communist, Socialist and Agrarian deputies elected to the *Verkhovna Rada* came from the five eastern regions, whereas the majority of national-democratic deputies were elected in four western regions (Holdar, 1995). In the presidential elections of 1994 the support base of the incumbent Leonid Kravchuk was firmly rooted in Western Ukraine, whereas support for Leonid Kuchma's Russophone, centrist and reformist platform was rooted in the populous south-eastern regions, which secured his victory. Ukraine's electoral geography seemed to suggest a clear-cut reinforcement of ethno-linguistic cleavages and led Western media to spread doomsday scenarios, for example about 'The Birth and Possible Death of a Country' (*The Economist*, 7 May 1994). The presidential elections of 1999 broke the electoral model of 1994 and resulted in a more complex regional distribution of votes. Kuchma's first term in office (1994–99) illustrated how Ukraine's regional diversity and the balance of power with parliament necessitate interregional compromises. By the end of his first term, Kuchma was more popular in the western parts of the country, while his electoral support base in the south-east, previously his stronghold, had become eroded.[9] Moreover, region and ethnicity have distinctive effects on different segments of the electorate. Age coupled with an interaction between language and education, for example, explains the leftist vote better than ethnicity or language alone (Birch, 1998b). The change of the electoral system in time for the 1998 parliamentary elections – half of the deputies were now elected on party lists – rendered the actual electoral dynamics at the regional level more visible. By 1998, as Craumer and Clem observed, 'economic reform questions had overwhelmed issues dealing with ethnicity and the Ukrainian state' (Craumer and Clem, 1999: 4). Birch suggests that cultural-historical experiences are strongly correlated with the support for national-democratic parties in the western regions incorporated into the USSR during/after the Second World War, whereas socio-economic factors are more salient in explaining the support for left-wing forces, such as the Communist Party (Birch, 2000). The lesson is that regional factors are significant in voting behaviour, but the regional effect on party preferences depends on the party.

Most factions in the Ukrainian parliament, in particular centrist groups, are formed around regional interest groups. Ideas about regionalization and autonomy tend to be subsumed under other pragmatic short-term interests and do not generate a broader political consensus due to inter- or intra-regional rivalries. Economic interests intersect the debate about autonomization and preclude a concerted attack on the centre's power. By 2001 there were two factions/parties in the *Verkhovna Rada* which explicitly play on Ukraine's regional diversity: the faction 'Revival of Regions' (*Vidrodzhennya Rehioniv*), led by one of Ukraine's most influential oligarchs and Kuchma supporter in 1999/2000, Oleksandr Volkov, and 'Regions of Ukraine' led by Mykola Azarov, the head of the State Tax Administration (UCIPR, 26 March 2001).

Ukraine's executive structures also reflect Ukraine's regionalization: by decree Kuchma set up a Council of Regions in 1994. It effectively replaced the presidential representatives at the regional and district level, who had been introduced in 1992 to ensure the centre's control over the local councils. The presidential representatives were abolished in 1994 when parliament reaffirmed the role of the councils.[10] The Council of Regions was conceived as a strictly consultative body under the auspices of the president. It brings together the heads of regional administrations, who are appointed by the president, the mayors of Kyiv and Sevastopol' and the Deputy Prime Minister of the Republic of Crimea, and its task is to coordinate regional and national interests, policies and priorities. While this body is clearly an extension of the president's executive, it nevertheless signals a political awareness that regions matter. So far the existence of powerful cross-cutting elite interests has meant that collective action by Ukraine's regions to secure more power or even a coherent regional policy from the centre has failed.

THE FEDERAL IDEA: PAST AND PRESENT

Different notions of federalism have been part of the Ukrainian political discourse since the nineteenth century when Mykhailo Drahomanov used the term 'federalism' to describe a new role and greater self-determination for Ukraine (consisting of the provinces Kyiv, Kharkiv and Odesa) within a federalized Russian empire (Rudnytsky, 1987: 243–4). His ideas were reflected in the political writings and acitivities of the historian Mykhailo Hrushevs'kyi in the early twentieth century. After February 1917 the Central Rada under Hrushevksyi first pushed for Ukrainian autonomy within a federalized Russia (Motyl, 1980: 11–12; Medvedchuk, 1996: 51). In response to revolution and war the Central Rada subsequently declared the independent Ukrainian People's Republic (UNR). Despite the claim to a unitary state, the draft constitution of the UNR of April 1918, which in the end was never enacted, incorporated Hrushevs'kyi's ideas of decentralization: the UNR was to be divided into 30 lands (zemli) plus the three cities Kyiv, Kharkiv and Odesa (Slyusarenko and Tomenko, 1993: 71). Moreover, the principle of national personal autonomy became one of its founding principles (Slyusarenko and Tomenko, 1993: 75). The short-lived Hetmanate under General Skoropads'kyi tried to square the circle by both proclaiming the 'Ukrainian state' (Ukrains'ka derzhava) and Ukraine's federation with an anti-Bolshevik Russian government (Motyl, 1980: 15). The subsequent Directorate under Vynnychenko and Petliura pushed the issue one step further in January 1919 through the proclamation of sobornist', borrowing the ecclesiastic term for 'unity' as a symbol for the agreement of the UNR and the Western Ukrainian People's Republic (ZUNR) to unite. The formal ratification of this union was left to the Ukrainian Constitutent Assembly (Motyl, 1980: 17; Slyusarenko and Tomenko, 1993: 123–4). Until then the ZUNR was to continue as the 'Western Oblast of the Ukrainian People's Republic' (ZOUNR), thereby adding a confederal element to the UNR. By the end of 1919 the idea of sobornist' had already become a victim of Petliura's political calculations: he tried to secure Poland's political and military support against Russia in return for granting Poland Eastern Galicia and the western half of Volhynia. His pact reinforced the rift that had occurred at the Paris Peace Conference where a separate Western Ukrainian delegation had formed (Motyl, 1980: 18–19). In the end, despite the collapse of the Russian and Habsburg empires, the ethnic Ukrainian territories remained fragmented between different states: the western borderlands became part of Poland, Czechoslovakia and Romania, and the Ukrainian SSR emerged as the new 'state' entity to the east. The special status of Crimea was also on the political agenda in the aftermath of the revolutions and during the early Soviet period. The Central Rada's sequence of proclamations reflects the indeterminate status of Crimea: the Third Universal Declaration of 20 November 1917 still explicitly excluded Crimea from the territory of the Ukrainian state (Slyusarenko and Tomenko, 1993: 74). The debates over Crimea's status – independence vs. autonomy within Ukraine vs. integration with Russia – in the aftermath of the revolution and under the German protectorate during World War I offer some striking parallels with the post-Soviet struggles over Crimea (Torbakov, 1996; Sasse, 1999: 216–26). In the years 1918–19 the Rusyns, who had been Magyarized after 1867, also managed to revive their demand for autonomy in their region south of the Carpathians (Magosci, 1978: 55–6). Out of the options they faced in 1919 – joining the Czechoslovak federation, autonomy within Hungary, a union with Ukraine or independence – only the first one emerged as a realistic scenario (Magosci, 1978: 91–101). Additionally, the Bolsheviks established a short-lived Donetsk-Kryvyi Rih Republic in the east of Ukraine in 1918 which was, however, primarily a means of undermining the Central Rada in Kyiv. The examples of the ZUNR/ZOUNR and Crimea, in particular, illustrate that the period 1917–21 saw a number of provisional institutional arrangements based on federal elements which were never realized due to the short life of the republic. Nevertheless, this period marks one of the few points of reference in the history of Ukrainian statehood, and the sheer fact that regional divisions were addressed during Ukraine's short-lived independence indicates the political significance of the country's regional diversity.

The establishment of the USSR transformed the meaning of federalism once again. The Soviet type of asymmetric, ethno-territorial federalism was by and large a façade for a strictly hierarchical system of state power overseen by the Communist Party at every level. This structure, aptly described by Brubaker as 'institutionalized multinationality', provided a platform for nationalist and anti-imperial mobilization during Gorbachev's liberalization and, thus, greatly contributed to the break-up of the USSR. As soon as the curious combination of an empire and a federation had collapsed, most of the successor states had to struggle with formal and informal Soviet institutional legacies, in particular with institutionalized Soviet autonomies. Initially, the Moldovan ASSR had been set up within the Ukrainian SSR in 1924 as the nucleus of a distinct Soviet Moldovan national identity which formed part of the USSR's strategy to acquire

Romanian territory (King, 2000). After the annexation of Bessarabia the new Moldovan SSR, established in August 1940, replaced the earlier autonomous construct.[11] Subsequently, Soviet Ukraine remained without any formal autonomies within its administrative-territorial boundaries until 1991, when a new ASSR status was conceded to Crimea.

In the post-Soviet period, the national Ukrainian political elite has shied away from federalism and, with the exception of Crimea, rejected autonomy as a principle of state-building. Centralization was inextricably tied to the overall rationale of consolidating the sovereign Ukrainian state and nation. The protracted political struggle over Crimea, in particular the brief phase of Crimean separatism in 1994, had demonstrated the potential for conflict. Simultaneously, it illustrated Kyiv's lack of control in the periphery and further discredited the idea of federalism at the centre of the new polity.[12]

Before the break-up of the USSR federalist ideas had been floated in the west of Ukraine with Vyacheslav Chornovil, the former dissident, leader of *Rukh* and chairman of the L'viv region council after March 1990, as its most prominent proponent.[13] The special *Rukh* meeting in Zakarpattya in March 1990, which marked the anniversary of the proclamation of the short-lived independent Carpatho-Ukrainian Republic (1938–39) fits this trend (Nahaylo, 1999: 259). Federalism has primarily been an idea of the political opposition in Ukraine (Zolotarev, 1995: 70). Prior to independence it was a means to emphasize the 'Ukrainian' character of Galicia, but once an independent Ukraine had been established, the idea was discarded as being too subversive of central state capacity. Chornovil and with him Ukraine's national-democratic political forces emerged as staunch supporters of a unitary Ukrainian state. The centre of political opposition and the pendulum of support for the federal principle gradually shifted to the east and south. In the 1994 presidential election, Kuchma's 'liberal' opposition based on the Interregional Bloc of Reforms (MBR) stressed the role of the regions.[14]

Academics and political analysts, most notably in Donets'k and Kharkiv (Bakirov, 1994; Miroshnik, 1995; Solov'ev, 1995: 14–15; Zolotarev, 1997), kept the issues of decentralization and federalism alive.[15] The need for special regional economic regimes was presented as a prerequisite for successful economic transition (Kravchenko, 1995: 33–7).[16] The most outspoken proponent of federalism in this period was Volodymyr Hryn'ov, the leader of the MBR. He played a crucial role in Kuchma's election campaign in 1994 when victory was gained on a platform of economic reforms and political and linguistic concerns in eastern Ukraine. Whatever Kuchma's real intentions were at the time, the fact that he successfully tapped into the concerns of the population and elites in the south-east and galvanized their support on the basis of a deliberately vague idea of regionalism underscores the political significance of Ukraine's regionalization. Once in office, Kuchma effectively sidelined Hryn'ov who merely became the president's adviser on regional questions without any direct influence on policy-making.[17] Influenced by Western thought, Hryn'ov elaborated on his ideas about federalism in his book *Nova Ukraina – yakoyu ya ii bachu* ['*The New Ukraine – how I see her*'] (Hryn'ov, 1995). The harsh public criticism he received demonstrated how much of a taboo federalism was for the political establishment.

Shortly after his re-election President Kuchma held a controversial referendum in April 2000, which aimed to increase the president's powers at the expense of parliament and gained the public's approval for complex institutional changes, such as the reduction of the number of seats in the national parliament (*Verkhovna Rada*) and the introduction of a bicameral parliament (*UCIPR Research Update*, 17 April 2000). The fact that an overwhelming majority of the population supposedly came out in favour of such an abstract concept as bicameralism casts a shadow over the legitimacy of this referendum. Despite a Constitutional Court ruling approving the referendum results, all the issues are pending and it seems highly unlikely that parliament will pass them voluntarily in the near future. In the context of Ukraine's regional diversity the introduction of a bicameral parliament constitutes the most interesting issue, as an upper chamber could dramatically increase the political leverage of regional representatives. At first glance, this institutionalization of regional interests does not seem to fit Kuchma's overarching attempt to weaken the legislature. The referendum was an example of Kuchma's ad hocism, for there was little prior discussion about the specifics of this proposition, and most importantly, about the question whether the deputies of the upper chamber would be appointed by the president or elected. The notion of bicameralism is closely associated with federal systems, but already during Ukraine's lengthy constitution-making process it had been discussed as a separate issue when President Kuchma himself had repeatedly supported a bicameral parliament in which the upper chamber would guarantee the representation of regional interests at the centre. Given the president's effective control of the regional administrations, and the lack of clarity over the composition of the upper chamber, it could end up being little more than an extension of the president's power base.

Despite ideas about federalism and autonomy being a constant in Ukraine's political debates, they have changed over time and failed to result in any substantive institutional change (with the exception of Crimea). They have been a marker of political opposition by strictly confined regional factions, and resonated with some ethnic minorities, but have not generated a cross-regional political strategy. Similar to regional elite groupings, national minorities adopted the political language of decentralization, tying their distinct national identities to different autonomy concepts. The highly politically mobilized Crimean Tatars made the strongest claim to self-determination as an indigenous population. After initially opposing Crimean political autonomy, they have increasingly tried to interpret Crimea's current autonomy status as a first step towards a Crimean Tatar national auotonomy. The Romanian minority in the Chernivtsi region and the Hungarian minority in Zakarpattya have also repeatedly supported the idea of national-territorial autonomies.

The rejection of federalism is one of the few issues on which there is a consensus among national-level elites in Ukraine. The experience with Soviet federalism and its ultimate collapse informs this view. Leftist parties do not oppose regional autonomy, in particular if asymmetrically applied to eastern and southern regions, but wholesale federalism is interpreted as a too radical reform of the inherited structures which could put central state authority at risk. The national democratic forces on the political Right, generally in favour of political reform, see federalism as an obstacle to state integration and national unity. Autonomy is associated with Ukraine's ethno-linguistic cleavages and strengthening of the Russophone regions in the south-east. The arguments against federalism are backed by a number of prominent constitutional lawyers. The ultimate fear is that Ukraine could be pulled apart by centrifugal tendencies in its borderlands in the west, east and south.

MANAGING REGIONAL AND ETHNIC CHALLENGES

In Ukraine the most serious political regional mobilizations occurred in the Donbas, Zakarpattya and, most importantly, in Crimea. Additionally, there was a small-scale movement in Odesa, trying to revive the idea of the old province of Novorossiya, including Transnistria, Odesa, Mykolaiv and Kherson regions as well as Crimea (Nahaylo, 1999: 322). In Chernivtsi *oblast* a question on a special regional economic status was added to the country-wide referendum on 1 December 1991 and approved by 89.3% of the voters (Nahaylo, 1999: 408, 419). The ethnic make-up of Crimea, the Donbas and Zakarpattya and their links – real or perceived – to neighbouring states gave these cases a particular momentum in asserting demands for autonomy or secession.

Zakarpattya (Transcarpathia)

Zakarpattya generated different demands for greater political autonomy based on the region's complex history and ethnic composition. The region had belonged to the Habsburg empire, then became part of Romania, Czechoslovakia, Hungary and Nazi Germany before being annexed by the

USSR in 1945. There was also a brief period of independence as the Republic of Carpatho-Ukraine in 1938–39. According to the last Soviet census of 1989, the Ukrainians constitute 78.4% of the regional population, while Hungarians are the biggest minority (12.5%) alongside smaller groups of Russians, Romanians, Slovaks and others. The region is extremely multi-ethnic; intermarriage has been widespread, making multiple identities one of the defining characteristics of the region and the basis for inter-ethnic peace (Batt, 2002). After proposals about regional economic powers had evaporated in the late Soviet period, the region as a whole launched one attempt at greater autonomy: the national referendum on Ukrainian independence on 1 December 1991 was supplemented by a referendum in Zakarpattya *oblast* on 'the status of a self-governing administrative territory'. 78% of those who participated came out in favour of this idea (Solchanyk, 1994: 62–3). President Kravchuk's earlier intervention had led the regional soviet to tone down the referendum question and avoid the term 'autonomy' (Nahaylo, 1999: 408).

The Ukrainian majority population in Zakarpattya has been divided within itself with one part declaring itself to be of a separate Rusyn ethnic identity and demanding political recognition. This movement had been involved in pushing the regional council into holding the region referendum in 1991. After the region's annexation by the USSR the Rusyns had been reclassified as 'Ukrainians'. It is difficult to pin down the distinct nature of Rusyn identity today, but the historical memory is still alive in the region, in Ukraine's western neighbours and especially among Rusyn émigrés in the West. Initial demands for autonomy were informed by the memory of the autonomous unit inscribed in the 1938 Czechoslovak constitution (Magosci, 1978). The Ukrainian state has so far only recognized the Rusyns as a sub-group of Ukrainians, but the fact that the tone of the debate has become less emotional over the years indicates that the Ukrainian state has been consolidated and that the Rusyn community is split within itself along cultural, political and generational lines (Batt, 2002).

In the Berehove district on the Ukrainian-Hungarian border, where the Hungarians are in the majority, yet another set of demands came to the fore when the district council held an additional local poll on 1 December 1991 on the creation of a Hungarian autonomous district. This proposal was met with the approval of 81.4% of the voters and, therefore, must have also appealed to non-Hungarians (Nahaylo, 1999: 419). Disagreements within the Carpathian Hungarian Cultural Association about the extent of 'anti-Ukrainian' demands subsequently weakened the movement's momentum (Batt, 2002). In the Soviet period the Hungarians in the region had been severely repressed. Only the collapse of communism enabled a revival of their national identity, which had a distinct international dimension to it.

Even before Ukrainian independence Hungary had begun to build friendly neighbourly relations with Ukraine in return for guarantees for the Hungarian minority in Zakarpattya. Bilateral treaties stipulate 'collective rights' for the Hungarian minority, which in Hungary is understood not only as cultural but also as national-territorial autonomy (Batt, 2002). In view of its EU aspirations, Hungary has not pushed for a quick implementation of these rights in Ukraine, Slovakia or Romania.

On the whole, the existence of sub-regional and sub-ethnic cleavages in Zakarpattya was instrumental in de-activating a range of different regional and ethnopolitical claims for special autonomy arrangements. Zakarpattya is a post-Soviet region with national minority issues but at this point the potential for radical claims against the centre is minimal, not least due to Zakarpattya's dire economic record.[18] With the region losing its role as the Soviet Union's western military outpost, the local population has become increasingly dependent on cross-border activities along the Hungarian and Slovak borders.

The Donbas

The Donbas region, consisting of the two regions Donets'k and Luhans'k, forms a key part of Ukraine's economic base. After Crimea it is also the region with the highest proportion – though not a majority – of ethnic Russians. According to the 1989 census about 45% of the population of Luhans'k region and 44% of Donets'k region identified themselves as Russians by nationality. Regional political mobilization, however, has occurred along different socio-economic, ideological and cultural faultlines only some of which have coincided and mutually reinforced one another. Already prior to the Soviet collapse the Donbas miners had emerged as one of the most vociferous constituencies of political opposition. From 1989 onwards they repeatedly staged strikes. The effectiveness of this political weapon began to wane only in the mid-1990s after they had forced President Kravchuk to agree to early elections in 1994 and formed an opposition to local party committees (Nahaylo, 1999: 213). The miners' movement was far removed from the Ukrainian national movement that had begun to crystallize in Western Ukraine and in Kyiv. In 1990–91 regional political mobilization, modelled on the Interfront movement in the Baltic republics, resulted in the demand to create a union of 12 regions in southern and eastern Ukraine. This proposal would have effectively split the country into two parts.

In the Donbas demands for regional autonomy were closely linked to socio-economic factors. By mid-1993 the repeated strikes had resulted in political demands for administrative autonomy for the region as a whole. This demand was picked up by the regional councils in Donets'k and Luhans'k *oblast* in conjunction with the question of making Russian the official language of the region alongside Ukrainian. Ultimately, the prolonged strikes and the threat to hold a referendum on the population's confidence in both the parliament and the president broke through the political stalemate at the centre, and forced early elections in 1994.

In the Donbas a local referendum was run concurrently with the 1994 parliamentary elections. The majority of the population approved all four proposals: making Russian the second state language alongside Ukrainian, making Russian the official language of administration in the region, federalization of Ukraine (this question was only asked in Donets'k *oblast*) and Ukraine's full membership in the CIS (Nahaylo, 1999: 466). Although this referendum and a similar one in Crimea held on the same day were downgraded to 'consultative' referenda, Kyiv could hardly ignore their results. The Donbas had also raised other issues, for example the notion of dual Russian-Ukrainian citizenship and a more open border with Russia. On the whole, political mobilization in the Donbas was primarily socio-economic or cultural in nature – these two cleavages did not always coincide – and concentrated on demands for more political, economic and cultural autonomy rather than outright secession. A vague consensus on some notion of greater regional autonomy was nurtured by a convergence of different regional interests: for parts of the regional elite a degree of autonomy was seen as a means of control over regional resources and policy-making, more specifically the protection of declining industries, such as the coal mines and the military-industrial complex (MIC); for conservative political forces it seemed to pave the way for closer integration with Russia; for the Donbas-based Liberal Party, representatives of small and medium enterprises and the technical intelligentsia regional autonomy was linked to forward-looking development strategies and investment plans, but their initiatives lacked the support of the local and regional administrations despite the fact that pro-reform forces were elected in Donets'k *oblast* and the city of Luhans'k (Nemyria, 1999b: 87). The majority of the regional administrative, industrial and agricultural elites (Labour Party, Inter-Regional Association of Industrialists, miners' trade unions) aimed to use an autonomy status for the exact opposite: the preservation of Soviet economic structures and subsidies. In opposition to both these economic interest conglomerates a circle of leftist, pro-Russian forces (Inter-Movement of the Donbas, Civic Congress, Congress of Russian Communities, Party of Slavic Unity) proved key in organizing the 1994 referendum (Nemirya, 1999a: 312–14). The Communist Party of Ukraine, which has repeatedly turned the Donbas into one of its electoral strongholds, tapped into this strand of regionalism.

Political mobilization in the Donbas has been closely linked to Soviet institutional legacies, in particular the region's socio-economic profile and the fact that Ukraine's industrial and administrative elites from Kyiv, Donets'k, Dnipropetrovs'k and Kharkiv formed an integral part of the Soviet nomenklatura and traditionally moved up the Soviet career ladder in Moscow. In the post-Soviet era, the regional nomenklatura in eastern Ukraine has tried to either maintain close links with Russia or reassert itself vis-à-vis the new centre in Kyiv, but the different orientations have prevented a coherent regional political stance. The existence of multiple political identities plus a Soviet socio-economic regional profile as opposed to clear-cut ethnic or ethnolinguistic identities have characterized the regional challenge posed by the Donbas (Nemyria, 1999b: 79). These intra-regional cleavages and conflicts of interest allowed Kyiv to neutralize the regionalist challenge. The presidential administration under Kuchma has been dominated by elites from Dnipropetrovs'k (*Dnipropetrovtsi*) who attacked regionalism as a product of 'corrupt' regional elites outside their home region. Once regional interests had translated into central power they were used to replace disloyal regional elites, in particular in Donets'k *oblast*.

Crimea

Crimea has a number of exceptional features which set it apart from all the other Ukrainian regions, secured its place at the centre of the Ukrainian state-building process and necessitated exceptional means of accommodation. Crimea's geographic location and the shape of the peninsula which juts out into the Black Sea and is connected to the rest of Ukraine only by a narrow isthmus, have compounded the image of Crimea as a separate entity and fuelled political mobilization. The region's distinct multi-ethnic population is a result of its complex history under the Crimean Tatar Khanate, the Russian Empire, the USSR and Soviet Ukraine (since 1954). Crimea is the only region in Ukraine with an ethnic Russian majority population (by now about 60% as compared to 23% Ukrainians), a significant Crimean Tatar segment (10–12%) and up to 100 smaller nationalities.[19] The Crimean Tatars have returned *en masse* from their places of deportation in Central Asia since 1990–91. This influx has confronted the authorities in Crimea and Kyiv with specific socio-economic and political problems and the potential for inter-ethnic tensions. Moreover, deeply rooted symbolic, literary and historical memories tied to the region form integral parts of the different national identities and claims to the region.[20] Crimea's economy was highly sovietized and dominated by the now bankrupt military-industrial complex and the Soviet tourism industry. The region is almost entirely dependent on energy and water from the centre (dual energy dependence on Kyiv and Russia).[21] The collapse of living standards and the lack of a regional cohort of reformers shaped the post-Soviet period. The regional population remained one of the most conservatively 'Soviet' parts of the new Ukraine in terms of its outlook and voting behaviour: with the exception of an interim period during which the Russian movement filled the regional power vacuum after the collapse, the Communist Party has retained its firm grip on the regional assembly. More than any other Ukrainian region Crimea has resonated in two post-Soviet transitions. Being a periphery within the former tsarist and Soviet imperial periphery, after 1991 Crimea emerged as a key interface between two interrelated state- and nation-building processes in Ukraine and Russia. Though not central to Western interests, Crimea is also at the centre of the geopolitical triangle formed by Ukraine, Russia and Turkey.

The first attempts at political mobilization in Crimea – a short-lived ecological movement and a small democratic group – were rather feeble. From 1990 onwards Crimean autonomy emerged as the first big issue in regional politics and, ultimately, as a test of Kyiv's authority in domestic politics and of its sovereignty in relations with Russia. What started as an issue of decentralized decision-making within the USSR carried over into demands for territorial autonomy in post-Soviet Ukraine at the end of 1991 and culminated in the Russian nationalist and separatist movement in 1994. The debate about autonomy was initiated in the second half of 1990 when the Crimean soviet set up a committee to study Crimea's future status involving deputies from all political levels (USSR, Ukrainian SSR and Crimean Soviet) alongside cultural and national organizations and journalists. Crimea's previous experiences with autonomy in the aftermath of the revolution and the early Soviet period were frequently referred to; the downgrading of the Crimean ASSR in 1945 to an ordinary region as well as the region's transfer in 1954 were deemed unconstitutional; and a possible referendum on Crimea's place within Russia or Ukraine was widely discussed.[22] These discussions prepared the ground for a regional referendum on 21 January 1991 on the establishment of Crimea's ASSR status within the USSR.[23] This referendum reflected both the genuine demand for regionalized decision-making in the USSR, a demand that had been encouraged by Gorbachev's 1990 law on autonomy, and fears of a growing Ukrainian national movement, epitomized by the restrictive 1989 Ukrainian language law.[24] The local media reports and the activities of the Crimean Communist Party in the run-up to the referendum highlighted the key issues: regional economic decision-making powers and a vaguely defined regional identity endangered by the new tide of Ukrainian nationalism elsewhere. This early referendum demonstrated a widespread consensus in Crimea: 93.2% out of 81.37% of the eligible electorate that participated came out in favour of the ASSR status within the USSR and the inclusion of this Crimean ASSR in

Gorbachev's plans for a Union Treaty.[25] The Crimean Tatars, the majority of whom was still to return to Crimea, were not yet represented in regional politics and had, therefore, boycotted the referendum.

The referendum results were not fully implemented by the Ukrainian Soviet authorities: an ASSR status within the Ukrainian SSR rather than within the USSR was affirmed by law on 12 February 1991 and incorporated into the constitution of the Ukrainian SSR in June 1991.[26] The subsequent discussions about the realization of the newly gained autonomy status were cut short by the August Coup 1991 and Ukraine's declaration of independence. The ethnification of the Crimean autonomy issue occurred in the wake of the 'yes-campaign' in the regional referendum and the support of 54.1% of the Crimean population for Ukrainian independence (Nahaylo, 1999: 419). Popular expectations about economic prosperity and an effective regional regime were quickly shattered. Regional elites channelled ensuing discontent along ethnic lines and demanded closer links with Russia. The democratic and centrist regional parties were too weak to counterbalance ethno-political mobilization in Crimea, and the infant regional party system ended up being skewed towards ethno-political mobilization.[27] A whole range of Russian nationalist political organizations flourished in 1993–94. Russian political organizations developed parallel to the large-scale return of Crimean Tatars and their political mobilization. Ethnic tension on the basis of a vaguely defined 'Russian' cleavage was the result of contingent political polarization. Even at its peak the regional Russian movement mobilized against the centre in Kyiv rather than ethnic Ukrainians in Crimea.

The Crimean Russian movement reached its apogee in 1994 with the election of a Crimean President, Yuri Meshkov, in January 1994. On this wave of Russian nationalism and separatism, Crimea held a 'consultative' referendum, coinciding with the Ukrainian parliamentary elections. The Crimean President, Yuri Meshkov, had called for a boycott of the national elections (with the result of 12 out of 23 seats in the national Rada remaining vacant) and concentrated on the election of a Crimean parliament instead in which his 'Blok Rossiya' secured 54 of a total of 98 seats, and a regional referendum which won approval for Crimean autonomy, dual Russian-Ukrainian citizenship and a widening of Meshkov's presidential powers.[28] By the end of 1994 the Russian movement was already deeply divided due to elite infighting. The quick rise and fall of Meshkov's movement demonstrated how easily a dormant ethnic sentiment can be mobilized in conditions of change and uncertainty, but also how unsustainable it is in the presence of cross-cutting cleavages, shifting political alliances and the lack of clear policy alternatives. Most importantly, the Russian separatist movement failed to address pressing socio-economic issues. Its haphazard privatization plan was blocked by parts of the regional elite and led to an effective moratorium on privatization for several years. This, in turn, created inroads for organized crime which came to dominate the regional political economy even more than in other Ukrainian regions (*Finantsova Ukraina*, 11 February 1997) The failure of the Russian movement to address the population's most pressing needs made it lose the electorate's support within less than a year.

The weakness of the Russian nationalist movement in Crimea contrasts sharply with the influential Crimean Tatar national movement with its different organizations and regional and national institutions.[29] The shared experience and memory of the ethnocide in 1994 has kept the Crimean Tatars united across generations, political orientations, social strata and business orientations, although the latter two differences have become more visible in recent years. The Russian nationalist movement lacked a comparable unifying element and was instead constructed on the basis of a blurred Soviet-Russian identity with vague political goals. Nostalgia for the 'glorious' Soviet past of the region was couched in the rhetoric of Russian nationalism and separatism. The movement lacked symbolic figureheads and competent political leaders who could have articulated a coherent political programme to sustain the movement's momentum in view of diverging interests among its key elite members. In Crimea, Russian nationalism was, therefore, a default option of political mobilization. Due to its inherent contradictions and regional sub-cleavages its political success was transitory.

Political mobilization in Crimea was hinged on the region's autonomy status, which emerged as the minimum consensus in the period 1990–98, although the term 'autonomy' was interpreted differently by the actors involved at different stages of the political process. Once a vaguely defined autonomy status was entrenched in the late Soviet period and inherited by post-Soviet Ukraine, it proved difficult to remove. Kyiv reacted hesitantly to the Crimean issue, but the early concession of an autonomy status helped to defuse the potential for an early escalation. Only in March 1995, when the Russian movement in Crimea had already fragmented, did President Kuchma crack down on what was coined 'Crimean separatism', abolished the Crimean presidency and set an ultimatum for the regional parliament to draw up a new constitution.

In the first post-Soviet Crimean Soviet, elected in 1994, a consociational quota guaranteed the political representation of Crimea's deported nationalities: the Crimean Tatars were given 14 of the 98 seats, and the Armenian, Bulgarian, German and Greek communities were guaranteed one seat each. The Crimean Tatar faction was the most consistent faction in the regional parliament. Although in the end the result of the constitution-making process fell short of their demands for a national-territorial autonomy, the quota gave them a voice during the critical phase of ethno-regional politics and defused conflict potential by locking them into the negotiation process. The national quota was abolished in the 1998 regional elections, a move that led to the renewed exclusion of the Crimean Tatar organizations from regional politics. This feeling of exclusion is somewhat counterbalanced by the fact that since the parliamentary elections of 1998 the Crimean Tatars are for the first time represented at the national level by two of their most vociferous leaders.[30] At the local and regional level the Crimean Tatars to some extent supported the Ukrainian national movement Rukh, a coalition which could mark the beginning of the end of ethnically defined party politics. Electoral sequencing at the national and regional level, which saw legitimacy shifting between the two levels of governance throughout 1990–98 ultimately helped to integrate Crimea into the Ukrainian polity.[31] By the 1998 parliamentary elections at the national and regional level, regional parties had officially been curtailed by the legal requirement to register as a national party in a number of Ukrainian regions, although pockets of the former Russian movement are still represented in the regional assembly.

In Crimea domestic politics and foreign policy issues are inextricably intertwined. The foreign policy dimension has continuously framed the Crimean issue but it has, on the whole, remained secondary to the domestic dynamics. The location and economic dependence of Crimea made reintegration with Russia a low priority on the agenda of the Russian Federation under President Yeltsin. For Moscow and, in particular, for individual populist politicians, the status of Crimea, Sevastopol' and the Black Sea Fleet are welcome symbols to manipulate in political rhetoric, but they have not provided the basis for an assertive Russian foreign policy towards Crimea. Moreover, the Chechen war sent at least two important signals to Ukraine: first, Russia's military capabilities do not match the neo-imperial rhetoric of some of its politicians and left the country struggling with its own centre–periphery problems. The Chechen war, therefore, established Crimea more firmly as a domestic Ukrainian issue. Second, the bloody consequences of Moscow's confrontational approach to Chechnya (as opposed to Tatarstan) seem to have fed into Kyiv's more gradual and bilateral approach to the issue of Crimean autonomy. The status of Sevastopol' and the Black Sea Fleet as well as a 20-year lease of its bases were clarified in the long-awaited Russian–Ukrainian Friendship Treaty of May 1997, the detailed provisions of which were eventually ratified by the Russian and Ukrainian parliaments in early 1999. Recently, the possibility of sharing the bases in Sevastopol' and control the remaining ships of the Black Sea Fleet jointly have been floated in

Russian–Ukrainian talk, but as of yet no new agreement has been reached. Whatever the outcome of any re-negotiation of the Sevastopol' bases may be, the sheer presence of the Russian neighbour provides a constant check on Ukrainian policy in the region. At the same time, Russia is bound by international agreements, such as the trilateral agreement with the US (1994) on the transfer of Ukraine's nuclear weapons in return for a guarantee of Ukraine's territorial integrity. The third potential foreign policy actor in the region, Turkey, has refrained from openly getting involved in Crimean politics. In general, Turkey regards Ukraine as an ally in the Black Sea littoral. The extensive Crimean Tatar diaspora in Turkey has mainly confined itself to humanitarian and cultural aid. Nevertheless, a certain fear of the unquantifiable 'Turkish influence' or 'Islamic factor' permeates the public discourse in Crimea despite the fact that military training of special Crimean Tatar units is as yet a marginal phenomenon. OSCE involvement in Crimea presents an important additional international dimension. In particular the personal involvement of the High Commissioner on National Minorities at the time, Max van der Stoel, helped to embed the Crimean issue as a domestic dispute over a constitutional autonomy arrangement, to preserve a regional autonomy status and to keep the Crimean Tatar issue on the agenda (Packer, 1998: 295–316).

Crimean Autonomy within a Unitary State

The single most important means of ethnic and regional conflict prevention in the Crimean case was the institutionalization of an autonomy status. While it was by no means a carefully designed strategy on Kyiv's part from the very beginning, the 'constitutional sequencing' of the national and regional constitutions (1990–98) as part of the protracted constitution-making process proved a vital mechanism in defusing conflict potential. Constitution-making in Ukraine took longer than in any other post-Soviet state. The constitution represents a minimum compromise and remains ambiguous in places. One of the contradictions inherent in the constitution is the attempt to reconcile the ideas of a unitary state and a federal element, the so-called 'Autonomous Republic of Crimea'. The label 'Autonomous Republic', the existence of a Crimean government, a regionally elected assembly as well as the possibility to build on regional tax and language provisions mark the constitutional starting-points of a territorial political rather than an ethno-political Crimean identity.[32]

The issue of Crimean autonomy came to the fore before Ukrainian independence and has since then passed through five stages. The first, preparatory phase led to the referendum in January 1991. The second stage lasted until early 1994 when the 'Russian wave' swept across the peninsula.

During this phase various attempts were made at adjusting the last-minute Soviet ASSR status to post-Soviet realities. Regional politicians, including the Crimean Supreme Soviet, jumped on the bandwagon of the autonomy movement, stressing cultural-historical or economic factors, respectively.[33] The emerging Russian nationalist faction initiated Crimea's declaration of independence in 1992, which was backed up by a first regional constitution on 6 May 1992 supported by the moderate regional parliament and representatives of the Russian movement alike. This constitution defined the Republic of Crimea as a 'state' (*gosudarstvo*) with sovereign powers on its territory and over its resources, law enforcement structures and independent foreign relations.[34] The Ukrainian parliament immediately rejected this constitution. A moratorium was imposed on a referendum on Crimea's status and a compromise constitution was drawn up by the Crimean parliament and enacted on 25 September 1992. This constitution emphasized that the 'Republic of Crimea' was a 'state' within Ukraine.[35] Both constitutions defined Crimea's status in territorial terms, referring to the 'multi-ethnic people of Crimea' (*mnogonatsional'nyi narod Kryma*) and 'the people of Crimea' (*narod Kryma*).

The third stage began in early 1994 with the election of the first and last Crimean President, Yuri Meshkov, and lasted until March 1995. This stage is best described as the rise and fall of Crimean separatism. At one point President Kravchuk was forced to admit to losing control over Crimea.[36] Presidential turnover at the centre coincided with Crimea becoming a policy priority in Kyiv. Against the backdrop of the ongoing constitutional tug-of-war between the president and the parliament at the centre, President Kuchma cracked down on Crimea in March 1995, placing the region firmly under his direct control, abolishing the Crimean presidency and setting an ultimatum for the Crimean parliament to draw up a new constitution.[37] By this time the Russian movement had already discredited itself in the eyes of the local population. The only change that outlived the Meshkov era for a few years was his switch to the Moscow time zone.

The fourth stage from March 1995 to June 1996 consisted once again of protracted negotiations during which Simferopol' regained parts of its lost status. Personal power struggles and the inexperience of many Crimean politicians, the delay of much-needed reforms in Crimea and the conflict between the regional executive and legislature had all contributed to the disintegration of the regional political alliance and had, thus, not only cost Crimea substantial parts of its autonomy, but they had also effectively undermined the legitimacy of the regional institutions.

The fifth and last stage in the constitution-making process began with the adoption of an incomplete Crimean constitution in April 1996 which left contentious issues such as a separate Crimean citizenship, Crimea's 'state' symbols and the explicit delineation of devolved powers to be decided. It was followed by the ratification of the Ukrainian state constitution in June 1996. In the end the majority of Ukrainian deputies accepted the phrase 'Autonomous Republic of Crimea', although the downgrading to an amorphous *avtonomiya* based on a statute rather than a regional constitution had already been on the cards.[38] The long night during which the Ukrainian constitution was finally passed saw a number of clever package deals: the vote on Crimean autonomy, for example, was tied to Ukraine's state symbols, thus appeasing communists and national-democrats alike.[39] The timing of the ratification of the incomplete regional constitution, followed by the national constitution guaranteeing a very basic autonomy status for Crimea including a regional assembly (*Verkhovna Rada*), government and constitution, further reduced the potential for conflict. Kyiv had repeatedly delayed decisions about Crimean autonomy. The Verkhovna Rada, for example, had waited five months before considering the Crimean draft constitution forwarded by the Crimean Supreme Soviet in November 1995. Although these delays were most likely not part of Kyiv's initial strategy, they paid off politically, as the final constitutional negotiations took place when the emotional dust had settled and the potential for conflict had by and large dissolved. The constitutional sequencing of the five stages from 1990 to 1998, which to some extent mirror the effect of electoral sequencing outlined by Linz and Stepan (Linz and Stepan, 1992: 123–39), generated different coalitions of regional interests and actors and allowed for the institutionalization of a minimum consensus: the preservation of Crimea's autonomy status. In effect, Crimea's special treatment has also increased Kyiv's control over the region through, for example, the presidential representative in Crimea, the regional branch of the Ukrainian Ministry of Internal Affairs and security forces staffed by Kyiv.[40] However, even a symbolic degree of regional autonomy can act as an important basis for conflict-prevention (Coakley, 1993: 14). After the 'ratification-in-parts' of the Crimean constitution in 1996 regional politics returned to economic-distributive issues, most importantly the struggle between two rival clans tied to the region's criminal structures and directly represented in the Crimean assembly. In the end, the regional Communist Party under its leader Leonid Grach, who is one of the key figures in the Ukrainian Communist Party, managed to capitalize on these rifts. The elections of 1998 saw the Communist Party regain the position it had only temporarily lost to the 'Blok Rossiya' in 1994–98 by securing the majority of seats in the regional assembly.[41] The Communist Party became the central player and stablizing force in this final phase of the constitution-making process culminating in the ratification of the revised Crimean constitution on 23 December 1998 by the Ukrainian Verkhovna Rada. This constitution refers to the Crimean assembly as a 'representative organ' with the right to only pass normative acts rather than laws.[42] The responsibilities of the Crimean Verkhovna Rada are limited, but frequent references to further specifications in Ukrainian laws introduce an element of flexibility and the possibility of subsequent modifications. The constitution does not only put the emphasis on Crimea's links with Ukraine and Kyiv's ultimate control over regional politics and security, but also repeatedly refers to the inviolability of the autonomy status.

While it would be too strong to say that institutional design led to successful conflict-management, the constitutional process locked most of the key actors into bargaining mode and eventually led to an institutional compromise. Crimea's autonomy status was primarily the effect of a protracted negotiation, which was shaped by the different political, economic and ethnic interests. The process itself, rather than the constitutional status, was the key to conflict-prevention. The Crimean Tatars are the key group alienated from the constitutional settlement. Their recurrent demonstrations illustrate that the Crimean Tatar issue remains the single most important potential for ethnic conflict in Crimea and in Ukraine as a whole.

CONCLUSION

Regional diversity has shaped Ukraine's history and vice-versa. The collapse of the USSR and Ukrainian independence saw centrifugal forces dominate in Ukrainian politics in the period 1990–94. While the historical memory of previous experiments with autonomy fuelled the imagination and mobilization of regionalist demands, the dismantling and reassembling of Soviet legacies was the driving force for these demands. In the three regions where the most serious political mobilization occurred – Zakarpattya, the Donbas and Crimea – these movements were intertwined with ethno-cultural demands.

Within and across regions elites have generally been divided among themselves in terms of their political, economic and foreign policy views (Nemyria, 1999a). This diversity of interests has facilitated the centre's ad hoc and 'divide and rule' approach. Moreover, mainly due to Soviet legacies, many Ukrainian regions are dependent on the centre: Crimea is highly dependent on water and energy supplies as well as subsidies, Zakarpattya is economically dependent, and even the ailing Soviet economic base in the Donbas' is ultimately in need of central restructuring programmes. So far Kyiv has managed – partly by defusing or buying off potential for conflict through a controlled institutionalization of regional interests, and partly by default and luck – to contain a range of centrifugal challenges and assert vertical executive control.

The political integration of Crimea into the new Ukrainian state has been one of the most significant cases of successful conflict-management in a post-communist state. Given that Crimea was considered Ukraine's biggest potential ethno-regional flashpoint, the prevention of conflict here puts the debate about conflict in other Ukrainian regions and the prognoses about the fracturing of the Ukrainian state in perspective. Four factors explain why ethno-regional conflict did not erupt in Crimea: first, the historically evolved instrinsically multi-ethnic setting lacked clear-cut ethno-political boundaries; second, Russian ethno-political mobilization proved unsustainable due to underlying socio-economic problems, a blurred Soviet-Russian identity and the internal fragmentation of the movement; third, an active external prop for nationalism or separatism was missing, as Russia – and even more so Turkey – refrained from supporting their ethnic kin groups as part of their official foreign policy; and fourth and most significantly, the dynamics of the protracted bargaining process over the institutionalization of regional autonomy provided the basis for effective conflict-regulation. In the case of Crimea three potential conflicts have been averted: a clash between Ukraine and Russia, intra-regional conflict and, most importantly, a centre–periphery conflict. A key issue – that of the Crimean Tatars (the question of their status as an indigenous people, minority representation, political integration and their socio-economic problems) – has yet to be addressed. The management of the Crimean Tatar issue and the implementation of long-postponed structural reform of the regional economy are the key to future stability in Crimea.

The institutionalization of Crimean autonomy has strengthened the notion of a civic Ukrainian state- and nation-building project. Ukraine began its nation-building with a zero-sum citizenship law and a gradual implementation of the Ukrainian language law. The resolution of the Crimean issue demonstrates that regionalism is not necessarily an obstacle to state- and nation building as such, but it is certainly an impediment to exclusivist ethnic nation-state building. Ukraine's regionalization has, in fact, played an important stabilizing role in Ukraine's transition and state- and nation-building. Of critical importance is the way in which ethnic and regional cleavages in Ukraine are cross-cutting, rather than reinforcing. Thus, they provide an effective equilibrium-making mechanism and a constant check on ethno-political mobilization. Ethnicity is only one of several cleavages that can be politically mobilized at the regional level, though it can temporarily gain in importance and disguise other, more deeply rooted regional or sub-regional cleavages, such as multi-ethnicity, cultural or socio-economic factors that cross-cut ethnic markers.

Post-Soviet Ukraine faced a myriad of political and economic challenges. The way in which it dealt with its ethnic and regional diversity and, above all, with its most precarious region Crimea, belongs to its political achievements. In Ukraine's current political system it is primarily the president who has to balance the different regional interests and provides an element of continuity into Ukrainian politics. There is no doubt that demands for regional autonomy were strengthened by the continuous tensions between the executive and legislature during the constitution-making process of 1991–96. There is a correlation, however, between the phases of presidential strength and improved management of regional demands, most notably in the Donbas and Crimea. The maintenance of political stability and the consolidation of the Ukrainian state, however, came at the price of postponing other major reform issues, and in particular the delay of macro- and micro-economic reforms.

Although the term 'federalism' is still highly stigmatized in Ukraine *de facto* the federal principle is already inscribed in Ukraine's Crimean Autonomy, and the regional diversity which permeates its policy-making, political bargaining, electoral politics and has left its mark on the transition process in general. This situation is aptly described by Livingston's concept of a 'federalized society' (Livingston, 1952). This concept describes the reality of territorial cleavages without implying the existence of matching political structures. A federal vs. unitary state are only the ideal-type end-points of a scale – between them lies a whole array of institutional arrangements. The institutional management of Ukraine's state of regions may still evolve towards an as yet unknown new equilibrium. In the meantime, Ukrainian policy-makers and analysts have to come to terms with its existence as a regionalized unitary state.

NOTES

1. Bukovina belonged to the Ottoman empire until the end of the Russian-Turkish war in 1774 when the Habsburg empire annexed the territory. See Magosci, 1996: 385.
2. For a detailed discussion of the 1954 transfer of Crimea on the basis of archival materials, see Sasse, 1999: 150–99.
3. For an overview of the different Crimean experiences with autonomy in the Soviet period, see ibid., chapter 6. For the parallels between the post-Soviet debates about Crimean autonomy and the period 1917–18, see Torbakov, 1996.
4. The support for independence in the western regions reached on average 95%, in the eastern regions over 80% and in Crimea a slim majority of 54.1%.
5. See Sasse, 1999: 313 (footnote 925).
6. For the regional breakdowns of economic indicators, see Derzhavnyi Komitet Statystyky Ukrainy, *Statystychnyi Shchorichnyk Ukrainy za 1999 rik*. Kyiv: Tekhnika, 2000.
7. These regular surveys represent one of the most reliable sources on Ukrainian public opinion. They are conducted by the Natsional'nyi Universytet Kyievo-Mohylyans'ka Akademiya i Kafedra Sotsiolohii, Kyivs'kyi Mizhnarodnyi Instytut Sotsiolohii.
8. Kubicek uses the term 'regionalism' to describe the existence of regional diversity (p.274). While his finding that regional divisions are here to stay is a well-founded observation, it

should not be taken as a reliable parameter of regional political mobilization, Ukraine's reform success or its survival as an independent state.

9. See data compiled by the Ukrainian Central Electoral Commission and the OSCE.
10. In Crimea the institution of the presidential representative survived the abolition of this position elsewhere. It demonstrates the recognition of both Crimea's exceptional role and the potential for conflict. The Crimean presidential representative was highly involved in the protracted regional elite bargaining process over the constitution.
11. The new Moldova SSR comprised six Bessarabian counties and the six western raions of the former Moldovan ASSR. Northern Bukovina, the rest of Transdnistria and part of the counties of Hotin, Akkerman and Ismail in northern and southern Bessarabia became part of the Ukrainian SSR. See King , 2000: 94.
12. According to Ukraine's first president, Leonid Kravchuk, federalism was never considered a realistic option for Ukraine. This was his response to the author's question following his talk at the conference 'From Soviet to Independent Ukraine', University of Birmingham, 13 June 1996.
13. See *Perturbatsii*, Warsaw, No.1, Autumn 1989, pp.70–76, quoted in a profile on Chornovil prepared by the *Nezalezhnyi Tsentr Ukrains'kykh Politychnykh Doslidzhen'*, Kyiv 1996. In this article Chornovil is even said to have supported the idea of Crimean independence. Volodymyr Hryn'ov, Adviser to President Kuchma on Regional Issues, confirmed Chornovil's early views on federalism in an interview with the author, Kyiv, 25 October 1996.
14. See *Mizhrehional'nyi Blok Reform: Prohramni partiini dokumenty*. Kyiv, 1995.
15. See, for example, the issue of the journal *Biznes Inform* (Kharkiv, 1995) titled 'Federativnaya Respublika Ukraina?', which discussed the advantages of political and economic decentralization.
16. A draft concept of regional policy in Ukraine was prepared by the Ukrainian National Academy of Sciences and the Institute of Economics; see *Kontseptsiya rehionaln'noi polityky v Ukraini*, Donets'k 1994.
17. Kuchma himself came to embody the dilemma of Ukraine's regionalization: on the one hand he recognized the importance of the regions, but on the other hand he was afraid of losing his grip on the regional administration. Author's interview with Volodymyr Hryn'ov in Kyiv, 25 October 1996.
18. Zakarpattya has consistently been one of the two or three weakest regions in terms of key economic indicators, such as the regional share in GNP or national income. For the economic data 1990–94, see A.P. Pavlyuk, 1996. For the more up-to-date economic developments, see Derzhavnyi Komitet Statystyky Ukrainy, 2000.
19. These figures are the estimates of the Crimean administration in 1998. In 1989 the Russians still accounted for 67% of the Crimean population. With the return of the Crimean Tatars the Slavic share of the regional population has dropped.
20. See Sasse, 1999: 102–49.
21. See ibid.: 298–307. For up-to-date comparison with other Ukrainian regions see the regional breakdowns in Derzhavnyi Komitet Statystyky Ukrainy, 2000.
22. For an overview of the main issues and positions emerging from these committee discussions, see *Krymskaia pravda*, 5 April 1990, 19 June 1990, 23 June 1990, 19 August 1990, 30 August 1990, 5 September 1990, 18 September 1990.
23. The wording of the key question about the 're-establishment' of Crimea's ASSR status was misleading: Crimea had previously existed as an ASSR within the RSFSR; the ASSR status within the USSR, envisaged by the referendum, was a new construct. It reflected Gorbachev's attempt to equalize the status of Union republics and ASSRs in order to secure support for a new Union Treaty.
24. Language had an even greater potential to become the key issue dividing Crimea and the rest of Ukraine, given that only about 4% of the regional population considered themselves to be Ukrainian-speakers. See Dawson, 1996: 158.
25. For the formulation of the referendum question, see *Krymskaia pravda*, 5 January 1991; for the official results see *Krymskaia pravda*, 22 January 1991.
26. See *Krymskaia pravda*, 13 February, 22 February, 23 February, 26 February, 14 June 1991.
27. For a detailed discussion of regional party development and political mobilization in Crimea, see Sasse, 1999: 251–88.

28. *Krymskaia pravda*, 18 January 1994, 1 February 1994, 13 March 1994, 17 March 1994, 6 April 1994, 8 April 1994, 12 April 1994; *Krymskie izvestiia*, 12 April 1994.
29. For the most systematic description and analysis of the Crimean Tatar national movement from their deportation to the 1990s, including key documents, see Guboglo, Chervonnaya (eds), 3 vols., 1992–96; I. Kuras (ed.), *Kryms'ki tatary: istoriia i suchasnist' (do 50-richchya deportatsii kryms'kotatars'koho narodu). Materialy mizhnarodnoi naukovoi konferentsii, Kyiv 13–14 travnya 1994r.*, Kyiv: Instytut Natsional'nykh Vidnosyn i Politolohii NAN Ukrainy, 1995; Y.Z. Adnylyuk (ed.), *Kryms'ki tatary 1944–1994rr. Statti, dokumenty, svidchennya ochevidstiv*, Kyiv: Ridnyi krai, 1995; Edward Allworth (ed.), *The Tatars of Crimea. Return to the Homeland*. London: Duke University Press, 1998 (2nd rev. ed.).
30. The two Crimean Tatar deputies in the national Verkhovna Rada are Mustafa Dzhemilev, the head of the Crimean Tatar Medzhlis, and his deputy Refat Chubarov. Dzhemilev was elected on the Rukh list; Chubarov was elected as an independent candidate.
31. For an analysis of these electoral dynamics and the change in elite composition, see Sasse, 1999: 251–88 and 329–52.
32. The Crimean constitution of 1998 allows for locally raised taxes to stay in the region. The Ukrainian constitution of 1996 stipulates that special language provisions are possible in regions with compact settlement of national minorities (Chapter 1, Article 10). This clause seems highly relevant to the Crimean case.
33. Author's interview with Nikolai Bagrov, Head of the Crimean Supreme Soviet until 1994, Simferopol', 5 April 1996.
34. See *Konstitutsiia Respubliki Krym*, Simferopol', 6 May 1992, Preamble and Part 1, Articles 1 and 10.
35. See *Konstitutsiia Respubliki Krym*, Simferopol', 25 September 1992, Article 1.
36. In his speech to the Ukrainian Parliament on 1 June 1994 Kravchuk said: '*De jure* Crimea is part of Ukraine...but *de facto* is already absent. ...It is neither in the state structures, nor in other organs, nor in any concrete questions', *Stenographic Report*, Bulletin 18. The author is grateful for this quote provided by Dominique Arel.
37. The 'Law on the Autonomous Republic of Crimea' of 17 March 1995 was published in *Holos Ukrainy*, 18 March 1995. For a collection of documents and reactions, see 'Chy rozhryt'sya kryms'ka kriza?', *Zapysky Ukrains'koho Nezalezhnoho Tsentru Politychnykh Doslidzhen'*, Kyiv, 1995.
38. Author's interview with Evgenii Suprunyuk, then Speaker of the Crimean Soviet, Simferopol', 8 April 1996.
39. Author's interview with Vladimir Yegudin, Crimean deputy in the Verkhovna Rada in Kyiv, Simferopol', 7 October 1996.
40. At the height of the Crimean separatist movement, the control of the security forces had effectively passed to the regional elites, signalling the centre's loss of control in the region.
41. *Krymskaia pravda*, 22 April 1998.
42. See *Konstitutsiia Avtonomnoi Respubliki Krym*, Simferopol', 23 December 1998, Article 1.

REFERENCES

Arel, Dominique and Andrew Wilson (1994), 'The Ukrainian Parliamentary Elections', *RFE/RL Research Report*, Vol.3, No.26.

Arel, Dominique (1996), 'A Lurking Cascade of Assimilation in Kiev?', *Post-Soviet Affairs*, Vol.12, No.1, pp.73–90.

Bakirov, V. (ed.)(1994), *Rehional'ne samovryaduvannya: problemy realizatsii vladnykh vidnosyn*. Kharkiv: Kharkiv State University.

Batt, Judy (2002), 'Transcarpathia: Peripheral Region at the "Centre of Europe"', in Judy Batt and Kataryna Wolczuk (eds), *Regions, State and Identity in Central and Eastern Europe*. London and Portland, OR: Frank Cass.

Birch, Sarah (1998a), 'Electoral Systems, Campaign Strategies, and Vote Choice in the Ukrainian Parliamentary and Presidential Elections of 1994', *Political Studies*, Vol.46, No.1, pp.96–114.

Birch, Sarah (1998b), 'Party System Formation and Voting Behavior in the Ukrainian Parliamentary Elections of 1994', in Taras Kuzio (ed.), *Contemporary Ukraine. Dynamics of Post-Soviet*

Transformation. Armonk: M.E. Sharpe, pp.139–60.

Birch, Sarah (2000), 'Interpreting the Regional Effect in Ukrainian Politics', *Europe–Asia Studies*, Vol.52, No.6, pp.1017–42.

Bojcun, Marco (1995), 'The Ukrainian Parliamentary Elections of March–April 1994', *Europe–Asia Studies*, Vol.47, No.2, pp.229–49.

Bremmer, Ian (1994), 'The Politics of Ethnicity: Russians in the New Ukraine', *Europe–Asia Studies*, Vol.46, No.2, pp.261–83.

Coakley, John (1993), *The Territorial Management of Ethnic Conflict*, London: Frank Cass.

Craumer, Peter R. and James I. Clem (1999), 'Ukraine's Emerging Electoral Geography: A Regional Analysis of the 1998 Parliamentary Elections', *Post-Soviet Geography and Economics*, Vol.40, No.1, pp.1–26.

Dawson, Jane I. (1996), *Eco-Nationalism. Anti-nuclear Activism and National Identity in Russia, Lithuania and Ukraine*. Durham: Duke University Press.

Derzhavnyi Komitet Statystyky Ukrainy (2000), *Statystychnyi Shchorichnyk Ukrainy za 1999 rik.* Kyiv: Tekhnika.

Hagen, Mark von *et al.* (1995), 'Does Ukraine Have a History?', *Slavic Review*, Vol.54, No.3, pp.658–719.

Hesli, Vicki L. (1995), 'Public Support for the Devolution of Power in Ukraine: Regional Patterns', *Europe–Asia Studies*, Vol.47, No.1, pp.91–115.

Hesli, Vicki L. *et al.* (1998), 'Political Party Development in Divided Societies: The Case of Ukraine', *Electoral Studies*, Vol.17, No.2, pp.235–56.

Hryn'ov, V.B. (1995), *Nova Ukraina – yakoyu ya ii bachu.* Kyiv: Arbis.

Huntington, Samuel (1996), *The Clash of Civilizations and the Remaking of World Order.* New York: Simon & Schuster.

Jackson, Louise (1998), 'Identity, Language, and Transformation in Eastern Ukraine: A Case Study of Zaporizhzhia', in Taras Kuzio (ed.), *Contemporary Ukraine. Dynamics of Post-Soviet Transformation.* Armonk: M.E. Sharpe, pp.99–113.

Khmelko, Valeri and Andrew Wilson (1998), 'Regionalism and Ethnic and Linguistic Cleavages in Ukraine', in Taras Kuzio (ed.), *Contemporary Ukraine: Dynamics of Post-Soviet Transition.* Armonk, NY: M.E. Sharpe, pp.60–80.

King, Charles (2000), *The Moldovans: Romania, Russia, and the Politics of Culture.* Stanford: Hoover Institution Press.

Kravchenko, V.I. (1995), 'Terytorial'nyi ustrii ta mistsevi orhany vlady Ukrainy', *Naukovi dopovidi.* Kyiv: Natsional'nyi Instytut Stratehichnykh Doslidzhen', No.43.

Kubicek, Paul (2000), 'Regional Polarisation in Ukraine: Public Opinion, Voting and Legislative Behaviour', *Europe–Asia Studies*, Vol.52, No.2, pp.273–94.

Kuzio, Taras (1994a), 'Russia–Crimea–Ukraine: Triangle of Conflict', *Conflict Studies*, Research Institute for the Study of Conflict and Terrorism, January.

Kuzio, Taras (1994b), 'The Crimea and European Security', *European Security*, Vol.3, No.4, pp.734–74.

Kuzio, Taras (1996), 'National Identity in Independent Ukraine: An Identity in Transition', *Nationalism and Ethnic Politics*, Vol.2, No.4, pp.582–608.

Larrabee, Stephen (1994), 'Ukraine: Europe's Next Crisis?', *Arms Control Today*, July/August.

Liber, George (1998), 'Imagining Ukraine: Regional Differences and the Emergence of an Integrated State Identity', *Nations and Nationalism*, Vol.4, No.3, pp.187–206.

Linz, Juan and Alfred Stepan (1992), 'Political Identities and Electoral Sequences: Spain, the Soviet Union and Yugoslavia', *Daedalus*, Vol.121, No.2, pp.123–39.

Livingston, William S. (1952), 'A Note on the Nature of Federalism', *Political Science Quarterly*, Vol.67, No.1, pp.81–95.

Magosci, Paul Robert (1978), *The Shaping of a National Identity: Sub-carpathian Rus' 1848–1948.* Cambridge, Mass.: Harvard University Press.

Magosci, Paul Robert (1996), *A History of Ukraine.* Toronto: University of Toronto Press.

Medvedchuk, V.V. (1996), *Konstitutsiinyi protses v Ukraini i orhanizatsiya derzhavnoi vlady ta mistsevoho samovryaduvannya.* Kyiv: Ukraina.

Miroshnik, O.S. *et al.* (eds) (1995), *Regional'noe razvitie Ukrainy: problemy i perspektivy*, Materialy Mezhdunarodnogo nauchno-prakticheskogo seminara, 25–28 May 1995, Kharkiv.

Motyl, Alexander (1980), *The Turn to the Right: The Ideological Origins and Development of*

Ukrainian Nationalism, 1919–1929. Boulder: East European Monographs.

Nahaylo, Bohdan (1999), *The Ukrainian Resurgence*. London: Hurst.

Nemyria, Hryhorii (1999a), 'Regional Identity and Interests: The Case of Eastern Ukraine', in Kurt R. Spillmann *et al.* (eds), *Between Russia and the West: Foreign and Security Policy of Independent Ukraine*. Bern: Peter Lang, pp.303–23.

Nemyria, Hryhorii (1999b), 'Regionalism as a Dimension of State Building in Ukraine', in Richard Sakwa (ed.), *The Experience of Democratization in Eastern Europe. Selected Papers from the Fifth World Congress of Central and East European Studies, Warsaw 1995*. London: Macmillan Press, pp.72–90.

Packer, John (1998), 'Autonomy within the OSCE: The case of Crimea', in Markku Suksi (ed.), *Autonomy: Applications and Implications*. The Hague: Kluwer Law International, pp.295–316.

Pavlyuk, A.P. (1996) 'Terytorial'na dynamika ekonomiky Ukrainy', *Rehional'nyi rozvytok*, Natsional'nyi Instytut Stratehichnykh Doslidzhen', No.1.

Rudnytsky, Ivan L. (1987), 'Drahomanov as a Political Theorist', in Peter L. Rudnytsky (ed.), *Essays in Modern Ukrainian History*. University of Alberta: Canadian Institute of Ukrainian Studies, pp.203–53.

Rumer, Eugene (1994) 'Will Ukraine Return to Russia?', *Foreign Policy*, No.96, Fall, pp.129–44.

Sasse, Gwendolyn (1999), *Bringing the Regions Back In: The Crimean Issue in Post-Soviet Ukraine*, Doctoral Thesis, University of London.

Solchanyk, Roman (1994), 'The Politics of State-Building: Centre–Periphery Relations in Post-Soviet Ukraine', *Europe–Asia Studies*, Vol.46, No.1, pp.47–68.

Slyusarenko, A.H., M.V. Tomenko (eds) (1993), *Istoriya ukrains'koi konstitutsii*. Kyiv: Znaniya.

Szporluk, Roman (1997), 'Ukraine: From an Imperial Periphery to a Sovereign State', *Daedalus*, Vol.126, No.3, pp.85–119.

Szporluk, Roman (1998), 'Nationalism after communism: Reflections on Russia, Ukraine, Belarus and Poland', *Nations and Nationalism*, Vol.4, No.3, pp.301–20.

Torbakov, Igor (1996), 'Russian–Ukrainian Relations 1917–1918: A Conflict over Crimea and the Black Sea Fleet', *Nationalities Papers*, Vol.24, No.4, pp.679–89.

Ukrainian Center for Independent Political Research (1997), *The Dnipropetrovsk Family-2*. Kyiv: UCIPR.

Ukrainian Center for Independent Political Research (2000), 'Referendum Questions that Remained Unanswered', *Research Update*, Vol.6, No.169.

Ukrainian Center for Indpendent Political Research (2000), 'Free Economic Zones in Ukraine: Genesis, Trends and Prospects', *Research Update*, Vol.6, No.189.

Ukrainian Center for Indpendent Political Research (2000), 'New 'Region' Formed in Ukrainian Parliament', *Research Update*, Vol.7, No.214.

Wilson, Andrew (1996), *Ukrainian Nationalism in the 1990s: A Minority Faith*. Cambridge: Cambridge University Press.

Zapysky Ukrains'koho Nezalezhnoho Tsentru Politychnykh Doslidzhen' (1995), *Chy rozhoryt'sya kryms'ka kriza?*, Kyiv.

Zolotarev, Vladimir (1995), 'Federativnoe ustroistvo Ukrainy kak sposob preodoleniia krizisa', *Krymskii kontekst*, Krymskaia Akademiia Nauk, No.3, pp.70–77.

Regionalism in Moldova:
The Case of Transnistria and Gagauzia

Since 1992, when the Moldovan–Transnistrian dispute erupted into violent conflict, Transnistria has remained virtually independent of Moldova.[1] While the Moldovan government has successfully resolved its other major regional conflict with Gagauzia, Transnistria has been an intractable problem. Gagauzia was the first region to declare its independence on 19 August 1990, however, the Moldovan and the Gagauzian leaderships agreed on the devolution of power and the creation of an autonomous territorial status in 1995. Consequently, the Moldovan case provides a unique opportunity to examine both successful and unsuccessful attempts at resolving regional conflicts. Why was an accommodation possible in Gagauzia, yet elusive in Transnistria? The first part of this essay examines Moldova's contemporary history and specifically addresses the development of inter-ethnic relations, elite mobilization and regionalism before independence in 1991, with a focus on how Moldovan and Transnistrian officials used history, language and culture to justify actions that ultimately led to the 1992 civil war. The next section discusses the origins and the consequences of the Transnistrian conflict. While this conflict was portrayed on both sides as an 'ethnic' struggle over linguistic and cultural issues, in fact, the competing political and economic interests of the Moldovan and Transnistrian elites propelled the conflict. This conflict is most appropriately characterized as one where ethnicity is instrumentalized in order to further rival political agendas. This is not to say that there were not legitimate concerns among the Moldovan population regarding linguistic and cultural freedom. Rather that elites exploited and manipulated these concerns in order to maintain or to attain power. The essay then examines the establishment of territorial autonomy in Gagauzia. The Moldovan government viewed the agreement on Gagauzia's autonomous status as the basis for future negotiations with Transnistria. This hope has so far not been realized as Transnistria's leadership has consistently regarded the Gagauzian autonomy as falling too far short of their aspiration for full statehood.

CONTEMPORARY MOLDOVAN HISTORY

The competing political agendas of Moldovan, Transnistrian and Gagauzian elites and their manipulation of ethnicity for political advantage is rooted in Moldova's contemporary history. Following the Russo-Turkish war of 1806–12 and the conclusion of the Treaty of Bucharest, the Moldovan area between the Prut and the Dniester rivers was annexed by Russia in 1812 and came to be known as Bessarabia. The region enjoyed considerable autonomy within the empire, and during this time, Moldovans comprised 86 per cent of the population (Hamm, 1998: 19). However from the mid-nineteenth century, Russia began to actively assimilate the Moldovan population of Bessarabia. Local government control was rescinded, and the Russian language supplanted the Romanian language in all legal proceedings. In addition, an influx of Russians and other ethnic groups significantly reduced the percentage of the ethnic Moldovan population. While they were still the largest language group, by the 1897 census their numbers had been reduced almost 40 per cent, and they comprised only 14 per cent of the urban population (Hamm, 1998: 25). The russification of Bessarabia intensified in parallel with the construction of a new 'Romanian' identity and state.

The Formation of Greater Romania

The First World War and the Russian revolution provided Bessarabia's pan-Romanian nationalists with an opportunity to press their claims for self-determination and integration with Romania. By spring 1917, public meetings were held throughout Bessarabia, and the cultural demands soon gave way to political aspirations. By the summer, a national assembly was formed (*Sfatul Tarii*) that was largely composed of pan-Romanianists. On 15 December, the Sfatul Tarii voted to form the independent Moldovan Democratic Republic of Bessarabia, with borders extending from the Prut to the Dniester River. Significantly, the area of modern-day Transnistria was not included in the new republic. On 27 March 1918, the Sfatul Tarii voted to unite with Romania, and by the end of 1918, the areas of Bukovina and Transylvania joined Bessarabia to form 'Greater Romania'.

In order to integrate the newly acquired population into Romania, the state greatly expanded the number of primary and secondary schools, instituted language tests and loyalty oaths for teachers and administrators and implemented ethnically-based quotas for admission to secondary schools and universities.[2] However the romananization policies did not lead to ethnic conflict. One reason why ethnic conflict did not occur was that the weakness of a Romanian identity and the weakness of the Romanian state meant that the romanianization efforts were not seriously enforced by the state. Russian language and cultural influences were still dominant during this period. For example, after 1918, except for a brief period between 1926 and 1927, there was no Bessarabian Romanian language daily newspaper (Livezeanu, 1995: 120). One of the reasons why the Romanian government was less than successful at integrating the Bessarabian population had to do with its perceived chauvinistic attitude towards locals. Romanian administrators were regarded as corrupt, inefficient and elitist. Whether real or imagined, many Bessarabians felt that the Romanians treated them unfairly.

The Soviet Socialist Republic of Moldova

By 1944, the Red Army was finally able to capture Bessarabia and later that year, the Soviet Socialist Republic of Moldova was formed by joining Bessarabia with the six districts that had constituted the Moldovan Autonomous Soviet Socialist Republic (MASSR). Consequently, Moldova inherited a large Russian-speaking community from the MASSR, and immigration, particularly of ethnic Slav industrial workers, furthered the russification of Moldova's urban areas. The percentage of ethnic Russians in Moldova almost doubled from 6.7 per cent in 1941 to 13 per cent by 1989. The actual number of ethnic Russians increased dramatically from just 300,000 in 1959 to over 550,000 in 1989 (Trebici, 1993). As elsewhere in the Soviet Union, ethnic Russians enjoyed disproportional representation in important political and economic institutions. As Kaufman points out, ethnic Moldovans perceived that they were under-represented in the more desirable professions while they dominated the inferior agricultural positions (Kaufman, 1996: 121). This ethnicized socio-economic cleavage became part of the demands for reform of the Popular Front movement of the late 1980s.

In the post-war period, the Soviet leadership encouraged the creation of a distinct Moldovan identity as one of the 'brother' nations of the USSR. New russification policies changed the alphabet for the Romanian language back to Cyrillic, and Russian was promoted as the dominant language of inter-ethnic communication, higher education and public life. A new mythology was created in which Soviet scholars spoke of a distinctive Moldovan language that was the foundation of a distinctive non-Romanian Moldovan national identity.[3] While today language does not constitute the basis of a separate Moldovan ethnicity, the legacy of the Soviet period has created a unique Moldovan ethnicity and identity apart from Romania.

Perestroika

As elsewhere in the Soviet Union, reforms introduced by Mikhail Gorbachev in the mid-1980s provided an opportunity for titular nations to express their resentment against Soviet russification policies. With the explosion of non-state controlled 'informal' groups in 1987, Moldovan intellectuals organized discussion groups that demanded greater cultural and linguistic freedom. By mid-1988, these informal pro-reform groups organized the Democratic Movement in Support of Restructuring to press for democratization and redress for discriminatory practices imposed upon the Moldovan majority and certain ethnic minority populations. While the Democratic Movement pressed for the recognition of Moldovan as the official state language (using the Latin rather than Cyrillic alphabet), it also articulated a linguistic agenda that focused on cultural and linguistic freedom for ethnic Gagauzi, Ukrainians and Bulgarians. In essence, this was a typical civic umbrella movement resembling that in other Soviet republics in the mid-stage of perestroika. The main division in Moldovan society was among the political elites and those counter-elites that aspired to power. As Kolstø, Edemsky and Kalashnikova argue, 'It is a gross simplification to present the conflict as a showdown between ethnic Moldovans and the "Russian-speaking" part of the Moldovan population it [the conflict] is essentially political in character' (Kolsto *et al.*, 1993: 975).

At this time, Moldova had no official language, though Russian was the dominant language of urban society, in administration, factories, commerce, and educational and political institutions. For example in 1989, only 10 per cent of Chisinau kindergardens conducted classes primarily in Romanian, and in Tiraspol there were no Romanian language elementary or secondary schools (Chinn and Roper, 1995: 299). By 1989, the Democratic Movement and its supporters had largely won the linguistic debate. The Scientific Council of the Moldovan Academy of Sciences recommended that Moldovan be made the official language, and the Democratic Movement was able to organize well-attended rallies and demonstrations in support of this demand.

In May 1989, individuals from within the Democratic Movement, Democratic League of Moldovan Students, Ecological Movement and other associations organized the Popular Front, and it quickly became the leading Moldovan opposition bloc. Its main platform was the promotion of linguistic and cultural freedom (Enciu and Pavelescu, 1998). While the Front spearheaded the opposition to Soviet policies of russification, several of its leading members were actually top-ranking ethnic Moldovan Communist Party apparatchiks. These reform party leaders recognized that to maintain power, they would have to join forces with the opposition.

In August 1989, the Moldovan Supreme Soviet proclaimed Moldovan (using the Latin alphabet) as the state language.[4] While the language law required those working in public services and education to acquire facility in both Moldovan and Russian, it allowed a period of five years to gain language facility. From this time the Front adopted a much more radical and ethnicized platform than the earlier Democratic Movement. The pan-reform agenda of the Democratic Movement was rejected in favour of a pro-Romania agenda. This shift in focus and the exclusivist elevation of the Moldovan language sparked an immediate response by the Russian-speaking community that Crowther has labelled 'reactive nationalism' (Crowther, 1991). According to Crowther, ethnic minority-led conflict was instigated because of a threat to the status quo (in this case a privileged elite). The promotion of the Moldovan language, particularly in an area such as Transnistria, threatened the existing Slavic elites. Transnistrians had dominated economic and political institutions in Tiraspol and in Chisinau. At the same time the newly dominant Moldovan elites in the Popular Front such as Mircea Druc, Iurie Rosca and others in Chisinau instrumentalized the language and cultural issues to consolidate their position in the fast-changing political environment.

In September 1989, Gagauzian leaders proclaimed the creation of an independent republic in the southern part of the country. In addition, ethnic Ukrainians and ethnic Bulgarians left the Front and joined with ethnic Russians to form the Internationalist Movement for Unity (*Edinstvo*) which was a pro-Russian culture and language organization. *Edinstvo* joined with the United Council of Work Collectives in Tiraspol to organize factory strikes and demonstrations against the language law. Transnistrians were the group most opposed to the language law because it was the most visible sign of the shifting balance of power away from ethnic Russian to Romanian-speakers (King, 2000: 186). This shift in power was also evident during the 1990 election to Moldova's last Soviet-era parliament. The Communist Party fractured into a country-wide reformist wing and a regionally concentrated conservative faction that consolidated its control over Transnistria and Comrat in Gagauzia. The reform communist faction cooperated with the Popular Front, and collaboration between these two groups extended into the electoral arena where one could find the names of leading Communists among the nominees of the Front (Crowther and Roper, 1996: 144). Unlike earlier elections to the Supreme Soviet, the March 1990 elections were generally free and fair. Following the election, the Popular Front formed a parliamentary coalition with other parties that held over 66 per cent of the seats. Popular Front member Alexandru Mosanu was named speaker, and the parliament confirmed a government composed almost entirely of ethnic Moldovans. Mircea Snegur, a leading Front supporter, was elected president by the parliament, and Prime Minister Mircea Druc was a strong advocate of union with Romania. During this period, Front MPs and the

Druc government pursued a pro-Romanian and pro-unionist agenda that further alienated the Russian minority. Iurie Rosca, president of the Front's parliamentary faction, stated that 'Moldova will unify with Romania – it is inevitable. We need time for Russia to lose power in Moldova. People do not remember what it is like to be part of Romania.'[5] However individuals such as President Snegur maintained a policy of 'one people, two states' that rejected reunification. While Romanian political leaders supported reunification, the Romanian public was much more ambivalent. In May 1990, the ethnic minority elites who controlled the city governments of Tiraspol, Bender[6] and Ribnita refused to accept the legitimacy of the new parliament and asserted 'sovereignty' over all local institutions. Tiraspol organized several referenda throughout Transnistria and Bender in which voters overwhelmingly favoured 'sovereignty' from Chisinau. It was from this foundation of two competing claims to 'sovereignty' that the conflict over the status of Transnistria developed during the following two years.

TRANSNISTRIA

The principal explanation for Transnistria's opposition to the agenda of the Popular Front was that the region's ethnic composition was unlike the rest of Moldova. In Transnistria, approximately 55 per cent of the population are ethnic Ukrainians and ethnic Russians, and aside from Bender and a few right-bank villages, the region had never been part of Romania.[7] Therefore pan-Romanian appeals by the Popular Front caused considerable fear among many Transnistrians. They refused to acknowledge the legitimacy of the 1989 language law. For Transnistrians, the return to the Latin script in the 1989 language law was unacceptable. While the Transnistrian constitution guarantees that Moldovan has an equal legal status with Russian and Ukrainian (Article 12), it is always written with the Cyrillic alphabet. In January 1990, a referendum on territorial autonomy was held in Tiraspol and passed by 96 per cent of the population. Even those who view the conflict as an 'ethnic' one admit that the 'Dniestrian Russophones are not, then, an ethnic group; they are a coalition of ethnic interests (Kaufman, 1996: 11). In essence, this is a conflict between Moldovans and a regionally concentrated Russophone population that has a 'Soviet' identity.

The Mounting Conflict

After the formation of the Transnistrian Moldovan Soviet Socialist Republic in September 1990, the conflict between Chisinau and Tiraspol quickly accelerated. By early 1991, several Transnistrian cities including

Tiraspol, Ribnita, Dubasari and Bender began to form paramilitary organizations (Nedelciuc, 1992: 70). The August 1991 Soviet coup clearly demonstrated the division between Moldova and Transnistria. While the Moldovan leadership denounced the coup leaders, the Transnistrian leadership, including future president Igor Smirnov, supported the coup. Transnistria attracted unreformed communists throughout the former Soviet Union. Shortly after the coup, Vadim Shevtsov, a former head of the Soviet OMON Special Forces in Riga, came to Transnistria and became head of the Ministry of State Security.

When Moldova declared independence on 27 August 1991, Transnistria quickly followed suit on 2 September. The Moldovan government viewed the new Transnistrian leadership, especially its leader Smirnov, as traitors and terrorists rather than as a legitimate government of a separate republic. The Moldovan government kidnapped Smirnov and leaders of the Gagauzian separatist movement on Ukrainian soil and brought them back to Chisinau but had to release them after one month following a Transnistrian railroad blockade. Later in December, Smirnov was elected President of Transnistria. During 1991 and 1992, the Transnistrian paramilitary force was strengthened by the transfer of men and arms from the Russian 14th Army, and from the huge stockpile of weapons and ammunition stored in the Transnistrian town of Kolbasnaia. The exact figures are unclear but approximately 40,000 tons of ammunition (much of it dating to the Second World War) are stored in Transnistria. Prior to 1992, there were approximately 10,000 servicemen and some 60,000 reservists. In practice, the distinction between the Transnistrian regulars and the 14th Army was blurred. Soldiers were often placed under the command of the Transnistrian military, and in December 1991, the 14th Army's commander, General Gennadii Yakovlev, accepted the position of Transnistrian Defence Minister. The Transnistrian military was also bolstered by a large contingent of Don Cossacks that arrived in late 1991. Military clashes occurred throughout 1992 along the Dniester River boundary between the Moldovan and the Transnistrian paramilitary units in which over a hundred people were killed. As a result Nationalists inside the Moldovan parliament were radicalized and brought intense pressure on Snegur to undertake decisive military action to resolve the conflict. In late March 1992, a state of emergency was declared, but military efforts to crush the separatist units were repulsed.

In the politics of the Russian Federation the conflict in Transnistria became an important test case for the defence of ethnic Slavs in the near abroad. In April 1992 Russian Foreign Minister Andrei Kozyrev warned that Russia could intervene to protect the rights of ethnic Russians, and Russian president Boris Yeltsin placed the 14th Army under direct

Russian control (the 14th Army had been to this point under CIS control). Effectively, Russian soldiers were now stationed on foreign territory. The Russian Congress of People's Deputies passed a resolution in support of the population in Transnistria and Russian Vice President Alexander Rutskoi visited Transnistria to provide his support. Rutskoi's visit occurred during the state of emergency, and he did not officially inform Chisinau. Thereafter, 14th Army commander Lieutenant-General Yuri Netkachev intervened actively on the side of Transnistria.[8]

While Russia figured prominently in the conflict, Ukraine and Romania were also important international actors. During March and April 1992, the foreign ministries of Moldova, Romania, Russia and Ukraine met on several occasions to create a framework for negotiations and a cease-fire. The Russians acted as proxy representatives for the Transnistrians. An agreement was finally reached, and a cease-fire commenced on 7 April 1992. The agreement established a four-party commission to monitor the cease-fire and the withdrawal of military forces. Russian demands that the 14th Army should be used as a peacekeeping force and that representatives from Transnistria be formally included were rejected by Moldova, Romania and Ukraine, and led to a break-down in the negotiations.

By May, the level of violence had greatly increased. The heaviest fighting occurred close to the border between Moldova and Transnistria, particularly in the cities of Dubasari and Bender. On 11 and 23 May, elements of the 14th Army reportedly attacked the villages of Cocieri and Cosnita which are located near Dubasari. While most of the population supported the Transnistrian leadership and the 14th Army, some Transnistrians declared their support for Moldova. In early June, several members of the renamed Christian Democratic Popular Front (FPCD) Tiraspol branch were arrested. These six members became known as the 'Ilascu group', named after their leader, Ilie Ilascu, who was the president of the FPCD Tiraspol branch. These six individuals were later convicted of terrorist acts against the state and given the death penalty. While the sentence was rescinded and two individuals were released, the other four have remained imprisoned since 1992. The arrest of these FPCD members eliminated the last major opposition within Transnistria.

In the summer of 1992 Bender became a flash point for the conflict. Bender's strategically important location on the right bank of the Dniester linked Moldova to the rest of the former Soviet Union. During the spring and summer, Transnistrian regulars captured most of Bender's police stations. On 19 June, Transnistrian elements attacked the last police station that was still loyal to Chisinau. Initially, the Moldovan military was able to repel the attack, but on the night of 20–21 June, 14th Army tanks rolled into the city and within a few short hours, Transnistria captured Bender. The capture of Bender was a turning point in the military conflict as the Moldovan side realized that it could not defeat the Transnistrians as long as they enjoyed the support of Russia's 14th Army. Estimates of casualities vary, but perhaps as many as a 1,000 died during the military conflict.[9]

The Agreement to Institutionalize Autonomy

The intensification of the conflict over Bender forced the Russian government to actively intervene to bring a settlement. In June, Yeltsin replaced Netkachev with Major-General Alexander Lebed, and in July 1992, Yeltsin and Snegur signed a cease-fire agreement that ended the hostilities. While Smirnov was present at the meeting, he did not sign the agreement. It contained a provision granting Transnistria a special status and guaranteed Transnistria the right of self-determination should Moldova change its statehood, something that had been offered to Transnistria much earlier. The agreement also established a security zone composed of Moldovan, Russian and Transnistrian forces. A tripartite Joint Control Committee (JCC) was formed to observe the military forces in the security zone and maintain order. The peacekeeping forces were first deployed on 29 July 1992 and consisted of six Russian, three Moldovan and three Transnistrian battalions.

The civil war, and particularly the violence in Bender, had an immediate impact on Moldovan overall domestic politics. In July almost all the members of the FPCD-dominated government resigned, and Andrei Sangheli was named Prime Minister. The Sangheli government chose to focus more on economic issues than regional issues. Also in July, President Snegur removed Defence Minister Ion Costas from his post, and in January 1993, Petre Lucinschi replaced Mosanu as parliamentary speaker. For many Moldovans, the strident nationalism of the FPCD was to blame for the escalation of conflict during the spring and the summer. The irony is that while the civil war forced a fundamental moderating change in the Moldovan government, it entrenched the militant Transnistrian leadership. As King notes, the conflict in Bender became part of the new mythology of Transnistria and its new identity construction (King, 2000: 197). Those that were associated with the conduct of the war in Transnistria, such as Smirnov, his advisor Valeri Litskai (later named Foreign Minister), Grigore Maracuta (speaker of the Transnistrian parliament) and Vladimir Atamaniuk (deputy speaker) were viewed as heroes. While Moldova has had four different governments since the war, there has been no significant change in the Transnistrian leadership.

The political fallout from the civil war continued throughout 1993. There were several defections from the FPCD, and Lucinschi's Agrarian Democratic Party (PDA) began to fill the political vacuum. While the FPCD no longer enjoyed its absolute parliamentary majority, the party had enough votes to block the passage of any constitutional or basic law. The legislative stalemate forced early parliamentary elections in February 1994. In order to prevent Transnistrians from participating in the elections, President Smirnov declared a state of emergency from January through March 1994. Although the Central Election Commission established alternative voting sites for Transnistrian residents, very few individuals participated.[10] The elections further signalled the de facto recognition of a separate Transnistria and marked a turning point in Moldovan domestic politics. The FPCD, which had held a majority of seats in the previous parliament, was reduced to less than nine per cent of the seats while the PDA captured an absolute majority. The success of the PDA signalled a fundamental shift in Moldovan politics. The 1994 parliamentary elections indicated that only a small minority of the Moldovan population embraced the pro-Romanian, anti-state position of the FPCD. In March, a non-binding referendum was held in which more than 95 per cent of voters favoured Moldova's continuing independent statehood, and in April, the parliament ratified CIS membership. The new Moldovan constitution adopted in July 1994 gave Transnistria a special form of autonomy (Article 111). The PDA's more balanced approach to Transnistria, overwhelming public support for statehood and CIS membership should have facilitated negotiations, however, the Transnistrian government steadfastly maintained that any final agreement had to be made between two sovereign states.

Aside from the political fallout, the loss of Transnistria had an enormous impact on the Moldovan economy. Most of Moldova's light industries and energy facilities are located in this region. Almost 25 per cent of the country's industrial production is located in Transnistria, and 87 per cent of Moldova's electricity and 100 per cent of its large electric machinery output come from this region. This is the reason why Transnistrians held so much economic power in Soviet Moldova and continue to have a negative economic influence on Moldova today. Transnistrian customs agents patrol the Moldovan border with Ukraine which not only accounts for a loss of tax revenues for Moldova but also contributes to organized crime and weapons smuggling. In addition, the Moldovan government has loss revenues because of the inability to privatize state-owned enterprises in Transnistria.

The Role of International Intervention

The OSCE: To bridge the gap between the two sides to the conflict, the Organization for Security and Co-operation in Europe (OSCE) established a mission in Chisinau in May 1993. This organization has been a significant actor during the post-military conflict period in Moldova by its encouragement of dialogue between Moldova and Transnistria. The OSCE itself has been a controversial figure within the negotiations. Some OSCE mission heads have been considered too supportive of either Moldova or Transnistria and not viewed as impartial. For example in 1997, Donald Johnson was declared *persona non grata* by the Transnistrian government because they felt that he was too favourable to the Moldovan side. The Moldovan government was equally critical of his replacement John Evans for being too sympathetic to the Transnistrians. On the advice of the OSCE, the two sides established 'expert groups' that were responsible for negotiations. Prior to this, negotiations occurred at an inter-parliamentary level but were not at all successful.[11] However, the creation of special negotiation teams did not end the stalemate. Philip Hahn, the head of the OSCE mission in Moldova in 1994, stated that the situation resembled 'a family feud – they will not see or speak to each other, and this will last for the next six to ten years.'[12]

The 14th Army: The July 1992 agreement left the status of the 14th Army unresolved. Yelstin's April 1992 decision to place the unit under Russian control was regarded in Moldova as tantamount to foreign military occupation. This issue was so sensitive for Moldova that an article was included in the new constitution forbidding the stationing of foreign troops on Moldovan territory. The Russians had consistently linked the withdrawal of the 14th Army to a settlement on the final status of Transnistria. This process came to be known as 'synchronization'. The OSCE, however, at its Budapest summit in 1994 rejected the linkage. After two years of negotiation, the presidents of Moldova and Russia finally signed an agreement in 1994 that called for the withdrawal of the 14th Army within three years 'from the date of entry into force' of the agreement. This clause was particularly important because Russian officials argued that the agreement only entered into force upon approval by the Russian Duma, which has steadfastly refused to ratify it. Another problem is that the agreement specifically refers to the withdrawal of the 14th Army. In 1995, the 14th Army was downgraded to an 'operational group of Russian forces' (OGRF), and therefore, it is unclear whether the agreement is legally binding on the renamed military force operating in Transnistria.

Transnistria's relationship with Russia and Ukraine: While Transnistrian officials enjoy a relatively close relationship with Moscow, especially with hard-line communists and nationalists in the Duma, their political agendas do not always coincide. In 1994, the Transnistrian parliament passed a resolution which stated that if the Russian forces should withdraw, all military equipment would revert to Transnistria. Russia, however, maintains the right to remove or to destroy the huge stockpile of weapons and ammunition. The status of this stockpile is just one of the issues that has caused disagreements between Tiraspol and local Russian military commanders. For example Lebed's replacement in 1995, Lieutenant-General Valerii Yevnevich, has antagonized the Transnistrian leadership by destroying military stockpiles.

For obvious geographic reasons, any discussion of removing weapons and ammunition by train from Transnistria to Russia must involve Ukraine. Because of its own separatist movement in Crimea, Ukraine has consistently supported Moldova's territorial integrity. The Ukrainian foreign ministry participated in the April 1992 cease-fire agreements. By 1995, Ukraine's visibility in the negotiation process became sharper, having resolved its own regional problems, most notably the Crimean issue, through an institutional accommodation. Moldovan–Ukrainian cross-border cooperation was strengthened (for example, on a new customs regime). Michael Wygant, head of the OSCE mission in 1995, stated that 'while Ukraine cannot replace Russia, it has a very important role to play in the negotiations'.[13]

The Memorandum: After months of negotiation, Moldovan and Transnistrian officials endorsed a memorandum in July 1996 on the settlement of the conflict. Although the two-page document contained much of the same text as found in previous agreements, the introduction of new concepts caused President Snegur to refuse to sign the document. Snegur was concerned about the Transnistrian interpretation of certain clauses. For example, the memorandum stated that the parties would 'continue the establishment between them of state-legal relations'. Transnistria interpreted this clause as establishing sovereign state-to-state relations. The clause that caused the most concern, however, stated that the parties would 'build their relations in the framework of a common state'. According to Grigore Maracuta, the speaker of the Transnistrian parliament, the concept of a 'common state' was first developed by Transnistrians and has four general elements: divided powers, delegated powers, unified powers and borders within the former Moldovan Soviet Socialist Republic.[14] Maracuta stated that a common state is defined as an equal partnership between two states.

The memorandum became an important issue during the 1996 Moldovan presidential election. Presidential candidate Lucinschi argued that Snegur's failure to sign the memorandum prolonged the conflict (Lucinschi neglected to mention that he and Snegur had both been members of the PDA). After Lucinschi's second-round victory in December, it was hoped that his leadership would put an end to the conflict. Many believed that his position within the former Communist Party would enhance his ability to work with the Transnistrians and enable him to resolve the stalemate.[15] Once in office, however, he also refused to sign the document because of concerns over its interpretation. Moldovan officials insisted that a separate annex be included that elaborated all of the disputed points. Although Lucinschi and Smirnov eventually signed the memorandum in May 1997, Smirnov and the Transnistrians never formally acknowledged the annex. Donald Johnson, head of the OSCE mission in 1997, believed that events had overtaken the memorandum and its defects were too many. Therefore, he recommended to the OSCE Permanent Council not to endorse the document.[16] Johnson was correct – the memorandum had no lasting influence on the negotiation process. Throughout 1997, meetings of the JCC or the expert groups occurred infrequently, and there was little progress on the final status of Transnistria. Part of the problem was that the composition of the Moldovan expert group changed after every presidential and parliamentary election, and these changes delayed the process.

Odesa and Kyiv Summits: The next stage of conflict resolution saw a bipartite intervention by Russia and Ukraine. With the active support of Russian Prime Minister Viktor Chernomyrdin and Ukrainian President Leonid Kuchma, Lucinschi and Smirnov concluded an agreement in Odesa in March 1998 that called for a reduction in the number of peacekeeping forces and the re-building of the bridges that were destroyed or damaged during the fighting in 1991 and 1992. While the two sides made no progress on the core issue of Transnistria's status, these confidence-building measures were important and by the summer of 1999, most of recommendations had been implemented. Nevertheless, the negotiations would sometimes lapse for months and only the intervention and pressure of Russia and Ukraine would force the Transnistrians back to the table.

Just as Chernomyrdin was instrumental in orchestrating the Odesa summit, Russian Prime Minister Sergei Stepashin was largely responsible for organizing the Kyiv summit a year later in July 1999. In Kyiv, the two sides agreed to establish five 'common spaces' including a common border, defence, judicial, economic and cultural space. Lucinschi and

Smirnov left it to the expert groups to elaborate these spaces, and even in Kyiv, it was clear that they had different interpretations. Lucinschi stated that a common defence space would be based on the creation of a single military force while Smirnov insisted that Transnistria would maintain a separate military. Moreover, Smirnov argued that any discussion concerning weapons and ammunition in Transnistria was a matter for Moscow and Tiraspol. The Moldovan press and news agencies were highly critical of the Kyiv summit, calling it 'resultless' and stated that the leaders 'did not sign any important documents'.[17] Ironically less than a week after the Kyiv summit, the Cuciurgan power station located in Transnistria cut off electrical power to Chisinau. Moldovan Prime Minister Ion Sturza claimed that the decision to cut off the electricity was not made by the power plant but by Transnistrian officials. The power station claimed that Moldova owed over $12 million, and unless it paid, no electricity would be delivered. The Moldovan response was to secure energy from Ukraine and Romania. Both Moldova and Transnistria are dependent on Russia, but because the Cuciurgan power station is located in Transnistria, the region was able to use its energy leverage over the rest of the country.

Economic issues have become extremely important during recent negotiations. While Moldova and Transnistria both owe debts to Gazprom, it is unclear how to settle the accounts. Moldova's energy debt to Gazprom is approximately $200 million while Transnistria's debt is more than $500 million. In the 1990s the Russian government subsidized Transnistria's energy needs, but recently the attitude of the Russian government and its energy suppliers has changed. In March 2000, Alexander Pushkin, deputy chairman of Gazprom, wrote a letter to the Transnistrian parliament in which he stated that 'Gazprom cannot be a donor for Transnistria. The reluctance to pay for gas is a gross political and economic blunder the entire responsibility for which shall be on the region's leaders.'[18]

The Istanbul Summit: Apart from the question of the status of Transnistria, the other key issue is the removal of the Russian forces from Transnistria. The agreement to withdraw all Russian forces was initially signed in 1994, and while there are less than 2,500 troops remaining, there is an immense stockpile of ammunition and equipment. While Russia has destroyed several tons of ammunition and has transported equipment from Transnistria, the status of the OGRF has not fundamentally changed since 1995. These forces are a tangible sign of Moldova's conditional sovereignty. Moldova's dependency on Russian energy as well as the Russian market has limited the country's ability to press for a conclusive agreement to resolve the status of these forces. A significant development came at the OSCE Istanbul summit in November 1999 when Russia agreed to a declaration to remove all forces from Moldova by the end of 2002, without any conditions and without any linkage to resolving Transnistria's status. With the coming to power of Putin in January 2000, however, the Russian Foreign Ministry backtracked from this commitment and made public a note addressed to the Transnistrian leadership stating that the military withdrawal would have to coincide with a political agreement on the status of Transnistria by 2002. The Moldovan Foreign Ministry was quick to point out that the Istanbul declaration made no mention of synchronization. Moreover, the Moldovan Foreign Ministry noted that the Istanbul declaration was a binding commitment within the OSCE framework.

Putin's role in resolving the conflict: The Russian president has been a significant actor in this conflict. It was Yeltsin who placed the 14th Army under his direct control, and he and his prime ministers were a party to every significant document signed by Moldova and Transnistria. Therefore, the election of Vladimir Putin was bound to impact on the negotiations. Prior to his June 2000 visit to Chisinau, many Moldovan politicians hoped that Putin would unequivocally support the Istanbul declaration and revitalize the negotiation process. In fact, Putin's discussions with Lucinschi focused on the rescheduling of Moldova's gas debt and the status of Transnistria. While Putin expressed his support for Moldova's independence and territorial integrity, he also stated that Russia would only 'try' to withdraw troops from Transnistria as required by the Istanbul declaration (*Basapress* 2000c). At the end of his visit, Putin announced the formation of a new commission to resolve the conflict. Significantly, he appointed Yevgenii Primakov, former prime minister and architect of the 1997 memorandum, the head the commission. Leading Moldovan politicians expressed anxieties over Primakov's ability to be even-handed. Gheorghe Marin, a leading Moldovan parliamentarian, stated that he was concerned whether Primakov would interpret the concept of a 'common state' from the Transnistrian perspective (*Basapress* 2000b). Putin's policy, consequently, appears to have returned to the pre-Istanbul position of Russia on the 'synchronization' of an agreement on the status of Transnistria with the removal of Russian forces.

A Change in the Regime: Implications for Settling the Conflict
Transnistria has continuously left its imprint on national-level transition politics in Moldova. Recent changes in Moldovan institutions have

become linked to the issue of Transnistria. In March 1999, Lucinschi issued a decree to conduct a consultative referendum at the same time as local elections schedule for 23 May. In his decree, Lucinschi proposed the creation of a presidential regime. One of the reasons offered by Lucinschi for this change from a semi-presidential to a strong presidential system was that it would place him in a stronger negotiating position with the Transnistrians.

Over 56 per cent voted yes in the referendum, and subsequently, Lucinschi proposed a draft law to give the president the sole authority to appoint and remove cabinet ministers. In addition, he proposed reducing the size of the parliament from 101 to 70 members and changing the electoral system from a strictly proportional representation system to one that combined proportional seats with single member district seats. Almost all of Moldova's political forces opposed the draft laws. International organizations such as the Council of Europe also expressed their concern over the constitutional change. In a speech delivered to the Parliamentary Assembly of the Council Europe on 25 June 1999, Lucinschi defended his proposal and explained that Moldova's political instability required the concentration of power in a strong executive. He argued that the inability of the Moldovan government to enact economic reform or resolve the status of Transnistria demonstrated the need for a presidential regime that would allow one individual to assume responsibility rather than a diverse group of parliamentarians and government officials.

Lucinschi failed not only to convince the Council of Europe but also Moldovan MPs. This was critical because in order to call a binding referendum, Lucinschi needed a parliamentary majority. By summer 2000, Lucinschi's support within the parliament was at its lowest point in almost four years, and finally on 5 July 2000, the parliament approved a series of constitutional amendments consolidating a parliamentary regime. Most importantly, the amendments stipulated that the president would be elected, and if need be, dismissed by the parliament. The amendments passed in the first reading by a vote of 92 to 5. Lucinschi failed to promulgate the law after the first vote (in essence vetoing the law), but the parliament re-voted the law 87 to 4. Once Lucinschi's term expired on 15 January 2001, the country became a parliamentary regime with an indirectly elected president. What impact will this change in the type of regime have on the negotiations with Transnistria and the prospects for conflict resolution? The president was responsible for assembling the expert group that negotiated with Transnistria, and predictably, Lucinschi argued that the parliament's decision was a retrograde step in the negotiation process: 'We were very close to resolving the conflict, but now I don't know what the parliament will do in the future.' On Moldovan television he warned that the parliament's decision 'may complicate the process of settlement of the Transnistrian conflict' (*Basapress* 2000a). The OSCE was divided on the issue. OSCE Chairwoman, Benita Ferrero-Walder, stated in a visit to Moldova immediately after the parliament's decision that she did not believe that the introduction of a parliamentary regime would have any negative impact on negotiations with Transnistria. In contrast, William Hill, head of the OSCE mission in Moldova, argued that the constitutional changes would delay the negotiating process since the Transnistrians would refuse to negotiate until the Moldovan side formalized a new procedure for selecting the expert group.[19]

GAGAUZIA: AN INSTITUTIONAL ACCOMMODATION

While Gagauzia's demographic and socio-economic background are different than Transnistria, the concentration of a russophone population made for some similar demands. However, unlike the conflict with Transnistria, Moldova was able to successfully resolve the dispute involving the ethnic Gagauzi located in the county's southern districts. The Gagauzi are a Turkic language-speaking people of Orthodox Christian faith who were highly russified during the Soviet period, and even today, Russian remains their primary language of commerce and education. As discussed previously, the Gagauzi initially participated in the meetings of the Popular Front under their umbrella organization, *Gagauz Halki* (the Gagauz People). However as the Front transformed from a reformist to a pan-Romanian organization, the *Gagauz Halki* demanded independence for the Gagauzi. In August 1990 the Gagauzi announced the formation of their republic with Comrat as the capital. There had never been any historical or institutional precedent for the creation of Gagauzia. They adopted national symbols and organized a local defence force. The Gagauzi and Transnistrians cooperated in several areas (such as defence and economic issues). As in Transnistria, Gagauzi elites supported the August 1991 coup, and the Moldovan declaration of independence only hardened the Gagauzi position on seeking greater autonomy.

The assertion of Moldovan sovereignty over Gagauzia, however, was not seriously contested. Unlike Transnistria, there was little armed conflict and violence. Regional governance in Gagauzia was not as developed as in Transnistria. The context of conflict with the Moldovan government was also very different. Gagauzia lacked an industrial base to its economy, was much more dependent on Chisinau for its economic viability and lacked a compelling foreign policy issue that would have been of interest to Russia (for example, a 14th Army or significant ethnic Russian population). These factors, combined with the Moldovan military defeat in Bender, created a positive environment for compromise. Discussions occurred throughout 1993, but after the February 1994 parliamentary elections and the repudiation of the Popular Front elites and overwhelming victory of the former nomenklatura, the Moldovan government entered into a final phase of negotiations with the elected Gagauz elite. A Moldovan law of January 1995 recognized *Gagauz Yeri* (Gagauz Land) as an autonomous territorial unit with a special status of self-determination. Individual villages, and not counties, are the administrative unit of *Gagauz Yeri*. Villages in which ethnic Gagauzi comprise over 50 per cent of the population needed to secure a majority in a referendum to join. Villages with less than 50 per cent Gagauzi could also hold a referendum if one third of the villagers agreed to the referendum. In the first referendum on 5 March 1995, three towns and 26 villages joined.[20]

At the same time, Article 1 of the law states that Gagauzia is a 'constituent part of the Republic of Moldova' (*Monitorul Oficial al Republicii Moldova*, 1995: 3). The Gagauzi elect a governor (*Baskan*) and a popular assembly. Elections for the *Baskan* and the popular assembly were held in 1995 and 1999. The Moldovan government and international organizations like the OSCE hoped that the special status of Gagauzia would serve as a model for Transnistria.[21] The irony is that many Transnistrians are unwilling to accept territorial autonomy precisely because of developments in Gagauzia since 1995. Almost all Transnistrians, and indeed most Gagauzi, believe that Gagauzia is not truly autonomous and that there has been a slow reconcentration of power back to Chisinau. Recently, Mikhail Kendigelian, chair of the popular assembly, told a sitting of the Transnistrian parliament that Gagauzia had decided to revise its relationship with Chisinau based on the Transnistrian concept of a common state (*Infotag* 2000a). The fact that there is still tension between Chisinau and Comrat should not be taken as a failure of Moldova's conflict resolution strategy to institutionalize autonomy. Political disagreements are inevitable, but a breakdown of the process would be marked by violence, and there is no evidence thus far of a danger of renewed violence in Gagauzia.

CONCLUSION

Since January 2000, the status of Transnistria has received a great deal of attention from international organizations. Representatives from the

OSCE and the U.S. State Department have come to Moldova to discuss a settlement to the conflict. At the Moscow CIS summit held in January 2000, the issue of Transnistria was discussed for the first time, and Putin's June visit highlighted Russia's renewed role in the resolution of the conflict. There has been little movement, however, on the fundamental issues. First, there is the issue of competing sovereignties. President Smirnov wants the Transnistrian and the Moldovan constitutions to have equal status. The Moldovan government has maintained that the Transnistrian constitution must be subordinate to the Moldovan one. Second, Transnistria wants its final status ratified as a state-to-state treaty. Smirnov wants all relations between Transnistria and Moldova based on a treaty rather than a law. The Moldovan government wants to grant Transnistria autonomy using a law, as in Gagauzia, rather than a treaty which denotes statehood. Third, the definition and division of economic, military, political and social competencies remains unsettled. It is unclear what impact the change from a semi-presidential to a parliamentary regime will have on the negotiation process. The president has been just as unsuccessful at negotiation as the parliament was in 1992 and 1993. However, the parliament's decision on constitutional changes is likely to delay the negotiation process at least in the short run as Moldovan and Transnistrian politicians accommodate to the political changes.

If the civil war had been exclusively an 'ethnic' war, then this conflict should have been resolved by now. Unlike ethnic conflicts such as Cyprus, there is considerable interaction among Moldovans and Transnistrians. There are packed buses that hourly transport people and goods back and forth between Chisinau and Tiraspol. Hundreds of students from Transnistria study at Moldova State University and the Free and Independent University of Moldova. The reality is that the nature of the conflict has evolved over time into a regional conflict. Initially in 1989 and 1990, there were legitimate linguistic and ethnic concerns on the part of many Transnistrians. However, the Transnistrian leadership used these concerns to solidify their position. The Transnistrian political and economic elites would have much to lose if the stalemate were to end, as they would not only lose their political influence but their economic privileges. Transnistria has become known as a haven for drug and weapons smuggling. Russia and the international dimension have always figured prominently in the Transnistrian conflict. Until Russia places significant political pressure on Transnistria, there is little incentive for these individuals to negotiate a change.

Aside from the international dimension, the conflict has domestic economic and political consequences. The Moldovan economy suffers because of the current stalemate. The government is unable to collect taxes, control important energy resources or privatize certain industries that are controlled by Transnistria. While there is a general political consensus that the resolution of the conflict should be based on a grant of autonomy, there is no consensus among the political elite as to who should be accountable for the process. President Lucinschi claimed that the lack of presidential power thwarted his attempts at conflict resolution. MPs, however, claimed that it was Lucinschi's inability to resolve the conflict which undermined his authority. The discussions over Transnistrian autonomy also have an impact on relations between Chisinau and Gagauzia. Not content with the autonomy granted in 1995, the Gagauzi argue that they want the same concessions and autonomy that Chisinau is willing to grant to Transnistria. Fundamentally, they want greater control over tax and revenue issues. The on-going struggle between Chisinau and Comrat illustrates that regional conflicts never truly end. There are always disagreements and conflicts between the centre and the periphery. The goal of conflict resolution should be to create a legal framework in which disputes can be peacefully negotiated.

NOTES

1. Moldavia was the Soviet-era name for present-day Moldova. In this article, I only use the name Moldova.
2. During this time, most Romanians refused to acknowledge a distinctive Moldovan ethnicity. Therefore, the term 'ethnic Romanian' was applied to any Romanian-speaker. Even today, many Romanians do not recognize Moldovans as ethnically distinct.
3. Dyer (1999) notes that the russification process was not linear. During the 1950s, Moldovan literature flourished compared to the 1960s and 1970s.
4. Kolsto, Edemsky and Kalashnikova (1993: 981) argue that the language law was not undemocratic and contained articles protecting the linguistic rights of other ethnic groups.
5. Iurie Rosca, president of the parliamentary faction and chair of the Executive Committee of the Christian Democratic Popular Front, interview with the author, Chisinau, 27 April 1994.
6. While the city of Bender is under the control of Tiraspol, it is actually located on the right bank of the Dniester and was part of Romania during the inter-war years.
7. Ethnic Ukrainians constitute approximately 28% of the Transnistrian population while ethnic Russians are 25%.
8. Some such as Kaufman and Bowers (1998) argue that Moscow provoked the violence in Bender in order to justify military intervention. However, there is no conclusive evidence that supports the contention that the 14th Army acted on the instructions of Moscow.
9. The Moldovan government claimed that 231 died during the conflict and another 845 were injured. The numbers reported by the Transnistrians were much higher.
10. Central Election Commission decision No.255 governed elections for 'citizens of the Dniester left-bank raions and the city of Bender.' See International Foundation for Electoral Systems (1994: 2–56).
11. Yuri P. Ataman, Chairperson of the Joint Committee for Democratization and Conciliation, interview with the author, Chisinau, 6 March 1997.
12. Philip Hahn, Former head of the OSCE mission in Chisinau, interview with the author, Chisinau, 4 June 1995.

13. Michael Wygant, Former head of the OSCE mission in Chisinau, interview with the author, Chisinau, 6 June 1995.
14. Grigore Maracuta, Speaker of the Transnistrian parliament, interview with the author, 22 May 1997.
15. Lucinschi was a first secretary in the Communist Party and the highest-ranking ethnic Moldovan in the Communist Party.
16. Donald Johnson, Former head of the OSCE mission in Chisinau, interview with the author, Chisinau, 8 August 1997.
17. Basapress went on to say that the 'talks in Kiev have not changed one little thing in the stance of the Tiraspol leadership'. See Basapress (1999).
18. As quoted in Infotag (2000b).
19. William Hill, Head of the OSCE mission in Chisinau, interview with the author, Chisinau, 21 July 2000.
20. The villages did not have to be contiguous, and therefore, there are some villages that joined that are surrounded by areas that are not part of Gagauz Yeri.
21. Michael Wygant, former head of the OSCE mission in Chisinau, interview with the author, Chisinau, 6 June 1995.

REFERENCES

Basapress (2000a), 8 July.
Basapress (2000b), 19 June.
Basapress (2000c), 17 June.
Basapress (1999), 20 July.
Basapress (1997), 15 August.
Chinn, Jeff and Steven D. Roper (1998), 'Territorial Autonomy in Gagauzia', *Nationalities Papers*, Vol.26, No.1, pp.87–102.
Chinn, Jeff and Steven D. Roper (1995), 'Ethnic Mobilization and Reactive Nationalism: The Case of Moldova', *Nationalities Papers*, Vol.23, No.2, pp.291–325.
Crowther, William and Steven D. Roper (1996), 'A Comparative Analysis of the Institutional Development in the Romanian and Moldovan Legislatures', in David M. Olson and Philip Norton (eds) *The New Parliaments of Central and Eastern Europe*. London and Portland, OR: Frank Cass.
Crowther, William (1991), 'The Politics of Ethno-National Mobilization: Nationalism and Reform in Soviet Moldavia', *The Russian Review*, Vol.50, No.2, pp.183–203.
Dyer, Donald L. (1999), *The Romanian Dialect of Moldova*. Lewiston, NY: Edwin Mellen Press.
Enciu, Nicolae and Ion Pavelescu (1998), 'Un miracol istoric: Renasterea romanismului in Basarabia', in Ioan Scurtu (ed.), *Istoria Basarabiei: De la inceputuri pana in 1998*. Bucharest: Semne.
Hamm, Michael F. (1998), 'Kishinev: The Character and Development of a Tsatrist Frontier Town', *Nationalities Papers*, Vol.26, No.1, pp.19–38.
Hitchens, Keith (1994), *Rumania 1866–1947*. Oxford: Oxford University Press.
Infotag (2000b), 16 March.
International Foundation for Electoral Systems (1994), *Republic of Moldova Parliamentary Elections: February 27, 1994*. Chisinau: Tish.
Kaufman, Stuart (1996), 'Spiraling to Ethnic War: Elites, Masses, and Moscow in Moldova's Civil War', *International Security*, Vol.21, No.2, pp.108–38.
Kaufman, Stuart J. and Stephen R. Bowers (1998), 'Transnational Dimensions of the Transnistrian Conflict', *Nationalities Papers*, Vol.26, No.1, pp.129–46.
King, Charles (2000), *The Moldovans: Romania, Russia, and the Politics of Culture*. Stanford: Hoover Institution Press.
King, Charles (1998), 'Ethnicity and Institutional Reform: The Dynamics of 'Indigenization' in the Moldovan ASSR', *Nationalities Papers*, Vol.26, No.1, pp.57–72.
King, Charles (1994), 'Moldovan Identity and the Politics of Pan-Romanianism', *Slavic Review*, Vol.53, No.2, pp.345–68.

Kolsto, Pal, Andrei Edemsky and Natalya Kalashnikova (1993), 'The Dniester Conflict: Between Irredentism and Separatism', *Europe–Asia Studies*, Vol.45, No.6, pp.973–1000.

Livezeanu, Irina (1995), *Cultural Politics in Greater Romania: Regionalism, Nation Building, and Ethnic Struggle, 1918–1930*. Ithaca, NY: Cornell University Press.

Livezeanu, Irina (1990), 'Moldavia, 1917–1990: Nationalism and Internationalism Then and Now', *Armenian Review*, Vol.43, No.2–3, pp.153–93.

Monitorul Oficial al Republicii Moldova (1995), Vol.2, No.3–4, 14 January.

Nedelciuc, Vasile (1992), *Republica Moldova*. Chisinau: Universitas.

Shishcanu, Ion and Vitaliu Varatec (eds) (1991), *The Pact: Molotov–Ribbentrop and Its Consequences for Bessarabia*. Chisinau: Universitas.

Trebici, Vladimir (1993), 'Basarabia si Bucovina: Aspecte demografice', in Adrian Pop (ed.), *Sub povara granitei imperiale*. Bucharest: Recif.

Multinationality, Regional Institutions, State-Building, and the Failed Transition in Georgia

MONICA DUFFY TOFT

This essay examines Georgia's stalled transition to democracy following the collapse of the Soviet Union. I argue that Georgia's failure to build a stable and unified state following its independence cannot be properly understood without considering the impact of regional institutions inherited from the Soviet Union. The dynamic process of independence turned Georgia's formally functional but largely moribund regional institutions into reactive instruments of fearful ethnic minorities and led to conflict.

Ironically, the reactive political mobilization within some of Georgia's regions was stoked by fear and resentment of Russian neo-imperialism within the central ruling elite in Georgia. Georgia responded to Russian hegemonic leadership of the 'Commonwealth of Independent States' with a form of nationalistic chauvinism of its own, which though defensive and integrative in its intent, proved threatening to national minorities within Georgia and disintegrative in its consequences. Abkhaz nationalists, for example, countered Georgian chauvinism with their own and threatened to secede, thus weakening the territorial integrity of Georgia. Ajars accepted that Ajaria belonged within the Georgian homeland, and rather than independence, Ajaria's primary concern was the maintenance and enhancement of its privileged regional position vis-à-vis the centre. A third group threatened by Georgian nationalism was the Ossetians, whose autonomous administrative status inherited from the Soviet era was threatened by dissolution from Tbilisi. Like the Abkhaz, the Ossetians felt threatened by the Georgian nationalizing state and sought to preserve their autonomy by separation. While Abkhazia and South Ossetia were largely conflicts over national autonomy, Ajaria was almost exclusively a conflict over administrative and economic autonomy. In the end, the combination of the shock of independence, combined with long simmering nationalist resentments and a large, powerful, imperialist neighbour, made it impossible for Georgia to establish stable institutions capable of moving it towards its goal of a strong, multinational and democratic state.

This essay proceeds in four parts. In the first part I present a brief theoretical discussion of 'stateness', a variable considered 'seriously under-analyzed' by Linz and Stepan, yet crucial to understanding transitions (Linz and Stepan, 1996). Stateness refers to the relationship between nation-building, state-building and democratization. Next there is an overview of four key national groups in Georgia – Georgians, Abkhaz, Ajars and Ossetians – in relation to the territory of Georgia. At the time of the dissolution of the Soviet Union there were three autonomous entities in Georgia: the South Ossetia Autonomous Oblast, the Ajarian Autonomous Soviet Socialist Republic and the Abkhaz Autonomous Soviet Socialist Republic.[1] The third part of the essay examines Abkhazia, Ajaria and Ossetia and how each region reacted to the nation-building and state-building efforts in the capital as Georgia sought independence from Moscow, largely from 1989 to 1994. The fourth part shows how national rivalry and Russian interference intensified the stateness problem, and how this in turn hampered a democratic transition in Georgia. The contribution concludes that understanding this transition requires us to trace the links between nationalism, regional institutions, state building, and finally, transition to democracy.

As elucidated by Linz and Stepan, the stateness problem relates how a polity's structure and identity affects its transition to democracy. When there is congruence between the identity of the nation and the borders of the state, then democratization and consolidation remain a distinct possibility:[2] 'This congruence empirically eliminates most stateness problems and thus should be considered supportive conditions for democratic consolidation.'[3] If congruence between a nation and the borders of a state is lacking however, then the democratic transition will be severely hampered.[4] Predicted difficulties arise because different nations within the borders of an emerging state are unlikely to accept the nationalist ideal and vision for the state as espoused by leaders of another nation. The state will be seen as illegitimate by a portion of the population. As a system of government that is premised on the consent of the governed, democracy and institution-building will remain contested and elusive.

In democratic transitions, emerging states need to legitimate authority among the governed. This process of legitimization often entails merging of a national conception of who should belong – who should be a full citizen – with the trappings of the state. This national conception hinges on particular characteristics, includes some and excludes others. Often the national conception includes a national majority, but it may not.[5] Those who find themselves outside the dominant conception are likely to characterize the emerging nation-state as non-representative and illegitimate. National minorities then face the question of whether to voice their concerns and/or choose to exit and form their own states.

The decision to voice or exit is not made in isolation. It is made in the context of a contest over who the state should properly govern. This contest usually involves give and take whereby voicing of fears of discrimination might be countered by reassurances that rights and privileges will be protected, regardless of national character. In these instances we should expect the national group not to pursue exit from the state. If, however, fears are not soothed through accommodative rhetoric and policies on the part of the nationalizing state, then voice might be abandoned in favour of exit. If the national group fears survival of its language, culture or religion, then it might perceive independence as the sole option to preserve identity. This is especially true if the state committed crimes against national groups.

In the next section we examine this voice-exit option among the Abkhaz, Ajars and Ossetians in the context of the nationalizing state of Georgia (Brubaker, 1996). The Ajars did not see themselves as ethnically distinct from the dominant Georgians, and as such, the conflict here was regional as opposed to ethnic. Once this was understood by both sides, a solution to this conflict based on coexistence within Georgia became relatively straightforward. Challenges to state authority persisted, but these challenges were never a hindrance to state-building because they were formulated as claims to administrative and economic rather than political autonomy. The Abkhaz and South Ossetians, by contrast, feared what they saw as a Georgian nationalizing state. For these ethno-regions, exit – even if it meant joining another state – became the preferred option.

REGIONALISM AND ETHNICITY IN GEORGIA

The first time Georgians had complete political control over their historic homeland was from 1918–21. Prior to the Bolshevik revolution ethnic Armenian businessmen dominated the urban environment, and along with ethnic Russians, occupied the most important posts in government. Independence marked an opportunity for ethnic Georgians to gain prominence (Suny, 1980: 207). Statehood, however, was short-lived: in 1921 Bolshevik troops invaded. Georgia became a Soviet Socialist Republic, first as part of the Republic of Transcaucasia, along with Armenia and Azerbaijan, then in 1936 it became a separate Union Republic. This consolidation was not welcome because it represented a threat to Georgian national identity as well as Russian domination (Pipes, 1997: 266–93).

Georgian national identity thus developed as national self-protection against feared domination of a Russian 'higher' culture and its potential for russification. As the system evolved, however, the titular nationalities, including Georgians, developed their own versions of national chauvinism. Within Georgia most national minorities perceived Georgia as a protected area of privilege for Georgians (Pipes, 1997: 290). Georgians received top political posts in the republic, the largest subsidies for cultural projects, and access to economic networks of illegal operations.[6] Close kinship ties, combined with the dominance of a distinctly Georgian caste within the republic's political elite, 'reinforced the exclusionary character of politics in the republic, the sense of superiority of the titular nationality and inferiority of the non-Georgians' (Suny, 1994: 318). The following three sections introduce the important geographical, demographic and historical context of the groups and regions which disrupted Georgian stateness, and as a result, Georgia's democratic transition.

Georgia and the Georgians

Due to its geostrategic location at the heart of the Caucasus, Georgia has been the site of competition of many empires seeking hegemony in the region. Conquered successively by the Persians, Byzantines, Arabs, Mongols and Ottomans, Georgia accepted Russian imperial domination in 1801.[7] During the Soviet period, Georgia was a Union Republic and a federation.[8] It contained three political-administrative subjects: two Autonomous Soviet Socialist Republics (ASSRs) – Abkhazia and Ajaria – and one Autonomous Oblast' – South Ossetia. The ASSRs were the most politically developed of the administrative entities due to the existence of republican legislatures and executive branches. Designed to give recognition to smaller ethnic groups, the Autonomous Oblasts (and Okrugs) were placed under the jurisdiction of either provinces or territories. Events in Georgia from 1990 mirrored those in other republics and regions that inherited autonomized structures from the Soviet era. Not only did Georgia, as a Union Republic, seek to leave the USSR, but its ASSRs, including Abkhazia and Ajaria, took advantage of the legal pretexts provided by Gorbachev to assert greater autonomy, and even secession in the case of the former, through the 'All-Union Law on the Demarcation of Powers Between the USSR and Members of the Federation' passed by the USSR Supreme Soviet in April 1990.[9]

Georgians represent an ancient Christian nation living in the southern part of the Caucasus. Ethnically they are part of the Kartvelian people, and call their land Sakartvelo and themselves Kartveli. Three groups make up the largest proportion of the Kartvelian group: Georgians (85%), Mingrelians (10%) and Svans (1%). Each group speaks a different language within the South Caucasian (Kartvelian) language group. Each language is quite distinct, and Georgian is the only written language in this group (Comrie, 1981: 197). The Georgians, Mingrelians and Svans are related ethnically. What has distinguished them since the eighth century is language. The Georgian language is one of the oldest in the region: the script has been traced back to at least the fourth century. The Georgians were united with Russians in Christianity (albeit under the Georgian Orthodox Church), so the primary characteristic that separated them from the Russians was language; and it was language that determined social, political and economic mobility (Suny, 1994: 128).

With the 1926 census, the Mingrelians and Svans had their own census grouping, but thereafter all three linguistic groupings were classified under the broader ethnic category of 'Georgian'.[10] Nonetheless, within Georgia there existed strong sub-ethnic or regional identities, including Ajarian, Imeretian, Kakhetian, Mingrelian and Svan. Because the Mingrelians, for example, speak a different language and the Ajars adhere to Islam, the distinction between these groups and the ethnic Georgians is more pronounced. The status of national minority is not conferred on these regional groupings, however, as each is seen as part of the larger Georgian national majority.

Well over 90% of all Georgians worldwide live in Georgia proper, and in 1989 Georgians constituted approximately 70% of Georgia's republican total population of 5.4 million. Given that almost all Georgians reside in what they see as their homeland, it is not surprising that Georgians have the highest levels of language retention. Over 98% of all Georgians consider Georgian to be their native language, while only a third claim Russian as a second language. These data suggest a nation with close and continued affinity to its homeland and language.[11]

Ajaria and the Ajars

The region known as Ajaria is located in the south-western part of Georgia. Its western border is the coastline of the Black Sea, to the south is Turkey, and to the east and north lies the rest of Georgia proper. The jurisdiction of Ajaria passed from the Ottoman to the Russian Empire to Turkey to Georgia, then finally to the Soviet Union. Ajaria's importance as a region can be traced to the latter part of the nineteenth century when Russia developed the capital Batumi, which became the third largest city in the province of Transcaucasia. As an important strategic and economic port and industrial centre, Batumi provided international rail and sea access, and oil pipelines were later constructed to Baku (Akiner, 1986: 243). In 1922 Ajaria became an ASSR subordinate to the Republic of Transcaucasia. In 1936 it was subordinated to Georgia, when Georgia achieved full Union Republic status separate from Armenia and Azerbaijan. The Ajarian ASSR was an anomalous entity of the USSR.

Whereas most of the autonomous entities were established on the basis of language or nationality, Ajaria was afforded autonomous status on the basis of religion.[12]

As mentioned above, the Ajars of Georgia were not considered a national minority for most of the Soviet period. Rather Ajars are considered to be ethnic Georgians, although they profess Islam as their faith. Conversion to Islam occurred during Ottoman rule from the sixteenth to the late nineteenth century. Ajars remain committed to Islam and there are few interfaith – Islamic–Christian – marriages (Bennigsen and Wimbush, 1986: 208). In the 1926 census, the Ajars were provided with their own national category, which distinguished them from the Georgians. This category was dissolved for the 1939 census, despite the fact that some continued to identify themselves as distinct from Georgians more broadly.[13] During this early Soviet period, Islam in Ajaria was severely repressed with mosques and religious schools closed and Islamic names georgianized. Derlugian called it 'a time of calamitous ethnic homogenization' that, for the most part, seemed to have succeeded (Derlugian, 1995: 33–5). As a consequence of the georgianization policies most Ajars were assimilated and came to recognize themselves as Georgians.

Because the census category for Ajars ended in 1926, it is difficult to estimate the number of Ajars. The 1989 census indicates that the Ajar Republic contained a total population of 381,000. Of this population, 'Georgians' constituted 317,000. The number of Ajars, or Muslim Georgians, in this last figure has been estimated to be around 130,000–160,000, or 34–42% of the regional population (Bennigsen and Wimbush, 1986: 208). Consistent with the non-migratory patterns of other Georgians, the total number of Ajars living outside Ajaria is very small.[14] In terms of national histories the Ajar–Georgian relationship is complicated because most Ajars today see themselves as Georgian. Georgians, in contrast, are reluctant to accept Ajars as belonging to the wider 'Georgian' identity due to religious differences. For most Georgians, Georgian means being Christian. The Ajars are Muslim and are, therefore, not considered 'real' Georgians.

Abkhazia and the Abkhaz

Abkhazia is located between the greater Caucasus mountain range and the shore of the Black Sea. It is bounded by the Psou River in the north-west and the Inguri River in the south-east. It is located in the north-west corner of Georgia, with the regions of Svanetia and Mingrelia to the east and south-east, respectively; and it shares its northern border with Russia. Authority over Abkhazia was won by the Russian Empire in its conquest of the Caucasus which led to the decimation of the Abkhaz population. Nonetheless during the Bolshevik revolution, the Abkhaz managed to gain status as a Soviet Republic, a founding member of the Union, on an equal footing to Georgia – a status codified in Abkhazia's Constitution of 1925. Abkhazia's separate but equal administrative status was annulled in 1936 when Abkhazia was subordinated to Georgia as an ASSR. Abkhazia's main economic and material contribution to the Georgian economy was in the tourism industry and agriculture. Its location along the Black Sea and corresponding tropical climate made it one of the most visited tourist areas during the Soviet era. Agricultural production consisted primarily of citrus, tobacco, tea and wine.[15] The port of Sukhumi was also an important transit point for the international shipment of goods, and the railway that connected Georgia to Russia in the north traversed Abkhazia.

Throughout their shared history Georgians and Abkhaz have contested each other's claim to whose ancestors constitute Abkhazia's original inhabitants. During the 1950s, 1960s, and then again in the 1980s, scholarly debates among Georgian historians challenged Abkhaz claims of being indigenous to the territory, arguing that Abkhaz were 'recent' settlers who had displaced Georgians.[16] For their part, Abkhaz scholars regard Georgians as the 'newly-arrived, non-native population of Abkhazia', and Abkhaz intellectuals, academics and politicians have attempted to prove the primordial history of the Abkhaz in this region.[17]

Contrary to Ajars, Abkhaz are classified as a national minority in Georgia. They are recognized as ethnically and linguistically distinct from Georgians. According to the 1989 census, the total population of the Republic of Abkhazia was 525,000. Abkhaz totalled about 93,000, constituting 18% of the Abkhaz republic population, compared with the Georgians who constituted 46%.[18] Whereas the Abkhaz population increased 9.2% between 1979 and 1989, Georgians increased by 13.6% in the same period. Abkhaz were a mere 2% of the total population of Georgia.

It was in the seventeenth and eighteenth century that some Abkhaz and Gurians (whose descendants are the Ajars) converted to Islam. After the suppression of two rebellions against imperial Russia in 1866 and 1877, large portions – half of all Abkhaz, and all the Muslims – of the Abkhaz population were exiled or left for the Ottoman empire. As a result there are more Abkhaz living in Turkey and other parts of the Middle East, 100,000–150,000, than in Abkhazia proper.[19] Both Christianity and Islam are thus present among the Abkhaz, with neither commanding strict adherence.[20]

The Abkhaz speak a different language than Georgians. Abkhaz is part of the North-West Caucasian branch, and had the status of a literary language in the Soviet Union (resulting in the publication of books, journals and a newspaper) and is written in the Cyrillic script. As the Soviet regime rationalized the multitude of languages, Abkhaz was scripted into Latin. This changed after the subordination of the republic to Georgia, and from 1938 Abkhaz was scripted in Georgian. A 'rapid process of "georgianization"' followed, with Georgian replacing Abkhazian as the only language of Abkhazia (Bennigsen and Wimbush, 1986: 214). Although use of Abkhazian was restored in 1956, it remained a minor language (Akiner, 1986: 224–6).

According to the 1989 census, 94% of Abkhaz consider Abkhaz to be their primary language, and another 79% consider Russian their second language. This figure reveals the depth of the cultural schism between Abkhaz and Georgians. Only 3% of Abkhaz claim a language other than Russian as their second tongue.[21] Although this language divide might be interpreted as the result of hostility of Abkhaz to Georgians, such an interpretation would be wrong. The divide has more to do with the lack of interaction between the nations. Those 'Georgians' who lived in Abkhazia, some 45% of the population, did not speak Georgian but rather Mingrelian. According to one estimate almost 25% of Abkhaz and 44% of Georgians (in 1979) living in Abkhazia could not communicate with one another. The language divide was reinforced, if not fully explained, by the territorial distribution of populations. The language issue reveals a deep divide between these two ethnic groups as the attempt to impose Georgian on the Abkhaz entrenched resentments, in particular, at discrimination in favour of Georgian speakers in access to higher education, government offices and professions (Hewitt, 1995: 225).

South Ossetia and the Ossetians

Ossetians live in the central Caucasus region on both sides of the Caucasus mountain range. This geographically divided region was separated administratively in the Soviet period, with North Ossetia as part of Russia and South Ossetia incorporated into Georgia. South Ossetia has an external northern border with North Ossetia. Ossetians are descendants of the Alans and trace their presence in Georgia to the thirteenth century when they were driven south by the Mongols. Despite the fact that a majority of Ossetians are Eastern Orthodox Christians (though there is a small minority of Sunni Muslim Ossetians), they 'are not strangers to Islam' (Omrod, 1993: 462). This is due to their shared history and interaction with other Muslim groups in the region as well as their Sunni Muslim ethnic kin.

Ossete is considered the primary language of 98% of Ossetians, with 60% claiming Russian as their second language (Henze, 1991: 166).

Ossete is a North-East Iranian language and is divided into two dialects: Digor and Iron. Iron is the literary language and is spoken by the majority of Ossetians, almost exclusively among the Ossetians in South Ossetia. The language was scripted into Cyrillic in the nineteenth century, and later into Latin for a brief period. As with Abkhaz, it was scripted into Georgian from 1938 to 1954, but later reverted back to Cyrillic (Comrie, 1981: 159–64). As with the Abkhaz language the imposition of Georgian was perceived as Georgian cultural hegemonism. According to the 1989 census there were about 164,000 Ossetians living in Georgia. The majority of Ossetians therefore do not reside in South Ossetia, but in districts bordering the South Ossetia Oblast' (Birch, 1995: 50). Within South Ossetia proper there were 65,000 Ossetians. They constituted two-thirds of South Ossetia's population of 98,000, with Georgians making up most of the remaining population.

The South Ossetian Autonomous Oblast' was formed in 1922 within the Republic of Transcaucasia. In 1925 North Ossetia (then an Autonomous Oblast' of Russia) and South Ossetia tried to unite (and join Russia), but were unsuccessful. This campaign was only one manifestation of the region's hostility to Georgian rule and show of loyalty to Moscow. During the Soviet period, Ossetia was considered to be one of the most Sovietized and pro-Russian regions of the FSU (Birch, 1995: 43–4). As with Abkhazia and Ajaria, South Ossetia was subordinated directly to Georgia when Georgia became a full Union Republic, separate from Armenia and Azerbaijan. As it was attributed the reduced status of an Autonomous Oblast in the Soviet Union, South Ossetia had a less institutionalized and weaker level of autonomy than did Abkhazia and Ajaria.

NATION-BUILDING, STATE-BUILDING, AND GEORGIA'S FAILED DEMOCRATIC TRANSITION

Georgia had to deal with political structures and institutions inherited from the Soviet Union: three autonomous entities that were established on the basis of recognizing a particular nationality.[22] This status privileged the titular nations of these autonomies and thus gave them institutional resources as well as legitimacy as nations (Roeder, 1991: 196–232, Treisman, 1997: 212–49). In Abkhazia, for example, the parliament passed its own legislation, subject to confirmation by the Georgian parliament. Additionally, given the procedures for electing republican officials, these officials had to be handled as legitimate representatives of at least part of the state's population. In negotiations with Vladislav Ardzinba, Chairman of the Abkhaz Supreme Soviet, over Abkhazia's status, Eduard Shevardnadze, himself in office following the coup that displaced the democratically-elected Zviad Gamsakhurdia, acknowledged the legitimacy of Ardzinba as the head of Abkhazia's Supreme Soviet and the fact that he represented the population of that republic.[23] Nonetheless, Shevardnadze remained committed to the idea that Abkhazia was an integral part of Georgia.

Could Gamsakhurdia or Shevardnadze have crafted the political situation in a way that would have dampened secessionist tendencies? Probably not, because tensions among the different groups had already reached breaking point. In every decade during the Soviet period, nationalist challenges were evident. In the 1930s and 1940s, language scripting and educational concerns increased friction, while historical challenges over who settled first in Abkhazia surfaced in the 1950s, 1960s and then again in the 1980s. From the national minorities' perspectives, the trappings of the formal and informal institutions of the republic seemed to favour the majority Georgians. Post-Soviet conflicts in Georgia thus arose from the perceptions of minorities that the newly independent Georgia would strengthen the Soviet era practices of privileging 'Georgians' at the expense of other ethnic groups, including by institutional means. The sentiments carried over from the Soviet period as most of Georgia's national minorities perceived Georgia as a realm of institutionalized Georgian ethnic privilege, where politicians in the centre sought to define an exclusivist conception of national identity which constantly reinforced a sense of 'a Georgia for Georgians'. In this light, Gamsakhurdia can be seen as a manifestation of processes and perceptions that were already in evidence.

Tensions among the national minorities, especially the Abkhaz, were apparent well before the era of perestroika and free elections. 1978 marked an important low point when the government of Georgia failed to revise Georgia's constitution. In a move to reduce tensions, the government sought the removal of a clause that guaranteed Georgian as the only official language of the republic. Mass demonstrations of Georgians objected to this measure and forced Shevardnadze, who was then First Party Secretary of the Georgian Communist Party (1972–85), to back down and retain the clause. Non-Georgians interpreted this capitulation ominously: it was widely viewed as a retreat in the face of nationalism and as evidence of a further increase in Georgian national chauvinism. This same incident played into majority Georgian fears of encirclement by minorities, whose patron and protector was assumed to be Moscow. This 1978 Constitutional debacle incited Abkhaz elites to seek Moscow's protection. Letters expressing grievances and concerns included a request that Abkhazia be removed from Georgia's jurisdiction and subjugated directly to the Russian Republic.[24] Moscow did not support Abkhazia's secession but did get Georgia to adopt a plan for bettering the economic and cultural conditions in Abkahzia.

Similarly, South Ossetia demanded unification with North Ossetia to form a single polity within Russia, effectively seceding from Georgia in 1989. The 1989 demand was rejected and violent clashes erupted between local Georgians (who feared unification with Russia) and Ossetians. The Georgian Supreme Soviet quickly rejected the South Ossetian 'declaration of sovereignty' and unilaterally abolished its autonomous status altogether. A state of emergency was declared: demonstrations were banned, newspapers were suppressed, and Georgian was declared the official language. Ossetians countered by declaring their language the official language of the *oblast*. Both examples of attempted de-institutionalization of the Soviet legacy – revocation of South Ossetia's autonomy status and language usage – seriously exacerbated relations between Georgia and South Ossetia.

On 28 October 1990 parliamentary elections were held in Georgia. Six Georgian nationalist blocs competed in the elections against the Communists. With 68% of the electorate participating (Abkhaz and Ossetian party candidates were prohibited from running), Gamsakhurdia's Round Table-Free Georgia bloc emerged victorious garnering 155 of 250 seats. The Communists finished second with 64 seats. Gamsakhurdia was elected chairman of the Supreme Soviet and he formed the first non-communist government from his Round Table/Free Georgia coalition with Tengiz Sigua as prime minister. Gamsakhurdia's ascendance in politics unnerved the national minorities. His dissident writings often invoked the idea of an imperilled Georgian nation, the destruction of its land, language and culture. He blamed both Moscow and the minorities. So his cry of 'Georgia for the Georgians' was interpreted as a battle cry for the suppression of minorities (Slider, 1997: 170–71). Gamsakhurdia had been elected on a platform that called for an independent Georgia, with a free market economy, a multiparty system and a legal system that protected the rights of all citizens. It also supported the strengthening of the rights of Georgians, restricted immigration and protection of the Georgian language. This part of the platform was common to all the parties competing in the elections (Jones, 1993: 297). What was not common was that Gamsakhurdia added his messianic message of not only a Georgia for Georgians, but a Georgia for Christian Georgians.[25] And it was not just rhetoric. The autonomous status of South Ossetia had already been abolished in December, and the status of Ajaria was also threatened. Gamsakhurdia justified the abolition policy by declaring that the Ossetians had the right to self-determination only in those lands that constituted the homeland of the Ossetian nation, namely in North Ossetia. South Ossetia, like Abkhazia and Ajaria, was Georgian land, Georgian homeland.

Thus, by the time the first democratic elections came in 1990, national divisions were sufficiently hardened. Electoral laws provide a case in point. Article 8 of the laws governing the election required all parties registered to have country-wide reach. Because national minorities in Georgia supported parties with limited regional reach they were threatened with being disenfranchised from the political process. To make matters worse, the one party which seemed to support the rights of the minorities, the Communist Party, added a clause in its platform which affirmed its commitment to Georgia's territorial integrity. The only way minorities could 'voice' their views was by boycotting the elections. Within a week the Supreme Soviet of Abkhazia declared itself a sovereign Soviet Socialist Republic. This declaration was overturned by the Georgian Supreme Soviet shortly thereafter.[26]

As with South Ossetia, Abkhazia's fate was partly tied to the inherited structures of the Soviet Union. Because Abkhazia was subordinate to Georgia during the Soviet period, the Georgians claimed that it should remain subordinate. Yet, Abkhazia's situation was a bit different than South Ossetia in that there was also an institutionalized precedent for its independence from Georgia, as codified in its 1925 constitution. Depending on the date, both sides' claims regarding Abkhazia's had clear institutional parameters that seemed equally legitimate and compromised as Georgia sought to shake off Soviet institutions.

From the very outset of Georgia's transition and through its first election, Tbilisi faced multiple ethnic and regional challenges. Although Georgians were two-thirds of the population, one-third was not. These groups perceived a Georgian state as a vital threat to their own ethno-national interests. From the Georgian perspective, these minorities were also perceived as a threat. Not only did they inhabit borderland areas that abutted Russia, but they directly appealed to Moscow for help and to be subordinated to the Russian Federation. Just as the minorities feared continuation of a perceived Georgian imperialism, so too did Georgians fear Russia's imperialism and seeming support for Georgia's minorities, especially Abkhazia.

Ajaria, the other autonomous region in Georgia remained peaceful, despite concerns that it too would succumb to violence and war. In the case of Ajaria, calls for greater autonomy were at first met with much resistance from Tbilisi. Whereas the fact of autonomy was not questioned for Abkhazia, just the degree of autonomy, in the case of Ajaria proposals were advanced in Tbilisi for abolishing Ajaria's autonomy altogether

(Fuller, 1990: 13–14). The chief proponent of abolishing Ajaria's autonomy was Gamsakhurdia himself.

Even under perestroika Ajars feared that as Georgia moved towards greater independence it was also moving towards a more exclusivist conception of what it meant to be a Georgian. Furthermore, the status of the Ajar Republic was directly and publicly threatened. During the 1990 Supreme Soviet elections, Gamsakhurdia's Round Table garnered only 24% of the vote, while the Communist Party came in first with 56% of the vote. The result was the reverse of the overall Georgian election outcome which gave 62% to the Round Table and 26% to the Communists. These election results soundly defeated Gamsakhurdia's view that Ajaria's autonomous status should be dissolved. Following these elections, Gamsakhurdia retreated. Abolishing Ajaria's autonomy would now have to be a local initiative.[27]

During the most tense period of confrontations between Ajaria and Tbilisi, Ajaria was accused of separatism. Yet the evidence indicates that Ajaria did not seek independence. The conflict centred on whether Ajaria would remain an autonomous republic (Fuller, 1990: 14). Despite Gamsakhurdia's rhetoric, therefore, the issue was one of territorial autonomy rather than ethno-religious difference. What accounts for this conflict and its resolution? The initial tension between Tbilisi and Batumi arose from the nature of Georgian nationalizing policies which emphasized a Georgianness that was tied explicitly to Christianity. Because the Ajars were Muslim, they were seen as falling outside this conception of national identity and, therefore, a threat to the unity and the legitimacy of the newly independent state. From the Ajar point of view, however, the religious distinction carried relatively little significance: Ajars considered themselves Georgians and their homeland of Ajaria was seen as an integral part of Georgia. The leader of Ajaria, Aslan Abashidze, frequently made his commitment to maintain Georgia's territorial integrity quite clear: 'Our republic is an administrative unit where members of various nationalities live, but all are citizens of Ajaria, and that means of Georgia as well. We have never had, and never will have, any territorial claims against Georgia ... Ajaria is historically a part of Georgia, and there has never been an instance in history in which Ajaria has created problems for its motherland' (*Nezavisimaia gazeta*, 27 June 1992: 3).

Rather than point to religious differences, Abashidze stressed the importance of advancing economic interests of the republic. Evidence of this can be found in the slogan adopted by his political party, Ajarian Revival: 'Wealthy people mean a wealthy state', which he extended during an interview to 'a wealthy state is a strong state' (ibid.). Although there was resentment in Batumi over the dominance of 'Christianity' in Georgia, the conflict hinged on an institutional issue, namely the region's autonomous status. Separatism was extremely limited, if not non-existent. In 1989 for example, the then Chairman of the Ajar ASSR Council of Ministers, Guram Chigogidsze, in a speech to the Georgian Supreme Soviet warned of the existence of a separatist organization in Ajaria. Yet he stated that at most it consisted of six persons and did not represent the views of the population at large. Similarly, the head of the Ajar Branch of the Georgian Writer's Union, Pridon Khalvashi, wrote that 'no separatist inclinations of any kind exist in Ajaria' (Fuller, 1990: 14).

Two key differences between the conflict with Ajaria and those with Abkhazia and Ossetia stand out. First, Ajaria remained loyal to Tbilisi's stated aim of maintaining the integrity of the Georgian state. At no time did it advance a claim or support secessionist claims by others. The reason for this is that although there was a religious difference and the nationalizing-Christian-Georgian state was seen as a threat, Ajars imagined themselves and their homeland as an integral part of Georgia. Protecting Georgia's integrity meant protecting Ajar integrity.

Second, the struggle between Ajaria and Tbilisi over time revealed to Tbilisi and Christian Georgians that unlike the Abkhaz, the Ajars had not in fact advanced its demands for more autonomy as a first step towards secession. The political goal for Ajaria was to protect its institutionalized regional status. Ethnicity, and in this case religion, did manifest itself, but the conflict was largely regional in nature, not ethnic. Over time, Tbilisi came to see the Ajars as the Ajars saw themselves: loyal Georgians who demanded nothing more than the re-institutionalization of their autonomous status. Exit was not pursued at any time, simply voice. In the case of the Abkhaz–Georgian relationship, neither Georgians, nor Abkhaz would deny that the Abkhaz are a distinct nation with a distinct language and culture which can trace its origins to lands in and around contemporary Georgia. Where disagreement lies is in the fate of Abkhazia, the territory. Both see this territory as constituting their homeland. This goes a long way to explain why the question of who settled first – whether an Abkhaz or Georgian – has remained such a volatile issue, before and during the transition. The dynamics of the conflict with Ossetia were similar with the exception that Georgia refused to acknowledge that the territory of South Ossetia was Ossetian homeland. Rather the Ossetians were viewed as interlopers whose true homeland was in the north. In these two cases, exit from Georgia was the preferred course of action, even if it meant subordination to Moscow.

CONCLUSION

As the Soviet Union dissolved, ethnic and regional conflicts in Georgia were intensified by nationalizing policies pursued by the centre which involved the de-institutionalization of Soviet institutionalized autonomies and brought to the fore ethnic and regional grievances. Both the Georgians and the Abkhaz viewed Abkhazia as rightfully belonging to them. In the case of South Ossetia, the Georgians viewed them as recent immigrants at best and invaders at worst. While it is difficult to disentangle nationalist from statist motivations in the struggle to prevent the secessions, it is clear that in South Ossetia, Georgian nationalism had been mobilized around the negative aim of maintaining the territorial integrity of Georgia against a perceived threat of Russian neo-imperialism. Because Abkhaz and South Ossetian separatists had come to be seen as agents of Russia, a secession would be simultaneously a reduction in state power, and a diminishing of Georgians' pride and national identity. With the collapse of the Soviet Union the Ajars advanced only moderate demands, seeking to sustain their administrative status first and economic concessions second. Given its own fight for independence, however, Tbilisi at first not only resisted such claims, but threatened to deprive Ajaria of its pre-existing rights and freedoms.

Georgia's interests vis-à-vis Moscow were simple survival: survival as a state with its pre-1991 boundaries intact. Georgia's leaders – Gamsakhurdia and Shevardnadze, each understood the Russian threat in a different way. Gamsakhurdia's response to the threat was to stimulate an aggressive Georgian nationalism. Shevardnadze's response was to negotiate with Russia, while attempting to capture Sukhumi and militarily crush the Abkhaz secession in a surprise fait accompli attack – perhaps hoping to remove any pretext for Russian intervention. This was a terrible miscalculation as Russia began actively arming and supporting the Abkhaz. Shevardnadze appealed to the United Nations, to no avail, and eventually was compelled to return to negotiations with Russia to resolve the conflict. During one of his weekly interviews, Shevardnadze put it in the following stark terms: 'Of course I think of the ideals of mankind because the implementation of these ideals depends significantly on Russia. But I also think of my motherland, my little country, first of all. Because, if democracy fails to win there, Georgia will be drowned in blood. It will find itself in an even deeper pool of blood.'[28] A month later he explicitly linked Georgia's survival with cooperation with Russia, 'We have to cooperate with Russia... otherwise Georgia will collapse and disintegrate.'[29] Despite Georgia's attempt to be independent of Moscow, Georgia was forced to work with Russia to stop the war raging in Abkhazia.

Georgia dealt harshly with Abkhazia and South Ossetia for three reasons. First, Georgian nationalism had been attached to the notion of a Georgian state free of patronizing Russian domination. Ardzinba made no secret of Abkhazia's desire to integrate with Russia, and this made it easy for Georgians to view Abkhaz resistance as a smokescreen for Russian neo-imperialism. In short, the loss of Abkhazia would have seriously diminished Georgian national identity. Second, Georgia felt threatened by Russian meddling in its affairs, and feared the loss of territory, however small its autonomies. Third, to have allowed the secessions would have set a bad precedent in multi-ethnic Georgia. If Georgia had allowed Abkhazia to join Russia or achieve independence, then it would have been very difficult for it to deny the same to South Ossetia.

In contrast to Abkhazia and South Ossetia, Georgia dealt leniently with Ajaria. The reason is that Ajaria did not make claims that threatened either the territorial integrity or national identity of Georgia. Initially, the non-threatening nature of these demands was drowned out by political struggles in Tbilisi. Once the idea of abolishing Ajaria's republican status had been defeated and the support of Ajaria for Georgia's national and state aims vis-à-vis South Ossetia and Abkhazia became obvious, Tbilisi was prepared to more readily accept Ajaria's autonomous status. In this essay we have been dealing with two cases of ethnic conflict and one case of regionalism within the multinational setting of Georgia. The conflicts in Abkhazia and South Ossetia are no longer violent for the most part, but they are far from being resolved. Tensions continue between Ajaria and Tbilisi, but these tensions do not revolve around issues of identity; rather, they are economic and regional in nature, and consequently more amenable to negotiation and compromise.

Ethno-regional division continues to be Georgia's most serious obstacle to state-building. These divisions make it extremely difficult to build the institutions necessary to stabilize the state and make it capable of supporting institutional and economic reforms. Moreover, until Russia can define a positive national identity independent of its historical tendency towards imperialism, the cascading insecurities which afflict Georgia's national minorities will continue to inhibit institutional solutions to Georgia's transition problems. Russia seems to have no interest in helping to permanently resolve the conflicts in Abkhazia and South Ossetia. Russian peacekeeping troops remain in Abkhazia and South Ossetia, while Russian-led negotiations on the repatriation of 250,000 refugees from Abkhazia (mostly Georgians) are stalled. Abkhazia and South Ossetia remain outside Georgia's control, having achieved de facto independence. Unless the minorities accept some degree of Georgian sovereignty over their regional territories and Moscow stops meddling in Georgian affairs, Georgia will continue to exist in a precarious and unstable transition.

NOTES

1. The capital of Georgia is Tbilisi; the other capitals are Sukhumi (Abkhazia), Batumi (Ajaria), and Ts'khinvali (South Ossetia).
2. According to this thesis, ethnic homogeneity is a prerequisite of democratic state building. This thesis can be traced back to John Stuart Mill, who claimed that 'Free institutions are next to impossible in a country made up of different nationalities.' Although contemporary scholars agree that national unity and consensus are important to the formation of democracy, most tend to ignore problems of national disunity or assume them away in the belief that with the proper institutional engineering, divisions in a society can be overcome. For the Mill quote, see John Stuart Mill (1869), p.310.
3. Linz and Stepan, p.25.
4. A contrary argument is offered by Raymond Basch who contends that heterogeneity might be a fundamental and positive causal factor of democratization. He compares three cases: Belarus, Moldova and Ukraine. These cases do not however substantiate his claims. The most diverse – or in his terminology ethnically separated – country, Moldova, underwent the most traumatic and violent transition. See Raymond M. Basch, pp.221–42.
5. In Burundi for example, during transition from colonial rule, a minority group of Tutsis promulgated a nationalist vision for the state of Burundi, that excluded and subsequently antagonized the majority Hutus.
6. Although the official rate of Georgia's national income grew at the third lowest rate in the USSR from 1960–1971, in 1970, Georgians had savings accounts nearly double those of average Soviet citizens (Suny, 1980: 213).
7. These lands had not been united under a single political authority since the fifteenth century. Eastern Georgia (Kartli and Kakheti) was absorbed into the Russian Empire in 1801, Mingrelia in 1803, Imeretia in 1804, and Abkhazia in 1810. See John F.R. Wright (1995), p.136.
8. Only the Union Republics were granted the right to secede as affirmed by article 80 of the Soviet Constitution.
9. In addition to this law, a related law – 'The Law on the Procedures for Resolving Questions Related to the Secession of Union Republics from the USSR' – was adopted (seemingly and hastily in response to the Baltic Republics' moves towards independence). This law was signed by Gorbachev on 3 April 1990. Article 3 stipulated: 'The peoples of autonomous republics and autonomous formations shall retain the right to decide independently the question of staying in the USSR or in the seceding Union republic, as well as to raise the question of their own legal state status.' For a discussion of the debates surrounding the adoption of this law see *Izvestiya*, 21 and 22 March, and 4 and 5 April 1990.
10. There is little evidence to support that members of these groups do not identify as Georgian. (I have not been able to determine precise numbers of Mingrelians, Svans and Kvartelians in these regions.) However, linguistic differences continue to influence the play of politics. This is due to language use and homelands. Many 'Georgians' living in Abkhazia spoke Mingrelian or Svanetian, and not the more dominant Kartvelian. Abkhaz nationals therefore had relatively little interaction with the official Georgian language, 'Kartvelian'. Furthermore, the homelands of Svanetia and Mingrelia are contiguous to Abkhazia. Svanetia is located long the southern slopes of the Caucasus range in western Georgia and shares its northern border with Russia, while Mingrelia is to south. Both share western borders with Abkhazia. Keeping these considerations in mind, I nevertheless refer to the Kartvelians, Mingrelians and Svans as Georgians, unless indicated otherwise.
11. *Narodnoe khoziaistvo SSSR v 1990 g. statisticheskiiezhegodnik* (1991), p.77.
12. The only other one was Birobidzhan, the designated 'Jewish' homeland.

13. A census was also conducted in 1937. A category of Ajar was included. There were a total of 88,230 Ajars in the Soviet Union, and of these 88,217 lived in the Georgian Republic. This census was not officially published or publicly available. The official reason provided was that it was statistically flawed in its underestimation of the total number of the population than was expected. See *Vsesoiuznaia perepis' naselniia 1937g.* (1991), pp.83 and 95. For a discussion of the 1937 Soviet census see Lee Schwartz (1986), pp.48–69.

14. Also recall from above the fact that over 90% of all Georgians worldwide and 95% of FSU Georgians live in Georgia. Data on the Ajars from personal correspondence with Zaal Anjaparidze of the Caucasian Institute for Peace, Democracy and Development, Tbilisi, Georgia, (CIPDD).

15. See *Narodnoe Khoziaistvo Gruzinskoi SSR za 60 let* (1980), pp.82, 125–6.

16. What is striking is that the Georgian historians have accepted that the Abkhaz have been in Abkhazia for at least 300–500 years, while the Abkhaz claim at least a 2000-year history. For frank discussions of these issues, see B.G. Hewitt (1996), pp.190–225.

17. cf. Zurab Papaskiri, 'Some Reflections on the Past of Abkhazia and Georgian-Abkhazian Relations', *Demokraticheskaia Abkhaziia*, 30 September 1989; as cited in Svetlana Chervonnaya (1994), p.2, fn.7. Also see Gueorgi Otyrba (1994), p.282.

18. Armenians constituted 15%, Russians 14%, Greeks 3%, and Ukrainians 2%.

19. According to one estimate there are some 250 Abkhaz-Abaza villages throughout Turkey and a rough estimate of 100,000–150,000 in Turkish cities and towns. There may be an additional 5,000 Abkhaz living in Syria, and a small number in Jordan and Iraq. Those Abkhaz (and Cherkess and Adyges) living abroad identify themselves as Circassians, however, and not Abkhaz. Data from personal correspondence with Zaal Anjaparidze of CIPDD, Tbilisi, Georgia, and Alexandre Bennigsen and S. Enders Wimbush (1986), p.213.

20. Official Kremlin International News Broadcast, 28 August 1992.

21. According to the 1989 Soviet Census. Data taken from *Narodnoe Khoziaistvo SSSR v 1990 g. Statisticheskiiezhegodnik* (1991), p.79.

22. For a discussion of the relationship between nationalism, democracy, and federalism see Juan J. Linz (1997).

23. Ardzinba was a member of the CPSU since 1967, and from 1988 he was a deputy in the Supreme Soviet of the USSR and chairman of the Commission for Autonomous Entities. He was elected on the basis of his position in the Communist Party, and as a legislator who sought to protect the rights of minorities more generally. He was a vocal advocate of the Abkhaz nation, but at a time and in a context in which such advocacy had little political impact. Ardzinba was also a Doctor of History, specializing in the history and culture of the peoples of the Ancient Orient and Asia Minor. He lived in Moscow until 1988, where he was with the Institute of Oriental Studies. In 1989 he became the director of the Abkhazian Gulia Institute of Language, Literature and History.

24. The actual degree of discrimination and equitable access in Abkhazia is unclear. According to Communist Party rolls in Abkhazia, Georgians constituted 51% of party membership, but only 44% of the population. Yet, according to another source, the Abkhaz constituted only 17% of the population, but occupied some 40% of the cadre positions. For the party figures see Darrell Slider (1985), p.53. For the cadre positions see *Pravda*, 21 September 1989, p.4. In terms of deputies to the Georgian Supreme Soviet and the contingent from the Republic of Georgia to the USSR Supreme Soviet, ethnic Georgians were 80% of the former and 66% of the latter. The Abkhaz were 8% of the former and 3% of the latter. Thus, the Abkhaz did seem to have less representation in the institutions at the republican level than at the all-Union level (although above the level of total Abkhaz population in Georgia of just under 2%). See *Narodnoe Khoziaistvo Gruzinskoi SSR za 60 let* (1980), p.31.

25. Shireen Hunter points out that as soon as the 'Georgians' were offered a chance to debate the nature of their political system, the idea of a 'theo-democracy', or 'a Christian state ruled on democratic but not secular principles' was advanced. Gamsakhurdia should be noted as important advocate of an independent Christian Georgia. He envisioned Georgia's spiritual role as meditating between East and West, Islam and Christianity. See Shireen Hunter (1994), p.112. Also see Jonathan Aves (1992), p.159.

26. On 25 August 1990, the parliament of the Abkhaz Autonomous SSR adopted a resolution on

'The Conception of the Abkhaz Autonomous SSR under the Conditions of Self-Management, Self-Financing and the Changeover to a Regulated Market'. It also approved a document entitled 'On Legal Guarantees to Protect Abkhazia's Statehood' and a declaration 'On Abkhazia's State Sovereignty'. The deputies of Georgian nationality refused to participate in the session. See *Pravda*, 26 August 1990, p.1.
27. Although he modified his position somewhat, Gamsakhurdia did not acknowledge publicly that his statement on the abolition of the republic caused the weak support for his Round Table-Free Georgia Coalition. Rather, he blamed it on subversive imperialist agents operating in the republic. See Ronald G. Suny (1994), p.400, fn.26 and Elizabeth Fuller (1990), p.14.
28. Georgian radio, Tbilisi, 4 October 1993. Transcript provided by British Broadcast Corporation, 6 October 1993.
29. As quoted in Dov Lynch (1998), p.28.

REFERENCES

Akiner, Shirin (1986), *Islamic Peoples of the Soviet Union*. London: KPI (rev. ed.).

Aves, Jonathan (1992), 'The Rise and Fall of the Georgian Nationalist Movements 1987–1991', in Geoffrey Hosking *et al.* (eds), *The Road to Post-Communism: Independent Political Movements in the Former Soviet Union 1985–1991*. New York: Pinter Press, pp.29–66.

Basch, Raymond M. (1998), 'The Effects of Ethnic Separation on Democratization: A Comparative Study', *East European Quarterly*, Vol.33, No.2, pp.221–42.

Bennigsen, Alexandre and S. Enders Wimbush (1986), *Muslims of the Soviet Empire*. Bloomington: Indiana University Press.

Birch, Julian (1995), 'Ossetia: A Caucasian Bosnia in Microcosm', *Central Asian Survey*, Vol.14, No.1, pp.43–74.

Brubaker, Rogers (1996), *Nationalism Reframed*. Cambridge: Cambridge University Press.

Chervonnaya, Svetlana (1994), *Conflict in the Caucasus: Georgia, Armenia and the Russian Shadow*, transl. Ariane Chanturia. Glastonbury: Gothic Images Publications.

Comrie, Bernard (1981), *The Languages of the Soviet Union*. Cambridge: Cambridge University Press.

Derlugian, Georgi M. (1995), 'The Tale of Two Resorts: Abkhazia and Ajaria Before and Since the Soviet Collapse', Working Paper 6, University of California: Center for German and European Studies.

Dunlop, John (1993), 'Russia: Confronting a Loss of Empire', in Ian Bremmer and Ray Taras (eds), *Nations and Politics in Soviet Successor States*. Cambridge: Cambridge University Press, pp.43–72.

Emizet, Kisangani N. and Vicki L. Hesli (1995), 'The Disposition to Secede: An Analysis of the Soviet Case', *Comparative Political Studies*, Vol.27, No.4, pp.493–536.

Fuller, Elizabeth (1990), 'Zviad Gamsakhurdia Proposes Abolition of Adzhar Autonomy', *Report on the USSR*, Vol.2, No.48, pp.13–14.

Fuller, Elizabeth (1991), 'Georgia's Adzhar Crisis', *Report on the USSR*, Vol.3, No.32, pp.8–13.

Gellner, Ernest (1983), *Nations and Nationalism*. Ithaca: Cornell University Press.

Henze, Paul B. (1991), 'The Demography of the Caucasus according to the 1989 Soviet Census Data', *Central Asian Survey*, Vol.10, No.1–2, pp.147–70.

Hewitt, B. G. (1996), 'Abkhazia: A Problem of Identity and Ownership', in John F.R. Wright *et al.* (eds), *Transcaucasian Boundaries*. New York: St. Martin's Press, pp.190–225.

Hunter, Shirin (1994), *The Transcaucasus in Transition*. Washington, D.C.: The Center for Strategic and International Studies.

Jones, Stephen F. (1993), 'Georgia: A Failed Democratic Transition', in Ian Bremmer and Ray Taras (eds), *Nations and Politics in Soviet Successor States*. Cambridge: Cambridge University Press, pp.288–310.

Linz, Juan J. and Alfred Stepan (1996), *Problems of Democratic Transition and Consolidation*. Baltimore: Johns Hopkins University Press.

Linz, Juan J. (1997), 'Democracy, Multinationalism and Federalism', Estudio Working Paper, 1997/103.

Lynch, Dov (1998), 'The Conflict in Abkhazia: Dilemmas in Russian "Peacekeeping" Policy', Discussion Paper 77. London: The Royal Institute of International Affairs.

Mann, Michael (1988), War and Capitalism, Oxford: Oxford University Press.

Mill, John Stuart (1869), Considerations on Representative Government. New York: Harper and Brothers, Publishers.

Narodnoe Khozyaistvo Gruzinskoi SSR za 60 let (1980). Tbilisi: Izdatel'stvo Sabchota Sakartvelo.

Narodnoe Khozyaistvo SSSR v 1990g. Statisticheskii ezhegodnik (1991). Moscow: Goskomstat.

Nezavisimaya gazeta, 27 June 1992.

Omrod, Jane (1993), 'North Caucasus: Fragmentation or Federation', in Ian Bremmer and Ray Taras (eds), Nations and Politics in Soviet Successor States. Cambridge: Cambridge University Press, pp.448–76.

Otyrba, Georgi (1994), 'War in Abkhazia', in Roman Sporluk (ed.), National Identity and Ethnicity in Russia and the New States of Eurasia. Armonk, NY: M.E. Sharpe, pp.281–309.

Pipes, Richard (1997), The Formation of the Soviet Union. Cambridge, MA: Harvard University Press (repr. ed.).

Pravda, 21 September 1989.

Pravda, 26 August 1990.

Roeder, Philip (1991), 'Soviet Federalism and Ethnic Mobilization', World Politics, Vol.43, No.2, pp.196–232.

Schwartz, Lee (1986), 'A History of the Russian and Soviet Censuses', in Ralph S. Clem (ed.), Research Guide to the Russian and Soviet Censuses. Ithaca: Cornell University Press, pp.48–69.

Slider, Darrell (1985), 'Crisis and Response in Soviet Nationality Policy: The Case of Abkhazia', Central Asian Survey, Vol.4, No.4, pp.51–68.

Slider, Darrell (1997), 'Democratization in Georgia', in Karen Dawisha and Bruce Parrott (eds.), Conflict, Cleavage, and Change in Central Asia and the Caucasus. Cambridge: Cambridge University Press, pp.158–98.

Suny, Ronald Grigor (1980), 'Georgia and Soviet Nationality Policy', in Stephen F. Cohen et al. (eds), The Soviet Union since Stalin. Bloomington: Indiana University Press, pp.200–226

Suny, Ronald Grigor (1994), The Making of the Georgian Nation. Bloomington, Indiana: Indiana University Press.

Treisman, Daniel S. (1997), 'Russia's Ethnic Revival: The Separatist Activism of Regional Leaders in a Postcommunist Order', World Politics, Vol.49, No.2, pp.212–49.

Volkan, Vamik D. (1990), 'Psychoanalytic Aspects of Ethnic Conflict', in Joseph V. Montville (ed.), Conflict and Peacemaking in Multiethnic Societies. Lexington, MA: Lexington Books, pp.81–92.

Vsesoiuznaia perepis' naseleniia 1937g. (1991). Moscow: Institut Istorii SSR.

Wright, John F.R. (1995), 'The Geopolitics of Georgia', in John F.R. Wright et al. (eds), Transcaucasian Boundaries. New York: St. Martin's Press, pp.134–50.

The Irony of Nagorno-Karabakh:
Formal Institutions versus Informal Politics

RAZMIK PANOSSIAN

For almost a decade now, the self-declared 'independent republic' of Nagorno-Karabakh (NK) has been engaged in a process of nation-state building in the context of post-Soviet transition. Karabakh is usually cited as a major instance of ethnic conflict within the crumbling Soviet Union, and the cause of war between Armenia and Azerbaijan. However, examined from the perspective of this volume, one can make the argument that Karabakh also serves as an example of a region which has been relatively successful in its transition to post-Soviet institution building and state-formation – at least in its formal institutional architecture. NK has given itself the status of a republic and acts as if independent, even though it is not recognized as such by any other country – even Armenia – or international agency. The micro-state of NK has a population of around 80,000 and an area of 4400 sq km.[1] It has the trappings of a market economy and democratic institutions, but it is far from being an 'open society' and is wholly dependent on Armenia economically.

In this essay, I will discuss the ambiguities relating to Nagorno-Karabakh's post-Soviet transition. The Karabakh case study is a good test case for a multi-dimensional analysis of a new entity that has emerged from the collapse of the Soviet Union. The war over the enclave, and its consequences, have had crucial and detrimental knock-on effects on both the Armenian and Azerbaijani transitions. The Karabakh 'problem' is simultaneously an ethno-nationalist conflict, a regional issue, and an attempt at state-building. The conflict over NK also has a very strong international dimension, being a cause of inter-state war. Finally, NK's status is a major unresolved legal problem in the OSCE area. The region of NK (formerly an autonomous *oblast'* in Azerbaijan) has formally become a *de facto* micro-state with an institutionalized statehood as a result of ethnic conflict. Informally, however, it functions as a dependent region of Armenia. At the same time, the regional elites of Karabakh have come to control key elements of the national political agenda of Armenia, 'taking over' the national centre.

In the study that follows, the first part provides an historical overview of the NK issue, and the second part analyses NK along four dimensions: (a) as a region of Azerbaijan, (b) as an 'independent' state, (c) as an informal 'region' of Armenia, and (d) as an ambiguous international entity caught between conflicting legal principles. The conclusion addresses some of the conceptual issues emanating from the case study of Karabakh.

THE ROLE OF HISTORY

There is a substantial body of literature on the historical and political dimension of the Karabakh conflict.[2] Administratively, NK had never been part of Armenia in modern history. Under the Tsarist empire it had been part of Baku province. The enclave was fought over by Armenia and Azerbaijan in the late 1910s and the early 1920s before the sovietization of the two republics. In 1923, it was formally declared an autonomous oblast' within the Azerbaijani SSR. Armenians never fully accepted this decision, and repeatedly questioned the enclave's status, demanding its transfer to the Armenian SSR in 1929, 1935, 1963, 1966, 1977, and 1987. The most notable of these political drives for reunification was in the early to the mid-1960s. The Armenian leadership cited anti-Armenian discrimination, economic underdevelopment, and demographic shifts to support its case (Ulubabian, 1994: 164–299). The Armenian population of the oblast' declined from 95 per cent in the early 1920s to 76 per cent in 1979 – that is, 123,000 out of a total of 161,000.[3]

The current conflict began on 20 February 1988 when the Soviet of NK, seizing the opportunity of greater openness under Gorbachev's glasnost' policy, passed a resolution asking for the transfer of the region to the Armenian SSR. On 13 June, the Supreme Soviet of Azerbaijan formally rejected the request, declaring NK's resolution null and void. Two days later, on 15 June, the Armenian Supreme Soviet, under tremendous popular pressure, passed a 'counter-resolution' giving its consent to the incorporation of NK into the Armenian SSR. A political impasse had been reached, and the onus fell on Moscow to 'settle' the conflict.

Moscow was resolutely against any type of border change throughout the USSR, and, in this case, refused to transfer the region to Armenia. Articles 73 and 78 of the 1977 USSR constitution stipulated that the consent of both republics was required to change borders, while the final approval came from the 'highest state bodies' – that is, the Supreme Soviet and the Congress of the People's Deputies in Moscow. On 18 July 1988, the USSR Supreme Soviet voted to keep the enclave within Azerbaijan. Due to civil disorder in NK, Moscow imposed direct rule on NK between January and November 1989, but the oblast' reverted to Azerbaijani jurisdiction by the decision of the USSR Supreme Soviet on 28 November 1989. In response, on 1 December 1989, the Armenian

Supreme Soviet declared the NK's unification with Armenia in a joint session with the Karabakh National Council. The Azerbaijani Supreme Soviet rejected this resolution as unconstitutional. Karabakh formally remained under Azerbaijan's jurisdiction until the disintegration of the Soviet Union in late 1991.

From the very beginning, the Armenian–Azerbaijani conflict degenerated into violence and ethnic-cleansing. In addition to armed skirmishes in and around NK, anti-Armenian pogroms took place in other parts of Azerbaijan, in Sumgait near Baku in February 1988, and in Baku in January 1990. Between 1988 and late 1991 Armenians in NK, and more generally in Azerbaijan, were attacked by Azeris. Almost the entire Armenian population of Baku (close to 220,000) was forced to flee, as were Armenians in other parts of Azerbaijan, except in parts of Karabakh where they resisted.[4] Simultaneously, the entire Azerbaijani population of Armenia (160,000) was intimidated to leave or forcibly expelled.[5] This mutual ethnic cleansing was the culmination of a decades-long process of homogenization in the two republics. As a result of these forced population transfers, a massive refugee problem emerged in both countries.

Until the dissolution of the USSR, the Soviet authorities sided, in general, with Azerbaijan. This was consistent with Moscow's policy of supporting the authorities in the capitals of the republics which had to deal with 'unruly' regions. Moscow's goal seemed to be the maintenance of existing institutional set-ups. Soviet troops sent to the conflict area to maintain order did prevent an all-out civil war, but often they either did not interfere, interfered too late, or, on numerous occasions, took the side of the Azerbaijani forces to 'punish' the Armenians for raising the NK issue. For example, Soviet and Azerbaijani forces attacked Armenians in August 1990 in the Noyemberian district, in Getashen, and in various other areas within NK. It was only after the collapse of the Soviet Union and the coming to power of Yeltsin in Russia that the balance began to shift in favour of the Armenians. Russian forces began to indirectly support the Armenian side of the conflict, supplying arms, fuel and logistical support. Russians were now 'punishing' the Azerbaijani side, under the leadership of Abulfaz Elchibey, for its extreme pro-Turkey and pro-Western policies.[6] Armenia was now viewed by Russia as its main strategic partner in the South Caucasus. Geopolitical calculations in relation to Turkey and Iran prompted Russia to support Armenia which, in turn, translated to military victories on the ground.

Between late 1991 and the spring of 1994 a full-scale but undeclared war was taking place between Azerbaijani and Armenian military units over Karabakh. In early 1992 Azerbaijani forces were in control of half of the territory of NK, and were expelling Armenian civilians. The spring of 1992 was the turning point, as an Armenian offensive began to push Azerbaijani forces out of the enclave. On 8 May 1992, the Azerbaijani stronghold of Shushi/Shusha in NK was captured by Armenian forces, followed ten days later by Lachin (the land corridor between NK and Armenia). By May 1994, when a Russian-brokered ceasefire was signed in the Kyrgyz capital Bishkek under the auspices of the CIS Parliamentary Assembly, Armenian forces had resoundingly defeated the Azeri army and controlled almost all of Nagorno-Karabakh, freeing the enclave from any kind of Azerbaijani rule or influence. In addition, the entire territory between Karabakh and Armenia (Kelbajar and Lachin), as well as areas in the east and south of NK (Aghdam and Fizuli to the border with Iran) were under Armenian control. In total, Azerbaijan lost about 15 per cent of its territory. As a result of the civil and military conflict, an estimated 25,000–30,000 people died on both sides.[7] Some 750,000 Azerbaijanis became internal refugees due to Armenian military advances.[8]

ONE CONFLICT – THREE ANALYTICAL APPROACHES

Karabakh's formal status as an 'independent' entity is quite ambiguous as far as international law and norms are concerned. Prior to the dissolution of the USSR, the constitutional position was quite clear – the Soviet constitution of 1977 allowed territorial changes only if the affected union republics and the USSR authorities agreed. After the failed August 1991 putsch in Moscow, as the Soviet Union began to quickly implode, Armenia and Azerbaijan declared their independence in August and September 1991. On 2 September 1991, four days after Azerbaijan's declaration of independence from the USSR, the Nagorno-Karabakh Oblast' Soviet declared its independence from Azerbaijan. The NK Soviet based its declaration on the USSR law on secession of April 1990 which stipulated that the secession of a union republic from the USSR gave an autonomous region within that republic the right to declare its own secession.[9] Although Soviet law was by this stage defunct given the collapse of the Soviet Union, the NK rushed to legitimize its secession on the basis of the April 1990 law. On 10 December 1991, a referendum in NK overwhelmingly affirmed the declaration of independence. Whereas from December 1991, the international community recognized the independence of all 15 former constituent republics of the USSR, no country, including Armenia, has recognized the independence of NK or established *formal* diplomatic links with it. Given the lack of a clear legal framework, Karabakh's status can be approached from three perspectives.

Nagorno-Karabakh as a Region of Azerbaijan

The first approach is centred on the fact that during the Soviet period NK was part of Azerbaijan, and had a well-defined administrative-institutional status as an autonomous oblast' within the Azerbaijan SSR. Until the collapse of the USSR, NK's budget, key policies and decisions, as well as important administrative positions, were sanctioned by the Azerbaijani authorities in Baku exclusively.[10] Although formally NK had the institutional mechanisms and status of an 'autonomous oblast', in practice its autonomy was a myth. NK had institutions such as a regional soviet, clearly demarcated regional borders, regional and local government agencies and other oblast'-based institutions. It was these regional institutions that provided the mechanisms through which Armenians could assert their demands once perestroika began. In fact, the single most important moment which 'launched' the 'Karabagh Movement' was the decision passed by the NK regional Soviet to unify with the Armenian SSR.

NK's administrative structure as an autonomous oblast' was a potent factor because it entailed the institutionalization of a very sharp ethno-national cleavage. It was this ethnic cleavage which led to the emergence of the 1988 nationalist movement for unification. NK Armenians cited discrimination, cultural impoverishment, economic backwardness and legal considerations in their demand for unification, but the crux of their argument was ethno-national – they wanted to live in one state with their ethnic kin in the Armenia SSR. In 1988–90 the demands of the 'Karabagh Movement' were expressed through the then existing Soviet institutional mechanisms. The emerging conflict was, therefore, a classic example of an ethnically defined region, with its own institutional structures, mobilizing along nationalist lines. Key protagonists of the 'Karabagh Movement', and many Armenian intellectuals, particularly from Karabakh, interpret the movement in the enclave in terms of a 'national liberation war' which the region waged against the repressive central authorities in Baku (Balayan, 1995; Ulubabian, 1994).

This view is rejected by the Azerbaijani side. Focusing on their defeat and loss of territory between 1992 and 1994, Azerbaijani intellectuals and officials see the conflict as a product of unprovoked Armenian aggression with the aim of creating a 'Greater Armenia'. They regard NK as Azerbaijani territory occupied by Armenian forces (Alijarly, 1996: 132–3; Dragadze, 2000: 157).[11] Azerbaijan's policy is that NK has an 'occupation regime' and there can be no peace until the region reverts to its jurisdiction. The status of the region, according to the Azerbaijanis, must be *de jure* similar to what it was during the Soviet period. The Azeri solution to the conflict is to grant the Armenians of Karabakh the 'highest level of autonomy', while rejecting any status other than autonomy as compromising the territorial integrity of the republic.[12] The Azerbaijan authorities have not, however, defined what this autonomy would consist of in practice.

Analysing NK as a region of Azerbaijan sheds light on two sets of factors. The first is the emergence of the nationalist movement in the enclave: regional Soviet institutions provided the mechanisms through which existing ethno-national discontent in the region was first expressed in response to the discriminatory pressures and policies of the central authorities in Baku. The second factor relates to current Azerbaijani approaches to the conflict, as the authorities in Baku still view NK as an integral part of the country and are reluctant to agree to any status for it beyond that of regional autonomy.

Nagorno-Karabakh as an Independent State

The second approach through which NK can be examined is that of a mini-state with its own institutions. This approach is particularly relevant to the case after late 1991, as NK, acting like a *de facto* newly independent state, engaged in a vigorous process of institution building based on Western models: parliamentary rule, direct elections, ministries, a *seemingly* open media and so on. However, it is important to note that these institutions do not have to cope with ethnic cleavages. The entire Azerbaijani population of the enclave was expelled during the war leaving no significant national minority. None of NK's new institutions have any relations to or connections with Azerbaijan.

Political institutions and elections: In the 10 December 1991 referendum, 99 per cent of voters opted for independence for NK.[13] Subsequently, the NK declared itself an independent 'Republic of Karabakh' on 6 January 1992. At first, the political elites decided to create a parliamentary republic. Elections to the new Supreme Council of the Republic of Nagorno-Karabakh were held on 28 December and when it formally convened on 18 January 1992, it became the supreme governing body of the republic. Its first significant act was to ratify the enclave's declaration of independence the day it convened. The parliament elected a president and prime minister, who ruled through a quasi-military body, the State Defence Committee. This committee was dissolved in December 1994, six months after the ceasefire, and was replaced by a civilian government. In late 1994, the governing elite decided to transform Karabakh from a parliamentary to a presidential republic. On 28 December 1994, parliament formally established the position of 'President of the Republic' and voted Robert Kocharian, a popular war hero who had considerable legitimacy due to his nationalist credentials, to the post. Kocharian formed a new government and appointed ministers. New parliamentary elections were held in April 1995, and 31 people were elected to the national assembly. On 24 November 1996, the first direct presidential elections took place, which Kocharian won with 89 per cent of the vote. When he resigned as President of Karabakh in March 1997 – to take up the post of Prime Minister of Armenia – his foreign minister, Arkady Ghukasian, was elected president in his place in August 1997 for a five-year term (also with 89 per cent of the vote). In June 2000, a new round of parliamentary elections was held for a slightly bigger 33-seat parliament, with 113 candidates contesting the seats. Thus, since late 1991, Karabakh has had three parliamentary elections and two presidential elections, giving its rulers a strong semblance of democratic legitimacy (Adalian, 1996: 108ff; Public International Law and Policy Group, 2000: 5–7).

The latest parliamentary elections are indicative of the seemingly successful democratic state-building process in Karabakh. The elections were considered to have been free and fair, with no significant or systematic malpractice reported. One international organization which monitored the elections observed, rather optimistically: 'Karabakh today is an oasis of good governance, respect for the law and decency by comparison with most of the rest of the post-Soviet Union' (British Helsinki Human Rights Group, 2000). The elections were conducted in an orderly, calm and competitive atmosphere, with no visible military presence or pressure on the voters. Voter turnout was officially declared to be 60 per cent. The pro-Ghukasian 'Union of Democracy Artsakh' won 13 seats (they had 26 candidates), the Armenian Revolutionary Federation (ARF or Dashnak) won nine seats (out of 22 candidates), the Ramkavar party won one seat, and the rest of the seats went to independents.

These elections were a significant advance from previous ones because for the first time in Karabakh the campaign was fought through party organizations and was based on party programmes, even though the parties did not have major differences over important issues. In particular, there was unanimity on the question of Karabakh's status as an independent republic. Party and individual differences were mostly related to economic issues and the best means to improve the social conditions of the population. Whereas the need for consensus during the war meant that the previous Karabakh National Assembly did not have formal political party or factional divisions, the demands of peace-time government have begun to nurture party politics. The ARF has assumed the role of opposition, albeit a loyal one, occasionally criticizing the leadership, especially over issues related to political appointments.[14] The

Karabakh government, however, does not tolerate sharp criticisms of the authorities. Despite the orderly conduct of elections and the *semblance* of democracy, Karabakh is far from being a 'model democracy'.

Military: The most powerful institution in Karabakh is the army, headed by the Minister of Defence, Seyran Ohanian. It is a well-equipped and well-trained force; and it pervades all aspects of society. The exact number of soldiers is not publicized, but the oft-cited figure is 20,000 men in active service. The army has stayed out of *formal* politics but no decision is made or activity undertaken which would undermine the power of the military. As an institution, it is above criticism. However, the army was the subject of an intense power struggle in the autumn of 1999 between its former head, General Samvel Babayan, and President Ghukasian, in alliance with Prime Minister Danielian. The civilian leadership prevailed insofar as Babayan, who was using the army as his support base for economic and political interests, was dismissed from his post as Defence Minister in December 1999.[15] Under Ohanian's command, the army has remained loyal to Ghukasian, despite some serious tensions within its general command. Moreover, Babayan was arrested (despite the lack of any convincing evidence) for the assassination attempt against Ghukasian in March 2000, put on 'trial', and sentenced to 14 years imprisonment. As such, the Babayan 'clan' has been eliminated as a serious contender in the economic, political and military arrangements within Karabakh and Armenia, but the enclave's army itself remains a unified and potent force.

Economic and social developments: As in Armenia, policies of privatization and the promotion of a market economy are espoused but little progress has been made in practice. The Karabakh government has a well-developed ministerial and administrative structure, it operates its own state budget approved by the parliament, it provides social services, runs the educational system, and even operates a university. It has embarked on an ambitious development programme to rebuild the republic, particularly the capital Stepanakert which was badly damaged during the war. All the trappings of an independent democratic state exist in Karabakh, albeit with a strong and relatively independent military. However, this is only part of the overall reality in terms of political dynamics.

Nagorno-Karabakh as an Informal Region of Armenia

The formal institutional set-up of Karabakh suggests that it is an independent self-governing statelet, based on democratic institutions. In reality, Karabakh is heavily dependent on Armenia, and on the support of the Armenian diaspora channelled through Armenia. Its policies are determined by a small group of people who control the political process. From this perspective, Karabakh may be regarded as an informal 'region' of Armenia, wholly integrated into the economy, and intertwined with its political dynamics. The informal nature of the relationship is crucial to understanding how these two entities cooperate in practically all spheres, while maintaining separate institutional frameworks.

There is only one major road that connects Karabakh to Armenia, and hence to the rest of the world, and that is the highway from Stepanakert, through Lachin, to Armenia. This is Karabakh's lifeline. Once a pot-holed secondary road suitable only for lorries, the road has recently been upgraded to one of the best highways in the South Caucasus, with the financial assistance of the Armenian diaspora. Telecommunications and transport all go through Armenia. Karabakh's currency is the Armenian Dram, and its budget is heavily subsidized by Armenia (Tchilingarian, 1997).[16] Its tax laws have been harmonized with Armenia. The salaries of its university teachers and some media workers are paid by ministries in Yerevan.[17] Since 1998, the Karabakh Interior Ministry has been issuing Armenian passports to inhabitants travelling abroad since 'all residents of this unrecognized state have been, in fact, considered as citizens of the Republic of Armenia [although] the Nagorno Karabakh Republic is still not included into Armenia's legal environment' (Petrosyan, 2000: 1). Similarly, its military, although with a separate command structure, is heavily dependent on Armenian equipment, soldiers and 'observers' (Harris, 1999: 4; Rieff, 1997: 122–3). The military cooperation between the two forces is such that it is implicitly understood that the Armenian defence minister has overall responsibility.

The political relationship between Armenia and Karabakh is more complicated. Again, there are no *formal* diplomatic relations between the two entities, but the presidents, prime ministers, and other ministers meet regularly to coordinate their activities. In May 1998 a protocol on consultation and cooperation was signed between the Armenian and Karabakh foreign ministers (Vardan Oskanian and Naira Melkumian, respectively). The most significant step towards formal cooperation came on 3 September 2000, when the Prime Minister of Karabakh, Anushavan Danielian,[18] and Prime Minister of Armenia, Andranik Margarian, signed an economic cooperation agreement between their two governments.[19] Azerbaijan denounced the agreement as 'a grave violation of Azerbaijan's national legislation, international legal norms and principles' (Azerbaijan News Service, as posted on Armenian News Network Groong, 10 October 2000). There are also similar links between the two parliaments. Much of these relationships depend on the personal networks and good will between the politicians involved, especially between the presidents. Not surprisingly, the institutional links and networks of personal ties have multiplied during Kocharian's presidency of Armenia.

It is clearly understood that the Armenian side of this equation is the more senior and powerful component, but Yerevan has never been able to dictate its will on Karabakh. In fact, with regard to the negotiations with Azerbaijan over Karabakh's status, Karabakh has been able to reverse the relationship and impose its position on Armenia. In this sense Karabakh has 'taken over' the political agenda of Armenia, and the 'regional' periphery is controlling the national political centre. In early 1997, *before* Kocharian's arrival in Yerevan as Prime Minister of Armenia, it was observed with reference to Yerevan's incapacity to impose a settlement on Karabakh hardliners: 'Frankensteins have a habit of losing control over their monsters' (Rieff, 1997: 126). This role reversal can be traced to the 1996 presidential elections in Armenia.

The incumbent president, Levon Ter Petrosian, ran for his second term in September 1996. Ter Petrossian had been one of the leaders of the 1988 'Karabagh Movement' in Yerevan, and rose to prominence on the nationalist wave in support of NK's unification with Armenia. He was elected as the first non-Communist president of the Armenian Supreme Soviet in the Summer of 1990, and as President of Armenia in direct elections in October 1991. By 1996, Ter Petrosian and the ruling party, the Armenian National Movement, had become very unpopular due to the economic crisis, deteriorating social conditions and widespread political corruption. After the military victory and ceasefire in 1994, Karabakh had ceased to be a major factor in Armenian domestic politics, and consequently the presidential elections of 1996 were fought over socio-economic issues.

Ter Petrosian rigged the election and claimed a first-round victory with 52 per cent of the vote. The opposition mobilized to unseat him, and when the National Assembly in Yerevan was attacked by angry protestors, Ter Petrosian, with the support of the army, initiated a military crackdown to stay in power. To regain popularity Ter Petrosian had to appoint a respected prime minister who could improve the economy. He first appointed, on 5 November 1996, the well-liked Armenian ambassador to Great Britain, Armen Sarkissian. When Sarkissian resigned due to ill health four months later, Ter Petrosian surprised everyone by appointing Robert Kocharian, the elected President of Karabakh, as Prime Minister of Armenia on 20 March 1997. Initially, Kocharian's appointment was popular. Ter Petrosian probably also calculated that a peace accord with Azerbaijan would need someone like Kocharian to 'sell' any compromises to the Armenian people, especially in Karabakh. Yet Kocharian's appointment to Yerevan proved to be Ter Petrosian's undoing, as it paved the way for the Karabakh elite to gain a foothold at the heart of political power in Armenia.

In 1997, both Armenia and Azerbaijan came under intense external pressure to come to an agreement over Karabakh. The basic elements of the peace agreement, however, could not be agreed. The four most difficult issues (in order of importance) were, and remain: (a) Karabakh's final status, (b) the return of the occupied territories, particularly the Lachin corridor, (c) the status of Shushi/Shusha (the predominantly Azerbaijani populated town within NK), and (d) the return of refugees. There were two approaches to the negotiations: a 'package' solution which dealt with all the issues at once, or a 'step-by-step' solution which would defer the most difficult question of status for a few years, and in the mean time permit progress on other issues so that the blockades would be lifted and confidence-building measures would be implemented. The OSCE Minsk group, the main mediating body, proposed the step-by-step approach as the best solution to the deadlock.

In September and November 1997 Ter Petrosian made two public pronouncements in which he advocated the step-by-step approach as a feasible alternative to the ongoing stalemate (Ter Petrosian, 1997a; 1997b).[20] He argued that in order to improve the economy, and to avoid war in the future, there had to be a final settlement of the Karabakh conflict soon. As he put it, 'Armenia will not become a modern state, there will not be economic development in Armenia, until the Karabakh question is solved, until the blockades are lifted' (Ter Petrosian, 1997a: 3). He tied Armenia's well-being directly to a permanent peace accord as soon as possible, even hinting that Karabakh was proving to be an unwarranted burden on Armenia's own development. He pointed out that once an agreement was reached immediate benefits would follow: the Azerbaijani-Turkish blockade on Armenia would end, and there would be a substantial increase in foreign investment.

The opposition in Armenia, still reeling from the presidential election in the previous year, immediately seized the opportunity to denounce Ter Petrosian for 'selling out' Karabakh, and for using economic problems to undermine 'national interests'. The Karabakh president, Arkady Ghukasian, opposed Ter Petrosian's approach as well, seeing it as the first step to keeping Karabakh formally a part of Azerbaijan. Being dependent on Armenia for its survival, the Karabakh leadership was not in a position to reject Ter Petrosian's proposals outright. However, in this instance, Karabakh had a powerful ally heading the Armenian government – Prime Minister Robert Kocharian. By the end of 1997, it was obvious that there was a clear division within the political elite in Yerevan over the proposed solution to the conflict. On the one hand, President Ter Petrosian and his allies were advocating the step-by-step approach, being more concerned with the immediate economic benefits an agreement would bring. On the other hand, key government figures who were from Karabakh, such as Prime Minister Kocharian and Armenian Interior and Security Minister Serge Sargsian (now Defence Minister), along with the Karabakh elite, resisted any settlement which might undermine the independent status of the enclave. The tensions led to political paralysis within the government of Armenia in January 1998. The political crisis ended when Defence Minister Vazgen Sargsian (not related to Serge) shifted his support from Ter Petrosian to the 'pro-Karabakh' group, thus forcing the president to resign on 2 February.

According to the Armenian constitution, the second person in line after the president is the speaker of parliament, and the third is the prime minister. Immediately after Ter Petrosian's resignation, Speaker of Parliament Babgen Ararktsian (a supporter of Ter Petrosian) also resigned. Hence, Prime Minister Robert Kocharian became Acting President. Other Ter Petrosian allies in the government also resigned, leaving Kocharian, in conjunction with the Interior and Defence Ministers, in full control of the government of Armenia. New presidential elections were called and after a second-round ballot on 30 March 1998 Kocharian was elected President of Armenia.[21] The election legitimized the 'velvet coup' by the opponents of Ter Petrosian and his plan to compromise on the Karabakh issue.

On 27 October 1999 the two most influential politicians from Armenia, Vazgen Sargsian, the former Defence Minister and Prime Minister (since June 1999) and Karen Demirchian, the popular former First Secretary of the Communist Party in Armenia and the Speaker of Parliament (since June 1999), were assassinated in parliament. This further strengthened Kocharian's hold on power. The initial challenges to the presidency of Kocharian by the supporters of the murdered Vazgen Sargsian came to naught.

By suggesting that Karabakh has 'taken over' the political agenda of Armenia, I am not suggesting that the leaders of the enclave are exclusively running Armenia or imposing all of their interests on the country. Aside from the fact that a Karabakh Armenian is the President of the Republic of Armenia, there are four components to this argument. First, although Kocharian has not proven to be the radical nationalist that many in the West feared, he is nevertheless much less willing to compromise over the status of Karabakh. He has delinked Armenia's economic well-being from a peace agreement with Azerbaijan. Kocharian has also adopted a harder position against Turkey, making the recognition by Turkey and the international community of the 1915 Genocide an important part of Armenia's foreign policy (Kocharian, 2000). Unlike the previous administration, Kocharian is not preoccupied with the possibility of cultivating closer relations with Turkey. He has met President Aliev of Azerbaijan on numerous occasions, but he has always maintained that Karabakh's final status must not subordinate the enclave to Azeri jurisdiction, and that he will not sign an accord which does not guarantee Karabakh's independence. Kocharian, together with the Karabkh leadership, has agreed to the OSCE's formulation that Karabakh and Azerbaijan can share a 'common state', but this has not been accepted by the Azerbaijani leadership. It does not seem that the Armenian side will compromise any further on the issue of the enclave's status. Kocharian and Arkady Ghukasian, the president of Karabakh, have close relations and have no significant disagreements on policy. The Armenian government no longer puts pressure on Karabakh to accept concessions for a final peace agreement. Gerard (Jirair) Libaridian, the Senior Advisor to Ter Petrosian, and Armenia's main negotiator on the Karabakh conflict until the autumn of 1997, characterized Kocharian and his supporters as the 'Party of Karabagh'. According to Libaridian, 'In most matters, the Party of Karabagh, whether in Karabagh or Armenia, is nonideological. Karabagh is at the top of the hierarchy of concerns; all else is subject to its logic. The leaders of the Karabagh party themselves, Kocharian [Samvel] Babayan [former Defence Minister of NK], Vazgen Sargsian, and Serge Sargsian, are essentially pragmatic people' (Libaridian, 1999: 94).

Second, as alluded to above, there are a number of powerful men from NK in positions of political and administrative influence in Yerevan. The most notable is Serge Sargsian, who in the past eight years has held the portfolios of Interior and/or Security Minister and Defence Minister.[22] Others include Leonard Petrosian, a former Prime Minister of Karabakh who at the end of 1998 was appointed Deputy Defence Minister of Armenia. At the time of his assassination on 27 October 1999, he was the Minister of Government Operational Issues. Currently, Slava Avanesian, the Secretary of the Karabakh's Security Council, is an advisor to Armenia's Prime Minister, Andranik Margarian. This Karabakh 'clan' is one of the few powerful groups within the Armenian political elite. In the past, it was kept in check by Vazgen Sargsian and his military-security apparatus. Since the assassination of Sargsian and the partial disintegration and cooption of his followers and allies (the Yerkrapah Union of War Veterans, the Republican Party, and Demirchian's Popular Party), the Karabakh 'clan' has consolidated its hold over politics in Armenia.

The anti-Kocharian and anti-Karabakh sentiment was very strong in the aftermath of the parliamentary shootings in October 1999. It was fuelled by the assumption that Kocharian and Serge Sargsian were behind the assassinations to consolidate their power in Armenia. The 'logic' behind the rumours was that by getting rid of the two most powerful and popular *hayastantsi* politicians (Armenians from Armenia), the *Karabakhtsis* (those from Karabakh) can have undisputed control of Armenia. In fact, Kocharian's adviser, Alexan Harutiunian, was arrested for colluding with the assassins, but later released in the absence of any evidence. Many supporters of the assassinated Premier are convinced of Kocharian's involvement, and are desperate to find 'proof' of it.[23]

Third, interlocked with the above political groups are a range of economic networks and interests. The situation in terms of economic 'clans' and alliances is more diverse and multifaceted. Nevertheless, the strength of the Karabakh 'clan' is also reflected in its control of certain economic sectors in Armenia, especially fuel supply, and to a lesser extent wheat imports. The Armenian economy, as is the case with other former Soviet republics, is divided into sectors which have a monopoly in certain economic domains. The so-called 'mafia' networks are linked to the political elite, and therefore the NK 'mafia' benefits immensely from the political power of the Karabakh 'clan' in governing structures.

Fourth, the above developments have led to a sense of resentment among many Armenians of Armenia – specifically among the business and political elites, as well as many Yerevan-based intellectuals – against the Karabakh Armenians' 'takeover' of Armenia. There is much anecdotal evidence for this sentiment, though it is not easily visible because it is not publicly articulated.[24] The tension inherent in this Karabakh–Armenia cleavage is obviously not an ethnic antagonism. It is, rather, very much a centre–region cleavage, reinforced by political, economic, cultural and stereotypical factors.

In conclusion, the approach to Karabakh as an informal 'region' of Armenia sheds light on the real power relations between the two entities. It is true that NK is administratively and legally separate from Armenia, but the politics and policies of Stepanakert and Yerevan are so intertwined that it is not possible to separate the interests of one from those of the other. The enclave has a paradoxical relationship with Armenia. On the one hand, it is very much dependent on the latter for its survival, and yet on the other it controls the political agenda of Armenia – at least when it comes to the most important issues facing the country, such as its relations with Karabakh, and by extension, the signing of a peace agreement, the lifting of blockades, relations with Azerbaijan and Turkey, and general foreign policy. The small region of NK has successfully imposed its interests and views onto Yerevan through the hold of the Karabakhtsi elite on the levers of political power in Armenia. At this point, public or organized political competition in Armenia does not reflect this cleavage because to do so would mean to oppose the sacred cow of 'Karabakh's security', and undermine 'national unity'. These issues go to the heart of Armenian nationalism since 1988.

The International Dimension

It is important to note that the unification of Karabakh with Armenia has been the main goal of nationalists since 1988. This unification has come about informally, as analysed above, and, since 1998, generally on terms set by the NK elite. The Karabakh elite sees NK's declaration of independence as a compromise to formal unification with Armenia in the face of international pressures. As the Patriarch of Karabakh put it, summing up the views of the *Karabakhtsis*,

> I know that the world community believes in the principle of territorial integrity, but I hope that justice will come to our land and that we will become independent. That is the only compromise that we are willing to make. Of course, we want to integrate with Armenia, but the world community will not allow us... We want to be part of Armenia. That is why the Karabakh Movement was started... One nation, one country, one people, one language, one faith, one church and one culture... We have declared an independent republic [as]... a compromise... Our compromise is to take the third way – not to integrate with Armenia or Azerbaijan but to become an independent republic (Krikorian, 2000).

The same sentiment was expressed by Samvel Babayan when he was the Defence Minister of Karabakh: 'I do not place any distinction between Armenia and Karabakh. For me, they constitute one state' (Alexandrian, 1999: 35). Karabakh's official position advocating international recognition of its independence uses historical, legal, demographic and moral arguments to justify its stance (Zargarian, 1999). This 'third way' has led to an ambiguous existence in international relations. Neither a region nor a recognized republic, Karabakh acts as and pretends to be a separate state. It has its own foreign minister who travels on an Armenian diplomatic passport, as does its president, and has 'consulates' (Information Offices) in Yerevan, Washington, Paris and Moscow. Although no state has formally recognized Karabakh's independence, occasionally there are gestures of semi-recognition and legitimacy granted by other countries. For example, President Ghukasian was formally received by the American State Department in 1999, and the American

Congress acknowledges Karabakh as a distinct administrative recipient of US aid. Armenian diaspora organizations welcome visits by Karabakh officials. Non-CIS citizens, including ethnic Armenians who are citizens of other countries (that is, diasporans), need a separate Karabakh visa in addition to the Armenian visa to enter the enclave.

In the absence of international recognition, Karabakh's foreign relations are mediated through Yerevan. Most importantly, this means that OSCE mediation and negotiations take place bilaterally between Yerevan and Baku, with Karabakh representatives playing no direct role. Although OSCE officials regularly visit Stepanakert to consult with Karabakh authorities, the enclave is not viewed as a *formal* party to the negotiations at the insistence of Azerbaijan. Baku portrays the conflict as one between Armenia and Azerbaijan rather than between one of *its* regions and *its* citizens and the Azerbaijani state. Karabakh is not officially recognized by the OSCE because, according to international law, it formally remains part of Azerbaijan (for an evaluation of the various mediators see Betts, 1999; Mooradian and Druckman, 1999). This is widely seen as an obstacle to the resolution of the conflict. Hence, the international system itself fosters the informal nature of Karabakh's international and domestic policies. Ironically, while Karabakh is developing its own institutions as a separate state to gain legitimacy, these institutions cannot play a formal role in the exclave's relations with the outside world. Policies and negotiations have to be conducted through Yerevan, although having a President from Karabakh in Armenia has facilitated communications between Stepanakert and Yerevan.

Currently, there are three main solutions proposed. The first is to postpone the question of the final status of NK. This was accepted by Azerbaijan in 1997, but rejected by the Armenians, who forced the resignation of President Ter Petrosian who favoured it. The second solution is to declare NK and Azerbaijan as part of a 'common state'. This was rejected by Azerbaijan in 1999. A third idea, suggested in the form of a trial balloon originating in the US, is that of a territorial swap – Armenia would obtain a land corridor to NK in exchange for a strip of land at its southern tip which would connect Azerbaijan and its exclave of Nakhichevan. The Armenian leadership dismissed this idea in 2000, although Azerbaijan has implied that it would not exclude such a solution. However, such a territorial exchange will alter the regional balance if it puts a hurdle at the Armenian–Iranian border. Academics too have been active in suggesting solutions. One set of ideas was put forth by David Laitin and Ronald Suny, advocating keeping Karabakh *de jure* in Azerbaijan, but with considerable Armenian autonomy and self-government, augmented by security guarantees and international protection (Laitin and Suny, 1999). Another study by international lawyers suggested the opposite view in the form of a two-phased approach. In phase one Karabakh would be granted 'intermediate sovereignty', with the right to enter into relationships with neighbouring states. Phase two would depend on the conflicting parties' behaviour and success in the first phase, and could lead to 'earned recognition' as an independent entity. Through various mechanisms (a mediation panel, commissions) the international community would be the ultimate judge, taking into account the wishes of the Karabakh Armenians (Public International Law and Policy Group, 2000).

Despite the various ideas and proposals, it is very difficult to negotiate a permanent solution to the conflict which would be satisfactory to the main parties. At the heart of the Karabakh conflict lies the classic contradiction inherent in the international system: territorial integrity versus the right of self-determination. The difficulty facing any peace agreement, and confronting the OSCE as mediator, is how to combine these two principles in a manner that is acceptable to the main parties to the conflict. The challenge is how a *de facto* independent entity can be made to appear to be *de jure* part of one state (Azerbaijan), while also being integrated into another state (Armenia).

CONCLUSION

From its very beginning in 1988, the Karabakh conflict was too historically entrenched and too radically disruptive to the very territorial integrity of Soviet Azerbaijan to be solved through existing institutional frameworks, and through institutional engineering and appeasement. Azerbaijan rejected the option of re-institutionalizing multinationality in any way that would acknowledge, let alone address, Armenian grievances. Armenians refused to entertain ideas of keeping NK in Azerbaijan. In this case, the historical record was too skewed and too tainted by the powerful homogenizing nationalism on both sides. The inherited Soviet institutions of 'national' autonomy provided a platform for political mobilization, though no institutional 'fix' based on compromise was going to satisfy the two sides. The conflict quickly turned violent, polarizing and hardening positions even further. Over the last decade, through war and state-building, Nagorno Karabakh has emerged as a *de facto* independent statelet, with developing political institutions and all the trappings of a seemingly functioning democracy. The question is how will this state-building affect the final arrangement of NK's status?

Two conceptual challenges emerge from the Karabakh case study. The first is related to the problem discussed in the preceding section: how to analyse a political system which appears to be institutionalized, but which is in fact highly informal and quasi-authoritarian in many of its power relations. Elections, parliaments, ministries and other similar state organs cloak behind-the-scenes power struggles, political manoeuvring and tensions. This interplay between informal power and institutionalized power is the key to understanding the relationship between NK and Armenia. Another dimension of informal power relations has to do with the political process *within* NK. In many instances, democratic institutions can be the facade for real power held by a few men and their supporters. There are many unwritten rules in Karabakh, and one of the important ones is that journalists must not criticize government officials too much. As with all unwritten rules, the limits are unclear and subject to interpretation and, of course, arbitrary abuse by the authorities. One journalist, Vahram Aghajanian, who pushed the limit too far by criticizing Prime Minister Anushavan Danielian, found himself arrested and charged with libel. He was sentenced to one-year imprisonment in April 2000, but after pressure from journalists in Yerevan and elsewhere, his sentence was changed to two years of probation. Strictly speaking, his arrest and trial were not illegal, but it was also clear that the existing state institutions – particularly the judiciary – were used by the authorities to silence him.

The second conceptual challenge relates to the ultimate solution to the Karabakh conflict and the appropriateness of this volume's theoretical framework as a 'guideline'. Admittedly, the authors of the introductory framework do not seek to provide a solution to ethnic conflict, but the framework itself has a remedial element in it. The problem in NK is how to deal with a successful secessionist movement that has achieved military victory, if that movement is itself resolutely against the re-institutionalization of multi-nationality or regional autonomy? In the case of NK, Armenian aspirations had been contained by Soviet power and its institutional arrangements for autonomy, though with a great deal of historical dissatisfaction. Any return to the Soviet legacy, especially if that institutionalization is going to be reminiscent of the old and discredited Soviet model of an autonomous oblast' under Baku's control, is unworkable. The de-institutionalization of the old has occurred and an alternative and new set of institutions is being constructed (re-institutionalized) which is different from the Soviet arrangements for managing multi-nationality. These new national(izing) institutions have become the basis of post-Soviet society in Armenia and Azerbaijan. Changing the current institutional arrangements of NK in a more multi-national direction would not, I suspect, lead to stability and accommodation, as the framework implies. However, the model set out in the introduction and conclusion of this volume does highlight the institutional basis of the conflict and shows that once the initial window of opportunity is lost, it can be very difficult indeed to renegotiate a multi-national institutional framework. The institutional arrangements valid in Soviet Armenia and Azerbaijan in 1988 might not be so appropriate after *de facto* secession has taken place. In short, the model is useful to explain the outbreak of secessionist conflict but does not offer a viable solution to the post-secessionist situation in NK.

NOTES

1. This is the area of the Nagorno-Karabakh Autonomous Oblast' as of 1988. It does not include the Azerbaijani territories outside NK (Lachin, Aghdam, etc.) currently occupied by the Armenian forces for strategic reasons and for the purpose of establishing a land corridor between Armenia and NK. The population is estimated by NK authorities at 120,000, but 70,000–80,000 is more realistic.
2. For general overviews see Astourian, 1994; Croissant, 1998; Rieff, 1997; Tololyan, 1995; Yamskov, 1991. For accounts sympathetic to the Azerbaijani position see Alijarly, 1996; Altstadt, 1992: 195ff. For accounts sympathetic to the Armenian side see Chorbajian, 1994; Walker, 1991. For an analysis of the perspective within Karabakh see Tchilingirian, 1999.
3. According to the 1989 census, the total population of the enclave was 189,000. Armenians numbered 145,450 or 76.9%, Azerbaijanis numbered 40,700. The 1989 figures are not as reliable due to the turmoil in NK and the beginning of the population transfers in and out of the region.
4. According to the 1979 Soviet census, there were 475,000 Armenians in Azerbaijan, of whom 123,000 lived in the Nagorno Karabakh Oblast'.
5. Systematic violence on a massive scale against Azerbaijanis living in Armenia never took place. There were isolated instances of murder, but no pogroms. Armenians, however, lost the moral high ground by massacring fleeing Azerbaijani civilians in Khojalu, Karabakh, in 1992.
6. A similar point is made by Betts, 1999: 172, but she overstates the argument when she says that Russia 'switched allegiances' when Azerbaijan joined the CIS in late 1993. Russia began selling arms and training the Azerbaijani military as well but maintained its support of Armenia without being as one-sided as before.
7. 30,000 killed is the oft-cited figure in news reports. MacFarlane and Minear (1997: p.1) give an estimate of 25,000 dead in the conflict, as do Mooradian and Druckman (1999: pp.712–3). Neither side have given an official casualty figure. Armenian casualties probably numbered 7,000–8,000 dead, those on the Azerbaijani side around 20,000–22,000.
8. Azerbaijani sources 'round up' these figures and constantly speak of one million refugees and 20% of Azerbaijani land being occupied. On the humanitarian dimension of the war, see MacFarlane and Minear (1997) and Human Rights Watch (1994).
9. For the Law of the USSR 'About the Procedure of Secession of a Soviet Republic from the USSR', passed in April 1990, see Public International Law and Policy Group and New England Center for International Law and Policy (2000), pp.5–6.
10. The exception was the ten-month period in 1989 when the oblast' was put under direct rule by the USSR government in Moscow.
11. This is a constant theme in the *Azerbaijani International Magazine* (see, for example, Vol.7, No.3 [Autumn 1999], pp.54ff.). A similar point regarding the contrasting views is made by Vaserman and Ginat, 1994, pp.358–9.
12. This point was made very clear by President Aliev in his speech at the Royal Institute of International Affairs, London, on 22 July 1998. See also 'Memorandum' (1999), submitted by the Azerbaijani Ambassador in London, pp.175–6.

13. Azerbaijanis living in NK at that point refused to take part in the referendum.
14. See, for example, *Asbarez Online*, 10 July 2000, and 31 July 2000; Aragil Electronic News Bulletin, Issue 2202, 7 July 2000.
15. The Defence Minister of Armenia, Vagharshak Harutiunian, played a decisive role at the height of this power struggle. He went to Stepanakert and on 15 December 1999 declared his 'strong support' for Arkady Ghukasian (*Transcaucasus: A Chronology* [on line], Vol.IX, No.1, January 2000).
16. Tchilingirian writes that in 1997 the NK budget was $20 million, $13 million of which was a subsidy from Armenia.
17. I am grateful to Hratch Tchilingirian for this information.
18. Before being appointed as Prime Minister of Nagorno-Karabakh Republic in June 1999, Danielian was the Deputy Parliamentary Speaker of Crimea and a major figure in the Crimean 'mafia' scene. He left Crimea before the crackdown of Ukrainian law enforcement agencies.
19. The agreement dealt with joint economic programmes in numerous policy areas such as hydro-electric power, industry, trade, tourism, health care (reported by Snark News Agency on 4 September 2000 and posted on *Armenian News Network Groong*).
20. The first was in the form of an extensive interview, given on 26 September 1997 (Ter Petrosian, 1997a). The second was an article devoted entirely to the Karabakh problem (Ter Petrosian, 1997b).
21. His main opponent was the former First Secretary of the Communist Party of Armenia (1974–88), Karen Demirchian, who came out from almost a decade of political retirement. He received 41% of the vote in the second round.
22. In the aftermath of the 27 October 1999 assassinations, he resigned as the National Security Minister. Never far from the levers of power, after spending some months as the Secretary of the National Security Council (based in the Presidential apparatus), he was once again appointed Defence Minister in May 2000.
23. Two Yerevan-based newspapers, *Chorord Ishkhanutiun [Fourth Element]* and *Haikakan Zhamanak [Armenian Times]*, constantly publish articles insinuating the involvement of the Kocharian administration – or of people close to him – in the assassinations; the Armenian Revolutionary Federation, a party supportive of the President, is particularly signalled out for its alleged involvement.
24. I was told this anecdote soon after Kocharian was appointed Prime Minister: 'These Armenians from Karabakh must really be dense; we told them to go and occupy Baku, instead they came and occupied Yerevan!'

REFERENCES

Adalian, Rouben (ed.) (1996), *Armenia and Karabagh Factbook*. Washington, DC: Armenian Assembly of America.

Alexandrian, A.H. (1999), 'Strong Man of Karabakh: Interview with Defense Minister Samvel Babayan', *Armenian International Magazine*, Vol.10, No.6, pp.34–5.

Alijarly, Sulejman (1996), 'The Republic of Azerbaijan: Notes on the State Borders in the Past and Present', in John F.R. Wright *et al.* (eds), *Transcaucasian Boundaries*. London: UCL Press.

Altstadt, Audrey (1992), *The Azerbaijani Turks: Power and Identity Under Russian Rule*. Stanford: Hoover Institution Press.

Astourian, Stephan (1994), 'The Nagorno-Karabakh Conflict: Dimensions, Lessons, and Prospects', *Mediterranean Quarterly*, Vol.5, No.4, pp.85–109.

Balayan, Zori (1995), *Dzhokhk yev drakht [Hell and Paradise]*. Yerevan: *Azg* Newspaper Publications.

Betts, Wendy (1999), 'Third Party Mediation: An Obstacle to Peace in Nagorno Karabakh', *SAIS Review*, Vol.19, No.2, pp.161–83.

British Helsinki Human Rights Group (2000), 'Nagorno Karabakh 2000', Report at www.bhhrg.org/nakorno-karabach.

Chorbajian, Levon *et al.* (1994), *The Caucasian Knot: The History and Geo-politics of Nagorno-Krabagh*. London: Zed Books.

Croissant, Michael (1998), *The Armenia-Azerbaijan Conflict: Causes and Implications*. Westport, CT: Praeger.

Dragadze, Tamara (ed.) (2000), *Azerbaijan*. London: Melizende.

Harris, Paul (1999), 'Nagorno Karabakh: Exclusive Report from Paul Harris in Stepanakert', *Combat and Survival*, Vol.11, Issue 5 (August), pp.5–10 (as posted on *Armenian News Network Groong*, 10 December 1999).

Human Rights Watch (1994), *Seven Years of Conflict in Nagorno-Karabakh*, New York: Human Rights Watch.

Kocharian, Robert (2000), 'Statement by H.E. Mr. Robert Kocharian, President of the Republic of Armenia at the Millennium Summit of the United Nations, 7 September 2000', posted on *Armenian News Network Groong*, 8 September.

Krikorian, Onnik (2000), 'An Interview with His Holiness Archbishop Barkev Martirossian, Primate of the Diocese of Artsakh' (22 July 2000), *Armenian Weekly On-Line*, posted on *Armenian News Network Groong*, 28 July.

Laitin, David and Ronald Suny (1999), 'Armenia and Azerbaijan: Thinking a Way out of Karabakh', *Middle East Policy*, Vol.7, No.1, pp.145–76.

Libaridian, Gerard (1999), *The Challenge of Statehood: Armenian Political Thinking Since Independence*. Watertown, MA: Blue Crane Books.

MacFarlane, Neil S. and Larry Minear (1997), *Humanitarian Action and Politics: The Case of Nagorno-Karabakh*. Providence, RI: Thomas J. Watson Institute for International Studies.

'Memorandum Submitted by HE Mr Mahmud Mamed-Kuliyev, Ambassador of the Azerbaijan Republic' (1999), *South Caucasus and Central Asia*, Vol.II, London: House of Commons Foreign Affairs Committee Report, July.

Mooradian, Moorad and Daniel Druckman (1999), 'Hurting Stalemate or Mediation? The Conflict over Nagorno-Karabakh, 1990–95', *Journal of Peace Research*, Vol.36, No.6 (November), pp.709–27.

Petrosyan, David (2000), 'Common Passport, Different Opportunities for Holders', *Review & Outlook – Armenian News Network Groong*, posted on 21 September.

Public International Law and Policy Group and New England Center for International Law and Policy (2000), 'The Nagorno-Karabagh Crisis: A Blueprint for Resolution: A memorandum based on the conference "The Nagorno-Karabagh Crisis: A Time for Resolution," Washington, DC, 17–18 May 2000', June.

Rieff, David (1997), 'Case Study in Ethnic Strife', *Foreign Affairs*, Vol.76, No.2, pp.118–32.

Tchilingirian, Hratch (1997), 'Karabakh: Internationalising the Enclave', *War Report* (IWPR), No.52, June–July.

Tchilingirian, Hratch (1999), 'Nagorno Karabagh: Transition and the Elite', *Central Asian Survey*, Vol.18, No.4, pp.435–61.

Ter Petrosian, Levon (1997a), 'Hajord serundneri gaghaparakhosutiune petk e lini mer petakanutian amrapndume [The Ideology of the Next Generation Must be the Strengthening of our Statehood]', *Hayastani Hanrapetutiun [Republic of Armenia]*, No.187, pp.1–3, 27 September.

Ter Petrosian, Levon (1997b), 'Paterazm, te khaghaghutiun? Lrjanalu pahe [War or Peace? The Moment to Get Serious]', *Hayastani Hanrapetutiun [Republic of Armenia]*, No.212, pp.1–2, 1 November.

Tololyan, Khachig (1995), 'National Self-Determination and the Limits of Sovereignty: Armenia, Azerbaijan and the Secession of Nagorno-Karabagh', *Nationalism and Ethnic Politics*, Vol.1, No.1, pp.86–110.

Ulubabian, Bagrat (1994), *Artsakhian goyapaikare [The Struggle for Survival of Karabakh]*. Yerevan: Gir Grots.

Vaserman, Arie and Rami Ginat (1994), 'National, Territorial or Religious Conflict? The Case of Nagorno-Karabakh', *Studies in Conflict and Terrorism*, Vol.17, No.4, pp.345–62.

Walker, Christopher (ed.) (1991), *Armenia and Karabagh: The Struggle for Unity*. London: Minority Rights.

Yamskov, A.N. (1991), 'Ethnic Conflict in the Transcaucasus: The Case of Nagorno-Karabakh', *Theory and Society*, Vol.20, No.5, pp.631–60.

Zargarian, Rouben (1999), 'Principles for Conflict Resolution in Nagorno Karabakh', *International Peacekeeping*, Vol.6, No.3, pp.129–33.

Patterns of Centre–Regional Relations in Central Asia: The Cases of Kazakhstan, the Kyrgyz Republic and Uzbekistan

NEIL J. MELVIN

During the years of Mikhail Gorbachev's programme of *perestroika* (1986–91), the territories of Central Asia were the location for some of the worst incidents of ethnic conflict experienced in the Soviet Union. In Osh in the Kyrgyz Republic, in Ferghana in Uzbekistan, in Dushanbe in Tajikistan, in Almaty in Kazakhstan, as well as other locations, violence erupted in response to perceived ethnic grievances. With the collapse of the Soviet state at the end of 1991, many of the conflicts that had appeared in the final years of the Soviet order seemed destined to become the basis for broader ethnic unrest and in particular ethno-regional struggles in the newly independent states.

Indeed, in the first decade of independence the struggle with regional political movements constituted one of the key elements in the drive to forge cohesive political entities from the diverse territories of each Central Asian republic. Regionally-based instability occurred in all of the Central Asian states, and in the case of Tajikistan the state disintegrated under the pressure of powerful regional movements (Rubin, 1998: 28–61; Lynch, 2001). Despite the importance of territorial issues during the first decade of independence, however, ethno-regionalism did not emerge as a leading cleavage in Central Asian society. In contrast to many of the other parts of the former Soviet Union, centre–regional relations in Central Asia followed a different trajectory of development.

Unlike the situation in many other areas in the former Soviet territories, formally institutionalized forms of multi-ethnicity (auto-nomous regions) did not serve as the driving force of centre–regional relations in Central Asia.[1] Second, despite the emergence of powerful regional movements and the rise of regional politics in Central Asia, the central elites of the new states resisted the federal or confederal solutions to regional pressure that were developed in other parts of the former Soviet Union. Rather than accommodating regional interests and identities, a powerful centralizing impulse developed in Central Asia that led to the construction of formally strong unitary states.

Below, the political dynamics that developed around the shifting geography of power in Central Asia will be examined to identify why the states of Central Asia emerged as a distinct sub-set of post-Soviet regime-types. It will be argued that in the first decade of independence the main contours of centre–regional relations reflected the Russian colonial and Soviet organization of power in Central Asia. In this period, state power was exercised to create and refashion political borders, social and economic institutions and identities set in place over the previous century (Beissinger, 1993: 93–115; Bunce, 1999: 790; Linz and Stepan, 1996).[2]

It will further be argued that the post-independence regional politics of three states of Central Asia – Kazakhstan, the Kyrgyz Republic, and Uzbekistan – demonstrate important divergences within the area.[3] Despite the shared heritage between the states of the region and a similar centralizing and authoritarian impulse, a variegated pattern of centre–regional politics emerged in Central Asia following independence (Melvin, 2001). It is argued that the colonial order in Central Asia forged less-articulated notions of ethnicity, nation and regionalism than in other parts of the Soviet Union. In particular, the colonial period did not provide a legacy in terms of exclusive 'regional' identities or institutions linked to specific territories that could effectively challenge the broad centralizing impulse that informed the state-building project undertaken by the newly empowered central elite networks following independence. At the same time, the diversity within the unitary state forms that developed in Central Asia reflected the variety of informal institutions, notably elite, ethno-linguistic, and social networks, which served as the basis for contesting the territorial division of power in each of the new states.

THE HISTORIC BASIS OF REGIONAL POLITICS

Immediately prior to Russian conquest, the single most important division in Central Asia was the socio-economic and political distinction between the sedentary populations of cities, towns and villages (*Sarts*), located primarily in Transoxiana (the area between the region's two principal rivers, the Amur Daria and Syr Daria), and the nomadic populations found predominately in the areas adjacent to the two river systems, but also intermixing with the settled populations. The complex religious, cultural and economic organization of the region ensured, however, that Central Asia was ordered by overlapping gradations based upon, among other factors, ethnic, political, geographical, linguistic, religious, and economic distinctions (Manz, 1994: 4–14).

In the early nineteenth century three agro-urban, multi-ethnic political principalities – the khanates of Khiva, Bukhara and Kokand – controlled territory in the central area of Central Asia. They dominated the Transoxiana region and together posed the greatest challenge to the conquering Russians. The remaining territories of Central Asia were controlled by loose tribal confederations, notably in the arid areas of the south, the mountainous Pamir region and much of the present day Kyrgyz Republic and Kazakhstan. The organization, functions and membership of tribal units was, however, fluid and the geographical area controlled by individual tribes was, on occasion, subject to rapid change.

Beginning in the 1730s, when the Kazakh tribes came under the 'protection' of the Russian Empire, the territories of Central Asia were gradually subordinated to Russia through military conquest, diplomatic pressure, and settlement. Central Asia was enclosed and then annexed by the Russian Empire. These actions established a set of defined borders around the southern and eastern perimeter of Central Asia, which while not closing off the territory to neighbouring communities, began a process of delimiting and restructuring the spatial organization of the area (Allworth, 1994).

The Russian colonial period initiated a series of significant changes in the distribution of political power within Central Asia. First, power was gradually transferred from elements of the local elite to the colonial administration within Central Asia and in the imperial metropole (St. Petersburg). The pattern of Russian rule in Central Asia varied, however, from territory to territory. The predominately nomadic areas of the north and west were placed under close Russian control. Initially, Transoxiana enjoyed a less intrusive type of rule, with considerable power remaining within traditional local institutions. While the Russian regime significantly curtailed the power of secular organizations, the Islamic religious authorities remained powerful actors in Central Asian society.

Second, power was concentrated in new geographic locations and among new social groups. Regions – initially defined by the military-colonial administrators – acquired new significance as centres for administering and controlling the territories under Russian control, notably the Tashkent region, the military garrisons of the northern Kazakh Steppe and in the south the town of Verny (Almaty) (Mackenzie, 1988: 208–34; Becker, 1988:235–56). The opening up of new territories for migration by European/Slavs – particularly the northern and eastern areas of the Kazakh Steppe and urban areas for administration, trade and industry – led to the emergence of important new centres of power. Many of these new centres served as links with the rest of the Russian empire, thereby challenging the position of the oasis towns that had built their power on control of Silk Road trade routes (Bacon, 1966; Seton-Watson, 1967). Under colonial domination the axis of power in Central Asia shifted firmly from a predominantly east–west to a north–south orientation.

The Soviet period continued the broad trends initiated during the Russian colonial regime; however, a set of radical policies also began to reshape fundamentally political power in the region. Not only was power concentrated in new political groups and geographic locations in Central Asia, but the identities, and the social and economic relations that had supported the traditional systems of political power in the region, were transformed. The Soviet programme involved two main elements: (1) the establishment of distinct administrative units within the region (the five Central Asian republics), each with a separate political and economic infrastructure and identity, and (2) the extension of a set of central institutions and identities into Central Asia to bind each of the republics to the Russian/Soviet political core.

The policies implemented by the Soviet regime in Central Asia owed much to the need to establish control following the revolts against Russian rule immediately prior to the Russian revolution. The weakening of political power in the imperial core during the Russian revolution and subsequent civil war opened the way for groups in the previously important regions to seize back power from the colonial administration and the new political centres it had established (Pipes, 1964). The challenge to the Soviet regime in Central Asia was not, however, simply a return to previous political arrangements. In many parts of the region a new political force animated resistance: pan-Turkic nationalism.

The series of compromises that the Bolsheviks agreed with the nationalists in the early years of the Soviet era initially preserved the traditional centres of power in the region, although within redefined political networks. The agreements proved, however, to be the preliminary stage of a process which was to refashion the political organization of Central Asia. The catalyst for the changes was the so-called programme of national delimitation that began in 1924 and continued until 1936 (Sabol, 1995).

National delimitation consisted of a division of Central Asia into distinctive administrative units based upon economic and trade sub-systems, the distribution of ethnic communities, geography, and geo-strategic calculations. The new Soviet republics formed as a result of this process were to function as homelands for their titular populations. In fact, the ill-defined notions of ethnic identification, lack of distinct social and economic boundaries, and complex patterns of cultural and linguistic interaction ensured that national delimitation could not be achieved without ignoring historic divisions between communities, overlooking non-ethnic identities, creating ethnically defined minorities and remodelling the traditional organization of the region.[4] In the decades that followed national delimitation in Central Asia, a series of border amendments and jurisdictional changes transferred strategic regions from one republic to another, serving to complicate further relations between the new republics, and between titular and ethnic minority populations.[5]

The formal delimitation of Central Asia into separate republics was a critical first stage in reshaping the region. Equally important, however, was the set of policies introduced by the Soviet authorities to reinforce the administrative division. The Central Asian republics served as the vessels into which new political identities were to be poured. The creation of national languages, the abolition of the Arabic script (to be replaced by Latin and then differentiated Cyrillic scripts), the elaboration of distinct national histories and theories of ethnogenesis, accompanied by literacy campaigns, policies of economic modernization and, importantly, the drive to destroy Islam as a coherent organization in the region, all served to undermine traditional loyalties, political networks, and social and cultural identities (Allworth, 1990: 210–48). The new republics were also awarded their own political and economic institutions in the form of republican Communist parties, and various other youth and workers movements, parliaments (Soviets), and ministries.

The Soviet project of socio-economic and political transformation in Central Asia achieved important success. The division of the region into five separate political units drove a wedge between the Central Asian populations, while the new republics provided the basis for a steady rise of new forms of nationalism focused on the titular populations and away from pan-Turkism. The project of fostering unity within the new republics was, however, less successful. The republican capitals created as a result of the delimitation programme were relatively new centres for political power, with little history of controlling and administrating the territories that were now subordinated to them.

While the Soviet nationalizing project was critical to the aim of dividing the Central Asian population, the policy was constrained by Moscow's interest in preventing the emergence of powerful nationalist movements aimed at securing independence for the republics. Independent political centres with significant national hinterlands could not be allowed to emerge. Running in parallel to the nationalizing agenda there was, therefore, a series of policies designed to check the rise of unified national movements in Central Asia.

Critical to the task of restraining Central Asian nationalism was Moscow's relationship with strategic regions within each of the Central Asian republics.[6] The sizeable concentration of Slavic/European settler populations in Central Asia, in particular in the leading urban centres and in the north and east of Kazakhstan, provided an important constraint on the ability of native elites to act independently. At the same time, Moscow pursued close relations with regions beyond the republican capitals, particularly regions with a tradition of political importance, as a means of checking the advance of unified national elites.

Moscow's manipulation of regional relations as part of a divide-and-conquer strategy was important in fostering a reshaping and strengthening of regionalism in Central Asia. This factor alone, however, cannot explain the importance of regional-based politics during the Soviet period. First, Moscow's close supervision of republican institutions located in each capital, and usually staffed by Russian and loyalist personnel, encouraged local political actors to build their careers through the regional power structures which were less open to central intrusion. Second, the nationalizing project as a whole served to entrench regional power structures. The symbols and dialects selected to constitute the new standardized national identities were frequently drawn from one particular region, usually the territories of the republican capital.

The final factor promoting the development of regional-based political sub-systems in Central Asia during the late Soviet period was the stability of cadres during the Brezhnev era (Critchlow, 1988: 142–61). With a set of barriers in place to prevent the emergence of national political movements, the security of tenure enjoyed by leading personnel within the party and state structures fostered a proliferation of patronage networks at a sub-republican level thereby entrenching regions as political mechanisms for resource distribution (Gleason, 1991: 613–28).

The experience of Russian and Soviet colonialism in Central Asia, therefore, fostered a contradictory set of processes. While the Soviets were able to effect a radical transformation of Central Asia they could not completely remake the area. Former identities, loyalties and values continued to inform the new social and political arrangements created in the area, and echoes of the previous period provided sources of resistance to the Soviet project. Further, in seeking to transform Central Asia, the Soviet authorities actually fostered new forms of political activity and a reconfiguration of former political systems. While the nationalizing process went ahead at one level, manipulation of regional relations by the central Soviet authorities created a set of incentives among local elites to mobilize against central control and the nationalizing agenda on the basis of regional networks.

In the early 1980s, as a new Soviet leadership sought to reassert control over Central Asia and still later as the Soviet system began to disintegrate, the fragile political balance between regions in Central Asia was disturbed. As the reform movement gathered pace across the USSR, centre–regional politics acquired an increasing salience, particularly where this issue intersected with ethnic questions.

REGIONAL MOVEMENTS DURING THE *PERESTROIKA* PERIOD

The earliest indication that fundamental change was coming to Central Asia was the onset of the so-called 'Cotton Affair' in Uzbekistan in 1982. The cotton affair marked the first attempt by Moscow to break up the considerable power that local elites had established in regional patronage networks. Following the death in 1983 of the long standing First Secretary of the Communist Party in the republic, Sharaf Rashidov, an extensive five-year-long purge of the republican elite was launched in Uzbekistan. Subsequently, the purges spread to all the Central Asian republics in the mid-1980s, sweeping away much of the former Central Asian political leadership. The political space that opened within the Central Asian republics as a result of the purges conducted during the perestroika period created an environment in which regional politics acquired an increased pertinence.

The Gorbachev agenda of political reform contained a drive to recentralize control and as such struck at the power concentrated within key regional groups. The principal impulse behind the rise of regional politics, however, was not always a reassertion of traditional power centres in Central Asia but the rise of ethno-nationalist politics. The growth of ethnic-based political movements in key regions within Central Asia had the effect of reinforcing the fragmentation of political life along regional lines.

As the nature of politics began to shift in the late *perestroika* period, the republican national capitals sought increased powers from Moscow, and centre–regional relations underwent a further shift. The response of the titular elites to the Moscow-imposed purges was the growth of a protective nationalism. The regions which had previously looked to Moscow to ensure their well-being now faced the prospect of new controls from republican capitals controlled by increasingly nationalist, ethnically constituted elites.

The process of reform initiated by the Soviet leadership in the early 1980s, therefore, had important consequences for regional politics in Central Asia. The reform process fragmented the complex and multi-level set of political arrangements that had bound Central Asia together. In particular, the quadripartite relationship between Moscow, republican capitals, administrative regions, and areas in neighbouring republics populated by co-ethnics was increasingly replaced by a bilateral link between each republican capital and its subordinate regions. The rapid concentration of power within republican capitals provoked considerable alarm in many regions.

The strongest reaction to the new situation occurred within regions with large non-titular ethnic communities, which suddenly had to face the prospect of minority status. The main catalysts for regional movements in such cases were the republican declarations of sovereignty, which cut off minority communities from their neighbouring 'home' republics and from Moscow, and legislation on the state language, which threatened the previous dominance of Russian as a *lingua franca* and challenged the ability of Russian-speakers to operate successfully within their republic. Ethnic mobilization was not, however, the only source of conflict with the republican capitals in Central Asia during this period.

The concentration of power in republican capitals also challenged a number of other important groups in each republic, in particular regional elites. The growing power of the central elites in Almaty, Bishkek, Tashkent, Dushanbe and Ashkabat posed a direct threat to the economic and political networks that had been built up elsewhere during the Soviet years. While most regional elites were in a weak position relative to the central elite, those that could utilize other political resources, such as Islam or ethnicity, were able to pose a challenge to the newly dominant groups.

THE DYNAMICS OF POST-INDEPENDENCE REGIONAL POLITICS

The collapse of the Soviet Union at the end of 1991 led quickly to the emergence of the republican capitals as principal repositories of power in Central Asia. The transformation of political arrangements in the area in a short space of time had an important influence on the significance and form of regional politics. The immediate legacy of the Soviet system in Central Asia was weak states, poorly developed national identities, and entrenched sub-national political networks that had become increasingly animated as a result of the developments of the perestroika period.

The position of the new ruling elites seemed tenuous because of the weak nature of the political units that they ruled. The republican capitals were ill-prepared in terms of institutions, trained personnel and resources for the new tasks that faced them. The principal challenge for the republican level Central Asian elite was to consolidate their positions by forging viable and strong states where previously there existed, at best, proto-states. Establishing centralized control over the regions and the elites that dominated them was viewed as one of the main goals of the state-building project of the central authorities. Within a few years of independence, unitary models of state-building had appeared in all three of the Central Asian states reviewed here.

The cultivation of nationalism and national identity provided a means to mobilize political support for the new regime and to forge unity within the republic. Nationalism served as an important resource by which to further concentrate power in the political and economic networks in the republican capitals and to break the power of competing political networks. Although at independence citizenship was offered to all residents of each Central Asian state, irrespective of ethnic origin, considerable contradictions developed between the official project of civic nationalism and the actual practices of the states of the region. In all of the states of Central Asia, policies to foster and consolidate national identities, defined primarily in ethno-national forms, were launched in the 1990s. National symbols, heroes, holidays and festivals, and histories were promoted. Plans for the expansion of titular languages were announced throughout the region.

New economic policies also played a central role in promoting regional politics in Central Asia. During the Soviet period, the republican economies of Central Asia operated at two distinct levels. The prestigious, industrial sectors were integrated into the overall Soviet economy and controlled from Moscow. Lower level activity, particularly agriculture, was largely managed within individual republics, often at the regional level. Establishing control over the national economy was one of the principal tasks of the newly empowered central elites. In regions that had traditionally enjoyed wealth and prestige as a result of their economic activity, new forms of control by the national capital often proved unwelcome. The onset of privatization in some countries marked a further challenge to the economic position of the regional elite, with ownership of enterprises, utilities and natural resources passing into the hands of individuals and groups outside the region.[7]

The final resource available to the central elites in the struggle with the regions was the exercise of coercion, in various forms. In the most mild cases, the state apparatus was used to force regions to adopt policies, to purge regional personnel, and to structure political processes and institutions (notably through laws on elections and party registration,[8] the creation of pseudo-democratic institutions, and territorial reorganization), to the advantage of the central elite. In its harshest form, violence was exercised through the military and security services against individuals and groups in the regions. Although a common set of factors informed regional politics in Kazakhstan, the Kyrgyz Republic and Uzbekistan in the first decade of independence, distinct patterns of centre–regional relations emerged in the three states.

Kazakhstan

In the ten years following independence, the Republic of Kazakhstan faced one of the most serious challenges in respect to regional politics in Central Asia. Centre–regional relations in the first decade of independence can broadly be divided into two periods. In the first five years, the central authorities developed a programme to contain the challenge of regional movements, particularly a potential ethno-regional challenge stemming from the concentration of European/Slavic communities in the north and east of the country. From 1995, a radical programme for restructuring the territorial organization of the state emerged, designed to undermine regional and ethnic threats to the central authorities.

The principal source of regional tensions in Kazakhstan following independence was the legacy of settlement and the structure of political power inherited from the Russian and Soviet periods. The expansion of the Russian Empire and the consolidation of Russian and then Soviet control over the Kazakh Steppe were greatly facilitated by waves of migration from European Russia. Over the course of 50 years in the late nineteenth and early twentieth century, the demographic balance in the north and east was shifted in favour of the Russian settlers as the Kazakh tribes were pushed from the region, forcibly settled and Russified (Demko, 1969). The industrialization and urbanization of the north and east during the Soviet years further ensured that there was an uneven process of modernization; heavily Russified regions enjoyed a disproportionately advantageous development compared to the predominantly Kazakh populated, poor and rural areas of the south.

During the perestroika period, the relationship between the south and the Russified areas of the north and east began to undergo important changes. The republican laws on language and sovereignty passed in the final years of the Gorbachev era demonstrated that Almaty was increasingly in a position to project a predominately southern defined Kazakh cultural identity onto the Russified areas of the north. Insecurity in the Russified regions as a result of these changes prompted the first stirring of local political mobilization against the growing power of the south.

With independence, power was increasingly concentrated in the hands of the president and the political networks emanating from his administration. The reach of the central authorities was, however, initially limited. Alternative centres of power existed at the regional level, particularly in the north and east. In this environment, the central authorities developed a range of policies to contain and co-opt the regional challenge. Pseudo-political parties organized by President Nazarbaev and his supporters and designed to co-opt key elements of the former nomenklatura in the regions were established. For example, the pro-presidential party SNEK that existed in the early 1990s contained many leading officials and enterprise directors from the north and east of the country.

At the same time, the appointment of local governors, key figures in the local administrations, and law and order personnel (judges, police, prosecutors) began to shift control of the regions into the hands of new, primarily Kazakh political networks. Control of enterprises passed to ministries in the south and to a new managerial class drawn predominately from amongst Kazakhs, particularly from the political centre. Constitutional provisions, electoral laws and fraud also structured elections to ensure that the regions were not able to attain powerful and independent representation. In the first parliamentary elections after independence, a quota system was established to ensure that at least two deputies loyal to the central authorities were elected from each region (Melvin, 1995).

With much of the Soviet era regional elite drawn into newly created political institutions, or replaced with regime loyalists, and lacking strong indigenous institutions following the demise of the all-Union Communist Party and state apparatus, independent representation for the north and east appeared to rest with ethno-political organizations. In the late 1980s, the shifting centre of political gravity in Kazakhstan produced the first attempts to mobilize an ethno-regional movement to protect the interests of the northern and eastern districts. In the early years of the independence period, the political movement LAD was established on the basis of the Russian cultural centres of the north and east. The movement, however, faced considerable opposition to its activities from local and central authorities, particularly when LAD sought to win political representation through elections. While a few LAD candidates were successful in elections, most faced illegal and semi-legal barriers to registration and harassment (Melvin, 1995: 100–23; Bremmer and Welt, 1995).

The lack of success of the Russian political movement in the early 1990s exposed the central weakness of the potential ethno-regional challenge to the central authorities. While the north and east of the country contained large numbers of non-Kazakhs, they lacked a consolidated ethno-political or regional identity or common set of interests that could serve as a basis for mobilizing opposition to the central authorities. The lack of a developed ethno-cultural basis amongst the Slavic population stemmed from the ambiguous nature of Russian ethnic and national identities in the Russian imperial and Soviet systems but was also the result of the lack of a strong ethno-nationalist identity amongst the Kazakhs themselves, at least in the early years of independence (Melvin, 1998: 27–57).

Although Kazakh ethnic identity had been consolidated during the Soviet years, division rather than national unity was the leading characteristic of the titular population at independence. Historically, three tribal groupings or hordes existed on the Kazakh territories. While it is difficult to identify tribalism in Kazakhstan in the early years of independence – socio-economic development and organization, modern communications, and new political forms meant there was little place for such forms of social organizations – the echoes of former identities and loyalties and the differing experiences of Russification amongst Kazakh communities meant that regional politics was informed by previous tribal divisions. Family and kin ties, local political and patron–client networks, and career patterns ensured that regions often served as semi-closed political systems for different Kazakh groups with local leaders frequently drawn from similar kin groups (Akiner, 1995: 75). With independence, these local political systems faced intrusion from the authorities in the republican capital on a scale not previously experienced, often reanimating or leading to a 'reimagining' of former identities and social structures (Schatz, 2000a: 489–506).

Earlier contact with the Russian Empire and the intensive process of Russification in the west, north and east ensured that Kazakhs from these areas were more closely linked to the political and economic structures of the Russified regions (that is, all-union institutions) than to those of the south. During the latter decades of the Soviet Union, the southern groups gradually took control of the republican institutions as a result of the policy of stability of cadres. With the collapse of the Soviet Union, the southern constituted networks of power were in a position to dominate the new state structures of independent Kazakhstan. Concern amongst Kazakhs in the northern, western and eastern regions about the growing dominance of southern groups prompted the emergence of a number of predominately Kazakh political movements with a strong regional flavour, although the central authorities subsequently undermined them.[9]

Thus, in Kazakhstan in the early years of independence a multi-level political struggle developed. At the end of 1991, the capital of Kazakhstan located in the south of the country with a hinterland of predominantly ethnic Kazakh patronage networks that stretched into the southern regions gained control over the territories of the country. While the president went out of his way to suggest that there were representatives from all communities and regions at the highest level of Kazakhstani politics, there is considerable evidence that the southern elite spread its network of power into the other regions, particularly through control over state appointments. At the same time, a process of Kazakhization heavily informed by a southern defined concept of ethnic and national identity, of many parts of the state apparatus, at both a central and regional level, threatened the previous position of the Russian community. By the mid-1990s, much of the Russified elite earlier co-opted by the new regime had been displaced.

In reaction to the growing redistribution of power, opposition began to mobilize on a regional basis, reflecting ethnic and social cleavages in

Kazakhstani society. Although the central authorities had considerable advantages in relation to the provinces, caution was exercised in relation to regional movements. In particular, the large size of the Slavic community and the Russian Federation's professed interest in 'protecting' its diaspora, coupled with the role of Kazakhs in regional movements, placed important limits on the degree to which Kazakh nationalism could be promoted as an official goal. In this environment, the central authorities became reliant on the newly constituted regional elite to contain or destroy regional political movements. For much of the early years of independence the regional elite enjoyed important levels of autonomy and stability. Indeed one writer argues that the early period of independence was marked by an accommodation of the pressures of diversity by instituting increased levels of informal ethno-regional autonomy (Cummings, 2000).

Ultimately, however, ethnicity failed to function as a political resource to mobilize the Russian population and the potential regional challenge, particularly based on ethno-political identities, faded. Instead, control of the institutions of the central state emerged as a far more potent political resource. From the mid-1990s, the transfer of the national capital and associated bureaucracy to the north, policies designed to promote the emergence of a national elite, and an extension of the policies of Kazakhization across the territory of Kazakhstan marked a new phase in the state-building project in the country.

The dissolution of the parliament in 1995 represented a turning point in centre–regional relations. With the ethno-regional challenge largely contained, and in some regions all but destroyed, the central authorities launched an ambitious rolling programme to reorganize the territorial structure of the state. The republican authorities sought to establish a strong central government and to adopt institutional procedures and practices commensurate with the new form of centralized territorial control.

In place of the single chamber parliament that had existed previously, the new parliament was bicameral in structure and contained an in-built pro-presidential bloc (Cummings, 1996). Together these changes served to weaken fundamentally the legislature as a political institution. The altered structure of the parliament and the mechanism by which deputies were elected helped to prevent the regions gaining high level independent political representation.[10] From the mid-1990s, the executive became the only significant political institution in the country.

A new constitution, approved by a national referendum of 30 August 1995, greatly strengthened the position of the executive, concentrating power in a network of regional prefects (*akims*), directly subordinated to the president.[11] Under article 2, Kazakhstan was for the first time formally identified as a unitary state (*Konstitutsiia Respubliki Kazakhstan*, 1996: 63–121). Also critical to the process of centralization was the transfer of the capital from Almaty, in the south of the country, to Astana in the north and a process of amalgamating regions beginning in 1997.

The drive to bind the regions more closely to the centre hinged upon an attempt to integrate the regional elite into a national elite structure. A new generation of akims loyal to the president was appointed in many regions and they were also granted important areas of local discretion, such as control over some important local enterprises. Unlike the early 1990s, however, greater efforts were made to prevent strong local patron–client networks developing, and the regional leaders, particularly from regions that demonstrated resistance to Almaty's rule such as East Kazakhstan, were subject to periodic replacement and rotation into the central state apparatus (Dave, 1996: 1–2).

By the end of the first decade of independence for Kazakhstan, the balance of power had begun to swing in favour of the central authorities. Power was concentrated in the hands of the president and his network and the central state was increasingly able to project its authority into the regions. Regions and regionally-based political movements, however, continued to constitute a potential threat to the regime, as highlighted by an alleged coup attempt by a small group of Russians in the north-east of the country in November 1999 (Cutler, 1999). Moreover, despite the efforts of the central authorities, the regional elite continued to exist as a distinct group with interests that frequently contradicted those of the centre. The uneasy balance between regions and centre led to speculation that the existing 14 regions would be consolidated as five large regions (RFE/RL Newsline, 2000).

THE KYRGYZ REPUBLIC

Like Kazakhstan, centre–regional relations in the Kyrgyz Republic following independence were primarily driven by a struggle between northern and southern groups with a regionally concentrated ethnic community (the Uzbeks in the south) providing the basis for a potential secessionist movement. Although the elements of centre–regional relations in the Kyrgyz Republic were similar to those of Kazakhstan, the political dynamics were in fact quite different. While the ethno-political structure and distribution of power established during the Russian and Soviet regimes provided the backdrop for post-independence centre–regional politics, it was political change in the latter years of the Gorbachev era, notably the emergence of Askar Akaev as president, that laid the basis for post-independence political geography of the Republic.

The creation of the Kyrgyz Soviet Socialist Republic in the 1930s involved binding together as a single administrative unit territories with similar ethnic characteristics (sizeable Kyrgyz populations) but with very different socio-economic and cultural traditions. In the south, the area around the city of Osh had historically been home to a variety of communities, although the Kyrgyz had become the most numerous in the latter decades of the twentieth century. In the urban areas in the south, however, Uzbek-speakers had dominated for hundreds of years. Prior to the territorial delimitation of Central Asia, geography, culture and history closely linked Osh and other southern areas to political centres in the Ferghana Valley and Transoxiana.

With the creation of the Kyrgyz SSR, the new capital Bishkek was granted considerable authority in relation to the territory under its control; however, the south remained significant because of the importance of agriculture and its large, and growing, population. In the late Soviet period, power in the republic was largely exercised through political networks originating in the south. Although largely composed of ethnic Kyrgyz, local Uzbeks (especially from the Osh City CPSY organization) attained high-level representation. These networks dominated republic-level institutions, particularly the Communist Party. A number of southerners attained the status of republican first secretary, including Absamat Masaliev who was republican leader from 1986 and prided himself on the maintenance of a highly conservative order in the republic. An open border between the Kyrgyz, Uzbek and Tajik republics ensured that groups such as the Uzbeks in the south of the country could maintain close contacts with co-ethnics in neighbouring republics, send their children to be educated in Uzbekistan and gain easy access to Uzbek language media.

In the 1970s, the ethnic balance in the south began to change as a result of differential birth rates between the Kyrgyz and the Uzbeks (the Kyrgyz were reproducing faster than the Uzbeks). The rapid population growth amongst both leading ethnic communities placed increased pressure on the critical resources of land and water, creating tension between the two leading ethnic communities in the south. Rising migration to urban areas amongst the Kyrgyz caused by high levels of rural employment made the cities and towns of the south the focus for tension between the two groups (Kostyukova, 1994: 425–34).

The onset of the perestroika era policies of elite replacement and increased central intrusion into localities further disturbed the fine balance that had existed between north and south, and between different groups in the south. The rise of Kyrgyz and Uzbek nationalist sentiments brought about by the rise in nationalist politics throughout the USSR and the declarations of sovereignty in the Kyrgyz Republic and Uzbekistan greatly exacerbated tensions in the south. Fears among the southern Uzbeks that the Kyrgyz would have increased power within a sovereign Kyrgyz Republic formed an important part of the background to ethnic rioting in 1990 between the two groups in Novyi Uzgen and Osh. Local Uzbeks also called for regional territorial autonomy and the adoption of Uzbek as the official language in the region.

While party and government elites in the Kyrgyz Republic had long been differentiated along a regional north and south cleavage, the events of the perestroika period greatly intensified the competition between the two areas. Tension between north and south surfaced at the end of 1990 following the removal of Masaliev as republican leader, in response to the ethnic rioting in the south, and his replacement with Askar Akaev. Alarmed about the erosion of the traditional dominance of key republican posts that the southern elite had enjoyed, there were increased calls for structural change that would guarantee greater autonomy for the south and thereby protect local political networks (Huskey, 1997: 665). A variety of proposals were made, including the idea of dividing the republic in two and the formation of a Kyrgyz Federation based on distinct northern and southern republics.

The rise to power of the political outsider Askar Akaev, who was elected president of the republic on 28 October 1990, signified an important shift of power in the Kyrgyz Republic. The emergence of Akaev marked the triumph of the minority Russified urban Kyrgyz of the north over the majority rural and largely southern Kyrgyz. The problems of governing in this situation, however, placed considerable pressures on the Akaev government and in the mid-1990s forced the regime into a series of important compromises with the regional elite. A defining moment for political development in the republic came at the end of 1993, when an increasingly isolated president forged an informal alliance with the regional executives. Akaev gambled that the popularity and patronage powers of the presidency would enable him to control the regional leaders.

In fact, the deal opened the way for a series of changes that strengthened the position of the regional elite as a whole. In late 1994, Akaev permitted regional executive officials to join one of the chambers of the recently created bicameral parliament. This chamber was modelled on the Federation Council of the Russian parliament. As a result of these changes, regional relations were institutionalized at the heart of political life in the republic with regional leaders enjoying important power at the political centre.

The regional elite also sought to enhance its local and national political position. In late 1993, the southern akims (Osh and Jalal-Abad districts) sponsored the formation of the Social Democrats, a new party that largely consisted of the leading members of the southern regional administrations. A central plank in the party's platform was the call for the direct election of regional leaders (*Slovo Kyrgyzstan*, 1994: 3). If enacted, this measure would have considerably strengthened the position of the southern leaders by breaking their dependence on presidential patronage.

Although the central government was prepared to grant important concessions to the regional elite, Akaev was also concerned to weaken the position of the southern groups. The president was particularly active in preventing the emergence of a broad-based challenge to his position from the south. Thus, Janysh Rustenbekov, the leader of Osh district, was replaced in July 1996, apparently because of an interview in which he outlined territorial disputes between the Kyrgyz Republic and Uzbekistan and spoke of the poor relationship between presidents Karimov and Akaev. As the centre sought to displace potential challengers from leading official positions in the south, the once powerful figures from the region were forced to rely on former Soviet organizations, primarily the Communist Party, to mobilize support. The growing ethnic polarization in the area, however, restricted the potential of this organization to attract popular backing from different groups.

Initially, the Uzbek minority community in the south served as an important ally for the north in its struggle with the formerly dominant southern elite. The rise of ethno-politics in the south during the late 1980s had produced an uncoupling of the Uzbeks from the leading regional political networks. In this situation the southern Uzbeks offered support to the central authorities, seen in its clearest form in the election of 1995. The Uzbek population offered support for Akaev, while the majority of the Kyrgyz in the south voted for Absamat Masaliev, the former first secretary of the republic and leader of Kyrgyz Communist Party.

In the latter years of the decade, despite the president's moves to prevent individuals emerging from the regional elite to challenge him, the importance of the regional elite as a whole and the post of the regional executive continued to grow in the Kyrgyz Republic. Chronic domestic socio-economic problems, the disputed southern borders with Uzbekistan, and the move by the president to further consolidate his political control, ensured that the Akaev regime relied more and more on the regional elite for support.

Beginning in late 1999, the drive to suppress opposition to Akaev in preparation for the presidential elections of 2000 drew the regional elite closer to the central authorities as the president was forced to rely upon regional groupings for repression and control. The creation of a new southern district (Batken) following an incursion in the summer of 1999 by armed Islamic militants from Tajikistan, and the manipulation of elections in the south in late 1999 to ensure political victory for Kyrgz candidates, made the centre further reliant upon the support of the regional elite.

Following Akaev's re-election, the close interdependence of the central and regional levels of executive power became even further apparent. In late December 2000, Kurmanbek Bakiev, a political figure from the south and former governor of the southern district of Jalal-Abad was appointed as Prime Minister (RFE/RL Newsline, 2001). The governor of Osh district was appointed finance minister. At the same time, the former minister for extraordinary situations became governor of Jalal-Abad, while the former minister of transport became mayor of the city of Osh.

Centre–regional relations in the Kyrgyz Republic, therefore, underwent a rapid evolution in the post-independence years. In the early 1990s, centre–regional relations were characterized by confrontation. The concentration of power around Akaev, a political figure with a small and relatively weak support base, was challenged by entrenched political structures in many of the Kyrgyz Republic's regions, ensuring a finely balanced relationship between the capital and the provinces. The weakness of the centre in relation to the regions, however, eventually led Akaev into a series of compromises with regional representatives, which accepted a growing role for regionally based politics in shaping the national political system.

By the late 1990s, the regional leadership had become critical to the president's drive to consolidate his control over Kyrgyz society. A general deterioration of the socio-economic situation and a worsening security problem in the south ensured that the regional elite was drawn further into the ruling regime. The emergence of this relationship formed part of the authoritarian political order that developed in the republic in the latter years of the decade (Melvin, 2002). Increased loyalty to the centre also ensured that the regional elite was granted greater discretion in running the regions and that they also gained institutionalized access (through the upper chamber of parliament), informal consultation (through regular meetings with the president) and high level appointments to the centre of decision-making.

The emergence of a ruling regime based on an alliance between the regional and central elite marked an important change for other leading regional interests. The Uzbek minority, which had been important in the early part of the decade as an ally of the president, was increasingly politically isolated. Much of the former southern elite that had challenged Akaev in the early years of independence was also marginalized. With Akaev loyalists occupying the key posts in the regions, the former southern elite was confined to the rapidly waning Communist Party and unable to exert significant influence over the politics of the republic.[12]

UZBEKISTAN

In Uzbekistan, the pattern of centre–regional relations that emerged in the post-independence period was significantly different from the cases of Kazakhstan and the Kyrgyz Republic. In particular, the central political authorities in Uzbekistan were more successful in asserting their dominance over the regions than in the other two Central Asian cases. Following independence, the elite in the national capital embarked at an early stage on a programme to destroy regional networks of power and replace them with a national elite controlled through the capital. This aim was pursued through a number of interrelated measures.

The political system that emerged in the first years of independence was in large part a product of the complex regional political balance that was informally institutionalized in the Communist Party in Uzbekistan during the Soviet period. In particular, during the Brezhnev era the first party secretary of Uzbekistan, Sharaf Rashidov, built up a powerful ruling group composed primarily of relatives and the regional leadership from Samarkand. The Tashkent regional elite was only included in this system in second-tier posts. The complex set of regional relations in Uzbekistan was critical to Moscow's power in the area, permitting it to act as the arbiter in the relations between competing elite networks in the republic (Vaisman, 1995: 105–22). The legacy of this arrangement was a republic fragmented into six distinct regions, with their own history, sub-culture and identity (Fane, 1996: 277–82).

The pattern of centre–regional relations was complicated by the Andropov era initiative to re-establish Moscow's control in the republic. In Uzbekistan, the campaign that began as an effort to catch a few local criminals eventually mushroomed into Central Asia's most extensive political purge (Carlisle, 1991: 23–44). Between 1984 and 1987, some 40 of 65 party secretaries in the UzSSR were replaced. Over 260 new secretaries of city and district party committees were elected. One third of all the chairmen and vice chairmen of regional party committees were changed (Gleason, 1997: 576). The shifting balance of power in the country had important effects on the regional situation in Uzbekistan. In 1989 and 1990 ethnic violence broke out in the Ferghana region. These changes prompted important shifts at the top of the political system in the republic. The weakening of regional political networks and the rapid rise of a younger elite opened the way for important changes in the structure of power in the republic after 1991.

Rashidov was initially replaced by Nishanov, a leader from the Ferghana area who brought with him leading representatives from the eastern provinces. The Ferghana riots in 1989, however, led to Nishanov's dismissal (by Moscow) and his replacement by Islam Karimov. Karimov was appointed as president by the parliament in March 1990, an election that prompted a struggle between Karimov and the leading representative of the former elite, Shukurulla Mirsaidov. Karimov's victory led quickly to the eclipse of Mirsaidov in 1992. This proved to be the final stage in the ascendance of Karimov and his supporters to undisputed dominance in Uzbekistan and the creation of a powerful, centralized system.

Following independence, strong unitary control was achieved in Uzbekistan through the construction of centralized executive power, the dismissal of opponents and the use of repression. A rigid vertical hierarchy of executive power was established in the constitution, particularly in respect to the regions of the republic. Although the constitution recognizes four major territorial divisions in the country – the Autonomous Republic of Karakalpakstan, the district, the region and the city – there is no provision for any meaningful lower tiers of independent authority. The Karakalpak Republic exists within the structure of the Republic of Uzbekistan and has its own constitution, parliament and president but the laws of Uzbekistan are superior to those of Karakalpak Republic. The Constitution specifies in a general way the 'competence' of the lower administrative units but makes clear that these are delegated from the centre, not independent (Hanks, 2000: 939–53).

Critical to the centralization of power in the republic was the creation of a prefectural (*hakim*) system. The new organization of administration shifted the 12 former oblasts to districts headed by a hakim. All of the hakim appointments announced in March 1992 were ethnic Uzbeks, all had previously been regional party committee secretaries, and all were members of the People's Democratic Party of Uzbekistan, the president's party. In the constitution, the president is given the power to appoint and dismiss the regional governors, and to suspend or repeal local acts passed by the hakims. The regional hakim simultaneously heads the local legislative council and appoints and removes the hakims of lower level units (makhalas/raions and cities).

The highly authoritarian nature of the political system in Uzbekistan and the anti-Islamic campaign that was waged by president Karimov made the regional leader increasingly important to the regime. With considerable power vested in the position of regional hakim, control over these positions was critical to the centre's ability to dominate the regions. President Karimov ensured that the hakims were loyal to him and subjected the regional leaderships to regular purges. The reasons cited for these dismissals included poor grain harvests, corruption and the slow speed of social and economic reforms. Frequently, the regional leaders were replaced with appointees from the centre.[13]

A serious regional challenge to Tashkent's authority came from Islamic movements in the Ferghana Valley.[14] In the early years of independence, the Ferghana region (traditionally the area for conservative Islam in Central Asia) emerged as an important area for an Islamic revival. Islam was used by the regional elite, which had lost power with the political ascent of Karimov, to mobilize support against Tashkent. The most significant Islamic political organization was the Adolat (Justice) Party.

The centre of Adolat's activities was in Namangan region where the Islamic movement briefly seized control of the city following independence. In the 1990s, Tashkent became steadily more involved in a struggle with the Islamic movement in the Ferghana Valley. The central authorities sought to control the regionally based Islamic revival through the projection of a state-sponsored 'official' Islam into the regions. Subsequent hakims of Namangan region, such as Tolkun Jabbarov, specifically targeted the remnants of Adolat in the region for 'adequate measures' (Clover, 1997).

Centre–regional relations in Uzbekistan, then, have followed a different course again to the cases of Kazakhstan and Kyrgyzstan. Although having one of the most entrenched systems of regional politics during the Soviet era, following independence the new central elite moved swiftly to destabilize and destroy sub-national political networks before rebuilding them as a single national system. The autonomy of the regions was severely proscribed through the constitution and the strict hierarchy of power that was established across the republic.

At the same time, measures to foster the creation of a new national elite were undertaken, including the establishment of training colleges in Tashkent and the circulation of leading figures through the national capital to the regions. Campaigns against corruption, nepotism, poor management, and radical Islam were used as the pretexts for removing key local figures. Uzbek nationalism and coercive policies against 'fundamentalist' Islam and localist sentiments were promoted together as a means to undermine regional value systems that might be used to mobilize resistance to the centre. Finally, the centre's firm control over all forms of economic activity ensured that the regions had few resources with which to challenge the centre.

While Tashkent was able to establish tight control over the territory of Uzbekistan, the state remained fragile and overly reliant on coercion to ensure regional compliance. As one commentator noted: 'While the process of building a national identity is moving forward rapidly, Uzbekistan still exists as a patchwork quilt of regions stitched together to form a single nation' (Fane, 1996).

CONCLUSIONS

Like other post-Soviet republics, in the first decade of independence the new states of Central Asia faced a variety of problems in structuring relations between the new centres of political power and the regions subordinated to them. The subsequent development of territorial politics and the form of state-building that emerged differed in important ways from that found in most other states in the former Soviet Union. Despite the ethnic conflicts that accompanied the breakdown of the Soviet order in Central Asia, the presence of regionally concentrated ethnic communities, territorialized nationality, and potential 'homeland' states for diaspora communities, in the first decade of independence significant secessionist or irredentist movements did not emerge to challenge the authority and boundaries of the newly independent Central Asian states.

Nor, indeed, did the central authorities offer significant concessions in the form of federal or confederal arrangements to regions with concentrations of ethnic communities. Instead, formally unitary states were established based upon strong executive power and programmes of nation-building through incorporation of different ethnic groups. Although strongly tinged with ethnic characteristics Kazakhstani, Uzbekistani and Kyrgyzstani 'civic' identities were formally promoted as the basis for state-building (Schatz, 2000b: 71–94).

The broad similarities that characterized territorial politics of the post-independence period stem primarily from the legacy of the Russian imperial and Soviet orders common to the states examined here. In the twentieth century, Central Asian society was thoroughly reshaped through contact with the Russian Empire, the territorial delimitation initiated from 1924, the programme of societal transformation launched in the late 1920s and the Stalinist purges of the 1930s. As a result of these radical changes, the previous territorial organization of power structures was broken and new patterns of loyalty, identity and subordination at central and regional levels were introduced. During the latter decades of Soviet rule, a complex relationship developed between the regions, republics, peoples and elites of Central Asia and Moscow. The breakdown of the Soviet order fostered a further reorientation of spatial relations and identities in the region.

In the 1990s, the central and regional elites of the newly independent states struggled to refashion the political, social and economic relations of previous orders in response to the changed circumstances of the post-

Soviet era. Four particular elements exerted a significant pull on determining the broad contours of territorial politics in this period:

First, despite Soviet programmes to foster nations and develop the Central Asia republics as proto-states, at the time of independence the regions within the new republics enjoyed considerable autonomy. Patron–client systems, cultural identities, language and economic networks reinforced cleavage structures at a sub-national level. During the latter years of perestroika, many of these elements became particularly animated, thereby presenting a particular challenge to the newly empowered central elites.

Second, although nationalism was a potent force in Central Asia in the late 1980s, it did not constitute a mass movement (Grant, 1994: 51–8; Brown, 1990: 87–96). On the one hand, this meant that minorities were not directly threatened by independence, while on the other hand, it meant that the titular population also lacked the unified identity and interests that undergirded the nationalist movements of the Baltic states and western territories of the Soviet Union. Many of the major social processes that lay behind nationalizing programmes in other parts of the world, notably the transformation of rural societies into urban ones, had yet to occur in Central Asia. The migration of titular rural populations into urban centres settled by different ethnic groups, and the tensions created as result of this change, was only beginning in parts of Central Asia as the Soviet order collapsed (Heleniak, 1997: 357–78). In the 1990s, potential ethno-regional movements were therefore undermined by the lack of ethnified territorial institutional structures and drawn into the centre–regional struggles instead. At the same time, without a powerful popular basis for nationalism within the titular populations, the three states of the region examined here developed official policies based upon inclusion, even if practice frequently fell short of the stated aims.

Third, a critical legacy of the Russian and Soviet orders for the new states of Central Asia was weak political centres. The Soviet-era institutions of state and party were quickly swept aside in the post-independence period. Despite attempts to foster new formal institutions, informal networks and patron–client systems quickly emerged as the basis of post-independence political life. Lacking adequate formal institutions to integrate regional and ethnic interests and to structure and contain conflict, post-independence politics quickly became a struggle by the central elites to exert their control over regional elites through the establishment of formally unitary states.

Fourth, there was a limited interaction of the elements of the 'triadic nexus' – home-state, host-state and diaspora communities – in terms of promoting nationalization and secession amongst ethnic communities in

Central Asia (Brubaker, 1996). In the case of Russia, important structural checks on the ability of the Russian state to pursue an aggressive policy towards its diaspora meant that 'exit' became the optimal decision for many of Central Asia's Russian population. Elsewhere in Central Asia, the complex nature of cross-border inter-ethnic relations and the weak nature of ethno-national identity in many areas limited the role of home and host states towards potential diaspora populations in the area.

While the factors identified above account for the emergence of the Central Asian republics as a distinct sub-set of the post-Soviet states, they do not explain the different patterns of centre–regional relations that emerged within this sub-group in the 1990s. In Kazakhstan the Russian question in the north and east, coupled with regional divisions within the titular elite, combined initially to impede the drive to centralize power. Regions were able to gain and protect informal types of autonomy. Eventually, to overcome regional resistance a state-building project emerged in Kazakhstan based upon a territorial re-organization of political space and policies of centralization. In this model, regional elite networks were either destroyed or incorporated into the new regime and new political centres created to challenge entrenched regional networks.

In the Kyrgyz Republic, the emergence of Akaev as president displaced the previous territorial organization of power. The ensuing struggle between former networks of power in the southern regions and the newly empowered but weaker networks based around the president in the north led eventually to the emergence of a ruling regime built on the incorporation of regional elites. Although relations continued to be characterized by important tensions, the regional elite and the president became increasingly interdependent as internal problems and external threats mounted. In this variant, regional power was largely preserved within a newly constituted unitary state.

In Uzbekistan, a different relationship between centre and regions emerged as the foundation for a unitary state. President Karimov rose to power through the Soviet era nomenklatura network (unlike Akaev in the Kyrgyz Republic), but a network that had been heavily purged. Moreover, although there was localized ethnic conflict in parts of Uzbekistan – indeed this was the catalyst for elite level change in the late Gorbachev period – the post-independence leadership did not face a serious ethno-regionalist challenge. Relying upon the Soviet era elite networks located primarily at the political centre, Karimov was able to overwhelm regionally based groups and impose a highly centralized state. Local networks were replaced with a regional elite appointed by the centre and loyal to the president. While essential to the project of consolidating president Karimov's rule, these actions have helped to promote the rise of radical Islam and further destabilize the Ferghana Valley.

Serious questions remain about the fragility of the unitary orders established in Central Asia. While inclusivist notions of nationality have been promoted to incorporate minorities and informal degrees of elite autonomy operate in several locations, the lack of serious concessions in terms of territorial autonomy to regions and ethnic communities has placed increased strains on existing political arrangements. At the same time, the rise of domestic tensions around centre–regional issues, particularly ethnic issues, points to a future where there may well be a growing engagement by home-states (notably Uzbekistan and the Russian Federation) with diaspora communities, raising tensions along borders and within ethnic enclaves. Instability in Tajikistan and Afghanistan, cross-border incursions and diaspora issues, ethnic tensions, socio-economic problems and the rise of regionally focused political Islam threaten the forms of territorial political arrangements that have been developed in the Central Asian states (Nunn et al., 1999). Regions remain a critical faultline in Central Asia that could well undermine or even destroy the current projects of unitary nation and state-building.

NOTES

1. Areas of territorialized ethnicity existed in Central Asia within two independent states, the Karakalpak Republic in Uzbekistan and the Gorno-Badakhshan Autonomous Oblast in Tajikistan. In the decade following the collapse of the Soviet order, neither region served as the basis for secessionist movements. Although Gorno-Badakhshan was closely engaged in the civil war in Tajikistan, this involvement reflected the fragmentation of the country along regional lines. Other regions of the country without particular administrative status also became the basis for political mobilization. The goals of conflict were not secession but control over the national capital and state.

2. Bunce has challenged the emphasis made in transitology on the importance of changes in the post-independence period. Instead, she has pointed to the role of legacies from the previous order in shaping and even determining outcomes in the post-communist states. Whereas, however, Bunce identifies state socialism as the principal source of legacies, in Central Asia the Soviet regime formed only a part of a broader development. It was the experience of incorporation into the Russian imperial and Soviet states, and the transformations – both direct in terms of the overt policies of control and management, and indirect in terms of deep-seated socio-economic and value change (modernization) brought about by this experience – that provided the main backdrop to the politics of the post-independence period. The identities, networks and institutions that shaped the politics of the newly independent Central Asia states were the products of over a century of transformation in the region.

3. Of the other two Central Asian countries, Tajikistan collapsed as a unified state in the early 1990s and has gradually been reconstituted around informally defined federal arrangements, and Turkmenistan has largely followed the pattern of centre–regional relations found in Uzbekistan.

4. A prerequisite for fixing the borders of national communities prior to delimitation was the construction of distinct ethnic groups in Central Asia. The Russian and Soviet census

played a fundamental role in this respect, requiring ethnic self-identification and steering individuals to adopt centrally defined and limited identities. Many potential identities, notably that of the sedentary and largely urban 'Sart', were not available as a choice within the census, causing groups to disappear into officially recognized categories.

5. In the first phase of national delimitation, the Uzbek SSR was established. The re-emergence of the traditional political centres of Central Asia as the location of the pan-Turkic nationalists constituted a major threat to Soviet rule in the area. The creation of Uzbekistan provided a means to replace the political alliances that had developed by the mid-1920s. The power centres of the Khiva oases, the Persian-speaking groups of the Samarkand and Bukhara oases, and Ferghana Valley were gradually subordinated to Tashkent and an Uzbek identity. Allworth argues that the creation of the Uzbek SSR formed the central part of an anti-Turkistan policy. If the creation of the Uzbek SSR formed the core of the delimitation project, establishing the Kazakh republic was critical to harnessing the core areas of Central Asia to the Russian Federation. Both Kazakhs and Uzbeks laid claim to the Syr Daria region and to Karakalpakia. The Kazakhs initially gained much of the former region, excluding the city of Tashkent, and also Karakalpakia. At the same time, Orenburg was removed from the Kazakh lands and the republican capital was initially transferred to Ak-Mechet (Kzyl-Orda) in the south and then in 1929 to the east to Alma-Ata (Almaty), a small largely Russian town. In 1932 Karakalpakia was awarded to Uzbekistan. The territories and peoples that had become the Kazakh ASSR in 1925 became the Kazakh SSR in 1936. Besides these two critical territorial divisions, the remaining Central Asia lands were also parcelled into republics. In 1924, alongside the creation of the Uzbek SSR, the Turkmen SSR was established on the basis of the Turkmen regions of western Bukhara, Khorezm and the former Transcaspian region. In August 1925, the Qara-Kirgiz autonomous region was transformed into the Kyrgyz Autonomous Oblast, and in May 1926 it became the Kyrgyz Autonomous Republic. In December 1936, the Kyrgyz SSR was established at the same time as the Kazakh SSR. In 1929, the Tajik Autonomous region within the Uzbek SSR was established as an independent republic in its own right.

6. Also important for containing nationalism were the penetration of central institutions into each republic such as the Communist Party, the system of all-union ministries, and the Soviet military and the security services. These institutions overlay republican institutions and, therefore, prevented the emergence of unified local political organizations and elites.

7. The forms of economic transformation were diverse across the region. In Kazakhstan areas of industrial development in the north and east lost control of local economies through a programme of liberalization and privatization that transferred ownership rights to groups based in the national capital and abroad. In Uzbekistan centralized control over lucrative sectors of agriculture (notably cotton) was expanded in the name of promoting an autarchic form of national economic development.

8. Laws on party registration generally required that in order to achieve official recognition, each party should have representation in every region of the country. For example, the 1997 law on political parties in Uzbekistan required that prospective parties must submit details of at least 5,000 members spread over eight provinces.

9. In the early 1990s, the leading poet, Olzhas Suleimenov was an important figure in the creation of a political movement that drew its support disproportionately from the Russified Kazakhs of the north and east of the country. However, this movement faced strong central opposition. The movement lost any significant influence when Suleimenov accepted the post of ambassador in Italy.

10. The new parliament was bicameral in structure with the senate consisting of two deputies from each region, city of republican significance and the capital. Deputies of local legislatures elected the senators. The lower chamber (Mazhilis) consists of 67 deputies elected from single seat constituencies.

11. Unlike Uzbekistan, where the regional executive head chairs the local legislature, in Kazakhstan there is an important formal separation of powers at the local level. The local

legislature (Maslikhat) is able to pass a motion of no confidence in the Akim if two thirds of the chamber votes for this decision.
12. The interdependence of central and regional elites in the Kyrgyz Republic encouraged the spread of patron–client networks throughout the new state. In his presidential campaign in the autumn of 2000 President Akaev identified regionalism and clan ties as a particular threat to the state. *RFE/RL Newsline*, Vol.4, No.197, Part 1 (11 October 2000). The critical role of regional networks and clan ties in binding the country together suggested, however, that removing these elements would be a difficult and hazardous operation.
13. In 1995 and 1996 the hakims of Khorezm, Syrdaria, Jizzak, Namangan, Samarkand and Bukhara regions were replaced. See 'Political Heads Role in Uzbekistan' *OMRI Daily Digest* (29 October 1996) and *Cyber Uzbekistan*. In February 1997, Mirzajon Islamov, the head of Ferghana region was removed on the grounds that he was 'no longer answering the needs of the time'. 'Regional Uzbek Boss Answers to Poor Economic Performance', *OMRI Daily Digest*, No.35, Part I (19 February 1997). In January 2000 Karimov dismissed the regional head for the Ferghana region. *Interfax* (18 January 2000). On 23 March 2000 Uzbek TV reported that President Islam Karimov had appointed a new governor for the southern region of Surkhandarya. During an extraordinary session of the Surkhandarya Regional People's Council President Karimov noted that such phenomena as nepotism, cronyism and bribery were flourishing in Surkhandarya.
14. Like the other two cases examined here, Uzbekistan also contains an important regionally concentrated ethnic minority, the Tajiks. The close social relations of Uzbeks and Tajiks, coercive measures against nationalist leaders amongst the Tajiks, and the fear of importing the conflict from Tajikistan into Uzbekistan ensured that a division between Tajiks and Uzbeks did not develop as a central cleavage in the Uzbek polity in the first decade of independence.

REFERENCES

Akiner, Shirin (1995), *The Formation of Kazakh Identity: From Tribe to Nation-State*. London: Royal Institute of International Affairs.

Allworth, Edward A. (1990), *The Modern Uzbeks: From the Fourteenth Century to the Present. A Cultural History*. Stanford: Hoover Institution Press; (1994) *Central Asia: 130 Years of Russian Dominance, A Historical Overview*. London: Duke University Press.

Bacon, Elizabeth (1966), *Central Asians Under Russian Rule: A Study in Cultural Change*. Ithaca, N.Y: Cornell University Press.

Becker, Seymour (1988), 'Russia's Central Asian Empire 1885–1917', in Michael Rywkin (ed.), *Russian Colonial Expansion to 1917*. London: Mansell.

Beissinger, Mark R. (1993), 'Demise of an Empire-State: Identity, Legitimacy, and the Deconstruction of Soviet Politics', in Crawford Young, *The Rising Tide of Cultural Pluralism: The Nation-State at Bay?* London: The University of Wisconsin Press, pp.93–115.

Bremmer, Ian and Cory Welt (1995), 'Kazakhstan's Quandary,' *Journal of Democracy*, Vol.6, No.3, pp.139–54.

Brown, Bess (1990), 'The Public Role in Perestroika in Central Asia', *Central Asian Survey*, Vol.9, No.1, pp.87–96.

Brubaker Rogers (1996), *Nationalism Reframed: Nationhood and the National Question in the New Europe*. Cambridge: Cambridge University Press.

Bunce, Valerie (1999), 'The Political Economy of Post-Socialism', *Slavic Review*, Vol.58, No.4, pp.756–93.

Carlisle, Donald S. (1991), 'Uzbekistan and the Uzbeks'. *Problems of Communism*, September–October, pp.23–44.

Clover, Charles (1997), 'Caught in a Struggle for Control of Islam', *Financial Times*, 22/23 March

Critchlow, James (1988), '"Corruption", Nationalism, and the Native Elites in Soviet Central Asia', *The Journal of Communist Studies*, Vol.4, No.2, pp.142–61.

Cummings, Sally N. (1996), *Kazakhstan's Parliamentary Elections and After*. London, Royal Institute for International Affairs Former Soviet South Briefing No.5; (2000) *The Dynamics of Centre–Periphery Relations in Kazakhstan*. London: Royal Institute of International Affairs.

Cutler, Robert M. (1999), 'Kazakhstan's Ethnic Mix: Recipe for a Shatterbelt in Central Eurasia', *Central Asia-Caucasus Analyst*, 8 December.

Dave, Bhavna (1996), 'More than a Cadre Reshuffle: Nazarbayev Appoints New Head in East Kazakhstan', *OMRI Analytical Brief*, Vol.1, No.74, pp.1–2.

Demko, George J. (1969), *The Russian Colonization of Kazakhstan 1896–1916*. Bloomington, IL: Indiana University Press.

Fane, Daria (1996), 'Ethnicity and Regionalism in Uzbekistan: Maintaining Stability through Authoritarian Control', in Leokardia Drobizheva *et al.*, *Ethnic Conflict in the Post-Soviet World: Case Studies and Analysis*. London: M.E.Sharpe, pp.277–82.

Gleason, Gregory (1991), 'Fealty and Loyalty: Informal Authority Structures in Central Asia', *Soviet Studies*, Vol.43, No.4, pp.613–28; (1997) 'Uzbekistan: the Politics of National Independence', in Ian Bremmer and Ray Taras (eds), *New States, New Politics: Building the Post-Soviet Nations*. Cambridge: Cambridge University Press.

Grant, Jonathan (1994), 'Decolonization by Default: Independence in Soviet Central Asia', *Central Asian Survey*, Vol.13, No.1, pp.51–8.

Hanks, Reuel R. (2000), 'A Separate Space? Karakalpak Nationalism and Devolution in Post-Soviet Uzbekistan', *Europe-Asia Studies*, Vol.52, No.5, pp.939–53.

Heleniak, Tim (1997), 'The Changing Composition of the Central Asian and Transcaucasian States', *Post-Soviet Geography and Economics*, Vol.38, No.6, pp.357–78.

Huskey, Eugene (1997), 'Kyrgyzstan: The Politics of Demographic and Economic Frustration', in Ian Bremmer and Ray Taras (eds), *New States and New Politics: Building the Post-Soviet Nations*. Cambridge: Cambridge University Press.

Kostyukova, Irina (1994), 'The Towns of Kyrgyzstan Change Their Faces: Rural-urban Migrants in Bishkek', *Central Asian Survey*, Vol.13, No.3, pp.425–34.

Konstitutsiia Respubliki Kazakhstan (1996), in Gisbert H. Flanz (ed.), *Constitutions of the Countries of the World*. Dobbs Ferry, N.Y: Oceana Publications, Inc.

Linz, Juan J. and Alfred Stepan (1996), *Problems of Democratic Transition and Consolidation: Southern Europe, South America and Post-Communist Europe*. London: John Hopkins University Press.

Lynch, Dov (2001), 'The Tajik Civil War and Peace Process', *Civil Wars*, Vol.4, No.4 (forthcoming).

Mackenzie, David (1988). 'The Conquest and Administration of Turkestan, 1860–85', in Michael Rywkin (ed.), *Russian Colonial Expansion to 1917*. London: Mansell.

Manz, Beatrice (1994), 'Historical Background', in Beatrice F. Manz (ed.), *Central Asia in Historical Perspective*. Cambridge, Mass.: Harvard University Press, pp.4–12.

Melvin, Neil (1995), *Russians Beyond Russia: The Politics of National Identity*. London: Pinter; (1998) 'The Russians: Diaspora and the End of Empire' in Charles King and Neil J. Melvin (eds), *Nations Abroad: Diaspora Politics and International Relations in the Former Soviet Union*. Boulder, Colorado: Westview, pp.27–57; (2001) 'New Authoritarianisms in Central Asia: A Comparison of Kazakhstan, The Kyrgyz Republic and Uzbekistan' in Yaacov Ro'i (ed.), *Democracy and Pluralism in the Muslim Regions of the Former Soviet Union*. London and Portland, OR: Frank Cass (forthcoming).

Nunn, Sam *et al.* (1999), *Calming the Ferghana Valley: Development and Dialogue in the Heart of Central Asia*. New York: The Century Press Foundation.

RFE/RL Newsline (2000), 'Is Kazakhstan Planning Territorial-Administrative Reform?', Vol.4, No.66, Part I, 3 April; (2001) 'Kyrgyz President Appoints New Prime Minister', Vol.4, No.247, Part I, 22 December.

Pipes, Richard (1964), *The Formation of the Soviet Union – Communism and Nationalism 1917–1923*. Cambridge, Mass.: Harvard University Press.

Rubin, Barnett R. (1998), 'Russian Hegemony and State Breakdown in the Periphery: Causes and Consequences of the Civil War in Tajikistan' in Barnett R. Rubin and Jack Snyder (eds), *Post-Soviet Political Order: Conflict and State Building*. London: Routledge, pp.128–61.

Sabol, Steven (1995), 'The Creation of Soviet Central Asia: the 1924 National Delimitation', *Central Asian Survey*, Vol.14, No.2, pp.225–41.

Schatz, Edward (2000a), 'The Politics of Multiple Identities: Lineage and Ethnicity in Kazakhstan', *Europe-Asia Studies*, Vol.52, No.3, pp.489–506; (2000b) 'Framing Strategies and Non-Conflict in Multi-Ethnic Kazakhstan', *Nationalism and Ethnic Politics*, Vol.6, No.2, pp.71–94.

Seton-Watson, Hugh (1967), *The Russian Empire 1801–1917*. Oxford: Oxford University Press.

Slovo Kyrgyzstan (1994), 'Rezoliutsiia II s'ezda SKPK', October.

Vaisman, Demian (1995), 'Regionalism and Clan Loyalty in the Political Life of Uzbekistan', in Yaacov Ro'I (ed.), *Muslim Eurasia: Conflicting Legacies*. London and Portland, OR: Frank Cass, pp.105–22.

The OSCE and Regional Conflicts in the Former Soviet Union

NATALIE MYCHAJLYSZYN

The international dimension is a crucial, albeit neglected, aspect of any meaningful analysis of the impact of ethnic and regional conflicts on post-communist transition. As the introductory essay to this volume notes, the necessity of incorporating the international dimension is emphasized in part by the role played by the Organization for Security and Co-operation in Europe (OSCE) in post-Soviet conflicts. The OSCE is a regional security organization of 55 states from Europe, the former Soviet Union, as well as Canada and the United States, concerned with a comprehensive and cooperative approach to security.[1] In addition to setting principles and norms on politico-military, economic and human rights issues and promoting their implementation by the participating states, an integral component of its activities has been the prevention, management and settlement of potential or actual conflicts in the OSCE area. Accordingly, since 1992 the OSCE has played an active role in trying to resolve regional and ethnic conflicts in the newly independent states of the former Soviet Union. It is in part due to the OSCE's activities that these conflicts have been elevated to the international level, where they are then influenced by external actors, whether states, other international organizations such as the United Nations, and the OSCE itself.

The main international principles and norms that inform the OSCE's interventions in post-Soviet regional conflicts offer solutions that uphold the right to self-determination (ethnic or otherwise) in correspondence with the territorial integrity of the state in question. Although self-determination in effect encompasses a range of options, from cultural autonomy through political autonomy (save for international personality) to secession leading to outright independence, the OSCE rejects the latter as being too radical a solution to the regional conflicts – particularly when executed through the use of force and without mutual consent. For the OSCE, secession violates a core international principle – respect for the territorial integrity of states. In other words, unilateral secessionist movements that lead to regional conflicts undermine the principles upon which post-Cold War European peace and stability has been constructed and, ultimately, threaten not only the existence of the state but also international security within the OSCE space.

And yet, the violation of a state's territorial integrity has been tolerated in those instances when secession is reached by way of mutual consent and, preferably, without the use of force. Nonetheless, its tolerance in international practice has been neither absolutely defined nor consistently applied, thereby blurring any understanding of what constitutes an acceptable secession. In fact, recent history demonstrates that the international community has recognized the secession of some newly independent states, which were achieved either by way of force or by peaceful means, while denying recognition to others which may have been equally, if not less, violent or even peaceful. For instance, the unilateral secessions of Croatia, Bosnia and Slovenia from Yugoslavia, and Ukraine and Kazakhstan (amongst other union republics) from the Soviet Union, and the mutually agreed division of Czechoslovakia into the Czech Republic and Slovakia, were tolerated and accepted by the international community. In contrast, there have been other secessions where the international community has strongly advocated solutions which accommodate self-determination *within* the territorial integrity of the state. Nagorno-Karabakh in Azerbaijan and South Ossetia in Georgia are examples of two violent conflicts, and Crimea in Ukraine a peaceful one, where this policy has been applied. It is the very absence of a consistent policy and confirmed basis according to which secession is internationally recognized and tolerated that leads to the emergence and prolongs the existence of separatist movements, thus undermining the OSCE's efforts to resolve post-Soviet regional conflicts. This ambiguity raises an important question about the impact of international practice as a limiting constraint on the OSCE in its conflict-resolution role. Its solutions are appropriate for situations where territorial integrity is not challenged and inappropriate where it is. Secessionists reject the OSCE's proposals and, in the end, conflicts remain unsettled and the OSCE's reputation and credibility as a regional security organization is questioned.

By comparing the OSCE's role in several conflicts (Ukraine, Moldova, Georgia, Tajikistan and Nagorno-Karabakh) we can evaluate the consistency and effectiveness of OSCE interventions from several perspectives. First, as the international organization present in all these cases, the OSCE provides a broad scope for a rich analysis of the international dimension in post-Soviet regional and ethnic conflicts. Second, such a cross-case comparison allows us to study the extent the OSCE is equipped to deal with the particularities of each regional and ethnic conflict. We can examine the response of the OSCE to regional particularities and the impact of this interaction on conflict resolution. Third, a study of the OSCE role in these conflicts reveals important insights into the ability of an international institution to influence domestic institutions in order to better manage regional conflicts and enhance security and stability. Fourth, we can identify those factors which influence (or limit) the OSCE's operational effectiveness in conflict resolution. It is important to note that as the OSCE and international organizations generally are simply one component of the international dimensions considered in this framework, the OSCE's interventions will be considered vis à vis the interdependence of conflicts within the post-Soviet states generally and the consequent impact of each specific case on others. In this respect, the role played by Russia in these conflicts merits particular attention.

Given the scope of the OSCE's interventions, the chapter will focus on three cases which are also considered in greater depth elsewhere in this volume: Ukraine (Crimea), Georgia (South Ossetia) and Azerbaijan (Nagorno-Karabakh). These three cases are selected primarily for their representation of similar conflicts among their subset. Crimea, for instance, is representative of the OSCE's efforts to *prevent conflict*, as are Estonia and Latvia. South Ossetia is representative of the OSCE's efforts to *manage conflict* as in the case of Moldova/Transnistria. Finally, Nagorno-Karabakh is representative of the OSCE's efforts at *conflict resolution*, as is Chechnya and Tajikistan. It is important to note that conflict prevention, management and resolution are distinct activities by virtue of the objectives sought: prevention is concerned with politically tense situations that have not yet escalated into violence; management is concerned with reducing or preventing the recurrence of violence after its cessation; resolution is concerned with violent situations and seeks to not only end the violence but also to reach settlement between the parties.[2] At the same time, the activities are not so distinct that they are not complementary. In fact, they frequently overlap and are undertaken simultaneously, as evident in the OSCE's involvement in Moldova, Nagorno-Karabakh and Tajikistan.

The analysis begins with a survey of the OSCE's involvement in regionalism and ethnic conflict in the post-Soviet area. This is followed by an assessment of the OSCE's efforts at preventing, managing and resolving the regional conflicts in Crimea, South Ossetia and Nagorno-Karabakh. The conclusion addresses issues raised by the introductory framework to this volume and offers some observations about the impact of the international dimension on post-Soviet transitions and ethnic and regional conflicts.

THE OSCE

The OSCE's involvement in post-Soviet regional and ethnic conflicts stems from its prominence in Europe's post-Cold War security architecture, for the OSCE is the primary institution for responding to sub-state sources of conflict and challenges to security. Conflicts are understood in terms of violations of OSCE principles and norms which govern sub-state behaviour and serve as the foundation for state stability and security. These sub-state principles were initially outlined in 'Basket Three' of the CSCE's (the OSCE's predecessor organization) Helsinki Final Act (1975) under the heading of human rights and fundamental freedoms.[3] The principles were expanded during the OSCE's particularly intense and rapid evolution in the late 1980s and early 1990s to become the 'human dimension,' that is, principles related to *inter alia* democratic institutions and the rule of law.[4] The protection of human rights, including the rights of persons belonging to national minorities, is considered by the OSCE to be 'an essential foundation of democratic civil society'. It is the neglect of these rights, in particular, that the OSCE views as among the key sub-state sources of conflict and threats to security (Budapest Document, 1994: 22). The 1999 Istanbul Summit reaffirmed that respect for human rights and fundamental freedoms, democracy and the rule of law is 'at the core' of the OSCE's comprehensive concept of security (Charter for European Security, 1999: 7).

The OSCE's response to conflict is guided fundamentally by the conviction that the implementation of the human dimension principles is the best form of prevention. However, as important as the human dimension commitments are to the OSCE's programme of action, other principles also figure prominently in its approach to responding to these conflicts when they emerge. In this regard, the principles of respect for the territorial integrity of the state and the right to self-determination are of particular relevance. Indeed, the violation of the respect for the territorial integrity of the state is frequently manifested in the form of a regional conflict where the region unilaterally seeks secession from the state in question. Moreover, the premise for seeking secession is frequently the exercise of the right to self-determination by the majority regional ethno-national population which fears or has experienced discrimination on the basis of its ethno-national identity at the hands of the central government with whom it does not share its ethno-national affinity. Thus, the OSCE advocates solutions to such conflicts which combine respect for the territorial integrity of the state while also respecting the regional minority population's right to self-determination.

The mechanisms by which the OSCE pursues its mission are necessarily wide-ranging in order to reflect the varying degrees of intensity of conflict situations and the implications for stability and security. Both CSCE and OSCE have focused considerably on simply identifying and setting the norms which would govern relations between states and their citizens, as realized in the 1975 Helsinki Final Act and the political agreements which proliferated in the years after the end of the Cold War: the 1990 Charter of Paris, the 1990 Copenhagen Document on National Minorities, the 1992 Helsinki Document, the 1994 Budapest Document, the 1996 Lisbon Document and the 1999 Charter on Security.

Other responses have consisted of regular and prominent reviews under the 1975 Helsinki Final Act of the implementation by the participating states of the OSCE's principles and human dimension commitments. For the most part, these reviews are carried out at the Summits of the OSCE, the meetings of the Ministerial Council, the weekly meetings of the Permanent Council, and at the alternating annual review conferences and the Human Dimension Implementation Review Meetings which, as is obvious by its name, is devoted specifically to the review of the implementation of the human dimension commitments. These reviews, usually held annually, involve discussion, an exchange of views and political consultation, but there is no concluding document, only a rapporteur's summary. When a more concentrated effort is required, the OSCE has developed a range of tools which it can apply as appropriate and promote the implementation of its principles. Three of these tools figure prominently in the cases examined here and will be featured accordingly: the High Commissioner on National Minorities (HCNM), the OSCE field mission and ad hoc measures.

First, the HCNM is exclusively concerned with the implementation of commitments pertaining to national minorities and violations of national minority rights. Established at the 1992 Helsinki Summit in order to enhance the OSCE's effectiveness where ethno-national tensions are concerned, the HCNM's mandate is to: 'provide "early warning" and, as appropriate, "early action" at the earliest possible stage in regard to tensions involving national minority issues which have not yet developed beyond an early warning stage, but, in the judgement of the High Commissioner, have the potential to develop into a conflict within the CSCE area' (Helsinki Document, 1992: 8). The HCNM is the only agent of the OSCE specifically involved in preventing ethno-national and minority conflicts (van der Stoel, 1994: 37). The HCNM is invited by the participating state experiencing such situations to use good offices, to play an advisory role, to mediate and to make recommendations in order to defuse tensions that arise from issues involving national minorities. In the context of regionalism and ethnic conflict, the HCNM's solutions emphasize the protection of minority rights, usually by institutional measures. Furthermore, they support those solutions that work within the framework of the state, such as harmonizing relations between majority and minority ethnic groups (Chigas, 1996: 55).

Second, the OSCE field mission is dispatched to participating states where there is a threat of or actual conflict. The field missions operate on mandates that are, generally, renewable every six months.[5] Broadly, the field missions review and assist in the compliance of participating states with their OSCE commitments (Kemp, 1996: 20). In this sense they are the most visibly intrusive aspect of the OSCE's work with member states. The field missions operate on-site, within the boundaries of the state and usually in the zone of conflict. By establishing an international presence in the areas of concern they reinforce the message that issues regarding human dimension commitments are of concern to the international community. Finally, ad hoc working groups can also be arranged to deal with a specific issue. Such working groups generally function independently and provide a forum for the negotiated settlement of a conflict.

THE OSCE IN UKRAINE, GEORGIA AND AZERBAIJAN

The newly independent states of the former Soviet Union joined the OSCE in 1992.[6] In the process, not only did these states commit themselves to implement the OSCE's principles, but they also legitimated the OSCE's involvement in their domestic politics. More specifically, the violation or weak implementation of human dimension and other OSCE principles were grounds for the OSCE's intervention. Indeed, the violation or poor implementation of these principles and their destabilizing consequences were already in evidence in many of these countries as discussed elsewhere in this volume. For the most part, these tensions and conflicts emerged along ethnic lines between the dominant, titular ethnonational group and regionally-concentrated minorities due to, *inter alia,* the perceived violation of national minority rights, unilateral claims of self-determination by regional authorities which violated the territorial integrity of the state, and immature and ineffective democratic institutions and rule of law which in many cases resulted in the use of force. Consequently, the OSCE became involved in many post-Soviet conflicts including the three conflicts relevant to this study. The HCNM became involved to prevent conflict between the secessionist Crimean Russians, the Crimean Tatars and the Ukrainian national government in Kyiv. In South Ossetia, the OSCE established a field mission in Georgia to reduce the violent conflict and stabilize the situation. To manage the Nagorno-Karabakh conflict, the OSCE created an ad hoc group, the 'Minsk process', which aimed to reach a political settlement of the conflict.

Ukraine and Crimea

Ukraine was facing a potential regional conflict and a threat to its territorial integrity from secessionist Crimean Russians who sought to exercise their right to self-determination by reunifying the overwhelmingly Russian populated peninsula with the Russian Federation.[7] The Crimean Russians were motivated by a perceived threat to their identity, language and culture from growing Ukrainian nationalism and Kyiv's nation-state building policies of 'Ukrainianization'. The Russian language, although spoken by many Ukrainians and a vast majority of the population of Crimea, was demoted from a state language to a cultural language; it could only be taught in schools where numbers warranted and was no longer the language of power and prestige. The Crimean Tatars, moreover, were attempting to reclaim Crimea as their historic 'homeland'. Having been deported by the Stalinist regime to Central Asia from Crimea in 1944, they began to return in large numbers in the early 1990s and demanded recognition of their special national minority status and the Crimean peninsula as their homeland (Sasse, 1996: 84–6). They have also sought guarantees of representation in the decision-making and political institutions of Crimea commensurate with their proportion of the Crimean population.[8]

All post-Soviet Ukrainian governments rejected the claims made by the Crimean Russians and Tatars. In this respect, it considered the secession of Crimea from Ukraine a threat to Ukraine's territorial integrity and a dangerous precedent, given that large parts of Ukraine's territory had been consolidated as recently as the Second World War, being formerly parts of Russia, Poland, Czechoslovakia and Romania. Moreover, Ukraine consistently denied that the Crimean Tatars were an indigenous people meriting special recognition or protection beyond that offered to other national minorities in Ukraine.

Tension over the peninsula's status escalated on the basis of unilateral declarations and policies. In February 1992 the Supreme Soviet of Crimea declared the peninsula the 'Republic of Crimea'; in May 1992, the Crimean parliament passed the Act of Independence of Crimea and adopted a Crimean constitution which established in effect Crimea's sovereignty from Ukraine. In January 1994, elections for the Crimean presidency were held against a strongly Russian chauvinist background; they were won by Yuri Meshkov, leader of the 'Rossiia' bloc which advocated Crimean unification with Russia, with 72.9 per cent of the votes (Sasse, 1996: 88–92). Statements made by the key actors suggested that ethno-national tensions in Crimea would explode into conflict. For example, Ukrainian parliamentarians warned that the 'situation in the peninsula is approaching that in Transnistria [sic]' (Ukrainian Center for Independent Political Research, 1996: 11).

Since the initial visit to Ukraine in February 1994, the HCNM actively promoted political solutions based on the implementation of OSCE principles. The HCNM focused on including clauses within the Ukrainian and Crimean constitutions to better reflect the peninsula's autonomy within Ukraine while also respecting its linguistic and cultural reality. For instance, he recommended that the reference in the Crimean Constitution to 'Republic of Crimea' be amended to the 'Autonomous Republic of Crimea' and 'citizens of Crimea' to 'citizens of Ukraine residing in Crimea'.[9] He also recommended that the Crimean constitution recognize Ukrainian as the state language and Russian and Crimean Tatar as official languages in Crimea on a par with Ukrainian, and the use of Ukrainian symbols and flags alongside those of Crimea. The HCNM also recommended that Crimea end its pursuit of a separate Crimean citizenship.[10] Ultimately, Ukraine's 1996 constitution recognized Crimea's autonomous status, and the Verkhovna Rada in December 1998 gave its approval of the Crimean constitution which recognized Crimea's subordination to Ukraine, elements which were encouraged by the HCNM in his interventions.

On the issue of the Crimean Tatars, the HCNM repeatedly urged Ukraine to facilitate fast-track and affordable citizenship acquisition for returning Crimean Tatars, thereby allowing them to participate in elections and benefit from other rights granted to citizens of Ukraine, such as employment and housing. Furthermore, he recommended that the Crimean constitution recognize Tatar as an official language in local authority areas where they composed at least 20 per cent of the population. The HCNM also suggested that Ukraine establish a permanent Inter-Ministerial Committee of Ukrainian and Crimean authorities as well as representatives of the Crimean Tatars to consider issues surrounding returnees, such as resettlement and employment opportunities, and to establish a formal consultative body in the Crimean Parliament with Tatar representatives who could express views on draft legislation of relevance to Tatars. Regarding Crimean Tatar political representation, the HCNM recommended (1) a proportional representation electoral system that would give Crimean Tatars 'near certainty' for representation in the Crimean parliament 'broadly commensurate to their percentage of the total population of Crimea,' (2) changes to the Ukrainian election law that discriminates against Crimean political parties and Crimean Tatar political parties by requiring registration in at least 13 oblasts, (3) formal and legal recognition of the Mejlis as the supreme representative college of the Crimean Tatars and protector of the Crimean Tatar identity, and (4) the Mejlis' being given responsibilities for Tatar culture and schools.[11]

Georgia and South Ossetia

Prior to the OSCE's intervention in Georgia in late 1992, armed conflict had been ongoing since 1988 between Georgia and South Ossetia, an autonomous oblast (region) of northern Georgia with an ethnic Ossetian majority population (60 per cent Ossetian and 30 per cent Georgian and 10 per cent others).[12] The Ossetians wanted independence from Georgia and unification with North Ossetia, an Autonomous Republic of the RSFSR until 1991 and a republic of the Russian Federation from 1992, to correct what they perceived to be an unnatural division of the Ossetian people and their homeland by an administrative border. The South Ossetians were also motivated by a fear of oppressive nationalizing policies pursued by the Georgian state from 1991. The nationalist controlled Georgian government of Zviad Gamsakhurdia in Tbilisi, elected in 1991, opposed the secession and independence of South Ossetia, considering it as part of the historic Georgian region of Shida Kartli. It argued that the Ossetians have never had a unified separate state and that the Autonomous Oblast of South Ossetia was an artifice created to fit the Soviet federal structure and nationalities policy. The very name 'South Ossetia', the Georgians argued, was itself misleading.[13] Furthermore, the secession of South Ossetia would have set a dangerous precedent for the Georgian state, where over 100 ethnic minorities might follow the example in a domino effect.[14] The Georgian nationalist government exacerbated the situation by pursuing nationalizing policies that conflated the dominant 'Georgian' ethno-national identity with the state identity. The nationalists felt that the Georgian nation was itself under threat from such secession movements in South Ossetia and elsewhere.

The conflict began to escalate when in September 1990 the South Ossetian leadership unilaterally declared South Ossetia to be an independent and sovereign Soviet republic. Subsequent elections to the South Ossetian parliament served as an informal referendum on South Ossetia's independence. Separatists triumphed in the elections and the South Ossetian parliament adopted a Declaration of Independence in December 1991 which was confirmed by referendum in January 1992, when 90 per cent of those who voted supported independence.[15] In parallel with the moves to legitimate the secession through the ballot box, there were regular violent armed confrontations between the Ossetian separatists and the Georgian nationalists. Heavy weapons shelled the civilian and military positions of both Georgians and Ossetians, though Georgian units were responsible for the most intense shelling of civilian areas in the South Ossetian capital, Tskhinvali, extensively damaging its buildings and infrastructure (Khustishvili and MacFarlane, 1994: 5). The conflict resulted in a massive flow of refugees from the area: approximately 40,000 Georgian refugees from South Ossetia to Georgian cities, mainly Tbilisi and Gori, and an estimated 100,000 Ossetians to North Ossetia (Khutsishvili and MacFarlane, 1994: 5). By June 1992, law and order had collapsed in South Ossetia, as drug and arms smuggling flourished and armed bandits and organized criminal groups dominated society.

Following the successful January 1992 coup against Georgia's nationalist president, Zviad Gamsakhurdia, the intensity of conflict between the Ossetians and the Georgians began to diminish. The new government negotiated a ceasefire with the Ossetian authorities and in June 1992, following the election of Eduard Shevardnadze as Georgia's new president, an agreement was brokered by Russia in the Russian Black Sea city of Sochi. Among its terms the cease-fire agreement called for the deployment of a Joint Peacekeeping Force (JPKF) to the Ossetian region, consisting of Russian, Georgian, and Ossetian troops.[16] The JPKF deployment stabilized the situation, although there are inherent problems with the low levels of professionalism and partiality of Georgian and South Ossetian troops.

The OSCE Mission to Georgia was established in November 1992, after the Russian-brokered agreement had been concluded.[17] Consequently, its main function has been to ensure that the agreement holds and that the weaknesses of the JPKF and its unusual composition do not seriously undermine the cease-fire. In this respect, the OSCE Mission was mandated, *inter alia*, to support the existing cease-fire, liase with the local military commanders of the JPKF, establish appropriate forms of contact with them, gather information on the military situation, investigate violent incidents and violations of the cease-fire, and monitor local tensions which potentially might destabilize the situation.

Azerbaijan and Nagorno-Karabakh

Since 1988 Karabakh Armenians and the Azeri government in Baku have been engaged in a violent sub-state ethno-national conflict over the status of Nagorno-Karabakh, a region located entirely within Azeri borders but with an ethnic Armenian majority population. In essence, the Karabakh Armenians demanded secession from Azerbaijan and unification of Nagorno-Karabakh with Armenia. In their view, this campaign aims to correct a historical anomaly whereby the Soviet leadership established the region as an autonomous oblast of the newly created Republic of Azerbaijan in 1923 instead of including it as part of the territory of the neighbouring Republic of Armenia. Moreover, the Karabakh Armenians argued that their rights were violated and that they faced repeated discrimination by the Azeri government in the fields of culture, religion and language policy. For their part, the Azeris opposed the secession of Nagorno-Karabakh and rejected any demographic or historical claims made by the Karabakh Armenians to support secession and unification with Armenia. Instead, the loss of Azeri territory was considered a serious violation of Azerbaijan's sovereignty since the Nagorno-Karabakh Autonomous Oblast was considered an integral part of Azeri territory based on historical and cultural linkages.[18] The unification of Nagorno-Karabakh with Armenia would also result in a loss of about 20 per cent of the territory of Azerbaijan, and thus threatened Azerbaijan's state- and-nation building.

The Karabakh Armenians declared Nagorno-Karabakh's unification with Armenia in February 1988, declared its secession from Azerbaijan in July 1988, and in September 1991 formally declared itself an independent state 'united' with Armenia. These unilateral declarations were accompanied by violent pogroms and armed conflict between the ethno-national communities which caused an estimated 10,000 dead.[19] The conflict escalated into an all-out war between Karabakh Armenia, supported by Armenia proper, and Azerbaijan, which involved large-scale ethnic cleansing by both sides. By late 1991 the Armenian forces had militarily defeated Azerbaijan and secured the de facto annexation of Nagorno-Karabakh, together with a strategically significant connecting land corridor (the Shusha or Lachin districts) across Azeri territory.[20]

The OSCE has followed a twin-track approach to resolve the Nagorno-Karabakh conflict within the OSCE's operating principles of balancing respect for Azerbaijan's territorial integrity with an acceptable autonomous status for Nagorno-Karabakh. The first track was to get the parties to negotiate. Referred to as the Minsk process and based on an ad hoc working group of the OSCE, it was named after the city in which the OSCE intended to convene a conference on the conflict based on its March 1992 decision to do so.[21] The second track concentrated on negotiations on a political settlement which aims to include the following key elements: the withdrawal of Armenian military forces from Nagorno-Karabakh, security guarantees for Nagorno-Karabakh and its population, respect for Azerbaijan's territorial integrity and the broadest possible self-rule for Nagorno-Karabakh. Once such a political settlement was reached, the conference in Minsk could then convene. Since 1997 the negotiations over Nagorno-Karabakh have been conducted primarily through the mediation of the co-chairmen of the Minsk Conference.[22]

ASSESSING OSCE CONFLICT MANAGEMENT

The international dimension of these post-Soviet conflicts is unmistakable in the form of the OSCE's efforts to prevent, manage and resolve them. What is the impact of ethnic and regional conflicts on post-Soviet transition from this critical, but neglected, perspective?

Consistency of Response

The OSCE's interventions in regional and ethnic conflicts in the former Soviet Union reveals a consistency across cases. In this respect, the OSCE's responses have consistently reflected its concerns and interests in promoting the implementation of its principles and norms to enhance peace and stability. The solutions advocated by the OSCE are informed by these principles and the view that their implementation would prevent, manage and settle the conflicts; these include, *inter alia*, respect for the territorial integrity of the state, self-determination, the peaceful settlement of disputes, and respect for national minority rights, including linguistic rights, education rights, citizenship rights, voting rights and access to political representation. These principles and norms, in particular the peaceful settlement of disputes, shaped not only the solutions advocated by the OSCE but also the process by which it sought to effect these solutions, which emphasizes dialogue and consultation rather than the threat or use of force and military coercion.

At the same time, it should be noted that in all these cases the OSCE did not deliberately seek out or pursue a regionalist solution. In other words, the OSCE does not advocate regionalism as a solution to conflicts where there is no foundation for it. The issues in Crimea, South Ossetia and Nagorno-Karabakh were framed by the existence of regionally-concentrated ethno-national minorities. The OSCE's advocacy of solutions that entail respect for the territorial integrity of states *and* autonomy for minorities resulted in a de facto strengthening of regionalism and the confirmation of autonomous status of the region as the core element of the OSCE's solution to such conflicts. In other words, the OSCE's impact on strengthening regionalism is a by-product of its attempts to resolve post-Soviet conflicts, that is, a conflict based on the status of a region that is dominated by an ethno-national minority. In addition, as it seeks to settle these conflicts, the OSCE by necessity includes the parties involved who in these cases happen to include regional elites.

In considering the comparability of cases where there is a significant international dimension, we should note the consistency of the OSCE's responses notwithstanding the differences among the cases. More specifically, the OSCE's interventions have taken place at varying points of the conflict cycle. With respect to South Ossetia and Nagorno-Karabakh, the OSCE intervened after an intense phase of the conflicts had been reached but before the collapse of the Soviet Union and the consolidation of the OSCE's role in European security. In the case of South Ossetia, its intervention took place following a de-escalation of the conflict and the conclusion of a cease-fire. In Nagorno-Karabakh, in contrast, the OSCE intervened during the war phase of the conflict. The OSCE's varying responses were shaped by the differences in the timing of its interventions. Furthermore, some specific conflict prevention tools were developed at a later date in the OSCE's institutionalization process. Thus, when the OSCE intervened in Crimea in 1994, it was on the basis of the HCNM, a position created in 1992 and tasked specifically with preventing the escalation of ethnic minority issues into violence.

However, these differences may not be revealing regarding the impact of the OSCE on regionalism and ethnic issues other than to indicate the versatility of the OSCE's capacity to intervene. At the same time, while the timing of the intervention may differ and the solutions advocated are ultimately similar, what is emphasized or prioritized in the solutions will naturally reflect the particular circumstances of a given conflict situation. In other words, the intervention of the HCNM into Nagorno-Karabakh would not be expected to be constructive or generate a positive impact relating to national minority issues given that other issues are more salient. This is not to say that the absence of the HCNM's involvement suggests that there are no ethnic issues to be dealt with but instead that their intervention is inappropriate and unlikely to be effective until an agreement on Nagorno-Karabakh's status is concluded.

The Limits of Response

The OSCE's efforts to deal with conflict in the post-Soviet area has exposed substantial limits to its capacity to deal with them. The conflicts have often been exacerbated by the weak level of economic development in the regions resulting from the demise of the Soviet Union and regional armed conflict. Parties to the conflicts frequently attempt to divert attention away from the weak economic conditions by appealing to ethnic identity. Moreover, weak regional and national economies have meant that domestic sources for funding the programmes, policies and legislation necessary to give effect to the OSCE's strategies for preventing, managing and settling these conflicts have been non-existent. For example, Ukraine has a chronic lack of funds for assisting in the repatriation of and citizenship acquisition for the Crimean Tatars returning to the peninsula, thereby delaying their integration and contribution to Ukraine's social, economic and political development. Similarly, weak economies have resulted in the proliferation of illegal economic activities, drug trafficking and arms smuggling, and institutionalized widespread corruption. Criminal groups have taken advantage of the unstable conditions resulting from the conflicts to expand their power and they have a stake in seeing settlement efforts fail. To overcome economic weaknesses, regions have often sought to build formal and informal economic relations with 'home' states, or neighbouring states, and in the process reinforcing their separation from the state in which they are located. Nagorno-Karabakh, for example, has even adopted the Armenian currency. Such ties may be as much a matter of geographic convenience and access as anything, but in cases such as those of South Ossetia and Nagorno-Karabakh, they *are* statements of intent for political unity. Crimea's economic dependence on Ukraine and its failure to build stronger economic relations with Russia, on the other hand, demonstrated that secession was not viable. A similar process may ultimately prevail in South Ossetia, which is weak economically and highly dependent on the Georgian economy and aid from international agencies who work through the central government in Tbilisi. Moreover, North Ossetia does not have the economic resources to support South Ossetia in its bid for unification. Thus, economic conditions strongly affect the credibility of the solutions advocated by the OSCE.

The OSCE has a very limited capacity to meet regional economic challenges such as these. For the most part, it lacks the mechanisms and the mandate by which it could provide financial assistance to the regions and promote regional economic development. Instead, its efforts are focused on the coordination of funding from abroad or facilitating contacts with international financial or donor institutions. For example, the OSCE arranged for a donor conference to raise funds for the repatriation and integration of Crimean Tatars in Ukraine. At the same time, the OSCE also cooperates with international donors in channelling funds, albeit inefficiently, through the central government rather than to the regions directly, and thereby weakening, not strengthening, regional tendencies. For the OSCE, the settlement of a conflict and the implementation of the rule of law and democratic institutions are the best means of combating the pandemic of crime associated with these conflicts.

Linking Institution-Building and Security

An examination of the OSCE's role in post-Soviet regional conflicts reveals important insights into the ability of an international institution to influence domestic institutions, especially where such efforts are made in the context of building security. More specifically, the OSCE's mandate in these regional conflicts is to deliberately promote the development of domestic institutions in a way that they will conform with international norms and standards and, in the process, enhance peace and stability. One of its methods for promoting domestic institutions in volatile and conflict-ridden areas has been by having the relevant principles and norms inform the solutions it advocates for these situations. Indeed, the security dimension of this effort to influence domestic institution-building should not be minimized as it reflects recent advances in security studies to move beyond traditional, military and inter-state conceptions of security to include non-traditional forms, such as those pertaining to domestic politics, including the political system of government, human rights and the treatment of national minorities. The linkage of security and domestic politics is part of a growing trend whereby international interference in domestic issues has been legitimated.

The OSCE has been at the forefront of a visible, albeit gradual, shift towards a more interventionist approach by international organizations in the domestic affairs of states under certain conditions and away from the absolute application of the twin principles of sovereignty and non-intervention. Indeed, the 1975 Helsinki Final Act and its acknowledgement of human rights issues as a matter of international security was the starting point for this shift in policy (Maresca, 1987: 154, 217). As the 1991 Moscow Conference on the Human Dimension noted: 'The participating States emphasize that issues relating to human rights, fundamental freedoms, democracy and the rule of law are of international concern, as respect for these rights and freedoms constitutes one of the foundations of the international order. They categorically and irrevocably declare that the commitments undertaken in the field of the human dimension of the CSCE are matters of direct and legitimate concern to all participating States and do not belong exclusively to the internal affairs of the State concerned' (Moscow Meeting of the Conference on the Human Dimension, 1991: 29).

Nonetheless, the OSCE's interventionist approach is balanced by a concern for state sovereignty. The OSCE ensures that its activities are sanctioned by a state, and are governed by the agreements and documents signed by its participating states. In fact, the OSCE intervenes only on the invitation of a state. The OSCE's entire approach to decision-making is based on the principle of consensus in order to avoid decisions that may be against the interest of a particular state because to do otherwise would undermine rather than strengthen security. Moreover, the OSCE has no power to impose solutions on a state.

Conflicting Principles?

OSCE intervention is characterized by a tension within the principles by which it informs its responses to these conflicts. The application of one principle, say state sovereignty and territorial integrity, clashes with the implementation of another principle, say protecting minorities through autonomization. To better understand this tension, it is necessary to appreciate that the OSCE's principles are not exclusively applicable to domestic situations; in other words, these principles have a dual purpose that reflect the OSCE's concern with not only sub-state but also inter-state security issues. Indeed, the conflicts in the post-Soviet region reflect the OSCE's comprehensive approach to security, as they involve inter-state aspects as well as sub-state ones. However, the application of inter-state principles to sub-state conflicts is not without its problems and, rather than stabilize the situation, these principles serve to raise greater uncertainty and questions about how to address conflicts in the post-Soviet area.

One way of illustrating this dilemma is to consider the contradictory principles of respect for the territorial integrity of the state and the right to self-determination to which the OSCE subscribes. For the most part, territorial integrity is considered to play a greater role in addressing a common source of inter-state conflict by prohibiting one state from making unilateral claims on and intrusions into another state. However, it also has valid application to regional conflicts by prohibiting secession movements that in effect violate a state's territorial integrity. Thus, where secession is an issue in a regional conflict, the OSCE's solution is predetermined to advocate maintaining the integrity of the state and opposing secession as an option.

The application of the territorial integrity principle clashes with the principle of self-determination which in essence provides for a national minority to be self-governed. The problem arises because self-determination covers a wide range of possibilities, from significant autonomy to secession and independence. Thus, while secession may be a recognized and accepted form of self-determination, it is an invalid solution to regional conflicts for the OSCE because it contradicts the principle of territorial integrity of states. The problem is exacerbated in international practice because claims to self-determination have been irregularly and inconsistently accepted. The OSCE has been much less receptive to self-determination and secessionism in the post-Soviet states compared with its recognition of declarations of independence by the union republics of the former Soviet Union. As the participating states themselves outlined in the Charter for European Security at the 1999 Istanbul Summit:

Full respect for human rights, including the rights of persons belonging to national minorities, besides being an end in itself, may not undermine, but strengthen territorial integrity and sovereignty. Various concepts of autonomy as well as other approaches outlined in [other OSCE] documents, which are in line with OSCE principles, constitute ways to preserve and promote the ethnic, cultural, linguistic and religious identity of national minorities within an existing State (Charter for European Security, 1999: p.8).

Mixed Results

Finally, in light of the foregoing, it remains to evaluate the OSCE's record in addressing post-Soviet regional conflicts and identify factors which influence or limit the institution's impact. In general, the record is mixed. In Ukraine, the overall potential for regional conflict over Crimea has receded dramatically since the intervention of the OSCE in February 1994 to the point where the mission established by the OSCE in 1994 was withdrawn in 1999.[23] Here the OSCE principle of respect for territorial integrity has been emphasized. Consequently, the Crimean Russians have accepted Crimea's status as an autonomous republic within Ukraine with its own constitution, parliament, flag and symbols that have been legally formalized in the Ukrainian Constitution adopted June 1996. Secession is no longer an issue in Crimea. The Crimean Tatars also have accepted Crimea's status as an autonomous republic within Ukraine and have pursued their interests for self-determination within this institutional framework. For example, they request guaranteed representation in the Crimean parliament, acceptance and promotion of the Crimean Tatar language and Crimean Tatar schools in Crimea, and recognition of the Mejlis as the political representative body of the Crimean Tatars. While there is substantial ground for optimism, the potential for ethnic tensions and conflict in Crimea has not been completely eradicated, especially as Ukraine's nationalizing policies are beginning to infringe upon national minority rights.[24] The extent to which Ukraine's territorial integrity continues to be accepted by Crimean Russians depends on a complex mix of factors including Kyiv's foreign policies regarding NATO, the EU and cooperation with the West; Ukraine's economic performance; and developments in Russia. Recent episodes of civil disobedience by Crimean Tatars, such as the May 1999 establishment of a tent-city as a form of protest outside the Crimean government building in Simferopol, are signs of a growing frustration at the lack of movement on their political and cultural rights. Notwithstanding these concerns, Crimea is widely regarded as one of the OSCE's successes.

Since the OSCE's intervention in June 1992 the cease-fire in South Ossetia has held, violence has not escalated and the overall military situation has remained stable. Independence and unification with North Ossetia is no longer considered the only option by South Ossetian authorities. Alternatives being considered include various models of autonomy, including confederation with Georgia. Under the auspices of the OSCE, since August 1996 South Ossetia and Georgia have been negotiating on a political settlement of the conflict through an agreement on the status of South Ossetia *within* Georgia. Political posturing on independence, particularly for electoral purposes, is still a feature of South Ossetian politics, where moderates are sensitive to the charge that they are making too many concessions to Georgia.[25] While the OSCE is considered to have had a positive impact on stabilizing the military situation in South Ossetia, it is debatable just how much this is due to the OSCE and how much is due to the Russian-led peacekeeping presence. The OSCE has not, however, managed to secure a final agreement on the status of South Ossetia.

The OSCE's role in Nagorno-Karabakh is by far the most complex. The cease-fire agreed to in 1994 has generally held, despite periodic violations by all sides. Armenia and Azerbaijan are engaged in a bilateral dialogue and have maintained negotiations for a political agreement under the auspices of the OSCE. After eight years of negotiations an agreement remains elusive. The Karabakh Armenians continue to advocate secession from Azerbaijan and the reunification of Nagorno-Karabakh with Armenia. Indeed, Nagorno-Karabakh is *de facto* part of Armenia. The recalitrant behaviour of the Karabakh Armenians in the negotiations noticeably reflects this situation. On one level, the Karabakh Armenians demand recognition by the international community as an equal to Azerbaijan and, therefore, the right to participate in the negotiations and in the Minsk Conference in a way which reflects this parity. On another level, the Karabakh Armenians oppose any proposal that pre-determines Nagorno-Karabakh's status as part of Azerbaijan and vertically subordinate to Baku. The Karabakh Armenians consider their current status of *de facto* independence from Azerbaijan as the basis for any negotiations. The OSCE's search for a settlement to the conflict has been hindered by the intense mutual distrust between the parties. Nagorno-Karabakh, for example, insists on security guarantees in the form of a Karabakh army to protect it against any possible Azeri military offensive. Indeed, the Karabakh Armenians insist that Nagorno-Karabakh will never again be part of Azerbaijan.[26] The threat of renewed military conflict is significant since Azerbaijan is thought to be buying weapons with its oil revenues and strengthening its military forces to retake Nagorno-Karabakh by force. Azerbaijan is prepared to accept a level of Karabakh autonomy within Azerbaijan, but thus far has not been willing to define what this might mean in reality.[27] Azerbaijan consistently opposes any solution, such as that proposed by the OSCE in late 1998, which is based on the concept of a common state, arguing that this is a violation of the OSCE's own principles regarding the territorial integrity of states.[28]

What factors account for this mixed record of the OSCE? In summary, the OSCE's ability to impact on these conflicts has been affected by the timing of its intervention (the earlier the intervention in the conflict process and after the conclusion of a cease-fire, the more likely its ability to influence the conflict), its own maturity and institutional capacity (the later the intervention in its maturity and institutionalization, the more tools and experience available for it to apply), the weak economic development in the regions (the poor economic conditions in the regions and in the states in question have been a major obstacle to the implementation and advancement of the OSCE's solutions), the degree of acceptance by the parties to the dispute of its intervention (the more acceptable the OSCE and its solutions, the more likely its ability to influence the conflict), and its own pre-determined solution to the conflicts (the wider distance between the objectives of the parties to the dispute and the OSCE's position, the less likely the OSCE's effectiveness in responding to the conflict).

The OSCE can only be as effective as the conditions allow it to be. This observation is particularly evident where the acceptance of the OSCE's interventions is concerned. Indeed, the cases of Crimea and South Ossetia demonstrate that progress on conflict resolution is accelerated by an acceptance by all parties of the OSCE role, and in particular by the state in question whose approval is required for the OSCE to intervene in the first place. Indeed, the HCNM was initially invited to Ukraine by the Ukrainian government and his visits were noted to have been greatly appreciated.[29] Likewise, the Georgian government has been supportive of the OSCE's intervention and its active role in monitoring the peacekeepers and the cease-fire agreement in South Ossetia.[30] Arguably, it is the OSCE's predetermined solution which favours the preservation of state integrity that lends the OSCE credibility from the state. Its main function, thereafter, is in effect to pressure the regional authorities to accept a 'within-state' solution.

Where the OSCE lacks credibility, whether from states or regions, its effectiveness is greatly reduced. In particular, regional actors often view the OSCE as biased, inflexible in its opposition to regional, secessionist ambitions and as a mouthpiece for the state. In Ukraine, for example, the

OSCE was perceived early in the process by Crimean authorities as an instrument of Kyiv that came to the problem with a predetermined solution, that is, that Ukraine's territorial integrity was not going to be violated by the secession of Crimea. Such a negative perception of the OSCE delayed the establishment of the branch office of the OSCE mission in Tskhinvali in South Ossetia until April 1997, after a three-year effort. The Karabakh Armenians believe that the OSCE's refusal to recognize their self-determination is simply freezing the conflict over its status, much as it was frozen during the Soviet period.[31] While initially supportive of the OSCE's efforts, Azerbaijan has become increasingly frustrated with the lack of progress under the OSCE framework and the promotion of the interests of the co-chairs at the expense of its state sovereignty.[32]

The role of the OSCE is very much interdependent on the reaction of other post-Soviet states not directly involved in conflicts, another aspect of the international dimension that influences regional conflicts and ethnic politics in the area. The most prominent of these factors is the role played by Russia. Russia impacted on the process in Ukraine positively, whereby it officially opposed Crimea's separation from Ukraine and unification with Russia, thereby removing a potentially explosive factor from the situation.[33] Russia's recognition of Ukraine's territorial integrity was included in the January 1994 Tripartite Agreement between Russia, Ukraine and the United States. Furthermore, Russia influenced the situation by making the signing of a Treaty of Friendship and Co-operation with Ukraine, an agreement that was critical to Ukraine in defining its relationship with Russia, conditional on the settlement of the status of Crimea. The Treaty was finally signed in May 1997 after Crimea's autonomous status in Ukraine was acknowledged in the Ukrainian constitution adopted in June 1996. With respect to the conflict in South Ossetia, the Russian battalion *is* essentially the JPKF, and its presence and discipline has been instrumental in stabilizing the conflict. Indeed, there is a perception among the South Ossetians and Georgians that whatever role the OSCE has played in managing the conflict, Russia is the key actor.[34]

Russia has also complicated the OSCE's interventions. In Crimea, nationalist elements in Russian domestic politics and in the Duma exacerbated the situation in Crimea by supporting Crimean independence and increasing tensions between Crimean and Ukrainian leaders. Leading Russian politicians of all hues have questioned the legality of the 1954 transfer of Crimea from Russia to Ukraine, and in May 1992 a Duma resolution even declared the transfer invalid. In July 1993, the Russian Duma adopted a resolution claiming that Crimea was a part of Russia, and in April 1995 it invited the separatist speaker of the Crimean parliament, Sergei Tsekov, and a Crimean delegation to Moscow to discuss the Crimean situation.[35] The mayor of Moscow, Yuri Luzhkov, made statements in 1995 claiming that Sevastopol, the headquarters of the Black Sea Fleet in Crimea, was a Russian city. In the case of Nagorno-Karabakh, Russia has challenged the OSCE framework for resolving the conflict. For instance, in order to enforce and legitimize the newly-established CIS and to allow for Russian control of the process, Russia insisted that Minsk be the location of the OSCE conference on the issue. Russia also regularly pursued its own mediation of the conflict parallel to and at the expense of the OSCE's efforts. It was Russia, not the OSCE that brokered the May 1994 cease-fire, shortly after Azerbaijan had joined the CIS in 1993. Russia's key role in managing the conflict was legitimized and reinforced when the chairmanship of the OSCE Minsk Conference was deliberately expanded to accommodate Russia. Consequently, most of the meetings of the Minsk Group have been held in Moscow. Russia has consistently favoured the Armenian side in the conflict since Armenia is its key strategic partner in the South Caucasus.

Other external actors have also impacted on these regional and ethnic conflicts. For instance, the persistent lack of political and economic support from North Ossetia for South Ossetia's campaign for independence and Ossetian unification affected the development of this conflict. Indeed, North Ossetia itself does not want to set a precedent of changes to territorial boundaries given its own domestic situation involving an Ingush campaign for independence from North Ossetia. Similarly, Armenia's support for Nagorno-Karabakh has seriously complicated the settlement negotiations under the Minsk process. For instance, Armenia has opposed any political agreement which pre-determines Nagorno-Karabakh's status within Azerbaijan. It has argued for Nagorno-Karabakh to be recognized in the negotiation process and in discussions on peacekeeping operations as a full and equal party to the conflict, arguing that the conflict is between Nagorno-Karabakh and Azerbaijan, not between Armenia and Azerbaijan. Furthermore, Armenia insists that any agreement must allow Nagorno-Karabakh full political and military control over its territory and must provide both security guarantees and a geographic contour that will end its exclave situation. Armenia doubts the ability of any country or international organization to secure Nagorno-Karabakh's safety from Azeri attacks. In May 1997 the Armenian Presidential Adviser on the conflict in Nagorno-Karabakh declared that the OSCE's principle of territorial integrity applied only to international conflicts between two recognized states and that there should be no expectations on Armenia and Nagorno-Karabakh to respect it.[36] In addition, in October 1997, the Armenian Defence Minister urged the Armenian people to 'fight our last war to the finish', and insisted that the strategic corridor of occupied territory, never mind Nagorno-Karabakh, will not return to Azerbaijani sovereignty.[37] The election of the former President of Nagorno-Karabakh, Robert Kochariyan, as President of Armenia in 1998, following the resignation of his predecessor due to criticisms that he was not doing enough to support Nagorno-Karabakh's independence, is a severe blow to a peaceful resolution of this conflict. A recent proposal based on two stages (first, withdrawal from some of the occupied territories and definition of some of the elements of Nagorno-Karabakh status within Azerbaijan; second, final withdrawal and final definition of Nagorno-Karabakh's status) was rejected by Armenian hardliners, including Kocharian.[38]

CONCLUSIONS

The OSCE's impact on post-Soviet regionalism and ethnic politics stems from its approach to security which prominently features a concern with sub-state threats arising from the failure to implement OSCE commitments, including respect for democratic freedoms, the rule of law and the protection of national minorities. On this basis, the OSCE has intervened to prevent, manage and settle regional conflicts featuring these elements, such as in Crimea, South Ossetia and Nagorno-Karabakh. In particular, its efforts have been based on a predetermined interpretation of the outcome of these regional conflicts whereby the state's territorial integrity must be respected at all costs. The OSCE has had a profound influence on the development of regionalism and ethnic politics in the post-Soviet area by delineating the limits of their valid expression. The OSCE actively discourages manifestations of regionalism that threaten state security, and by implication European security. While the intended consequence of this pre-determined interpretation is the promotion of peace and stability, in fact, if applied rigidly it acts as a severe constraint on conflict resolution. The case of Nagorno-Karabakh demonstrates the inherent contradiction of the OSCE's two key operational principles: respect for state sovereignty and respect for the self-determination of minorities. By giving precedence to the former over the latter the OSCE has created a formula for continued instability.

NOTES

1. The 55 participating states of the OSCE are as follows: Albania, Andorra, Armenia, Austria, Azerbaijan, Belarus, Belgium, Bosnia and Herzegovina, Bulgaria, Canada, Croatia, Cyprus, Czech Republic, Denmark, Estonia, Finland, France, Georgia, Germany, Greece, Holy See, Hungary, Iceland, Ireland, Italy, Kazakhstan, Kyrgyzstan, Latvia, Liechtenstein, Lithuania, Luxembourg, Macedonia, Malta, Moldova, Monaco, Netherlands, Norway, Poland, Portugal, Romania, Russia, San Marino, Slovakia, Slovenia, Spain, Sweden, Switzerland, Tajikistan, Turkey, Turkmenistan, Ukraine, United Kingdom, United States of America, Uzbekistan. The Former Republic of Yugoslavia (Serbia and Montenegro) had been suspended from the OSCE since 1992, but its status as a participating state was reinstated in October 2000.

2. *Conflict prevention* is generally defined as 'efforts to avoid the development of contentious issues and the incompatibility of goals' and/or 'measures which contribute to the prevention of undesirable conflict behaviour once some situation involving goal incompatibility has arisen'. (Reychler, 1994: p.4; see also Lund, 1996; Carment and James, 1996). *Conflict management* is defined as action taken to arrest the expansion and escalation of a conflict and to stabilize the situation, rather than ending the conflict or removing its sources (Bercovitch, 1984: p.9; Laue, 1990: p.258; Rabie, 1994: pp.50, 53). *Conflict resolution* essentially comprises action to achieve 'a durable agreement that deals with, to the satisfaction of all concerned, the issues that lead to the violence.' (Sandole, quoted in Rabie, 1994: p.53). It attempts to undermine, remove, or eliminate the sources of the conflict as thoroughly and as permanently as possible (Rabie, 1994: p.57).

3. From 1973 to 1994, the OSCE existed as the Conference on Security and Co-operation in Europe (CSCE). The name was changed at the 1994 Budapest Summit to 'Organization' to better reflect its new institutionalized presence in European security, *1994 Budapest Document: Towards a Genuine Partnership in a New Era*, p.7. Principle seven of the Final Act (1975) enshrines *Respect for human rights and fundamental freedoms, including the freedom of thought, conscience, religion or belief.* Basket Three alludes to *Co-operation in Humanitarian and Other Fields* in such areas as human contacts, information, culture and education.

4. The 1989 Vienna Summit first referred to the human dimension, stating 'the undertakings entered into in the Final Act and in other CSCE documents concerning respect for all human rights and fundamental freedoms, human contacts and other issues of a related humanitarian character, …which are hereafter referred to as the human dimension of the CSCE…' *The 1989 Vienna Summit Concluding Document*, 1989, p.30. Subsequent documents and meetings expanded the meaning to include democratic institutions, the rule of law and the protection of national minority rights among other matters. See in particular the comprehensive *Document of the Copenhagen Meeting of the Conference on the Human Dimension of the CSCE*, 1990.

5. Some field missions, such as fact-finding or rapporteur missions, are shorter in duration and have specific mandates.

6. Of the cases relevant to this study, Ukraine, Armenia and Azerbaijan joined in January 1992 and Georgia in March 1992. Russia directly succeeded the USSR as a participating state.

7. By 1989, Russians formed 68% of the population of Crimea. Until 1954, the Crimean peninsula had been part of Russia.

8. Since 1989, 250,000 Crimean Tatars have returned to resettle in Crimea and now comprise 10% of the Crimean population. Although exonerated in 1967, the Crimean Tatars were given the right to return to Crimea only in 1989.

9. Letter from the HCNM to the Minister for Foreign Affairs of Ukraine, 19 March 1996.

10. Letter from the HCNM to the Minister for Foreign Affairs of Ukraine, 12 October 1995; Letter from the HCNM to the Minister for Foreign Affairs of Ukraine, 5 April 1996.

11. Letter from the HCNM to the Minister for Foreign Affairs of Ukraine, 15 May 1995; Letter from the HCNM to the Minister for Foreign Affairs of Ukraine, 12 October 1995; Letter from the HCNM to the Minister for Foreign Affairs of Ukraine, 5 April 1996.

12. Out of South Ossetia's total population of 100,000, Ossetians comprise 60% and Georgians about 30%, with 10% others. Revaz Gachechiladze, *The New Georgia: Space, Society,*

Politics (London: University College London Press, 1995), pp.79, 87.

13. Interview with Zurab Lomashvili, Georgian Delegation to the OSCE, Vienna, Austria, February 1997.

14. At the time, the Abkhazians were also demanding secession. Georgians feared that other ethnic groups residing in compact regions, such as the Armenians and Azeris, would make similar demands for secession and unification with their home-state.

15. Report of the CSCE Rapporteur Mission to Georgia, 17–22 May 1992, pp.6–7. The parliamentary elections and the referendum were boycotted by the ethnic Georgians residing in South Ossetia.

16. The JPKF consisted of roughly equally sized battalions of 500 personnel from Russia, Georgia and South Ossetia, deployed in mid-July (Aves, 1995). Other terms of the cease-fire agreement included the withdrawal of armed formations from the region as well as the disarmament and disbandment of militias. A Joint Control Commission (JCC) was to be set up to implement these obligations and to provide the framework for a negotiated settlement of the status of South Ossetia.

17. Established in November 1992, the OSCE Mission to Georgia has been based in Tbilisi; in April 1997 a branch office was established in Tskhinvali.

18. Many generations of Azeris have resided in Nagorno-Karabakh, whence come many of Azerbaijan's great literary and cultural figures.

19. *Interim Report by the CSCE Rapporteur Mission on the Situation in Nagorno-Karabakh*, 26 February 1992, pp.2–3.

20. In April and May 1991, Azeri units attacked and destroyed a number of Armenian villages in Nagorno-Karabakh. Other Armenian regions in Nagorno-Karabakh were constantly raided and several cases of murder, torture and multilation were reported.

21. The Minsk conference consisted of representatives from Armenia, Azerbaijan, United States, Russia, France, Turkey, Belarus, Germany, and the OSCE Troika. As Nagorno-Karabakh is not a state it was not represented. This conference has yet to convene.

22. The co-chairmen are appointed by the Chairman-in-Office of the OSCE and work in close contact with the relevant OSCE institutions and structures, and regularly reporting to the OSCE. There was originally only one chairman until the 1994 Budapest Summit when the decision was taken to have two co-chairmen, with one reserved for Russia. A third co-chairman position was added in 1997; since then, the co-chairmen of the Minsk Conference have been the United States, France, and Russia. It is important to distinguish between the participants of the Minsk Conference and the Minsk Group, the primary difference being that Nagorno-Karabakh is represented in the Minsk Group.

23. In place of the field mission, the OSCE has established the position of a Project Co-ordinator Office whose mandate is to support democracy-building projects. http://www.osce.org/ukraine/overview.htm.

24. An October 1998 draft of the Crimean constitution was criticized by ethnic Russians for depriving the Russian language of official status and by the Crimean Tatars for failing to recognize their indigenous status.

25. Such sensitivities were in evidence in the 1999 parliamentary elections in South Ossetia during which time candidates declared their continued support for South Ossetian independence and that progress on negotiations depended on Georgia's efforts to meet its economic commitments to South Ossetia.

26. Interview with Nayra Melkumian, Permanent Representative of the Nagorno-Karabakh Republic in Armenia, Yerevan, Armenia, June 1997.

27. Interview with Vagif Sadykhov, Azeri Ambassador to Austria, Vienna, Austria, February 1997.

28. Ilgar Mamedov, Counsellor, Azeri Delegation to the OSCE, personal interview with author, Vienna, Austria, December 1999.

29. Letters from the Minister of Foreign Affairs for Ukraine to the HCNM, 7 June 1994, 30 June 1995, 14 November 1995.

30. Interview with Georgi Burduli, Deputy Minister of Foreign Affairs, Republic of Georgia, Tbilisi, Georgia, June 1997; Interview with Zurab Lomashvili, Georgian Delegation to the OSCE, Vienna, Austria, February 1997.

218   ETHNICITY AND TERRITORY IN THE FORMER SOVIET UNION

31. Interview with Nayra Melkumian, Permanent Representative of the Nagorno-Karabakh Republic in Armenia, Yerevan, Armenia, June 1997.
32. Interview with Ilgar Mamedov, Counsellor, Azeri Delegation to the OSCE, Vienna, Austria, 16 December 1999.
33. The Russian president repeatedly made statements recognizing Ukraine's territorial integrity and Crimea as part of Ukraine. The Russian foreign minister stated to the Ukrainian foreign minister that 'Russia will not interfere into the Crimean situation'. The Crimea: Chronicle of Separatism, p.90.
34. Interview with Zurab Lomashvili, Georgian Delegation to the OSCE, Vienna, Austria, February 1997; Interview with Kaha Chitaia, Chairman, Parliamentary Foreign Relations Committee, Parliament of Georgia, Tbilisi, Georgia, June 1997; Interview with Stanislav Kochiev, First Secretary, Communist Party of South Ossetia, Tskhinvali, South Ossetia, June 1997.
35. The Crimea: Chronicle of Separatism, p.136.
36. RFE/RL Newsline 1:40, Part I, 28 May 1997.
37. RFE/RL Newsline 1:146, Part I, 24 October 1997.
38. Interview with Ilgar Mamedov, Counsellor, Azeri Delegation to the OSCE, Vienna, Austria, 16 December 1999.

REFERENCES

Aves, Jonathan (1996), *Georgia: From Chaos to Stability?* London: Royal Institute of International Affairs.
Azar, Edward (1990), *The Management of Protracted Social Conflict: Theory and Cases.* Brookfield, VT: Gower Publishing Company.
Azar, Edward and John Burton (eds) (1986), *International Conflict Resolution: Theory and Practice.* Boulder, CO.: Lynne Rienner.
Bercovitch, Jacob (1984), *Social Conflicts and Third Parties: Strategies of Conflict Resolution.* Boulder, CO: Westview Press, 1984.
Carment, David and Patrick James (1996), 'Ethnic Conflict at the International Level: Causes, Prevention and Peacekeeping', in David Carment and Patrick James (eds), In *The International Politics of Ethnic Conflict; Prevention and Peacekeeping.* Unpublished manuscript.
Chigas, Diana (1996), 'Preventive Diplomacy and the Organization for Security and Co-operation in Europe: Creating Incentives for Dialogue and Co-operation', in Abram Chayes and Antonia Handler Chayes (eds), *Preventing Conflict in the Post-Communist World: Mobilizing International and Regional Organizations.* Washington, D.C.: The Brookings Institution.
Gachechiladze, Revaz (1995), *The New Georgia: Space, Society, Politics.* London: University College London Press.
Goldenberg, Suzanne (1994), *Pride of Small Nations: The Caucasus and Post-Soviet Disorder.* London: Zed Books Ltd.
Hunter, Shireen (1994), *The Transcaucasus in Transition: Nation-Building and Conflict.* Washington, D.C.: Centre for Strategic and International Studies.
Kemp, Walter (1996), *The OSCE in a New Context: European Security Towards the Twenty-First Century.* London: Royal Institute of International Affairs.
Khutsishvili, George and S. Neil MacFarlane (1994), 'Ethnic Conflict in Georgia'. Unpublished manuscript.
Laue, James H. (1990), 'The Emergence and Institutionalisation of Third Party Roles in Conflict', in John Burton and Frank Dukes (eds), *Conflict: Readings in Management and Resolution.* New York: St. Martin's Press.
Lund, Michael (1996), *Preventing Violent Conflicts: A Strategy for Preventive Diplomacy.* Washington, D.C.: United States Institute of Peace Press.
Nodia, Ghia (1996), 'Political Turmoil in Georgia and the Ethnic Policies of Zviad Gamsakhurdia'. Unpublished manuscript.

Rabie, Mohamed (1994), *Conflict Resolution and Ethnicity*. Westport: Praeger.
Reychler, Luc (1994), 'The Art of Conflict Prevention: Theory and Practice'. In Werner Bauwens and Luc Reychler (eds), *The Art of Conflict Prevention*, New York: Brassey's.
Sasse, Gwendolyn (1996), 'The Crimean Issue', *Journal of Communist Studies and Transition Politics*, Vol.12, No.1: 83–100.
Ukrainian Centre for Independent Political Research (1996), *The Crimea: Chronicle of Separatism, 1992–1995*. Kyiv.
van der Stoel, Max (1994), 'The Role of the CSCE High Commissioner on National Minorities in CSCE Preventive Diplomacy', in Staffan Carlsson (ed.), *The Challenge of Preventive Diplomacy*. Stockholm: Ministry of Foreign Affairs, Sweden.
OSCE (1992), *Helsinki Document: The Challenges of Change*.
OSCE (1994), *Budapest Document: Towards a Genuine Partnership in a New Era*.
OSCE (1999), *Charter for European Security*.
OSCE (1975), *Helsinki Final Act*.

Conflict and Accommodation in the FSU: The Role of Institutions and Regimes

JAMES HUGHES AND GWENDOLYN SASSE

It is not surprising that the collapse of a multinational empire like the Soviet Union gave rise to political instability and conflicts over territory as this conforms to a pattern set by the historical experience of the fall of other great empires. The contributions in this volume have examined cases of post-Soviet states where there are simultaneous nation- and state-building dilemmas arising from the problems of new state formation during transition, in particular those of identity, territorial definition, building state capacity, and international recognition. These problems have interacted with and accentuated ethnic or regionalist challenges 'from below', and in some cases 'from outside'. There is an observable trend for post-Soviet states to engage in 'nationalizing' projects which have as their goal the recasting of the newly independent state in the mould of the predominant ethnic group. This trend enacts a preference for homogenization and a tendency for discrimination against minorities. The scale and intensity of these 'nationalizing' projects have varied across the FSU as the time frame or temporal sequence of certain policies, such as citizenship or language laws, have often revealed marked differences.

No single factor from the list of conventional causes of conflict, whether structural, geographical or identity-related, appears to convincingly account for the causation of all post-Soviet conflicts. The contributions in this volume illustrate this wide diversity of factors in the causation and dynamics of post-Soviet conflicts. The significance of the key causative factors – such as the historical legacies and memories of ethnic strife, international conditions, demography and settlement patterns, the degree of societal homogeneity and the nature of cleavage structures, geography, the political economy of transition, institutional engineering, the role of the military/security forces, elite and popular perceptions and practice, and cultural proximity or difference – have varied depending on the case. The contributors have analyzed these diverse conflict cases by focusing on the four underlying questions outlined in the introduction. First, the causes and distinctiveness of the territorial challenges; second, their nature: are they essentially ethnic, regional or driven by some other factors, or indeed some combination of elements? Furthermore, what is the relationship between territorial challenges and the process of post-Soviet transition and state- and nation-building? Third, why have some conflicts been amenable to accommodative strategies, while others have been violent and protracted, and yet other predicted conflicts have not materialized? Fourth, how have international and domestic factors interacted in the shaping of conflict trajectories and outcomes?

STANDARD EXPLANATIONS

The key works on ethnic and regional conflicts in the FSU generally offer two types of explanation. Brubaker and Bunce take a neo-institutionalist approach and emphasize the importance of the Soviet institutional architecture for ethno-political mobilization during the breakdown phase of the Soviet Union. Linz and Stepan follow the conventional liberal argument about the incompatibility of sustainable democracy and multi-ethnicity, particularly where the latter is institutionalized in a constitution or other superior political arrangement. Both of these categories of explanation share an underlying assumption about the inefficacy, if not undesirability, of institutional arrangements for managing multi-ethnicity in a divided society. The transitology approach, in particular, reflects the liberal precept that assimilation into the hegemonic group is the most democratic way to achieve inter-ethnic peace, presupposing that this is always possible, and assuming that the ethnification of politics in democratizing states precludes a stable democratic outcome or 'consolidation'. The ethnically complex transitioning states of the FSU are regarded as a significant testing ground for these assumptions, yet they appear to have been presented with a logically inconsistent Catch-22 formula for democratization. To reformulate Barrington Moore, we summarize this prescription as: *no homogeneity, no democracy*.

The contributions to this volume have contested these assumptions. Brubaker and Bunce have rightly emphasized, in our view, how the 'institutionalized multinationality' embodied in Soviet federalism created a specific 'breeding ground' for ethno-political mobilization during the breakdown phase of the Soviet Union. Our framework goes one step further than this by analyzing not only the post-collapse deconstruction of the old system by nationalists, but the reassembly and construction of the new post-communist systems. Similarly, we believe that one of the basic assumptions of transitology – that to successfully establish themselves newly democratizing post-Soviet states must first eradicate institutionalized multi-ethnicity and homogenize their populations and state structures – is deficient. This assumption is derived from fundamental levels of analysis problems inherent in Western liberal thinking on transition and nationalism. One of the key assumptions of many of the core writings of transitology, that the fall of the Soviet Union initiated a 'transition to democracy' process, is tautological. The regime change from Soviet authoritarianism that began in the mid-1980s developed along different roads of new state formation and state building, and this process was accelerated after the collapse of the Soviet Union in 1991. This process of change is multi-dimensional and cannot be reduced to 'democratization', even of a problematical variant. In a considerable number of post-Soviet states, most obviously in Central Asia where varieties of sultanist dynasticism and authoritarianism rendered democratic transition an ephemeral phenomenon, transitions were transient. Post-Soviet 'democratization' is a process along a spectrum, where even two of the most widely accepted consolidated democracies, Estonia and Latvia, reveal clear evidence of privileging of the hegemonic ethnic group and systematic institutionalized discrimination against their large Slavic minorities. Transitology proposes that transition is universally a 'state' process where integration is achieved by national level elites. These core premises of transitology are deficient for understanding the complex processes of regime change in a multi-ethnic conglomerate like the FSU, particularly given the legacy of formal and informal institutionalized and territorialized multi-ethnicity. In our view, the adoption of nationalizing and homogenizing policies in divided societies is likely to intensify minority discontent and sow conflict. The threat of, or actual eruption of conflict, in turn, leads to a temptation among hegemonic elites to opt for an anti-democratic oppressive control regime, unless there are countervailing disincentives (such as international pressures). Consequently, the challenge for political elites is to engineer a state institutional architecture which manages to accommodate multi-ethnicity.

Our analysis examines various dimensions, not only the state level process, but also the relations between territorial authorities within states, as well as the role of external states, regions, and other actors on developments. We support the view that post-Soviet regime change constitutes a specific 'regional' category because these states share a common legacy and were affected by distinct domestic and international 'regional' factors.[1] The critical role played by a common Soviet structural and institutional legacy is one of the most distinctive traits of post-Soviet conflicts which strengthens the validity of a distinct intra-regional comparative approach. Furthermore, the Soviet-era legacy made for a particular type of interdependency of institutions and regimes among the successor states, and this continues to reverberate in the demonstration and contagion effects of conflict, conflict management and strategies of accommodation.

INSTITUTIONS AND REGIMES

The contributions to this volume suggest that while there are obvious differences in the contexts and participants, there are some common causes and similar dynamics to many post-Soviet conflicts. Previous studies, such as that by Roeder, have stressed the significance of the size of an ethnic minority and the cultural distance between the core nation and the minority as the pre-eminent factors in the causation of post-Soviet conflicts (Roeder, 1999). The relative population size of a particular group is most relevant when it is associated with the spatial concentration of a group. The bigger and more concentrated an ethnic minority is in a given territory, the greater the likelihood for conflict. Even then, Abkhazia is a clear exception to this rule since conflict began despite the fact that the Abkhaz population accounted for only 18 per cent of the population of the Abkhaz Autonomous Oblast in 1989, though the proportion soared rapidly after the mass ethnic expulsions of Georgians and Mingrelians in 1992. In Crimea, the share of the returning Crimean Tatars today accounts for only about 10–12 per cent of the regional population, but their high degree of political mobilization and intense motivation has given them a political significance in ethnic conflict potential far outweighing their numbers in Crimean and Ukraine as a whole.

In comparing the outcomes of the different strategies of coercion and accommodation pursued in post-Soviet conflicts, we have attempted to draw together the rather compartmentalized literatures on transition, nationalism, ethnic conflict regulation and regionalism. Our analysis attempts to interlink these conceptual approaches and by concentrating on their shared emphasis on mobilization, institutions, elites and historical legacies, we have identified four defining traits of post-Soviet ethnic and regional conflict.

- The context of post-imperialism
- The combination of territorial and ethnic challenges
- The impact of transition regime type on institution building
- The interaction of internationalization and interdependency

The Context of Post-Imperialism

Empire is a regime of hegemonic control, which tends to act as a limiting constraint on ethno-territorial conflicts. One of the characteristic features of the decline of empires is the rise of such conflicts (Lustick, 1979 and 1993; Horowitz, 1985; Lieven, 2000). This is not to say simply that imperial breakdown opens a lid and releases ancient hatreds. Instead post-imperial conflicts thrive on the multi-dimensional nature of the imperial legacy and the difficulties of regime change in conditions where the systemic stress levels of managing the demographic, territorial, cultural, functional and institutional remnants of empire cause overload and breakdown. It is the 'detritus of empire', as Snyder observed, that 'constitutes the building blocks of the new political arrangements that are constructed out of the rubble' (Snyder, 1998: 1). Any edifice constructed from rubble is bound to be messy, if not inherently unstable, and the historical lesson of state-building on the detritus of empire is that it is conducive to instability, if not to failed states. If the end of empire is sudden the subsequent political vacuum and weak institutional capacity can render the conflicts with an explosive quality. Europe has been one of the most significant zones of such conflicts given the confluence of several major empires: the Ottoman, Habsburg, German, British and Russian-Soviet empires. The ethnic conflicts that have arisen after the end of the Soviet empire fit within a broader historical pattern and may persist over the *longue durée* (Rubin and Snyder, 1998; Lieven, 2000).

The collapse of the Soviet empire in the late 1980s and early 1990s resembles earlier periods characterized by the disintegration of great European empires, after the First World War (the Habsburg, Ottoman, and Tsarist empires), and the Second World War (the German empire in Europe, the British and French empires outside Europe). Each of these periods was an apogee of international involvement in a highly selective policy of nation state-building in the emergent successor states. What is arguably different about the end of the Cold War and the collapse of the USSR, however, is that Russia's inheritance of the Soviet nuclear arsenal has severely weakened the capacity of outside powers to reshape the post-Soviet order. The enlargement of NATO and the EU are types of third-party intervention aiming to reshape the political order in Central and Eastern Europe, but the capacity of these blocs to project their power into the FSU is limited. One of the fundamental criteria of membership of both regional organizations is the acceptance of existing territorial boundaries and internal guarantees for ethnic minorities. This kind of Western conditionality, however, has not been extended to the FSU, with the exception of the Baltic states. In the FSU Russia retains its influence as an unrivalled regional power, and the West has been hesitant or incapable of intervention, as demonstrated by the renewal of war in Chechnya in late 1999. Geographical proximity and the persistence of Soviet era dependencies have allowed Russia to stay deeply involved in all of the violent and some potential post-Soviet conflicts, whether providing military, economic or political support, managing negotiations or organizing peacekeeping forces with UN tacit approval (as the CIS forces in Abkhazia and Tajikistan) or without (as the Russian military in Transdnistria).

Potential for conflict after the end of the Soviet empire has been more acute because of a number of key differences compared to preceding end-of-empire processes. Most empires have collapsed as a consequence of military defeat, and arguably, the Cold War depleted the capacity of the Soviet Union and the will of its elites to compete with the West. First, however, the nature of the Soviet collapse differed from its predecessors by its speed. It was extraordinarily fast by comparison with other empires, including the British, taking little more than two years in 1990–91. This rapid deflation allowed virtually no time for conflict potential to be planned for, channelled or managed. In any event, empires are rarely deconstructed according to a plan and disengagement tends to be most problematic the closer the periphery of empire is to the imperial core, as the anti-colonial struggles in Ireland and Algeria demonstrate. Second, the geographical proximity of core and periphery tends to be correlated with deep historical and cultural ties and the blurring of identities. The fact that Russia's empire was the most contiguous in modern history, with its core and periphery coterminous, inevitably made for a much more complex and destabilizing disengagement. Territorial proximity was a ready-made rationale for continued Russian *droit de regard*, interference and, when deemed necessary, direct intervention in the affairs of successor states in the 'near abroad'. Contiguity explains why Russia has retained a considerable influence over developments in many successor states, since proximity is not merely an excuse for interference but creates security imperatives and national interest dilemmas that, taken together, constitute a logic for it. Third, the sheer scale of the disintegration, the Soviet Union being one of history's greatest land empires, created a chaotic surge of demonstration and contagion effects among the new states. Fourth, the Soviet empire was organized in an ethno-federal structure, many of the units of which were highly multi-ethnic within their administrative boundaries. Thus, the Soviet collapse released pre-institutionalized, but still immature, nation-states in embryo, most of which had no historical provenance as independent entities. Whether or not the new state did have a history of independent statehood, the nationalizing state-building policies pursued after independence broke their Soviet territorial and identity templates. The task of building or consolidating nations and states in such conditions was a formidable one. International norms of recognition in the post-imperial phase were intended to embed new states in the international system, but these norms also created an enduring problem of frozen conflicts, with many secessionist entities surviving *de facto* independent and *de jure* unrecognized. Fifth, and most importantly, the configuration of the collapse was exceptional as the imperial core, Russia, played a central part in the dismantling of its contiguous empire.

Post-Soviet state-building has been conditioned by an intricate interplay of path-dependent and contingent endogenous and exogenous factors. On the one hand, a path-dependent endogenous factor is evident in the way that nation- and state-building proceeds within multi-national institutionalized and territorialized political-administrative constructs inherited from the imperial era. How the institutional legacies have been disassembled and reassembled affects, and is affected by, competing territorial, ethnic or separatist challenges, and has a crucial bearing on the likelihood of conflict. The exogenous factor is evident in the fact that nation- and state-building occurs not only in a post-imperial but also in a truly international and global context where international intervention to regulate conflicts has acquired a new legitimacy, although not necessarily with a more effective capacity for enforcement. We should also take note of the changing impact of international competition over time, in particular between Russia and the USA/NATO/EU, in determining how and when conflicts will be settled.

The context of post-imperialism allows us to compare the post-Soviet conflicts with previous and ongoing conflicts over imperial legacies elsewhere. Furthermore, the emphasis on the role of institutional change and design opens the way for a meaningful integration of the post-communist cases into theories of ethnic conflict, nationalism and regionalism. It is also apparent, however, that the concurrence of post-imperialism with the legacy of communist federalism is a fertile ground for ethnic and regional conflict and, as one of the most distinguishing features of these cases, makes for useful intra-regional comparisons.

We have sought to move beyond the cruder end-of-empire theses used to explain post-Soviet conflicts, which often have a primordialist undercurrent that overstates the importance of the upsurge of 'ancient hatreds' once the communist control regime was removed. Clearly, historical memories shape identities and political behaviour. In some cases, such as Nagorno-Karabakh, Chechnya, Abkhazia and South Ossetia, historical animosities are salient factors. The question is, were the historical elements of these conflicts primary agents of causation, residual factors, or mobilizing and radicalizing features after the initiation of the conflicts? The evidence from the contributions suggests that, on balance, history was a residual factor and was drawn on more for its mobilizing power once the conflicts were under way. The trigger in most cases appears to have been the centre–periphery elite conflicts over attempts to modify or disassemble Soviet-era autonomies or otherwise distinctive territorialized structures by nationalists and nationalizing states.

The Combination of Territorial and Ethnic Challenges

The role of regions is one of the least studied, yet fundamental, factors in post-Soviet conflicts. Although nationalism, ethnic mobilization and regionalism are conceptually distinct, in many studies the regional factor to the conflicts is either ignored altogether or is subsumed under the generic term 'ethnic conflict'. The contributors have examined the substantive nature of the regional cleavages feeding into conflicts. We suggest that many of the violent and non-violent post-Soviet conflicts are regional rather than clear-cut ethnic conflicts, or are impelled by regionalist factors in addition to the ethnic dimension. The widescale destabilization that accompanied the post-Soviet transition has often led to political mobilizations around secessionist and substantively regionalist issues, but these were often disguised and voiced in the rhetoric of inter-ethnic competition. Tatarstan, Crimea, and Transdnistria best illustrate this phenomenon, as these were all cases where elite mobilizations of ethnicity against the central government were initiated and strongly impelled by political economy distributive issues (oil resources in the case of Tatarstan, and the protection of outdated Soviet industries and regional assets in the others). In particular, an inherited Soviet regional socio-economic and demographic structure are key elements of some conflicts, nurturing them in Transdnistria, Northern Kazakhstan, and in the Ferghana Valley, and defusing them where there are economic dependencies on the central state, as in Gagauzia and Crimea.

Multi-ethnicity has been a major challenge for many post-Soviet states, as it was for the totalitarian and authoritarian periods of Soviet power. In many cases of post-Soviet conflict clear-cut inter-ethnic competition eludes definition, but rather we are dealing with complex compounds of regional, cultural and economic grievances that were generally triggered into conflict by attempts to alter the institutional arrangements for managing multi-ethnicity inherited from the Soviet era. While it is not our aim to either downplay the significance of ethnicity in causing, fostering and prolonging conflict in general or to suggest an extremely narrow definition of 'ethnic conflict', it seems appropriate to shift the focus from the generic label 'ethnic conflict'. The contributions in this volume offer a detailed analysis of the important but partial role that ethnicity plays in many of the actual or potential conflicts under scrutiny. Similarly, we do not view ethnic and regional conflict as mutually exclusive categories, as both ethnic and regional issues can overlap or activate one another as the conflict arises and develops over time. Ethnic and nationalist mobilization have diverse causes, modes of articulation and forms of accommodation, but we distinguish them from regionalism by the latter's mobilization around primarily territorial interests, the absence of an overarching ethnic cleavage, and the absence of an aspiration for a nation-state.

In all of the real and potential conflicts considered in this volume, ethnic and/or linguistic issues were instrumentalized as one of several mobilization strategies advanced by the elites. In four of the five violent conflict cases considered (Chechnya, Abkhazia, South Ossetia and Nagorno-Karabakh) ethnicity was one of the defining markers of the conflict from the very beginning, but the intensity of this marker sharpened as a consequence of the radicalization induced by the conflict process itself. The post-Soviet conflicts in Transdnistria, Gagauzia, Crimea, Tatarstan, Bashkortostan, Ajaria, Northern Kazakhstan and, potentially, the Ferghana Valley involve mobilizations around a complex range of regional, ethnic, linguistic, socio-economic and pragmatic elite concerns as well as security considerations. On the whole, all of these conflicts could more appropriately be described as regional rather than clear-cut ethnic conflicts, despite their ethnic overtones. In fact, with the exception of Ajaria, the above cases have occurred in multi-ethnic settings, although a high degree of sovietization conceals this underlying trait. While the overarching 'Soviet' identity had a moderating and stabilizing effect on ethno-political mobilization in the USSR, this role came under extreme pressure with the collapse in 1991. Those successor states that have been most aggressive in the pursuit of nationalizing projects to construct their new identities have, by definition, had to decisively destroy the previously hegemonic 'Soviet' identity. Regions where residues of the Soviet identity persist strongly, however, have tended to have limited or no violent conflict. In Crimea, Gagauzia, Transdnistria, and Northern Kazakhstan, minority groups exhibit a strong 'Soviet' identity that counterbalances the potential for an ethnic political mobilization. In some cases, such as Crimea and Gagauzia, constitutional autonomization designs have accommodated these conflictual identities. In others, such as Transdnistria, conflict resulted from the attempted nationalizing project, while in the case of Northern Kazakhstan a strongly oppressive control regime coupled with a gradualist nationalizing project has kept the region subdued.

In disentangling the regional and ethnic issues, our conclusion is that in most cases an 'ethnic' veneer hides more deeply embedded regional issues. Some conflicts have a double 'regional' dimension as they have occurred in regions that are not simply located within one successor state, but also are ethnic exclaves or 'external peripheries' that were dislocated from potential 'homeland' states by Soviet boundary-making policy: for example, Nagorno-Karabakh, Crimea, Transdnistria and South Ossetia. The irredentist potential of such double regions is enhanced by their geographic location on or at the new international frontiers of the successor host state and adjacent to their potential 'homeland' state.

The Impact of Transition Regime Type on Institution Building

It may seem that post-Soviet conflicts have occurred irrespective of regime type. For example, there have been violent conflicts and peaceful accommodations in both presidential and mixed systems. Equally, we can observe a similar pattern in federal and unitary states. Only Russia is a constitutionalized federal state, though other successor states, such as Georgia, Moldova and Ukraine, have federal elements to their constitutional arrangements. Consequently, state type – unitary or federal – does not appear to be significantly correlated with conflict, though power-sharing arrangements of a federal or quasi-federal type do appear to be an effective means of managing such conflicts.

Similarly, regime type is not clearly correlated with conflict. The impact of presidentialism, parliamentarism or some form of mixed regime type on state stability is much debated. The importance of constitutional design is an axiom of transitology. As was noted in the introduction to this volume, the assumption is that institutional choices matter for democratic consolidation and economic performance over time, and that parliamentarism is 'more conducive' to building democracy. How countries are constitutionally equipped, that is, the choice of regime type, is seen as being critical for their state capacity to manage the problems of transition. We may summarize this as the effectiveness and stability thesis. One of the problems in this literature, however, is that attempts to measure the comparative advantages and disadvantages of presidential, parliamentary or mixed systems, are frequently characterized by definitional blurring. One indication of the blurring of distinctions between the systems is the increasingly widespread use of the term 'semi-presidentialism'. Furthermore, the influential study by Shugart and Carey identified two additional intermediate regime types between pure presidentialism and pure parliamentarism: the 'premier-presidential', defined as a regime where the president has some significant powers but the cabinet is responsible to the assembly; and the more unstable 'president-parliamentary' type, defined as a regime with shared or 'confused' responsibility over cabinets between president and parliament (Shugart and Carey, 1992: 15). On applying this framework to the FSU, Shugart found a trend from the former to the latter along a west–east axis into the FSU (Shugart, 1996).

The variety of regime types in the FSU lie along a spectrum from democratic to authoritarian, and even to, in the case of the Central Asian states, sultanistic regimes.[2] This reality makes the application of terms such as president and parliament frequently merely shorthands for leaders and assemblies. The leader of Turkmenistan, Saparmurat Niyazov, for example, is widely referred to as 'president' by Western commentators and analysts. In fact his official title, 'Turkmenbashi', should be translated as 'leader of all Turkmen, and he is president for life. This concept of leadership has more in common with authoritarian and totalitarian regimes than it does with the concept of presidentialism.

As important as institutional frameworks are for democratic consolidation, their performance is determined by the actors and elites that operate them and their political values and modes of behaviour. Personalities, leadership style and character issues can be as or more important than the formal rules of the game. Institutionalist studies of post-Soviet constitution-making have tended to stress the path dependencies arising from inherited rules and recirculated actors and elites. Elster's metaphor compares the challenge of constitution-making in post-communist states with 'rebuilding the ship in the open sea' (Elster et al., 1998). The constitution-making process began under old communist era rules and – to varying degrees – with the same old elites involved. The paradox of post-Soviet change was that the political actors had to redefine the constitutional rules of the game while themselves playing that game. Similarly, Easter suggests that the structure of old regime elites as they emerge from the breakdown phase determines the institutional choices of the transition phase. Distinguishing between three types of old regime elites emerging from the post-communist transitions (consolidated, dispersed and reformed), Easter argues that the regime type chosen was determined by the elite structure: presidentialism in the cases of consolidated and reformed elites, and parliamentarism in most cases where there were dispersed elites. Elite preferences for one regime or the other, according to Easter, are shaped by how they affect power resources. Presidentialism (decree powers, fixed term in office, personalization of power) is better suited to establish a proprietary claim on power resources, denies new political actors access, and provides a buffer against the new forces released by democratization and the market. Parliamentarism, on the other hand, is preferred where old elites have been dispersed and politics is dominated by new political actors, whose concern is to establish open access, largely guaranteed by electoral competition (Easter, 1997: 189).

A major weakness of the debate over regime type in the transition states of the FSU is that there is a tendency to overlook Horowitz's thesis on the importance of presidentialism as a potentially critical stabilizer in ethnically divided societies. The question is whether regime type is a significant factor in conflict causation or management. The dimensions of the question can be considered as follows: do similar regimes have similar outcomes; do similar regimes have different outcomes; do different regimes have similar outcomes; and, do different regimes have different outcomes? Of the post-Soviet states Estonia and Latvia have strong parliamentary systems, though even here presidential veto powers have been crucial for the management of minority issues through legislation rather than constitutional enactments, and in accordance with OSCE recommendations. Moldova, Ukraine and to some extent Russia have mixed systems, while the rest have strongly presidential leader-dominated regimes. In focusing on the institutional dimension of the management of multi-ethnicity as a key level of analysis, the studies presented in this volume have followed a broad interpretation of what institutions are and how they function, as outlined in the introduction, rather than a narrow focus on the presidential–parliamentary spectrum. Irrespective of regime type, nation- and state-building in the successor states has interacted with the legacies of the old Soviet system by discarding it in whole or part, or recycling it in some form. Thus, the experience of how nation- and state-building projects in post-Soviet states have dealt with ethnic and regional challenges may be examined as a model of two trends: de-institutionalization and re-institutionalization.

The first trend involved the de-institutionalization of different Soviet legacies, including attempts to alter the formal arrangements of 'institutionalized multinationality' at the regional level by changing the status or eradicating autonomous areas (Autonomous Republics, Autonomous Oblasts and Autonomous Okrugs). For example, the conflict between Georgia and South Ossetia in December 1990 hinged on the nationalizing project of Gamsakhurdia's parliamentary nationalist regime. In response the Ossetians attempted to opt out of Georgia but stay within the USSR, while the Georgian parliament revoked the autonomy status of South Ossetia. A similar dynamic led to the conflict with Abkhazia in 1990–91. Alternatively, in Chechnya and Nagorno-Karabakh there were attempts to eliminate autonomy status 'from below' in preference for secession at a time when Russia and Azerbaijan were predominantly parliamentary regime types. Other substantive changes to inherited institutional legacies included policies to undo Soviet language policy, economic structures and practices, eliminate or constrain settler-colonialism, the de-privileging of certain regions or groups that were beneficiaries of the Soviet regime (such as the Russian or Slavic diasporas), and installing a new privileging regime for the hegemonic ethnic group, in particular through laws on citizenship, voting rights, language, residence and employment. The parliamentary regime types in Estonia and Latvia and the mixed regime in Moldova presided over such a de-institutionalization and attempted to privilege the hegemonic ethnic group in the initial stages of transition. In the latter it provoked the secessionist movement in Transdnistria and the autonomist challenge from Gagauzia. In the former, the process was relatively successful, partly because of subdued mobilization on the part of the large Slavic minority and partly because the ethnic privileging by Estonians and Latvians was constrained and monitored by international organizations such as the OSCE and EU which exercised leverage because of the Baltic states international aspirations to 'rejoin' Europe.[3] Virtually unconstrained programmes of ethnic privileging, in contrast, were implemented in the Central Asian states, though more gradually.

De-institutionalization of the inherited structures for managing multi-ethnicity in the early phases of transition tended to provoke a reactive mobilization from the region or regions affected, and was usually elite-led and framed in ethnic rhetoric. Where territorial autonomy was threatened, the typical trajectory of this reactive mobilization developed from an initial aim of protecting the autonomy status, to demands for enhanced autonomy, and then to the extreme option of secession. Thus, the conflict dynamic itself appears to be a critical factor in transforming and radicalizing demands.

The second trend involves a reassembly of the inherited institutional legacy, whether by institutional, constitutional or other structural devices. The reaffirmation of formal or informal ways of power-sharing and accommodation is termed here a re-institutionalization. This type of re-institutionalization should not be confused with democratization, as in some cases, such as in Tatarstan, Bashkortostan, Ajaria and Central Asia, political and inter-ethnic stability correlate with the consolidation of new forms of authoritarian politics. The establishment of a control regime, in our view, is a form of re-institutionalization. In many post-Soviet states the management of ethnic and regional challenges by reinstitutionalization is, in practice, the prerogative of presidents and leaders. The para-constitutional new Federal Treaty of 1992 in Russia was adopted at a time when the state was formally still a parliamentary system. The asymmetric power-sharing treaties for Tatarstan, Bashkortostan and Sakha of 1994–95, in contrast, were executive agreements between President Yeltsin and the strong presidents of these republics. The constitutional accommodation between Ukraine and Crimea was achieved at a time when President Kuchma's power was strong vis-à-vis the Ukrainian parliament. On the other hand, Yeltsin had a prominent role in the launching and pursuit of war against secessionist Chechnya. Similarly, the second war in Chechnya initiated by Russia in late 1999 was a conflict primarily driven by the presidential ambitions of Putin. More recently, strong presidents such as Aliev in Azerbaijan, Kocharian in Armenia and Shevardnadze in Georgia, have taken the lead in the negotiations to reach accommodations to the conflicts in the Caucasus.

Repressive control regimes have been most strongly consolidated in the sultanistic regimes of Central Asia since the early 1990s. While there is no clear correlation between regime type and conflict or accommodation over ethnic and regional challenges to the state, it does appear that strong control regimes, such as those of Central Asia, can manage ethnic and regional challenges without necessarily addressing or even attempting to resolve the issues at stake. In the short and medium term they may succeed in neutralizing reactive mobilizations from minority groups by coercion, or some measure of informal accommodation in a patrimonial system of elite cooption, or through strengthened central administrative control through regional governors appointed by the presidents. Comparative experience indicates that such regimes can persist, but they are notoriously unstable as they preside over an immense potential for opposition and mobilization.

Consequently, the institutional legacy of the Soviet era, in particular 'institutionalized multinationality', may not only explain the patterns of the breakdown of the communist system, as Brubaker and Bunce have argued, but also the patterns of nation- and state-building during post-communist transition. In fact, the Soviet institutional legacy was an important constraint on nationalizing projects. Nagorno-Karabakh is a special case in that it is the only post-Soviet conflict where a territorialized ethnic group which enjoyed an institutionalized status that was not threatened by a nationalizing state took the initiative to secede to join a nationalizing project in a neighbouring ethnic kin state. While the reasons for this conflict are essentially historical, even this case confirms the general argument made by the case studies of conflicts in this volume, that the 'making' of new post-Soviet states could not proceed in a stable or peaceful manner on the basis of a rapid 'unmaking' of the Soviet structures by nationalizing projects, and that regional and ethnic factors are intertwined.

THE INTERACTION OF INTERDEPENDENCY AND INTERNATIONALIZATION

A recurrent theme of the multi-level analysis presented in the contributions is the high degree of interdependence of transitioning states in terms of the causes and dynamics of their conflicts. The interdependency has two dimensions. The first dimension involves the impact of successor states and their conflicts and non-conflicts on each other, including most importantly the role of the Russian Federation in all of the violent and potential conflicts in the FSU. The second dimension concerns the impact of the international system and its organizations on potential and violent conflict. The conflicts do not occur in a vacuum but are processed within the wider context of post-imperialism and transition. Consequently, post-Soviet conflicts are as much influenced by inter-state relations and the interdependencies among transition states as they are by intra-state and international factors. The fundamental interdependency is the Soviet legacy of interconnected economies. Crimea's economic dependence on Kyiv is one example; Moldova's dependence on Transdnistria for electricity is another; Tatarstan's landlocked location and dependence on Russia for oil processing and transhipment is yet another.

The interdependence of post-Soviet conflicts is reflected in their contagion or demonstration effects. The Russian military intervention in Chechnya in 1994-96, for example, was a powerful deterrent for the resumption of other potential conflicts, demonstrating the enormous costs of all-out war. In contrast, Tatarstan's power-sharing agreement of 1994 was widely perceived beyond Russia as an institutional innovation that could be a precedent for conflict resolution. Crimean elites drew on the experience of Russia's accommodation with Tatarstan for settling the Crimea issue, while Georgia and Azerbaijan have offered similar autonomy arrangements to resolve their secessionist problems, though as of yet without success. The fact that Russia under Putin is now attempting to dilute many of the autonomous arrangements of the power-sharing treaties with Tatarstan and Bashkortostan, and has returned to a coercion strategy in Chechnya, is not a good advertisement for the durability of such institutional devices, and will undoubtedly make institutional accommodations based on autonomy appear less attractive and less viable elsewhere. The dynamics of conflict interdependence in Moldova, however, have exhibited the reverse tendency. Rather than the autonomy arrangement of 1995 with Gagauzia acting as a precedent and an incentive for conflict-resolution in Transdnistria, Transdnistrian elites have rejected the constitutional arrangement as falling too far short of their demands. Concurrently, the Gagauz elites are increasingly dissatisfied by the discussions of more extensive powers for Transdnistria, which could lead to a reopening of the autonomy issue in order to secure even more powers. Thus, unresolved regional problems have a contagion effect to destabilize other regions that seemed to have been successfully accommodated. The demonstration or contagion effect can, therefore, work both ways: it can shape perceptions and provide an example of institutional means of conflict-management, but it can also revive debates and tensions based on new expectations or the perceived ill-functioning of existing autonomies.

Russia has played an ambivalent role in the regions in conflict. On the one hand Russian control and conditionality have had a stabilizing effect on some of the conflicts and, for example, prepared the basis for OSCE and CIS/UN peacekeeping; on the other hand there has been a tendency for Russia to freeze conflicts by pressurizing both parties to the conflict and thereby helping to maintain the *status quo* (especially in Abkhazia and Nagorno-Karabakh). Ironically, its involvement on the Abkhaz side in the conflict with Georgia was effectively sanctioned by the UN's recognition of the CIS peacekeeping mission after the 1994 truce.

Once conflicts have erupted, however, they may develop a different dynamic altogether. There was a discernable snowball effect on the radicalization of conflicts after 1991. Once elites and society as a whole become radicalized by conflicts the parameters of any settlement can be subject to wild fluctuation and bidding games. Consequently, institutional designs for managing ethnic and regional challenges to the state, such as autonomy, which may have been acceptable at the outset of a conflict, become wholly unacceptable. An autonomy agreement could well have stabilized Abkhazia and Transdnistria in 1991, but by 1992 such arrangements were unworkable. In Nagorno-Karabakh, however, the prospects for a settlement within the institutional architecture of the state of Azerbaijan evaporated with Armenia's military intervention, supported by Russia. The specific historical circumstances and political dynamics of this conflict, in particular the rise to power of the secessionist Karabakhtsi in Armenian politics, may well have rendered any settlement internal to Azerbaijan impracticable, as it may cause a civil war in Armenia.

All of the violent post-Soviet conflicts have been shaped by the interaction of domestic and international factors. In addition to the role of interdependency discussed in the previous section, the international dimension of post-Soviet conflicts principally consists of the influence of, and intervention by, states external to the FSU and international organizations. International influence on post-Soviet conflicts from outside the FSU has been weak and ineffective. Western states have tended to channel their influence on conflicts through the key international organizations for conflict management and resolution, the OSCE and UN. To some extent the OSCE's mission is constrained by the contradictory international principles on self-determination and territorial integrity. In practice, the OSCE as a representative body of states and state interests promotes territorial integrity. When it comes to conflict resolution, this emphasis leads to a prioritization of autonomy arrangements within the existing post-Soviet state boundaries. Indirectly, the solutions suggested by the OSCE are, thus, framed by the Soviet legacy of institutionalized regions and autonomies and help to further embed and legitimize them. The OSCE is often not seen as a neutral actor by the conflicting sides in post-Soviet conflicts, as it tends to be associated with Western influence or one of the parties to the conflict. It has been most successful in cases of conflict-prevention where the parties are already negotiating over constitutional devices, rather than in the resolution of conflicts which are ongoing and where the parties are radicalized. Generally, the OSCE employed a gradualist strategy of pressure, using the personal diplomacy of the OSCE High Commissioner of Nationalities, Max van der Stoel, as its most effective instrument. The results, however, indicate that the OSCE seems better equipped to protect minorities when the regime is compliant and receptive to pressure for some ulterior policy motive as in Latvia and Estonia.

Neither the OSCE nor the UN has been involved in a single case of conflict resolution in the FSU, though they are active in conflict regulation, managing those conflicts which are frozen, such as in Abkhazia and South Ossetia and in Nagorno-Karabakh. Here the focus is on the stabilization of conflicts, the maintenance of ceasefires, and the facilitating of negotiations by round-tables and mediating groups, such as the 'Minsk' group for the Nagorno-Karabakh conflict. Russia has been the key arbiter of many of the violent post-Soviet conflicts, mediating between the parties and brokering ceasefires in Abkhazia, South Ossetia, Transdnistria and Nagorno-Karabakh. It is on the basis of Russian arbitration that OSCE negotiations usually follow. Furthermore, states where there are conflicts have become more dependent on Russia as a result of its interference. Some parties to the conflicts have relied heavily on Russia for economic and military assistance, most obviously Armenia whose military victory over Azerbaijan and survival of an economic blockade was critically dependent on its alliance with Russia. Russian support has been crucial also for secessionists in Abkhazia, South Ossetia and Transdnistria. Ironically, even Georgia and to a lesser extent Azerbaijan, two victims of Russia's support for secessionists, became more subject to Russian influence as the price for a freezing of the conflicts at a time when the military advantage lay with the secessionists. Post-Soviet conflicts, consequently, by subterfuge have given Russia a greater leverage over the state-building and transition of many post-Soviet states.

Although the FSU is scattered with several important diaspora groups, most importantly Russians living outside Russia, cases of active support from ethnic diasporas or homeland states are rare. The strong influence of diaspora groups is evident in only one conflict: Nagorno-Karabakh. In the case of secessionist Nagorno-Karabakh, support has been given by the Armenian diaspora which has provided extensive financial assistance and significant political lobbying in the USA, where it is concentrated. In contrast, Turkey has played a restrained political lobbying role on behalf of its 'ethnic' kin in Azerbaijan and to a much lesser extent in Crimea. An 'ethnic' factor in direct military intervention by an outside state occurred in just two conflict cases: Armenia's military aggression in support of Karabakh's secession, and Russian military intervention in support of the secessionists in Transdnistria.

The trend in post-Soviet conflicts conforms to a global trend identified by Gurr's updated 'Minorities at Risk' project, which states that: 'In most recent wars of self-determination, fighting usually began with demands for complete independence and ended with negotiated or de facto autonomy within the state.' Gurr believes that from the mid-1990s there has been an emerging international consensus on the idea that disputes over self-determination 'are best settled by negotiation and mutual accommodation'. He may well be also right in arguing that negotiating regional and cultural autonomy is cheaper than rising instability and insurgencies in the long-run, as well as the costs of incurring international opprobrium. The constraining network of international organizations, mutual obligations and dependencies that Gurr identifies as being crucial for conflict resolution, however, are essentially tools for the projection of the influence of the leading Western powers. Similarly, his claim that with 'international engagement, ethnic conflict's heyday will belong to the last century' is dubious (Gurr, 2000: 54–8, 61, 64). The logic of the above views is belied by the reality of continuing competition between Russia and the West for influence in the post-Soviet space, particularly where significant economic resources are involved, as in the Caspian Basin. Both, moreover, have very different interests in the outcome of post-Soviet conflicts. This international competition is a hindrance to conflict resolution, since a mutually agreeable solution for the parties to the conflict is complicated enough but is made even more complex by the need for Russian and US consent, most notably in Nagorno-Karabakh.

CONCLUSION

The complexity of the challenges to the post-Soviet successor states has been a major contributory factor in obstructing their overall reform process, not only in constitutional design but also in the fields of economy and social issues. Where conflicts have been managed peacefully or resolved by institutional devices, the negotiation process itself has been a positive development and helped to cement a more stable civic definition of the successor state. That, of course, is provided that national and regional elites are willing to negotiate and engage in compromise.

Confederal, federal, and common state solutions which promote and institutionally entrench autonomy arrangements at the regional level are widely recognized to be the most productive basis for future accommodations and settlements of conflicts in the FSU. The obstacles to such arrangements appear to be twofold. First, there is the post-imperial context. By definition empires are often quasi-federal in that they are multinational and local governance is devolved to authorities within specific colonies, while matters of more general importance (foreign policy, defence, trade, taxation) remain centralized under the control of the imperial government. Federalism as a state organizing principle fits more readily with the logic of empire, whereas unitary systems accord with the logic of nationalism. The post-colonial experience in Africa and Asia with federalism demonstrates that there can be a significant disincentive for successor states to adopt it after independence, particularly if the pressure for this originates from external sources such as the former imperial power or international organizations, thus suggesting a continued paternalistic threat to sovereignty.

Second, the radicalization that inevitably intensifies during conflicts can trap transition states in a downward spiral of non-resolution and dysfunction that may be accelerated by the weakening of the state and other key institutions during the transition process. In particular, the economic dimension of transition tends to be disastrously affected by conflicts, even in those cases where institutionalized accommodation strategies prevailed. Whether violence erupted or conflict management succeeded, the conflicts led to a postponement or deflection of much-needed economic reforms at the national and sub-national levels. In fact, institutionally embedded autonomies often did little to progress economic reforms in the regions concerned since they entrenched old elites in power, though obviously they avoided the crippling costs associated with military conflict. In Crimea, Gagauzia, Tatarstan, Bashkortostan and Sakha, accommodation strategies tended to consolidate the power of regional rent-seeking elites who stalled any reforms that threatened their hold on power.

The studies presented here have attempted to illustrate the wide array of institutional devices and policies employed to manage regional and ethnic challenges to the states of the FSU, examining why particular arrangements have worked in some cases, while similar or other designs have been inoperable elsewhere. There is no doubt that the successful management of ethnic and regional diversity and conflict-potential is a prerequisite for political stability as well as the foundation for successful democratic consolidation and economic transition – though not necessarily for the onset of the transition process itself. To reiterate the problem of Gellner's rejection of a 'third way', we suggest that in the absence of forced assimilation or ethnic-cleansing, the pre-requisite for the transition to a stable democracy in a multi-ethnic state is an institutional architecture that recognizes diversity and manages territorialized minorities and secession-potential. In the more democratic post-Soviet states this has been achieved by a re-institutionalization of multi-ethnicity through legislation and institutionalized autonomies. Where conflicts have not been managed by a re-institutionalization of multi-ethnicity the outcome is a fractured state and a deflected transition process, with mass ethnic expulsions or discriminated and disgruntled minorities, and frozen conflicts where unreconciled secessionist entities exist in a Nether World of the international system. Depending on one's perceptions, Nagorno-Karabakh, for example, can at present be interpreted as a secessionist region of the Azerbaijani state, an informal region of Armenia or an independent state though unrecognized by the international system.

Post-Soviet state-building in a context of territorialized multi-ethnicity tended to begin with a de-institutionalization of the legacies of the old system. Thus, the ethno-territorial structures of 'institutionalized multinationality' inherited from the Soviet period had a major impact not only on the collapse of the USSR, but also on post-Soviet state-building. They not only undid the Soviet past but also disrupted the post-Soviet future. In this sense the post-Soviet successor states became disassembled states. While conflicts tend to be radicalizing events, the effect of which may make an institutional 'fix' ineffective or inapplicable, the extent to which these states have been successful in stabilizing their conflict potential has been largely determined by their state capacity for creating a new institutional architecture. There are two main variants for this: either the establishment of a new 'control' regime, or the reassembly and re-institutionalization of provisions for multi-ethnicity in ways which may or may not draw on the autonomy arrangements of the discarded old regime. Both variants may be effective at managing multi-ethnicity, but only the latter comes with an international seal of approval.

NOTES

1. See Bunce's critique of transitology in the extensive Slavic Review debate of 1994–95 with Schmitter, Karl and others.
2. We employ Sultanism as a regime category in the Weberian sense of an 'extreme case of patrimonialism' where the public and private domains are fused, the polity is the personal domain of the ruler, there is no rule of law and a low level of institutionalization. In sum, an arbitrary and personalistic regime.
3. David Laitin's study of the Russian diaspora claims that Russian and Soviet settlers are often content to assimilate to the post-Soviet nationalizing state (Laitin, 1998).

REFERENCES

Bunce, Valerie (1995), 'Should Transitologists Be Grounded?', *Slavice Review*, Vol.54, No.1, pp.111–27; 'Paper Curtains and Paper Tigers', *Slavic Review*, Vol.54, No.4, pp.979–87.

Easter, Gerald M. (1997), 'Preference for Presidentialism: Postcommunist Regime Change in Russia and the NIS', *World Politics*, Vol.49, No.2, pp.184–211.

Elster, Jon, Claus Offe and Ulrich K. Preuss (1998), *Institutional Design in Post-Communist Societies: Rebuilding the Ship at Sea*. Cambridge: Cambridge University Press.

Gurr, Ted Robert (2000), 'Ethnic Warfare on the Wane', *Foreign Affairs*, Vol.79, No.3, pp.52–64.

Horowitz, Donald L. (1985), *Ethnic Groups in Conflict*. Berkeley: California University Press.

Laitin, David (1998), *Identity in Formation: The Russian-Speaking Population in the Near Abroad*. Ithaca: Cornell University Press.

Lieven, Dominic (2000), *Empire: The Russian Empire and its Rivals*. London: John Murray.

Lustick, Ian (1979), 'Stability in Deeply Divided Societies', *World Politics*, Vol.31, No.3, pp.325–44.

Lustick, Ian (1993) *Unsettled States, Disputed Lands: Britain and Ireland, France and Algeria, Israel and the West Bank-Gaza*. Ithaca: Cornell University Press.

Rubin, Barnet and Jack Snyder (eds) (1998), *Post-Soviet Political Order: Conflict and State Building*. London: Routledge.

Shugart, Matthew and John M. Carey (1992), *Presidents and Assemblies: Constitutional Design and Electoral Dynamics*. Cambridge: Cambridge University Press.

Shugart, Matthew (1996), 'Executive-Legislative Relations in Post-Communist Europe', *Transition*, December 1996, pp.6–11.

Snyder, Jack (1998), 'Introduction: Reconstructing Politics amidst the Wreckage of Empire', in Barnet Rubin and Jack Snyder (eds), *Post-Soviet Political Order: Conflict and State Building*. London: Routledge, pp.1–13.

Abstracts

Comparing Regional and Ethnic Conflicts in Post-Soviet Transition States
James Hughes and Gwendolyn Sasse
This comparative study of post-Soviet conflicts stresses the role of political-institutional changes and adjustments to Soviet legacies made during transition in the causation, prolongation and accommodation of ethnic and regional conflicts. The main theoretical assumptions of the diverse literatures on transition, ethnic conflict and regionalism, are evaluated to highlight both their shortcomings and their potential usefulness for understanding post-Soviet conflicts. Four main questions are investigated: the causes and distinctive features of post-Soviet conflicts, the distinction between ethnic and regional conflicts, the impact of the conflicts on broader processes of transition, in particular institutional engineering, and the interaction between domestic and external factors as a formative dynamic of the conflicts.

Managing Secession Potential in the Russian Federation
James Hughes
The survival of the Russian Federation is an exceptional case since all other multi-ethnic communist era federations in Europe have collapsed. Theory suggests that the Russian Federation should have been subject to the same corroding effects of Soviet 'institutionalized multinationality'. This contribution explains its survival by examining the inherited structural constraints which limited the potential for a disintegration along ethnic lines, and the new post-Soviet institutional designs which led to the development of a stabilizing partial asymmetric federalism to manage the most serious cases of ethnic mobilization. The essay also focuses on the critical role played by Russia's powerful presidency under Yeltsin and Putin in the redesigning of Russian federalism, and analyses why presidentialism facilitated an accommodation with the elites of some ethnic republics, while being a major causative factor in the failure to manage the secession of Chechnya.

The 'New' Ukraine: A State of Regions
Gwendolyn Sasse
Post-Soviet Ukraine is composed of regions which historically have never been united within one independent state. The contribution argues that the 'new' Ukraine has had to face several regional rather than clear-cut ethnic

challenges since gaining independence in 1991. Rather than being a destabilizing factor, the regionalization of Ukraine's political, socio-economic and administrative structures has contributed to its political stability. Regional political mobilization occurred in only a few regions, with Crimea posing the only serious ethno-regional challenge to Ukrainian state-building. Conflict in Crimea was widely expected but did not occur due to the absence of clearly demarcated ethno-political boundaries and the weakness of Russian nationalism both in Crimea and in Russia. Most importantly, the protracted process of negotiation at the regional and national level channelled the Crimean issue into a constitutional settlement.

Regionalism in Moldova: The Case of Transnistria and Gagauzia
Steven D. Roper

This article demonstrates how differently the demands of Transnistria and Gagauzia have been managed by the Moldovan centre. Despite Gagauzia declaring independence as early as 1989, Moldova did not perceive it as a threat to its territorial integrity and embarked on a negotiation process which resulted in a limited but constitutionalized autonomy arrangement in 1995. In contrast, accommodation failed in Transnistria. While the linguistic concerns of the Russophone population of Transnistria were a salient factor underlying the outbreak of conflict, pragmatic considerations of the regional elite make this conflict a regional rather than an ethnic issue. The as yet unresolved conflict has had a direct effect on Moldova's transition politics, contributing to the resignation of the government in 1994, the neglect of socio-economic issues and the attempt of both the Moldovan executive and legislature to use the conflict as a justification to expand their powers.

Multinationality, Regional Institutions, State-Building and the Failed Transition in Georgia
Monica Duffy Toft

The Georgian case illustrates the 'stateness' problem inherent in the combination of ethno-regional heterogeneity and central nationalizing policies. Institutional referents from the Soviet period informed the conflicts in Abkhazia and South Ossetia: in the 1920s Abkhazia was a Soviet SSR alongside Georgia before being downgraded to an ASSR in 1935, and South Ossetia became an Autonomous Oblast' in 1922 only after attempts to unite North and South Ossetia had failed. The essay illustrates how Gorbachev's reforms and revived claims for autonomy or reunification led to Tbilisi unilaterally abolishing South Ossetia's autonomy status in 1990, while Abkhazia effectively lost its status through a deliberate manipulation of the election rules. Conversely, Ajaria's demands proved easier to accommodate, as the emphasis was put on being 'Georgians with a different religion' and the strong regional leadership maintained close ties with the controlling networks at the political centre.

The Irony of Nagorno-Karabakh: Formal Institutions versus Informal Politics
Razmik Panossian

To analyse the ambiguities related to the status of the self-proclaimed 'independent republic' of Nagorno-Karabakh, and its relationship to Armenia, this contribution examines Karabakh from four perspectives: (a) as a region of Azerbaijan, (b) as an 'independent' state, (c) as an informal 'region' of Armenia, and (d) as an ambiguous international entity caught between conflicting legal principles. The essay argues that it is essential to examine the informal nature of the relationship between Armenia and Karabakh, in addition to the formal institutional set-up. Moreover, it suggests that although Karabakh is almost wholly dependent on Armenia for its survival, yet its elites and interests have come to dominate key areas of Armenian politics. In this sense, the 'periphery' has 'taken over' the national centre.

Patterns of Centre–Regional Relations in Central Asia: The Cases of Kazakhstan, the Kyrgyz Republic and Uzbekistan
Neil J. Melvin

Since the collapse of the Soviet order, the countries of Central Asia have emerged as a distinct sub-group of post-communist states. The state-building policies of the political elites of Central Asia have aimed to fashion strong unitary systems. The contribution explores the development of state forms in the region and examines in detail the case of Kazakhstan, the Kyrgyz Republic and Uzbekistan. The diversity of political relationships that has emerged within these centralized states points to a complex interaction of post-colonial legacies, informal institutions and evolving identities as being the principal agents shaping territorial politics in the region.

The Osce and Regional Conflicts in the Former Soviet Union
Natalie Mychajlyszyn

The OSCE's interventions in post-Soviet ethnic and regional conflicts reveal important insights into the impact of the international dimension on post-Soviet transition. While the impact of the OSCE has been positive in a few cases, as in Crimea, for the most part it has been ineffective in conflict resolution and prevention. The contribution argues that the weakness of the OSCE is mainly due to the tension between competing principles of respect for territorial integrity and the right of self-determination which inform the OSCE's activities. The OSCE seems to be most effective in situations where territorial integrity is not challenged, and its solutions are inappropriate where it is. As a result, instability in the area is expected to continue and the OSCE's credibility as an institution for preventing, managing and resolving regional and ethnic conflicts is ultimately undermined.

Notes on Contributors

James Hughes is a Senior Lecturer in the Department of Government, London School of Economics. His research interests include the politics of transition in Russia, with special reference to the transformation of Russian federalism, ethnic conflict and the role of elites.

Gwendolyn Sasse is a Lecturer in the European Institute at the London School of Economics. Her research concentrates on post-communist transition, state- and nation-building, regionalism and ethnic conflict, with special reference to Ukraine.

Steven D. Roper is an Assistant Professor of Political Science at Eastern Illinois University. His research interests include electoral and parliamentary formations and conflict resolution in Eastern Europe and the former Soviet Union. He is the author of *Romania: The Unfinished Revolution* (Harwood Academic Publishers, 2000).

Monica Duffy Toft is an Assistant Professor of Public Policy at the John F. Kennedy School of Government and the Assistant Director of the John M. Olin Institute for Strategic Studies, Harvard University. Her research interests include ethnic violence, and military and strategic planning.

Razmik Panossian is a Tutorial Fellow in the Department of Government, London School of Economics. His research concentrates on Armenian nationalism and nation-building in the Soviet, post-Soviet and diasporan contexts. He is the co-editor (with Donald Schwartz) of *Nationalism and History: The Politics of Nation Building in Post-Soviet Armenia, Azerbaijan and Georgia* (University of Toronto CREES, 1994).

Neil J. Melvin is a Senior Lecturer in the Institute of Political and International Studies at the University of Leeds. His research is focused on territorial and identity politics with special reference to the new states of Central Asia and Russia. He is the author of *Uzbekistan: Transition to Authoritarianism on the Silk Road* (Harwood Academic Publishers, 2000).

Natalie Mychajlyszyn is an Assistant Professor in the Department of Political Science, Concordia University, Montreal. Her research interests include the international relations of the former Soviet Union, international regimes, ethnic conflict, conflict prevention and settlement, and civil–military relations.

Index

Printed in the United States
87812LV00002B/274/A

TESTIMONIALS

Legalese with Ease will definitely become the standard Human Resources reference for every H.R. Professional keen on making sure that they have all the knowledge they need at their fingertips.

Darlene Brushett
Managing Director of Human Resources
BMO Nesbitt Burns

Legalese with Ease will definitely stay on my desk as a quick reference tool. Malcolm and Adrian have provided an exhaustive list of legal terms and have managed to use plain language to describe these terms.

Varta Bruce
Human Resources Director

Malcolm and Adrian have done a great job with their latest text, *Legalese with Ease.* With over 25 years of combined experience they have succeeded in compiling a comprehensive list of terms that will provide a useful guide for anyone working in Human Resources.

Michael Annable, CHRP
VP-Human Resources
Linamar Corporation

Legalese with Ease delivers what every busy Human Resources Professional needs. A clearly written, comprehensive, plain English dictionary of relevant legal terms.

Shelly Rae
VP-Human Resources
Dominion of Canada General Insurance Company

 **hr**WORKS®

Legalese with Ease
Legal Terms for Human Resources Professionals

FRASER MILNER CASGRAIN LLP

Malcolm MacKillop B.A., LL.B.
Adrian Miedema B.Math, LL.B.

Contributor: **Janine Geddie** B.A., LL.B.

CCH CANADIAN LIMITED
90 Sheppard Avenue East, Suite 300
Toronto, ON M2N 6X1
Telephone: (416) 224-2248 Toll Free: 1-800-268-4522
Fax: (416) 224-2243 Toll Free: 1-800-461-4131
www.cch.ca

A WoltersKluwer Company

Published by CCH Canadian Limited

Edited by:
Janine Geddie, B.A., LL.B.

 The CCH design is a registered trademark of CCH Incorporated.

National Library of Canada Cataloguing in Publication

MacKillop, Malcolm
    Legal terms for human resources professionals / MacKillop, Malcolm
Includes Index.
ISBN 1-55367-181-3

    1. Law — Canada — Terminology. 2. Personnel management — Canada — Terminology. I. Title.

KE3107.3.M32 2003   349.71'01'4   C2003-904885-3
KF3320.ZA2M32 2003

ISBN 1-55367-181-3
© 2003, CCH Canadian Limited

Typeset by CCH Canadian Limited.
Printed in Canada.

DEDICATION

To Evan Batten-Cotte, the boy who has changed my life.

MJM

To my brother Brian, whose life speaks words that a voice cannot. And to Suanne deBoer-Miedema, my "wife of noble character".

AJM

FOREWORD

Over the past quarter century, the jurisprudence in the emerging field of employment law in Canada blossomed. With this developed a large number of new terms, both in the human resources field and in the law.

The publication of *Legalese With Ease* will address a real need for human resource professionals, lawyers & business executives. Under one cover, the reader can now reference succinct and understandable definitions of key words and phrases.

This book covers the landscape from employment law to labour law to health & safety issues. In addition to a complete compendium of definitions, this work is most useful for its list of statutes and charts relating to legislative requirements.

The authors, Adrian Miedema and Malcolm Mackillop are to be highly commended for their efforts in taking complicated concepts and providing crisp and understandable definitions. In some instances specific examples are offered to the reader (see: "compressed work week"). Also useful is the system of cross-referencing.

Adrian Miedema's practice at Fraser Milner Casgrain LLP involves employment, labour, and health and safety matters. He is a contributor to FOCUS ON CANADIAN EMPLOYMENT AND EQUALITY RIGHTS. Over the past six years, he has developed considerable experience in this field, while at the same time giving freely of his time to the not-for-profit sector through the Scott Mission and the ALS Society of Toronto.

Malcolm Mackillop is highly respected as a Leader of the Employment Law Bar in Canada. Over the past decade and a half I have marvelled at his creativity, intensity, and industry. As one of the driving forces in the Employment & Labour Group at Fraser Milner Casgrain LLP, he brings a wealth of experience and perspective to the practice. Malcolm is a prodigious writer, lecturer and commentator in the field. He is regularly consulted by the Canadian print and electronic media for his views.

It is little wonder that the Mackillop/Miedema team has produced a very useful book which will serve the business community, employers, employees, and the human resources and legal communities well.

Both are to be commended for their efforts in creating this most significant contribution to the ever growing literature in the field. I expect that it will grace many workplace shelves as an often-referenced resource.

The Honourable Mr. Justice Randall Scott Echlin,
Ontario Superior Court of Justice,
Toronto,
September, 2003.

PREFACE

In April, 2003, after 14 years with the same law firm, I joined the Employment and Labour group at Fraser Milner Casgrain. When I told Jamie Knight, the Manager of our group, that I had been approached by CCH to write a book on legal terms, he encouraged me to accept the offer and was extremely enthusiastic about the project. Jamie, also a celebrated author and well known labour lawyer, has shown his support not only for this book, but has repeatedly shown us his commitment and dedication to all of our writing initiatives for which we are very grateful. We are also fortunate that David Fuller, C.E.O. of Fraser Milner Casgrain, has been very supportive of this project and understands the importance for us to publish in our practice area. Our goal in writing this book is a modest one. We hope that *Legalese with Ease* will provide Human Resources Professionals with a dependable guide that can be used on a daily basis. Obviously, it would be difficult to cover all the sub-practice areas of employment law, but we have attempted to cover the four areas which are the most common, and we believe that we have provided a comprehensive list of terms in these four practice areas. I would be remiss if I did not thank my legal assistant Janki Chowbay for her hard work and dedication. Janki has worked countless hours under demanding circumstances during the last five months of transition, for which I am truly grateful. Finally, I have been blessed by the loving support of my life partner, Judy Cotte, herself an accomplished securities lawyer, for all her patience and understanding. She understands the importance of my writing projects and importantly, in times of despair, she helps me appreciate all the gifts in my life.

Malcolm J. MacKillop

September 2003

I have always enjoyed words. To a certain extent I cannot understand where this comes from. It was not a necessary product of my mathematics studies at University of Waterloo where I studied as many formulae as I did words. My best guess is that it flowed from my parents' constant encouragement to study hard, and my attempts to figure out the meaning of the Dutch words they used when they didn't want me to understand what they were saying. I owe them my thanks.

We live in an era of word bombardment. We have a constant flow of words across our desks every day. The proliferation of caselaw in the area of labour and employment law has helped define certain terms while introducing new, and sometimes unsatisfactory, words. This book is an attempt to provide plain language definitions of labour and employment law terms.

Lawyers know that no definition can be comprehensive. In litigation, a single dictionary definition rarely suffices, and an in-depth review of caselaw and context is necessary. But I hope that this book provides a useful reference for Human Resources Professionals who are confronted with legal terms, and perhaps a launching point for practitioners digging into a word.

I would particularly like to thank Janine Geddie for her tireless efforts in helping to prepare this book. As well, I would like to thank my assistant and law clerk, Melissa O'Connor, who often helps me choose the right words to use. Lastly, I am grateful to my colleagues in the Employment and Labour Law group at Fraser Milner Casgrain LLP for their encouragement of writing projects and contributions to the employment and labour law community.

Adrian Miedema

September 2003

TABLE OF CONTENTS

v

EMPLOYMENT

A

ADOLESCENT

A person who is between childhood and adulthood. In certain jurisdictions, adolescence is specifically defined to include people falling within a specific age range, who have certain restrictions on the hours of work or types of work they may perform.

For example, in Alberta an adolescent is defined as an individual 12 years of age or older, but under 15 years of age. For most jobs, adolescents in that province may only be employed outside of school hours, with parental consent, and for no longer than two hours on a school day or eight hours on a non-school day. Manitoba defines an adolescent to be a person between the ages of 16 and 17, and deems them to be an adult for employment standards purposes.

See also: CHILD, MINIMUM AGE, YOUNG PERSON

ADOPTION LEAVE

The ability of a parent to take unpaid time off from work upon the adoption of a child. Adoptive parents have the same rights as natural parents, and adoption leave is covered under the parental leave provisions for each province.

> *See also:* LEAVES OF ABSENCE, CHILD CARE LEAVE, PARENTAL LEAVE

AGENCY EMPLOYEE

> *See:* ASSIGNMENT EMPLOYEE

AGGRAVATED DAMAGES

In a wrongful dismissal action, extra damages may be awarded in order to compensate an employee who has suffered mental distress as a result of being treated in an unacceptable manner by the employer on termination. The purpose behind allowing such damages is to compensate for hurt feelings, anxiety and stress that is felt by the employee for actions that the employer should have known would be hurtful. The mental distress must be more than the basic feelings of hurt or anger that most employees feel when their employment is terminated. For example, an employer who alleges incompetence as a reason for dismissal, when there is no evidence of the employee's incompetence, might be liable for aggravated damages. Whether aggravated damages will be awarded by a court depends on the individual circumstances of each wrongful dismissal action where it is brought up as an issue.

> *See also:* DAMAGES, MENTAL DISTRESS DAMAGES, PUNITIVE DAMAGES, *WALLACE* DAMAGES

ASSIGNMENT EMPLOYEE

An employer may contract with an employment agency for certain services. The agency will then hire employees to perform those services for the employer, and they are called assignment employees or agency employees. Given their unique employment situation, assignment employees may receive less notice of termination in a wrongful dismissal action than a regular employee.

> *See also:* EMPLOYEE

ASSIGNMENT OF WAGES

A transfer of the right to collect wages from the employee who earned the wages to a creditor to whom the employee owes money. With written

Employment

authority from the employer, an employer may be required to transfer an employee's wages to another person or corporation, usually to satisfy a debt that the employee owes. Statutes generally govern the extent to which such assignments may be made. In particular, such deductions are specifically permitted in British Columbia, the Northwest Territories and the Yukon, and may include payments to unions, charitable organizations, pension or superannuation plans, or those authorized by collective agreement, as well as compliance with a maintenance order, to an insurer, or for any other purpose authorized by the Director of Employment Standards for the employee's benefits.

See also: DEDUCTIONS FROM WAGES

ATTACHMENT OF DEBT

The process of taking property from a person who owes money, in order to ensure that the person's debt will be paid. This may be accomplished by a writ, summons, or other order of the Court.

In the employment law context, an attachment of debt may be used in a case where an employer owes money to an employee, likely for unpaid wages. If a person or corporation is in debt to the employer for a certain amount of money, the Director of Employment Standards may be allowed by legislation to take that debt, and use it to pay the employee the wages that he is owed. Therefore, the debt would be paid to the Director of Employment Standards, instead of to the employer, and the Director would then distribute the wages to the employee.

See also: PRIORITY OF WAGES, RECOVERY OF UNPAID WAGES

AVERAGING AGREEMENTS

Employers may choose to average out the number of hours that their employees work over a number of weeks, so that overtime pay is not owed to the employee, even though she may have worked more than the standard overtime threshold in one week. Permission from the relevant employment standards officials, or agreement with the affected employees, will generally be required.

Using averaging agreements, an employee could work 50 hours one week, 10 the next, and 45 the next, and still not be entitled to overtime

A

if the threshold is 40 hours per week, since the average weekly hours of work over the three week period is only 35 hours.

See also: HOURS OF WORK, WORK WEEK

B

BAD FAITH DAMAGES

See: WALLACE DAMAGES

BALLPARK NOTICE

In determining reasonable notice for a dismissed employee, some courts have used the concept of ballpark notice. This concept is based on the idea that determining an appropriate notice period for a wrongfully dismissed employee is inherently uncertain. So, under this approach, the court will look at whether the severance offer by the employer was reasonable, and within the range of awards given to similar employees in similar situations. If it is, the court will not interfere, even if the severance offer was not exactly what the court would have awarded as reasonable notice.

This approach to determining reasonable notice is problematic, and has been specifically rejected by a number of courts. Some have rejected this approach because it gives too much weight to the employer's initial offer, and puts too much of a burden on the employee to show that the offer was unfair. Similarly, determining an appropriate "range" for a particular employee may result in vastly different notice awards, depending on the views of an individual judge. As an example, say that an employee is offered 9 months' salary in lieu of notice, and it is determined that the traditional range for this class of employee is 8 to 10 months' notice. On the ballpark notice doctrine, the trial judge may choose not to interfere with the 9 month offer as it is within the reasonable range.

See also: DISMISSAL, REASONABLE NOTICE, WRONGFUL DIS-MISSAL

BENEFITS

Indirect compensation given to an employee as a condition of employment. Also known as "fringe benefits", benefits are usually not directly related to job factors or performance but are offered to employees as incentives beyond basic salary and wages.

Employers may make deposits in the employee's name into pension plans, employment insurance, workers' compensation plan membership, or provincial health care plans as indirect benefits. More direct benefits that may be offered to an employee include:

- life or health insurance

- extended health care plans

- drug plans

- dental care plans

- vision care plans

- travel accident plans

- income replacement plans

- supplemental unemployment benefits

- other miscellaneous group benefits

    See also: BONUS, SALARY, WAGES

BEREAVEMENT LEAVE

A leave of absence granted to an employee when a family member dies. Nine jurisdictions specifically provide for bereavement leave, as set out in the table below. The duration of the leave varies from one to five days, and a qualification period is frequently part of the bereavement requirements. Most jurisdictions state that the bereavement leave can be unpaid, although some state that one day must be paid, and the federal jurisdiction requires the whole bereavement leave to be paid.

BEREAVEMENT LEAVE

Jurisdiction	Qualifying Period	Length of Leave	Paid or Unpaid	Timing Restriction
Federal[1]	3 mos	3 days	paid	Immediately after death
Alberta	n/s	n/s	n/s	n/s
British Columbia	n/s	3 days	unpaid	n/s
Manitoba	n/s	n/s	n/s	n/s
New Brunswick	n/s	5 days[2]	unpaid	No later than day of funeral

B

Jurisdiction	Qualifying Period	Length of Leave	Paid or Unpaid	Timing Restriction
Newfoundland	30 days	3 days	1 day paid 2 days unpaid	n/s
Nova Scotia	n/s	1 or 3 days[2]	unpaid	n/s
Ontario	n/s	n/s	n/s	n/s
Prince Edward Island	n/s	3 days	unpaid	No later than day of funeral
Quebec	n/s	1 or 5 days	1 day paid 4 days unpaid	n/s
Saskatchewan	3 mos	5 days	unpaid	Within 1 week of funeral
Northwest Territories and Nunavut	n/s	n/s	n/s	n/s
Yukon	n/s	1 week	unpaid	Funeral must be within the week.

[1] The three-month qualifying period is for paid leave. If under three months' employment, employee is still entitled to unpaid leave.
[2] Varies depending on relationship of employee to deceased.

See also: EMERGENCY LEAVE, IMMEDIATE FAMILY, LEAVES OF ABSENCE

BONUS

An addition to the salary or wages that are normally paid to an employee. A bonus may be given for extraordinary work, or as an incentive to employees to encourage them to be more productive or effective in their work. Some bonuses are based on the employee's performance, while others are based on the employer's profitability, and still others are based on a mixture of both.

See also: BENEFITS, SALARY, WAGES

BUSINESS HOURS

The official hours of operation of a company. In certain positions, employees will be required to be present in the office during normal business hours, such as businesses involved in customer service.

BURDEN OF PROOF

In a legal matter, one of the parties will be required to prove a fact or facts in dispute on an issue raised between the parties in order to succeed. Usually the person who brings the dispute forward will have the burden of proving the facts that form the basis for the allegation, unless the circumstances require the other party to justify its actions. For example, if an employee is dismissed for just cause and brings a wrongful dismissal action, once the employee proves that he was employed and was subsequently dismissed, the burden shifts to the employer to demonstrate that there was just cause to dismiss the employee.

C

CALL-BACK PAY

Wages, usually above an employee's regular wage rate, for workers who are called back on the job outside of their scheduled working hours. Contract provisions usually provide for a minimum number of hours of pay, regardless of the number of hours actually worked.

CALL-IN PAY

The minimum payment that employees are entitled to if they are called into or report to work, but are not given the opportunity to work an entire shift or normal work day. It protects workers from being called into work at the employer's discretion, and then being sent home without any compensation.

The call-in amount ranges between two and four hours of pay, although in most jurisdictions employees are entitled to three hours of call-in pay, whenever they are called in to work. In Manitoba, New Brunswick, Nova Scotia, Nunavut and the Northwest Territories an employee is only entitled to call-in pay if the employee is summoned to work outside of regular work hours. In British Columbia and the Yukon, employees are entitled to two hours of call-in pay, although in British Columbia employees must be paid for four hours of work if the employee was scheduled to work on that day for more than 8 hours. In the Northwest Territories and Nunavut employees are entitled to four hours of call-in pay.

It should be noted that, in some jurisdictions, there are special provisions regarding call-in pay for certain types of workers. In addition, if the cancellation of work is beyond the employer's control, call-in pay provisions may not always apply. Finally, exceptions may be made for cases where an employee reports to work, but is unfit to work.

C

CHILD

In Manitoba and Newfoundland, a person under 16 years of age is defined to be a child. Across the country, people below a specified minimum age are prohibited from working, or they are only allowed to work in certain fields and under certain restrictions.

See also: ADOLESCENT, MINIMUM AGE, YOUNG PERSON

CHILD CARE LEAVE

Parental and adoption leaves in New Brunswick are called child care leaves. In New Brunswick, employees who become a father or mother to a newborn or adopted child are entitled to child care leave without pay of up to 37 weeks.

See also: ADOPTION LEAVE, PARENTAL LEAVE

CIVIC HOLIDAY

In Ontario, many employers and employees observe the first Monday in August as a public holiday, even though it is not specifically defined as a provincial holiday.

The term "holiday" in Ontario includes a day appointed as a civic holiday by a council for a municipality, city, town, or district. Historically, the City of Toronto originated a midsummer holiday for a "day of recreation" on August 18, 1869. This was the first official recognition of an annual event that had started back in 1861. In 1871 Lord Lubbock of the British House of Lords proposed to make the first Monday in August a civic holiday based on the Toronto example of a midsummer holiday. In 1875 Toronto began observing the civic holiday on the first Monday in August, and that was the beginning of the tradition that continues to this day. In 1968, Toronto City Council officially named the civic holiday "Simcoe Day", although now it is known throughout the province as the civic holiday. Therefore, the civic holiday is a municipal, not a provincial holiday, although many municipalities do choose to observe it.

See also: STATUTORY HOLIDAY

COMMON ANNIVERSARY DATE

An employer may set a common date for all employees, for the purposes of determining a year of employment. The number of years of employment is then used to determine an employee's entitlement to vacation. In many cases, an employer will choose January 1 as the common anniversary date, regardless of the actual starting date for a particular employee.

> *See also:* VACATION, VACATION ENTITLEMENT, VACATION ENTITLEMENT YEAR, VACATION PAY YEAR, YEAR OF EMPLOYMENT

COMMON LAW

Rules developed by courts of law, or laws that are made by judges over time, based on precedent. They are distinct from statutes, which are laws made by legislatures.

COMMON LAW PARTNER

A person living with another individual in a conjugal relationship, where they are not legally married. Legislation differs in terms of how long one has to live with a partner in order to be considered part of a common law relationship. It is usually defined as at least one year of living together, although it may be as long as three years.

COMPRESSED WORK WEEK

Employees may schedule their work so that they work the same number of hours as they would during a regular work week, but in fewer days. Since employees under this schedule are working fewer days in a week, the employer can extend their workday beyond 8 hours usually without having to pay overtime. Compressed work week agreements are permitted in all jurisdictions across Canada.

Some pros and cons of the compressed work week for employers and employees include:

Pros:

- extension of the workday without overtime required to be paid;

- allow employees more time off;

- employees who live further away will have less commuting to deal with each week.

C

Cons:

- possibility of reduced staff on Mondays or Fridays, so cross-training, back-up training, and a good communication system are required to ensure that production or service do not suffer during these low times;

- possible stamina issues, since it is generally true that productivity drops off when longer hours are worked;

- some people with young families may resist being away from their family for extended periods of time, or they may experience difficulties with their day care arrangements.

EXAMPLE — COMPRESSED WORK WEEK POLICY

Please note that the following policy is provided for sample purposes only. It does not necessarily comply with your current jurisdictional legislation.

Compressed work week at a 340-employee marketing firm.

Policy

In the spirit of reducing commuting time and offering our employees the best possible balance between work and personal interests, our company offers a choice of two compressed work schedules.

4/40

With this schedule, you work no longer than 4-10-hour days in one week, for a total of 40 hours. For example, you could work 8 a.m. to 7 p.m. with an hour for lunch Monday to Thursday, and get every Friday off. A sample schedule is presented below.

Week	Mon	Tues	Wed	Thurs	Fri
1	10	10	10	10	Off
2	10	10	10	10	Off
Etc.					

9/80

By opting for this schedule, you will work eight 9-hour days and one 8-hour day in two weeks, for a total of 80 hours. For example, you could work 8:00 a.m. to 6:00 p.m. with a one-hour lunch break on Monday through Thursday.

On the first Friday, you will work a normal 8-hour day and get the second Friday off.

Week	Mon	Tues	Wed	Thurs	Fri
1	9	9	9	9	8
2	9	9	9	9b	Off
Etc.					

Procedure

Department supervisors, based on assessments of the workloads and hours of operation, will determine the number of compressed work week schedules available. They will continually assess workloads and adjust the number of compressed work weeks, as necessary. It is the supervisor's job to ensure a proper staffing balance among employees in terms of skill level and experience at all times to achieve effective customer service and productivity targets.

To apply for a compressed work week, submit a written request to your department manager. If arranged, your manager will sign approval and place the document in your employee file for reference.

Your supervisor will keep you informed about the development and posting of schedules. Your performance will also be screened for performance problems. The compressed work week will be removed as appropriate. It may also be discontinued at anytime, based on operational needs.

> *See also:* HOURS OF WORK, OVERTIME, WORK DAY, WORK WEEK

CONSTRUCTIVE DISMISSAL

It is generally clear when an employer has ended an employment relationship. However, sometimes an employer may legally terminate an employment relationship without necessarily intending to, or even being aware of it. For example, if the employer unilaterally alters a material term of the employee's contract of employment without providing reasonable notice, that change may be seen by the employee as legally ending the employment contract. The employee may either accept the new employment contract, with the new terms, or he may claim compensation for constructive dismissal.

C

There are a number of unilateral changes which may constitute a constructive dismissal, although all of the circumstances surrounding the change must be considered. Some examples may include:

- A major change in compensation, job duties or responsibilities, or reporting arrangements; or

- A change in location.

There are some things that an employer can do in order to prevent a claim of constructive dismissal. First of all, before making major changes to the conditions of employment for an employee, or group of employees, an employer should be sure to give reasonable notice. In basic terms, the employer is giving the employee notice of termination of the current employment contract, at which point it is replaced with a new employment contract with new terms. The employee can then use the notice period to decide whether she wishes to continue working under the new conditions. Also, an employer should create a carefully drafted contract of employment at the beginning of the employment relationship for new employees to sign. The contract should deal with situations such as the possibility of transferring the employee from one location to another, altering the employee's responsibilities, or any terms which the employer may reasonably expect to want more flexibility in determining from time to time.

> *See also:* CONTRACT OF EMPLOYMENT, DEMOTION, PROMOTION, REASONABLE NOTICE, RESIGNATION, WRONGFUL DISMISSAL

CONTINUOUS OPERATIONS

Includes industries or services which continue operations day and night during a seven day period, without stopping until the regularly scheduled work for that period has been completed. Examples would include a grocery store open 24 hours, an all-night gas station, or a hotel. These industries may not be required to follow certain employment standards requirements, such as certain statutory holiday requirements, as they remain in operation during holidays.

CONTRACT OF EMPLOYMENT

Every employee has an employment contract with his employer, whether it is explicitly set out in writing, or implied by the relationship between the parties. It is an agreement by the employee to do certain work, and an agreement by the employer to pay the employee for that work. Beyond that, it can deal with all aspects of the employment relationship including the nature of the work, any reporting relationships, duties of the employee, salary, bonuses, allowances, confidentiality of information, length of the contract and termination clauses.

Under the common law of contract, parties are generally free to contract as they choose. If questions about the contract arise, it will be important to determine what the parties actually agreed to. Using common law principles, one or more of the parties cannot make fundamental changes to the agreement without providing reasonable advance notice of the changes. Similarly, an employment contract may be found to be unenforceable if there was no actual agreement between the parties, if the agreement was involuntary or one of the parties was forced into the agreement, or if the agreement was imposed on the employee without any benefit or consideration being given to him or her by the employer.

All jurisdictions have introduced employment standards legislation setting out minimum requirements. No contract of employment, whether oral or written, may contract out of these minimum requirements.

COURT LEAVE

Employers are required to provide employees with an unpaid leave of absence from work if they have been summoned or selected to perform jury duty, or if they are required to attend court as a witness. Employers are not required to pay for the leave although many employers do, viewing it as part of their civic duty.

See also: LEAVES OF ABSENCE

D

DAMAGES

An amount owing to a person for breach of a legal right or obligation.

In the employment context, when an employer terminates an individual's employment, reasonable notice or an amount equal to the employee's compensation during the reasonable notice period should be paid to the employee. If the employer does not provide the employee with adequate notice, the employee may be entitled to sue the employer for damages for wrongful dismissal. In order to determine the amount of damages that are owed to an employee, the court will determine what constitutes reasonable notice in the particular situation.

Other forms of damages beyond reasonable notice may be awarded to an employee in certain situations. If the employer behaves in a particularly harsh, reprehensible, or malicious manner, aggravated and/or punitive damages may be awarded to the employee.

> *See also:* AGGRAVATED DAMAGES, MENTAL DISTRESS DAMAGES, PUNITIVE DAMAGES, REASONABLE NOTICE, *WALLACE* DAMAGES, WRONGFUL DISMISSAL

DAYS OF REST

Historically, Sunday was considered a day of rest in Canada. On Sundays, shops were closed, business was not conducted, and employees rested.

There have been numerous Charter challenges to legislation prohibiting work on Sundays. In particular, the federal *Lord's Day Act* was found by the Supreme Court of Canada to be invalid law. As a result, the federal *Lord's Day Act* is no longer in force, although some provinces continue to have their own legislation restricting what businesses may open on Sunday. Provincial retail business shopping legislation details when retail shops are allowed to be open and closed, and which stores are exempted from these requirements. Some jurisdictions also protect the right of employees to refuse to work on Sundays, or statutory holidays.

DEDUCTIONS FROM WAGES

In general, an employer is not allowed to take off any money from an employee's wages that is not specifically set out in legislation, in a court order, or authorized in writing by the employee.

Deductions that are specifically allowed by some legislation include:

- Union dues: employers must deduct union dues according to collective agreements between an employer and a union, or with the written authorization of the employee;

- Room and board: employers can make deductions from wages for the cost of room and board which they provide to an employee, although the amount that can be deducted is limited by legislation;

- Uniforms: in many jurisdictions, employers can make deductions for uniforms, although the amount that can be deducted is limited by legislation;

- Charity: employees may provide written authorization allowing deductions to be made for charity; this is specifically permitted in British Columbia, the Northwest Territories and the Yukon;

- Pension plans: employees may provide written authorization to permit deductions for pension and superannuation plans; this is specifically permitted in British Columbia, the Northwest Territories and the Yukon;

- Insurance: with employee's written authorization, an employer may deduct premiums for insurance; this is specifically permitted in British Columbia, the Northwest Territories and the Yukon;

- Credit obligations: deductions to meet credit obligations may be made with employee authorization; this is specifically permitted in British Columbia, the Northwest Territories and the Yukon; or

- Direction to pay spouse or other immediate family member: the Northwest Territories and the Yukon specifically permit employees to authorize the payment of wages to a spouse or other member of the immediate family.

Many deductions will not be permitted. An employer's business costs can never be deducted from an employee's paycheque. Written authorization will not be enforceable for agreements that will reimburse an employer for property or money loss, when another person beside the employee had access to the property or money in question. In several provinces, such as Alberta, an employer cannot deduct for faulty workmanship, although many provinces are silent on this issue.

See also: ASSIGNMENT OF WAGES

DEFINED INDUSTRIES

In Ontario, defined industries are specified to be the women's coat and suit industry, and the woman's dress and sportswear industry. Employees in these particular industries within the province of Ontario have a special set of employment standards requirements as set out in Ontario's Terms and Conditions of Employment in Defined Industries Regulation under the *Employment Standards Act.*

D

DEMOTION

A transfer to a lower-level position within a company. It may involve a substantial change in job responsibilities, or a decrease in salary and benefits. Demotions may result in constructive dismissal in certain circumstances, although not all changes to an employment relationship will be deemed to be demotions, and not all demotions will be seen as constructive dismissals. It will depend on the nature of the changes to the employment situation, and the individual circumstances of each case.

Some job changes that may result in a demotion include: (a) changes in job title; (b) changes in reporting function; and (c) changes in substantive duties. In particular, transferring an employee to a position in the company with lower prestige or status will likely be seen as a demotion. If a unilateral change is made to a central term of the employment contract, it will most likely be considered a constructive dismissal.

See also: CONSTRUCTIVE DISMISSAL, PROMOTION

DEPENDENT CONTRACTOR

An individual, whether employed by a contract of employment or not, who performs work or services for another person for compensation or reward under such terms and conditions that the individual is in a position of economic dependence on, and under an obligation to perform duties for, that person, more closely resembling the relationship of an employee rather than that of an independent contractor. This applies whether or not the individual furnishes her own tools, vehicles, equipment, machinery, or material or any other thing.

See also: EMPLOYEE, INDEPENDENT CONTRACTOR

DIRECTOR

A member of the board of directors of a corporation who is usually elected at an annual meeting of shareholders of the corporation. Directors are responsible for making important business decisions, such as deciding to borrow money, or buying property for the benefit of the corporation. The day-to-day management of the corporation is left to employees and managers. In many corporations, especially smaller ones, directors may also be involved in the daily running of the corporation as officers or employees as well.

See also: MANAGER, PROFESSIONAL EMPLOYEE

DISCHARGE

See: DISMISSAL

DISCIPLINE

Action taken by an employer against an employee for contravening expressed or implied terms of the employment agreement. This may include the breach of a workplace rule or policy. The conduct may include theft, dishonesty, incompetence, personality conflict, harassment, and more.

Company policies should be clear and readily available to all employees, so that employees know what is required of them. If a situation arises where discipline is required, an employer should act early and fairly in order to stop the conduct in question before it becomes a habit. Some types of misconduct will always be cause for discipline even if they do not violate any specific written rule or policy. Employers should also help the employee to improve his performance by providing appropriate support and guidance. The best approach to solving a discipline issue before it gets to the dismissal stage is to develop and utilize a process of progressive discipline, but this depends on the severity of the misconduct.

See also: PROGRESSIVE DISCIPLINE

DISMISSAL

A release or discharge from employment. A dismissal occurs when the employee's employment is at an end. In order for an employee's actions to constitute dismissal for cause, there must be some act or series of acts by the employee that amounts to a repudiation of the original contract of employment with the employer. A dismissal should be clearly indicated to the employee, such as in a direct letter from the employer telling the employee that he has been fired. In some cases, though, acts of the employer may constitute dismissal of the employee, whether or not the employer intended to dismiss the employee.

See also: CONSTRUCTIVE DISMISSAL, RESIGNATION, WRONGFUL DISMISSAL

DUTY OF CONFIDENTIALITY

An employee has a duty not to reveal certain information learned from her employer. This duty of confidentiality may be contained in a contract of

D

employment, which explicitly sets out what information may not be revealed by an employee, or it may arise from the general common law duties of loyalty and good faith that an employee owes to an employer.

See also: FIDUCIARY DUTIES

E

EDUCATION LEAVE

It is not legislated in any jurisdiction, but a collective agreement or any other agreement between the employer and a group of employees may provide for leave, with or without pay, for employee retraining or skills updating.

See also: LEAVES OF ABSENCE

EMERGENCY

An unexpected, urgent situation where an employer may require an employee to work overtime. The definition of what constitutes an emergency varies from jurisdiction to jurisdiction, but it includes such things as accidents; interruptions to the supply of essential services, such as utilities; and urgent or essential work that must be performed on machinery or equipment in order to prevent a serious interference with the functioning of the employer's business. Circumstances that will qualify as an emergency will usually be unforeseen or unpreventable, and an employee's hours may be extended only as required to prevent serious interference with the company's ordinary operations.

EMERGENCY LEAVE

In Ontario, an employee is entitled to up to ten days of unpaid leave from work for personal illness, injury, or medical emergency, or death, illness, injury, medical emergency or urgent matter with respect to certain family members. Family members include a spouse or same-sex partner, parent, child, grandparent, grandchild, child's spouse or same-sex partner, sibling, or dependent relative.

See also: BEREAVEMENT LEAVE, LEAVES OF ABSENCE, SARS-RELATED EMERGENCY LEAVE, SICK LEAVE

EMPLOYEE

A person engaged in work for an employer who is entitled to wages for labour or services performed. An employee is distinct from an independent contractor who is considered "self-employed".

The term employee is defined in employment standards legislation across the country, which set out minimum requirements and working conditions for all workers who are classified as employees.

> *See also:* ASSIGNMENT EMPLOYEE, DEPENDENT CONTRACTOR, EMPLOYER, FULL-TIME EMPLOYEE, INDEPENDENT CONTRACTOR, PART-TIME EMPLOYEE, PROFESSIONAL EMPLOYEE

EMPLOYER

A person or corporation that employs one or more workers, and pays their wages.

> *See also:* EMPLOYEE

EMPLOYMENT INSURANCE

A system of insurance, financed jointly by employers and employees, to provide income to people who are unemployed in order to assist them while they look for another job. Regular benefits are available for employees who lost their job through no fault of their own, due to such things as a shortage of work, or seasonal or mass lay-offs, and who satisfy certain minimum hours of work requirements. Maternity, parental or sickness benefits are available to employees who are off work as a result of pregnancy, caring for a newborn or adopted child, or unable to work because of illness. There are also special benefits available to persons who are engaged in fishing. The system of granting employment insurance is based on the federal *Employment Insurance Act*, S.C. 1996, c. 23, and is run by Human Resources Development Canada — Développement des ressources humaines Canada.

> *See also:* MATERNITY LEAVE, PARENTAL LEAVE, RECORD OF EMPLOYMENT (ROE)

EMPLOYMENT RECORDS

> *See:* PERSONNEL RECORDS

E

EMPLOYMENT STANDARDS

Essentially, employment law is a form of contract law. In general, two people may make whatever agreement they wish, and include any terms they would like. However, if a person is hired as an employee of a company, then specific employment standards legislation will also govern that relationship. Employment standards legislation is designed to do two things. First, it provides protection to the individual worker, and second, it creates certainty in the labour market by requiring basic employment practices. The legislation requires that all employers establish employment conditions that meet at least the minimum standards set out in the legislation.

All jurisdictions in Canada, whether federal, provincial or territorial, have employment standards legislation in place providing for minimum wages, minimum age of employment, maximum hours of work, overtime pay rates, entitlement to annual paid vacation, statutory holidays, leaves of absence and protection on termination of employment. It should be noted that the federal government has jurisdiction over matters of a general or national interest, which includes banks, railroads, nuclear power facilities and telecommunications operations, along with other national businesses. Other employment relationships are governed by specific provincial or territorial legislation. The main employment standards legislation in Canada include:

❑ Federal: *Canada Labour Code*, R.S.C. 1985, c. L-2

❑ Alberta: *Employment Standards Code*, R.S.A. 2000, c. E-9

❑ British Columbia: *Employment Standards Act*, R.S.B.C. 1996, c. 113

❑ Manitoba: *Employment Standards Code*, S.M. 1998, c. 29

❑ New Brunswick: *Employment Standards Act*, S.N.B. 1982, c. E-7.2

❑ Newfoundland and Labrador: *Labour Standards Act*, R.S.N. 1990, c. L-2

❑ Nova Scotia: *Labour Standards Code*, R.S.N.S. 1989, c. 246

❑ Ontario: *Employment Standards Act, 2000*, S.O. 2000, c. 41

❑ Prince Edward Island: *Employment Standards Act*, S.P.E.I. 1992, c. 18

❑ Quebec: *Labour Standards Act*, S.Q. 1979, c. 45

❑ Saskatchewan: *The Labour Standards Act*, R.S.S. 1978, c. L-1

❑ Northwest Territories and Nunavut: *Labour Standards Act*, R.S.N.W.T. 1988, c. L-1

❏ Yukon: *Employment Standards Act*, R.S.Y. 1986, c. 54

  See also: CONTRACT OF SERVICE, EMPLOYEE, EMPLOYER

F

FAMILY CARE LEAVE

In Quebec, an employee can be absent from work for ten days without pay during each year of employment for matters relating to the care, health or education of the employee's child. The circumstances must be unforeseen, or beyond the employee's control, and the employee must take all reasonable steps to limit the amount of leave that she requires.

An employee with three months of uninterrupted service may be absent without pay for up to twelve weeks in a year, in order to care for a child, spouse, spouse's child, father, mother, brother, sister or grandparent who is seriously ill. With a medical certificate, the leave may be extended for up to 104 weeks in the case of a serious and potentially mortally ill child of the employee.

  See also: EMERGENCY LEAVE, FAMILY RESPONSIBILITY
  LEAVE, LEAVES OF ABSENCE

FAMILY RESPONSIBILITY LEAVE

In British Columbia, an employee is entitled to up to five days of unpaid leave during each year of employment in order to meet the responsibilities related to the care, health or education of a child in the employee's care, or the care or health of any other member of the employee's immediate family. An immediate family member includes a spouse, child, parent, guardian, sibling, grandchild or grandparent of the employee, along with any person living with the employee as a member of the employee's family.

In New Brunswick, an employee may take up to three day's unpaid leave to meet the responsibilities related to the health, care or education of a person in a close family relationship with the employee. In Newfoundland and Labrador, an employee who has completed 30 days of continuous service with the same employer may take seven days of unpaid sick leave or family responsibility leave in one year.

Employment

F

FAMILY CARE LEAVE in Quebec provides a similar leave provision for employees.

> *See also:* EMERGENCY LEAVE, FAMILY CARE LEAVE, LEAVES OF ABSENCE

FIDUCIARY DUTIES

All employees have a duty of loyalty and good faith toward an employer, which will also include a duty of confidentiality with respect to information related to the employer. Certain employees, because of the nature of their position and their ability to harm the employers, also owe "fiduciary duties" to the employer. Fiduciary duties include the duty to avoid conflict between their duty to their employer, and possible self-interest for personal gain. The extent of the fiduciary duties that an employee will have toward an employer will depend largely on the position that the employee holds in the company. They will often include the duty not to solicit employees or customers of the employer for a reasonable time after termination of employment.

> *See also:* DUTY OF CONFIDENTIALITY

FIXED-TERM CONTRACT

A contract of employment between an employee and an employer for a limited period of time. Since the employment relationship ends once the contract is over, the employee is considered to have been given notice of termination when the contract was signed.

> *See also:* CONTRACT OF SERVICE

FULL-TIME EMPLOYEE

An employee who is hired by an employer to work a certain number of hours in a work day or work week. Different employers set different thresholds for "full time" work, although 24 hours per week is a common threshold.

> *See also:* EMPLOYEE, PART-TIME EMPLOYEE

G

GARNISHMENT OF WAGES

Taking a person's wages for the purpose of paying off a debt. A court order is required before a garnishment of an employee's wages may occur. For example, the garnishment process may be used to enforce child support orders. If an employee is refusing to make his required child support payments, an employer may be required by court order to subtract a certain percentage of the employee's wages, which will then be given as child support.

GROUP TERMINATION

Termination of the employment of a large number of employees at the same time. Most jurisdictions have enacted special laws to govern these situations, although the specific criteria for group terminations differ in each region.

The federal jurisdiction, Alberta, Manitoba, Newfoundland and Labrador, and Ontario define group termination, or "mass termination" as 50 or more employees being terminated within a period of not more than four weeks. In British Columbia it is 50 or more employees at a single location within a two-month period. New Brunswick defines group termination as more than ten employees in a four-week period, where the affected employees represent at least 25 per cent of the work force. Group termination in Nova Scotia is ten or more employees in a period of four weeks or less, while in Quebec it is ten or more employees in a period of two consecutive moths. In the Northwest Territories, Nunavut and the Yukon, group terminations occur when 25 or more employees are fired within a four-week period.

In general, the issues surrounding group terminations are similar to those encountered by employees who are terminated individually, except that employers will also have the responsibility of notifying the Minister of Labour about the group terminations, and longer minimum notice periods for affected employees may be required to be paid. Employers may also be required to take responsibility for organizing a joint planning committee to consider ways that the terminations may be avoided, or help employees find other employment. Group terminations are sometimes called collective dismissals or mass terminations.

See also: INDIVIDUAL TERMINATION, TERMINATION

G

H

HIGH TECHNOLOGY COMPANY

In British Columbia, a high technology company is defined as one with more than half of its employees classified as high technology professionals, including their managers and company executives.

See also: HIGH TECHNOLOGY PROFESSIONAL

HIGH TECHNOLOGY PROFESSIONAL

In British Columbia, a high technology professional is defined as an employee working in the computer science industry. Specifically, these professionals include people employed in the investigation, analysis, design, development, implementation, operation or management of computer information systems, using specialized computer knowledge, and professional judgment. As a result of the special demands of employees working in the computer science industry, high technology professionals in British Columbia are exempted from certain employment standards requirements, such as the hours of work, overtime and statutory holiday provisions.

See also: HIGH TECHNOLOGY COMPANY

HOURS OF WORK

The time during which an employee is required to work for the employer. Laws dictate how employees should be scheduled for work, and how they should be paid for the hours that they actually work. All jurisdictions set maximum hours of work for employees, provide for extra payment to employees who work more than a certain threshold number of hours, and require that employees be given regular rest and meal breaks. Where specified, the standard overtime threshold is generally eight hours of work in one day, and can range from 40 to 48 hours of work in a week. Any time worked beyond the overtime threshold must be paid at overtime rates.

In Ontario, if an employee agrees, he may work up to 60 hours per week; in New Brunswick there is no limit set on the number of hours of work in a day, week or month, but overtime is required to be paid after 44 hours worked in a week.

HOURS OF WORK CHART

Jurisdiction	Maximum Hours Permitted
Federal	8 per day; 48 per week
Alberta	8 per day; 44 per week
British Columbia	8 per day; 40 per week
Manitoba	8 per day; 40 per week
New Brunswick	No limit on the number of hours in any day, week, or month; overtime paid after 44 hours
Newfoundland and Labrador	40 per week
Nova Scotia	48 per week
Ontario	8 per day; 48 per week; up to 60 per week with employee agreement (overtime payable after 44 hours in a week)
Prince Edward Island	48 per week
Quebec	40 per week as of Oct. 1, 2000
Saskatchewan	8 per day; 40 per week
N.W.T./Nunavut	8 per day; 40 per week
Yukon	8 per day; 40 per week

See also: AVERAGING AGREEMENTS, COMPRESSED WORK WEEK, OVERTIME, WORK DAY, WORK WEEK

Employment

H

I

IMMEDIATE FAMILY

The definition of what constitutes the immediate family of an employee varies from jurisdiction to jurisdiction. Immediate family will often include such relationships as an employee's spouse, common-law partner, or same-sex partner; parents; children; grandchildren; siblings; grandparents; in-laws; or relatives who are living with the employee. Certain rights, such as EMERGENCY LEAVE, are based on which relationships are considered to be immediate family.

In order to determine whether a particular relation of an employee qualifies as immediate family, be sure to check the relevant employment standards legislation.

> *See also:* BEREAVEMENT LEAVE, EMERGENCY LEAVE, LEAVES OF ABSENCE

INDEPENDENT CONTRACTOR

A person who contracts with an employer to do a particular job, but who is not controlled by the employer or subject to the employer's right to control with respect to completing the terms of the contract. An independent contractor is not an employee, and therefore has fewer, and more limited, legal rights than an employee.

A number of tests have been developed in order to determine whether a person is an employee or an independent contractor. The "control test" looks at the level of control that the employer has over the person in question. The factors involved in the control test include: (1) control; (2) ownership of the tools; (3) chance of profit; (4) risk of loss. Another test that has been used to determine a person's employment status is the "organization test". This test looks at whether the person in question is employed as part of the business and her work is done as an integral part of the business, or whether the person works under a contract for services where her work is done for the business, but is not an integrated part of it. Finally, courts have used the "enterprise test", which states that a particular situation involves an employer and an employee if the employer (1) controls the activities of the worker; (2) is in a position to reduce the risk of loss; (3) benefits from the activities of the worker; and (4) the true cost of a product or service is borne by the enterprise offering it.

> *See also:* DEPENDENT CONTRACTOR, EMPLOYEE, EMPLOYER

INDIVIDUAL TERMINATION

A non-union employee's employment may be ended by an employer at any point, either for just cause, or without cause, by giving reasonable notice of termination, or notice in accordance with a written contract.

Every jurisdiction in Canada sets out minimum statutory notice requirements, based on the employee's length of service. These minimum notice requirements are set out in the chart below. There may also be an employment contract in place, with terms governing how an employee may be terminated, and how much notice of termination will be required. If there is no written contract, a court will look at common law reasonable notice requirements in order to determine an appropriate notice period.

Some employees are not entitled to notice of termination under employment standards legislation. Workers who have been hired for a fixed term, who have been offered and refused alternative work, whose contract has become impossible to fulfill, seasonal employees, or those who work in the construction industry, may not be entitled to notice of termination according to legislation. Employees who have not worked for a minimum period of time for the employer may also not be entitled to notice of termination.

INDIVIDUAL TERMINATION NOTICE REQUIREMENTS CHART

Jurisdiction	Length of Service	Required Notice	Notice by Employee
Federal	3 mos	2 weeks	none
Alberta	more than 3 mos, less than 2 yrs	1 week	1 week
	2 yrs or more, less than 4 yrs	2 weeks	2 weeks if employed 2 yrs or more
	4 yrs or more, less than 6 yrs	4 weeks	
	6 yrs or more, less than 8 yrs	5 weeks	
	8 yrs or more, less than 10 yrs	6 weeks	
	10 yrs or more	8 weeks	
British Columbia	3 to 12 mos	1 week	none
	12 mos to 3 yrs	2 weeks	
	3 yrs	3 weeks	
	4 yrs or more	1 additional week for each subsequent yr up to a max. of 8 weeks	
Manitoba	30 days	where wages are paid once a month or more often, notice equals one pay period; where wages are paid less frequently than once a month, at least 30 days	same as notice by employer
New Brunswick	6 mos to 5 yrs	2 weeks	none
	5 yrs or more	4 weeks	

Jurisdiction	Length of Service	Required Notice	Notice by Employee
Newfoundland and Labrador	3 mos or more, less than 2 yrs	1 week	same as notice by employer
	2 yrs or more, less than 5 yrs	2 weeks	
	5 yrs or more, less than 10 yrs	3 weeks	
	10 yrs or more, less than 15 yrs	4 weeks	
	15 yrs or more	6 weeks	
Nova Scotia	3 mos or more, less than 2 yrs	1 week	1 week's notice if 3 mos or more & less than 2 yrs service; 2 weeks' notice if 2 yrs or more service
	2 yrs or more, less than 5 yrs	2 weeks	
	5 years or more, less than 10 yrs	4 weeks	
	10 years or more	8 weeks	8 weeks
Ontario	3 mos or more, less than 1 yr	1 week	none
	1 yr or more, less than 3 yrs	2 weeks	
	3 yrs or more, less than 4 yrs	3 weeks	
	4 yrs or more, less than 5 yrs	4 weeks	
	5 yrs or more, less than 6 yrs	5 weeks	
	6 yrs or more, less than 7 yrs	6 weeks	
	7 yrs or more, less than 8 yrs	7 weeks	
	8 yrs or more	8 weeks	
Prince Edward Island	6 mos or more, less than 5 yrs	2 weeks	same as notice by employer
	5 yrs or more	4 weeks	

Employment

I

Jurisdiction	Length of Service	Required Notice	Notice by Employee
			Civil Code:
Quebec	3 mos or more, less than 1 yr	1 week	domestics, ser- vants, labourers & journeymen: 1 week's notice if hired by week; 2 weeks' if hired by month; 1 month if hired by year (same for employ- er or master)
	1 yr or more, less than 5 yrs	2 weeks	
	5 yrs or more, less than 10 yrs	4 weeks	
	10 yrs or more	8 weeks	
Saskatchewan	3 mos or more, less than 1 yr	1 week	none
	1 yr or more, less than 3 yrs	2 weeks	
	3 yrs or more, less than 5 yrs	4 weeks	
	5 yrs or more, less than 10 yrs	6 weeks	
	10 yrs or more	8 weeks	
N.W.T./ Nunavut	90 days or more, less than 3 yrs	2 weeks	none
	3 yrs or more, less than 4 yrs	3 weeks	
	4 yrs or more, less than 5 yrs	4 weeks	
	5 yrs or more, less than 6 yrs	5 weeks	
	6 yrs or more, less than 7 yrs	6 weeks	
	7 yrs or more, less than 8 yrs	7 weeks	
	8 yrs or more	8 weeks	

Jurisdiction	Length of Service	Required Notice	Notice by Employee
Yukon Territory	6 months or more, less than 1 yr	1 week	1 week if employed less than 2 yrs
	1 yr or more, less than 3 yrs	2 weeks	2 weeks if employed
	3 years or more, less than 4 yrs	3 weeks	2 yrs or more, less than 4 yrs
	4 yrs or more, less than 5 yrs	4 weeks	3 weeks if employed
	5 yrs or more, less than 6 yrs	5 weeks	4 yrs or more, less than 6 yrs
	6 yrs or more, less than 7 yrs	6 weeks	4 weeks if employed
	7 yrs or more, less than 8 yrs	7 weeks	6 yrs or more
	8 yrs or more	8 weeks	

See also: GROUP TERMINATION, PROFESSIONAL EMPLOYEE, TEMPORARY LAYOFFS, TERMINATION

INEXPERIENCED EMPLOYEE

In Nova Scotia, an employee who has not worked in his current job for more than three months. Inexperienced employees have a lower minimum wage rate than other employees.

See also: MINIMUM WAGE

J

JOINT AND SEVERAL LIABILITY

A liability is said to be joint and several when the injured party can obtain compensation from each party separately, or all parties together, at the option of the person who is suing.

Specifically in the case of unpaid wages owing to an employee, directors of a corporation may be found jointly and severally liable for wages that remain

J

unpaid. There may be a maximum limit placed on how much wages directors can be found personally liable for.

> *See also:* ASSIGNMENT OF WAGES, DIRECTORS, RECOVERY OF UNPAID WAGES

JURY DUTY

> *See:* COURT LEAVE

JUST CAUSE

Legal justification for terminating an employee's employment without notice, or pay in lieu of notice. Just cause for dismissal includes any act by the employee that fundamentally breaches her employment contract. If just cause does not exist, then the employer is required to give the required notice of termination, or compensate the employee instead of giving notice.

A court may look at a number of factors when considering whether there was just cause for dismissing an employee, such as:

- if the employee was warned about the alleged behaviour in the past;

- if the employee knew that her job was in jeopardy if the alleged behaviour continued;

- if the employee's behaviour was condoned or ignored by the employer over a period of time;

- if the employer allowed other employees to act in a similar manner; and

- the length of time that the employee had been working for the employer, since it is often more difficult to terminate a long-term employee for cause.

Some acts that may constitute just cause include: incompetence, insubordination, absenteeism or lateness, illness, intoxication or addiction, dishonesty, sexual harassment, criminal activity, conflict of interest, or breach of an employee's fiduciary duties toward an employer. Whether a particular action will result in a finding of just cause depends on the circumstances of each individual situation.

It should be noted that in a wrongful dismissal action, the employer has the burden to demonstrate that there was in fact just cause for dismissing the employee.

> *See also:* GROUP TERMINATION, INDIVIDUAL TERMINATION, REASONABLE NOTICE, TERMINATION, WRONGFUL DISMISSAL

L

LABOUR STANDARDS SUSPENSE ACCOUNT

Under the *Canada Labour Code*, the Receiver General is required to manage a Labour Standards Suspense Account, containing all money paid to the Minister of Labour by employers as liability for unpaid wages. Money is then paid out of this account to employees who are owed wages from the employer.

> *See also:* ATTACHMENT OF DEBT, RECOVERY OF UNPAID WAGES

LAYOFFS

> *See:* TEMPORARY LAYOFFS

LEAVES OF ABSENCE

Employers are required by employment standards legislation to allow employees time off from work for specific reasons. The time off may be with or without pay. Leaves of absences offered to employees in various jurisdictions include:

- maternity or pregnancy leave
- parental or child care leave
- paternity leave
- adoption leave
- bereavement leave
- family responsibility leave

L

- special occasion leave

- medical examination leave

- sick leave

- emergency leave

- leave to vote in an election

- jury duty or court leave

- education leave

LENGTH OF SERVICE

Amount of time that an employee has worked for a particular employer. It is often an important factor in determining how much notice is required when an employee is terminated without cause.

LIVING WAGE

An estimate of the minimum amount of money an employee should be paid for basic living expenses. This idea was the motivation behind the creation of minimum wage in the province of Ontario. Back in 1920, the province of Ontario passed the *Minimum Wage Act*, in order to provide a living wage for females in the province.

See also: MINIMUM WAGE

M

MANAGER

A person who is chosen or appointed to manage, direct, or administer the affairs and day-to-day requirements of an organization or company, or a group within an organization or company. People in managerial positions are often exempted from some requirements under employment standards legislation.

See also: DIRECTOR, PROFESSIONAL EMPLOYEE

MATERNITY LEAVE

Every jurisdiction legislates a protected leave of absence for a pregnant worker to have a baby. However, many jurisdictions do require an employee to have worked for her present employer for a specific period of time in order to be eligible for maternity leave. Alberta, Nova Scotia, the Yukon, Nunavut and the Northwest Territories require a one year qualifying period. Newfoundland and Labrador and Prince Edward Island require 20 weeks of work prior to the birth. Saskatchewan has a 20-week qualifying period in the 52 weeks prior to the leave. Ontario requires 13 weeks of work before the due date, while British Columbia, New Brunswick, and Quebec have no qualifying period before being eligible for maternity leave.

The length of maternity leave in most areas is 17 weeks, except in Alberta where it is 15 weeks, and Quebec and Saskatchewan, where it is 18 weeks. Most women who take maternity leave will also be entiteld to parental leave, with the combined leaves adding up to one year. Some jurisdictions also allow these periods to be extended for medical reasons. An employee is required to notify her employer in writing of when her last day of work will be, and the notice requirements range from two to six weeks, in general. The employer has the right to request a medical certificate certifying the fact of the pregnancy and giving an estimated date of birth.

Employees on maternity leave have the right to return to their position, or an equivalent position, upon the end of their leave, and their employment is deemed to be continuous during the leave. While employers are required to give protected time off to pregnant employees, they are not required to pay the employee's salary during her leave. Employees may receive partial compensation through Canada's federal Employment Insurance Plan by collecting employment insurance while they are off of work.

See also: LEAVES OF ABSENCE, MATERNITY-RELATED REASSIGNMENT, MEDICAL EXAMINATION LEAVE, PARENTAL LEAVE

MATERNITY-RELATED REASSIGNMENT

In the federal jurisdiction, a pregnant or nursing employee may be reassigned or have her job duties modified if her work is posing a risk to the health of the mother, foetus, or child. It applies from the start of the pregnancy up to 24 weeks after the birth of the child. If it is not practical to modify the job functions or to reassign the worker, the employee can take a

Employment

M

leave of absence without pay for the duration of the risk. A medical certificate will likely be required in these circumstances.

In Quebec, a pregnant employee may be granted special maternity leave without pay if she has a medical certificate indicating that the health of the mother or unborn child is at risk by remaining at work. This leave will be considered regular maternity leave from the fourth week preceding the expected delivery date.

Even in jurisdictions without express maternity-related reassignments, human rights legislation will impose a duty to accommodate.

See also: MATERNITY LEAVE

MAXIMUM HOURS

Some jurisdictions have placed absolute limits on the number of hours of work that an employee can be required to work in a day or a week, even when overtime pay is provided. These upper limits are put in place in order to protect employee health and welfare.

The federal legislation stipulates that an employee may not work more than a maximum of 48 hours in a work week. In Alberta, an employee may not work more than twelve consecutive hours in a workday. An employee in Ontario, if a standard work day of more than eight hours has been set, can work longer than eight hours in a day, as long as she has a period of eleven consecutive hours free from work each day, and an employee can agree to work longer than 48 hours in a week, up to a maximum of 60 hours.

See also: HOURS OF WORK, OVERTIME

MEAL BREAK

Employees are entitled to a break from work during the day to eat and rest. These breaks usually do not have to be paid. A meal break is also known as a meal period.

Alberta, British Columbia, Manitoba, Ontario, Prince Edward Island, Quebec, Northwest Territories and Nunavut all allow for a one-half hour break if the employee has worked for five hours. Saskatchewan requires that the employee work more than six hours total in the day to get the one-half hour break after five hours worked, while in the Yukon an employee will get a one-half hour break after five hours if he works less than ten hours in total, but only after six hours if he works more than ten hours in total. In Newfoundland, an employee is entitled to one hour off for every five hours worked.

See also: WORK DAY

MEDICAL EXAMINATION LEAVE

In Quebec, a pregnant woman who requires a medical or midwife examination as a result of her pregnancy can take time off from work, without pay, in order to attend the examination.

See also: LEAVES OF ABSENCE, MATERNITY LEAVE

MENTAL DISTRESS DAMAGES

In a wrongful dismissal action, an employee may claim that she suffered from mental distress, anxiety, vexation or frustration as a result of the manner in which she was fired by the employer. Anyone who is fired will feel some sort of mental distress at the loss of her job. A court will look at all of the circumstances of a particular situation in determining whether mental distress damages should be awarded. Damages for mental distress are rarely awarded, except where the employer's conduct was severe enough to be capable of creating an independent cause of action. An example would be where the employer intentionally and wrongfully accuses the employee of theft.

See also: AGGRAVATED DAMAGES, DAMAGES, PUNITIVE DAMAGES, *WALLACE* DAMAGES

METHOD OF PAYMENT

Every province excluding the federal jurisdiction, which is silent on the issue, requires wages to be paid to an employee by cash, cheque or direct deposit. In Quebec, direct deposit can only be used if the parties have signed a written agreement. Some parts of the country specify the types of financial institutions on which employers are allowed to draw cheques, or to which they may directly deposit wages.

See also: PAYMENT OF WAGES, WAGES

M

MINIMUM AGE

A legislated restriction on the hiring of employees to those who are over a specified age. Individuals who are younger than the specified age may be allowed to work in certain fields and under certain restrictions, with parental consent. Restrictions for such individuals may include a limit on the number of hours that may be worked during the day, or a limit on the times during which he will be able to work.

MINIMUM AGE CHART

Jurisdiction	Minimum Age
Federal	17
Alberta	15
British Columbia	15
Manitoba	16
New Brunswick	16
Newfoundland and Labrador	16
Nova Scotia	14
Ontario	16
Prince Edward Island	16
Quebec	14, if no consent
Saskatchewan	16
N.W.T./Nunavut	17
Yukon Territory	17

See also: ADOLESCENT, CHILD, YOUNG PERSON

MINIMUM WAGE

The lowest rate of pay that an employer can pay an employee for working. Every province and territory sets its own rate, and it ranges from $5.90 per hour in Alberta to $8.50 per hour in Nunavut. Most provinces do not have a special minimum wage rate established for employees under 18 years of age, although the minimum wage for employees under 18 is set at $6.40 in Ontario.

MINIMUM WAGE CHART

Employees 18 Years of Age and Over

	Rate	Effective Date
Federal*......................................	see below	July 1, 1996
Alberta...	$5.90	October 1, 1999
British Columbia**............................	8.00	November 1, 2001
Manitoba	6.75	April 1, 2003
New Brunswick................................	6.00	August 1, 2002
	6.20	January 1, 2004
Newfoundland and Labrador..................	6.00	November 1, 2002
Nova Scotia† ································	6.00	October 1, 2002
	6.25	October 1, 2003
	6.50	April 1, 2004
Ontario	6.85	September 4, 2001
Employee serving liquor on licensed premises.......................................	5.95	September 4, 2001
For hunting and fishing guides, domestics, homeworkers and harvester workers, see ¶5461.		
Prince Edward Island	6.25	January 1, 2003
	6.50	January 1, 2004
	6.80	January 1, 2005
Quebec	7.30	February 1, 2003
Saskatchewan..................................	6.65	November 1, 2002
N.W.T.***††	6.50	April 1, 1991
	8.25	December 28, 2003
Nunavut	8.50	March 3, 2003
Yukon Territory...............................	7.20	October 1, 1998

* Federal minimum wage aligned with rate in each province and territory. No special rates established with respect to age.

** The minimum wage is $6.00 for an employee in B.C. who has no paid employment experience before November 15, 2001 and has 500 or fewer hours of paid employment with one or more employers.

*** Applies to employees 16 years of age and over. This age distinction will be eliminated on December 28, 2003.

M

† Nova Scotia also sets out minimum wages for "inexperienced employees" (see ¶5456 for the definition). The current minimum wage for inexperienced employees is $5.55. It will increase to $5.80 on October
1, 2003, and will increase again to $6.05 on April 1, 2004.

†† For those who live along the N.W.T. highway system. Minimum wage is $7.00 for employees else-
where in the N.W.T. This geographic distinction will be removed on December 28, 2003.

See also: LIVING WAGE, INEXPERIENCED EMPLOYEE

MITIGATION

Acts taken to minimize a loss or damages. An employee who is wrongfully
dismissed ususally has a legal duty to minimize the losses that she may suffer
as a result of the termination, by attempting to find a comparable job in the
shortest possible period of time. In most cases, this duty does not require an
employee to take a position that is at a substantially lower salary or level of
responsibility just in order to mitigate her damages. In a wrongful dismissal
claim an employee will not be able to recover losses that could have been
avoided if the employee had taken reasonable steps to find another job. But,
this also means that an employee may be able to recover the costs of finding
another job, even if these costs are greater than if the employee had not
attempted to mitigate her damages. If the employee is able to find another
job, the salary from the new job will be taken off any wrongful dismissal
damage award, often called "mitigation income".

See also: REASONABLE NOTICE, WRONGFUL DISMISSAL

N

NON-COMPETITION CLAUSES

Employers may include a clause in an employment contract that limits the
right of an employee to compete against the employer within a certain area,
for a certain period of time. In general, the law is reluctant to permit
restrictions on the right of an employee to compete with a former employer,
even if the restrictions are agreed to in writing. Employees should have the
right to practice their trade or earn a living, so generally employees will be
allowed to compete with their former employers, and bring to a new business the knowledge and skills that they acquired in their former job. But in
certain situations, an employment contract may contain a term that limits
the right of the employee to work for a competitor of the employer within
certain limited situations. In order to be enforceable, these non-competition
agreements must balance the right of individual employees to use their skills
and knowledge in a new job, with the interest of employers in preventing

activities on the part of former employees which could unfairly expose trade secrets, or damage their competitive edge.

Non-competition clauses can take various forms. Some prevent competition in the industry, while others prevent the employee from doing business with customers of the employer. To determine whether a particular non-competition clause is reasonable, there are three main questions to ask. First, does the employer have an interest in the employee's particular knowledge or skills? Second, is the length, geographical area, and scope of the non-competition agreement too broad? Finally, is it a general barrier to competition, or is it limited to not taking clients from the former employer?

See also: CONTRACT OF SERVICE

NON-SOLICITATION CLAUSES

See: NON-COMPETITION CLAUSES

O

OVERTIME

The hours worked by an employee beyond the overtime threshold hours of work, which are generally eight hours in a day, and between 40 to 48 hours in a week. In almost all jurisdictions, the rate of pay for overtime work is one and one-half times the employee's normal rate of pay. Exceptions are set out in the chart, below. Many unionized employees are not required to work overtime unless they or their union have agreed to it, except in the case of an emergency or accident.

Some provinces set both daily and weekly overtime thresholds. For example, in British Columbia an employee will be paid overtime for working more than eight hours in one day, or for working more than 40 hours in one week. That means that if an employee works eight hours on Monday, Thursday, Friday and Saturday, ten hours on Tuesday, and four hours on Wednesday, the employee will be owed two hours of daily overtime for Tuesday, and four hours of weekly overtime for exceeding 40 hours (excluding the daily overtime on Tuesday).

OVERTIME PAY CHART

Jurisdiction	Overtime Rate
Federal	more than 8 hrs. in a day or 40 hrs. in a week: $1^1/_2$ times regular wage
Alberta	more than 8 hrs. in a day or 44 hrs. in a week: $1^1/_2$ times regular wage
British Columbia	more than 8 hrs. in a day or 40 hrs. in a week: $1^1/_2$ times regular wage; more than 12 hrs. in a day: double regular wage
Manitoba	more than 8 hrs. in a day or 40 hrs. in a week: $1^1/_2$ times regular wage
New Brunswick	more than 44 hrs. in a week: $9.00 per hour
Newfoundland and Labrador	$9.00 for each hour in excess of 40 in a week; expected to be effective April 1, 2003, but now deferred, more than 40 hours in a week: $1^1/_2$ times regular wage
Nova Scotia	more than 48 hrs. in a week: $1^1/_2$ times minimum rate
Ontario	more than 44 hrs. in a week: $1^1/_2$ times regular wage
Prince Edward Island	more than 48 hrs. in a week: $1^1/_2$ times minimum rate
Quebec	more than 40 hrs. in a week: premium of 50 per cent of prevailing hourly wage
Saskatchewan	more than 8 hrs. in a day or 40 hrs. in a week: $1^1/_2$ times regular wage
N.W.T./Nunavut	more than 8 hrs. in a day or 40 hrs. in a week: $1^1/_2$ times regular wage
Yukon Territory	more than 8 hrs. in a day or 40 hrs. in a week: $1^1/_2$ times regular wage

See also: HOURS OF WORK, MAXIMUM HOURS, PREMIUM PAY, TIME OFF IN LIEU OF OVERTIME, WORK DAY, WORK WEEK

P

PARENTAL LEAVE

All jurisdictions grant both the mother and the father unpaid leaves of absence to care for, and to adjust to new family responsibilities upon the addition of a new child to their family through childbirth or adoption. The amount of leave to which parents are entitled varies between jurisdictions from 34 weeks to 52 weeks. Both parents may wish to take parental leave, although in some jurisdictions there is a limit on the combined length of the leave which the two parents may take. An employee wishing to take parental leave must provide written notice, usually two to four weeks before the leave is taken. In the notice, the employee must specify their intent to take parental leave, as well as the dates on which the employee proposes the leave will start and end. A medical certificate might also be required, confirming the pregnancy and anticipated birth date. If the employee is adopting a child, proof of the adoption must be provided to the employer.

A mother who takes maternity leave may also take parental leave, but she must take the two leaves consecutively. As a result, she cannot take her maternity leave, return to work, and then take parental leave later on. Many jurisdictions put a limit on the length of the combined maternity and parental leave, usually between 50 to 52 weeks maximum combined leave.

See also: CHILD CARE LEAVE, LEAVES OF ABSENCE, MATERNITY LEAVE

PART-TIME EMPLOYEE

Someone who is employed to work less than a certain number of hours in a work day or work week. Different employers set different thresholds. Many define "part time" as less than 24 hours per week.

See also: EMPLOYEE, FULL-TIME EMPLOYEE

PATERNITY LEAVE

In Quebec, an employee is entitled to be absent from work for five unpaid days after the birth of his child, or upon the termination of pregnancy in or after the 20th week of pregnancy. Once the employee has worked 60 days for the employer, he is entitled to the first two days of leave with pay.

See also: MATERNITY LEAVE, PARENTAL LEAVE

PAYMENT IN LIEU OF NOTICE

An amount paid to a terminated employee instead of providing advance, or working notice of termination of employment during the notice period.

See also: REASONABLE NOTICE, TERMINATION

P

PAYMENT OF WAGES

Employees must be paid all wages that are owing to them for services performed. There are detailed requirements for employers setting out how long the period between these payments can be, how the money is required to be paid, and what can be deducted from an employee's wages.

When an employee quits or is terminated, all applicable wages including vacation pay, overtime wages, bonuses and other pay, must be paid within a certain time, often the employee's last day. Ontario, for example, requires payment within 7 days of termination, or by the day that would have been the employee's next pay day.

PAYMENT OF WAGES CHART

Jurisdiction	Regular Payments	Payment Upon Termination
Federal	on regular payday within 30 days of entitlement arising	within 30 days of entitlement
Alberta	within 10 days of each pay period; pay periods not to exceed one month	within 3 consecutive days after last day of employment where employment terminated with notice or pay in lieu of notice; within 10 consecutive days after last day of employment where employment terminated without pay or notice
British Columbia	to be paid at least semi-monthly within 8 days after the expiration of each pay period	within 48 hours of termination; where employee terminates, within 6 days after the termination
Manitoba	to be paid at least semi-monthly, and within 10 working days after the expiration of each pay period	within 10 working days of termination

Jurisdiction	Regular Payments	Payment Upon Termination
New Brunswick	payment at least every 16 days which is to include all wages earned up to a day no more than 7 calendar days prior to the date of payment	no later than the next regular payday; never more than 21 days from date of termination
Newfoundland & Labrador	payment at least half-monthly and within seven days after the end of the pay period	within 1 week of the date of termination
Nova Scotia	to be paid at least semi-monthly within 5 days after the expiration of each pay period	payment on expiry of termination notice
Ontario	wages to be paid on regular payday established by employer	within 7 days of date of termination; or by the day that would have been the employee's next pay day
Prince Edward Island	intervals between paydays cannot be more than 16 days; pay must include all wages earned up to and including a day that is not more than 5 working days prior to the date of payment	payment to be made no later than the last day of the next pay period after termination
Quebec	regular intervals of not more than 16 days or 1 month if employee is an executive or party to a contract	not specified
Saskatchewan	wages to be paid at least semi-monthly or at the end of every 14-day period, to include all wages earned up to 6 days before payday	within 14 days of the termination

Employment

P

Jurisdiction	Regular Payments	Payment Upon Termination
N.W.T./Nunavut	pay periods not to exceed 1 month; all wages earned during a pay period are due within 10 days after the end of the period	within 10 days after termination
Yukon Territory	pay periods not to exceed 16 days; payment no later than 10 days after end of pay period	within 7 days of the date of termination

See also: DEDUCTIONS FROM WAGES, METHOD OF PAYMENT, PAY PERIOD, WAGES

PAY PERIOD

The permitted length of time between payment of wages to employees.

British Columbia, Manitoba, New Brunswick, Prince Edward Island, Quebec and the Yukon require the pay period to be not more than 16 days long. Newfoundland and Labrador, Nova Scotia, and Saskatchewan require a pay period at least semi-monthly. Alberta, Nunavut and the Northwest Territories stipulate not more than 1 month between payments. Federally, and in Ontario, the employer can determine the pay period, as long as it remains consistent.

See also: PAYMENT OF WAGES

PERSONAL INFORMATION

Information about an employee which is provided to an employer that should not be released without consent. Personal information may include such things as the employee's address, telephone number, race, religious or political beliefs, age, marital or family status, medical condition, or views and opinions given by the employee, or by other people with respect to the employee.

Determining what sorts of things will be seen as 'personal' may depend on where the employee works, and whether the employee works for the government in the public sector, or for a corporation in the private sector. The federal government, some provinces, and the territories have already enacted privacy legislation applicable to public sector employees. The federal government has enacted the *Personal Information Protection and*

Electronic Documents Act, and this Act already applies to personal information that is collected, used, or disclosed in the course of commercial activities by federal companies, such as banks, airlines, telecommunications companies, broadcasters and transportation companies. It also applies to the personal information of employees in those organizations. Beginning in January 2004, this act will begin to apply to all private "commercial" sector employers across the country, unless a particular province has already enacted substantially similar legislation by that time. Some provinces have enacted general privacy legislation that may be applied to private sector employees.

> *See also:* PERSONAL INVESTIGATION, PRE-EMPLOYMENT INVESTIGATION

PERSONAL INVESTIGATION

An employer may want to look into the background of a person, in order to obtain factual or investigative information about them before deciding whether to hire him or her for a job. Manitoba is the only province that has legislation dealing specifically with these pre-employment investigations (for further information, see PRE-EMPLOYMENT INVESTIGATIONS below). In general, if an employer wants to conduct a personal investigation, it should receive the person's consent before beginning the investigation, and it should also consult the relevant privacy legislation dealing with personal information to know what information can actually be collected, and what can be done with the information once it is received.

> *See also:* PERSONAL INFORMATION, PRE-EMPLOYMENT INVESTIGATION

PERSONNEL RECORDS

Records that an employer keeps for every employee. Generally, an employer will be required to keep on hand records indicating such things as how many regular and overtime hours each employee has worked, wage rates, dates on which the wages are paid, and information on annual vacations and statutory holidays.

Every province is different in terms of what information an employer will be required to keep, and for how long. Employers should develop a comprehensive system of record-keeping, based on what information is required to be kept, and how long the information must be kept. Closely following the legislative requirements is key for all employers, because it is

P

these records that will be looked at if an employment standards complaint is brought forward by an employee.

PORTAL-TO-PORTAL

The definition of a work day for forestry or silviculture workers in British Columbia. The work day for these employees begins at the time that the workers leave the camp, motel, or other pick-up point — the "portal" — to be taken to the worksite, until the time that the workers are returned to that same point at the end of the day.

See also: SILVICULTURE WORKERS, WORK DAY

PRE-EMPLOYMENT INVESTIGATION

An investigation to learn more information about a person, usually for the purpose of determining whether or not he should be hired for a particular position.

Generally, an investigation would be conducted in order to create a personal report, setting out the factual, medical, or investigative information that the employer is entitled to know about. Factual information may include name, address, professional qualifications, previous places the person has worked, estimated income, paying habits, possible outstanding credit obligations, cost of living obligations, public information, and any information voluntarily supplied by the person being investigated. Medical information may include any information that is obtained from members of the medical profession, with the consent of the person being investigated. Investigative information means any other information about the person being investigated that is not included within factual or medical information. The personal report may not include such private and irrelevant information as references to race, religion, ethnic origin, or political affiliation, or bankruptcies that occurred more than 14 years ago.

Manitoba is the only province that has legislation dealing specifically with the case of personal investigations related to employment, entitled *The Personal Investigations Act,* R.S.M. 1987, c. P34. In Manitoba, pre-employment investigations may not occur without the written consent of the person who is being investigated, or unless the employer provides written notice to the person that an investigation was conducted within 10 days of a decision being made with respect to the employee.

See also: PERSONAL INFORMATION, PERSONAL INVESTIGATION

PREGNANCY LEAVE

See: MATERNITY LEAVE

PREMIUM PAY

The wage given to employees for working overtime hours. Generally, it is one and one-half times the employee's normal rate of pay.

See also: OVERTIME

PRIORITY OF WAGES

If an employer corporation is involved in bankruptcy proceedings, unpaid wages that are owing to employees are given a certain priority over other entities that are also owed money by the bankrupt employer. The debt is usually deemed to be a secured charge against the property and assets of the employer, up to a maximum amount. In many provinces, the charge has priority over all other liens or claims. Sometimes, though, the amount of the claim for unpaid wages will be limited to a particular time frame of wage earnings. For example, in New Brunswick only the first three months of wages have priority over other claims. The rest of the debt is handled as if the employee was an ordinary creditor.

PRIORITY OF WAGES CHART

Jurisdiction	Priority	Amount Recoverable
Federal	fourth	wages for 3 months prior to bankruptcy to a maximum of $500; valid disbursements for travelling salespeople not exceeding $300
Alberta	priority over every claim except for a purchase money security interest*	up to a maximum of $7,500
British Columbia	first priority	not addressed
Manitoba	first priority except for mortgages or a purchase money security interest*	up to a maximum of $2,500

* Subject to certain conditions. Please see relevant legislation for complete details.

P

Jurisdiction	Priority	Amount Recoverable
New Brunswick	— first priority — rank as general creditor	— 3 months' wages — remainder of claim
Newfoundland & Labrador	first priority	up to a maximum of $7,500
Nova Scotia	first priority (except for wages owed to other workers)	not addressed
Ontario	— first priority — rank as general creditor	— 3 months' wages — remainder of claim
Prince Edward Island	first priority	up to a maximum of $5,000
Quebec	not addressed	not addressed
Saskatchewan	first priority except for mortgages or a purchase money security interest*	not addressed
N.W.T./Nunavut	first priority	not addressed
Yukon Territory	first priority	up to a maximum of $7,500

See also: ATTACHMENT OF DEBT, RECOVERY OF UNPAID WAGES

PROBATIONARY EMPLOYEE

An employee working within a probationary or trial period. An employee may be offered a position on the basis that the first few months of employment will be a trial period for the employer and the employee, during which the performance of the new employee will be monitored closely. If the employer determines that the new employee is not suitable for the position he was hired for during his probationary period, the employee may often be dismissed without notice being given, depending on the wording of the clause. Regardless of how long an employer deems the probation period to be, employment standards legislation permits dismissal without notice only during the first three months. If the employee is terminated after that time period, the employer is obligated to comply with the appropriate employment standards minimum notice requirements.

The terms of a probationary period must be clearly communicated to the new employee right from the start, including the length of the probationary period, the basis of the employer's assessment of the employee's performance, the standards that the employee will be expected to meet, whether there may be an extension of the probationary period, and any

Employment

assistance that may be available to the employee during the probationary period.

A probationary employee should be given a fair chance of success. An employer can assist an employee by giving information about potential performance issues to the employee regularly and documenting them well, in case the employee is let go. An employer should extend a probationary period only in exceptional circumstances.

PROFESSIONAL EMPLOYEE

An employee who works in a position requiring advanced education or skill. Professional employees include doctors, lawyers, architects, and dentists, among others. They are exempt from many of the requirements of the relevant employment standards legislation, such as hours of work, minimum wage and overtime requirements.

See also: DIRECTOR, EMPLOYEE, MANAGER

PROGRESSIVE DISCIPLINE

A step-by-step method for dealing with employee misconduct or incompetence in the workplace. A process of progressive discipline usually involves a series of progressively more serious warnings and punishments. Discipline may progress from verbal warnings to written warnings, followed by progressively longer suspensions, ultimately resulting in termination if the actions of the employee do not improve over a period of time. The goal of this form of discipline is correcting poor behaviour, and creating a better and more productive work environment, rather than simple discipline or dismissal. Depending on the nature of the misconduct, often an employer will not be able to show JUST CAUSE for dismissal unless the employer has provided progressive discipline.

Some factors that should be kept in mind when a company is developing a progressive discipline process include:

- be sure to set out clear, reasonable job expectations in the company policy;
- communicate job expectations to all employees clearly;
- provide reasonable supervision, training and instruction;
- bring unacceptable work to the attention of the affected employee immediately;

P

- give an employee the opportunity to tell his story if misconduct is alleged;

- give verbal and written warnings; and

- most importantly, keep complete written records.

   See also: DISCIPLINE

PROMOTION

A movement to a higher level position within a company. It may involve a substantial change in job responsibilities, and a corresponding increase in salary or benefits. Promotions are seen to be positive moves for employees, but there have been very rare situations where promotions were found to be constructive dismissals. An employee may be upset by a promotion that involves substantial changes to her hours of work, days of work, location of work, or the nature of the work that she is required to perform.

   See also: CONSTRUCTIVE DISMISSAL, DEMOTION

PUBLIC HOLIDAY

   See: STATUTORY HOLIDAY

PUNITIVE DAMAGES

Punitive damages are damage awards that may be made by a court. Unlike most damage awards, which are made to compensate an injured party for actual losses suffered, punitive damages are awarded in order to punish a party that has acted in a harsh, reprehensible, or malicious manner. An employee may claim punitive damages in an action for wrongful dismissal, claiming that the actions of the employer were particularly harsh or vindictive. Courts are generally reluctant to award such damages unless the employer has acted in an extremely egregious manner. These damage awards are also called exemplary, vindictive, penal, or retributory damages. To obtain punitive damages, an employee must show that the employer committed an "independent, actionable wrong".

   See also: AGGRAVATED DAMAGES, DAMAGES, MENTAL DISTRESS DAMAGES, *WALLACE* DAMAGES

Q

QUALIFYING PERIOD

The amount of time that an employee is required to have worked for a particular employer in order to be eligible to receive certain rights under employment standards legislation. For example, in many provinces an employee is required to have worked for her employer for a specific length of time before being eligible for maternity leave. A full description of maternity leave qualifying periods is included in the MATERNITY LEAVE definition. There are also qualifying periods in many provinces before an employee is entitled to be paid for statutory holidays. Many group insurance plans also have qualifying periods during which new employees cannot enroll.

R

RATE OF PAY

Amount of money an employee is paid by the hour, week, month, or year. The amount must be equal to or greater than the minimum wage rate set for each jurisdiction.

See also: MINIMUM WAGE

READY ACCESS

A term used in the silviculture or forestry industry, indicating a worksite that an employee can get to by car, van, or truck. If an employee must be taken to the worksite by specialized transportation, such as in an airplane, helicopter, barge, or boat, it will be deemed a worksite with no ready access.

See also: REMOTE WORKSITE, SILVICULTURE WORKERS

REASONABLE NOTICE

Notice owing at common law to non-union employees with no contractual notice entitlement. If an employee is terminated without just cause, he is entitled to notice of termination of employment unless a contract provides otherwise. The rationale for providing reasonable notice is to give the terminated employee time to look for a similar position, at a similar salary, in the same geographic region if possible.

R

The amount of reasonable notice that will be required to be paid depends on the individual circumstances of each case, and is influenced by a number of factors. Reasonable notice is almost always greater than, but inclusive of, the minimum statutory notice.

Some of the main factors a court will look at to determine reasonable notice at common law include:

- How long the employee has been working for the company — long-term employees tend to get more notice;

- The position held by the employee — higher level positions, such as management positions, will usually require more notice;

- The availability of similar employment — particularly when the possibility of finding similar employment is restricted by geographical location or the nature of the industry;

- The age of the employee — employees who are older or close to retirement age will get more notice because of the difficulty for them of finding another job;

- The employee's history with the company — employees with a good or excellent employment record will likely get longer notice periods than employees with poor work records;

- Inducement of the employee to leave a prior job — if an employee was recruited to leave a secure job, and is terminated from the new job after a short period, that will likely lengthen the required notice period; and,

- Possible acts of bad faith — bad faith actions by the employer at the time of termination may lengthen the notice period. Bad faith actions may include refusing to give reasons for termination, using false accusations, refusing a reference, or acting insensitively to an employee.

It should be noted that in some situations a "rule of thumb" formula has been used by courts as a starting point, although it is not necessarily applicable in all circumstances. The rule of thumb formula equates approximately one month's notice for each year of service. This estimate is then adjusted up or down, depending on the employee's particular situation.

> *See also:* BALLPARK JUSTICE, CONSTRUCTIVE DISMISSAL, GROUP TERMINATION, INDIVIDUAL TERMINATION, JUST CAUSE, MITIGATION, PAYMENT IN LIEU OF NOTICE, TERMINATION, WRONGFUL DISMISSAL

RECORD OF EMPLOYMENT (ROE)

A Human Resources Development Canada form used for the purposes of applying for Employment Insurance benefits. It is required to be completed by employers for each employee who stops working for them. It indicates how long the employee worked for the employer, how many weeks the employee paid Employment Insurance premiums, the amount of insured earnings, and the reason why the employee no longer works for the employer.

The Employment Insurance office uses the ROE to determine if an unemployed worker who applies for Employment Insurance qualifies for benefits, how much the benefits will be, and for how long they can be paid. Forms can be obtained by viewing the Human Resources Development Canada — Développement des ressources humaines Canada Web site at **http://www.hrdc-drhc.gc.ca/ae-ei/**.

Employers must take time to finish the ROE completely and accurately. A government official will call if the hours and insurable earnings are not reported correctly. These specifications must be precise because Employment Insurance entitlement is based on the number of hours worked, as well as the reason for termination. Voluntary quits are not eligible for EI, but terminations will be unless the employee was terminated for "misconduct". The ROE must be completed following a termination of employment and should accurately state the reason for the cessation of employment.

See also: EMPLOYMENT INSURANCE

RECOVERY OF UNPAID WAGES

If an employer fails to pay money that is owed to a past or current employee, the employee may bring a complaint before an employment standards officer. Generally, an Employment Standards officer determines any complaints for unpaid wages, and the officer's order or decision may be appealed. If no one appeals, or if the ruling is upheld on appeal, the officer may then issue an order to pay against the employer, and this order is enforceable as if it were a court order. Payment of the debt may be enforced by issuing a court order, which provides the power to garnish, seize and sell property and assets. Some provinces allow the employee to register the order with the Land Titles Office, creating a lien against the employer's interest in the employer's land.

In some circumstances, company directors may be held personally liable for unpaid wages accumulated while they were directors. The Director of

R

Employment Standards has the authority to garnish, seize and sell personal property and assets of the company directors. The maximum amount a director will be liable for varies by jurisdiction, and in some cases the law specifically states that the employee must seek payment from the company first.

Employers should be aware that the most common employment standards complaint is for unpaid wages. When a complaint is brought, the employer should ensure that it was filed within the correct time frame for the jurisdiction, and whether the employee has also started civil proceedings. In some provinces, it is illegal to pursue both a common law action and an employment standards complaint.

See also: ATTACHMENT OF DEBT, PRIORITY OF WAGES

REMOTE WORKSITE

A place where silviculture work is being performed that cannot be accessed by a normal road, or highway. An employee would have to be taken to such a worksite by specialized transportation, such as an airplane, a helicopter, a barge, or a boat. A remote worksite would also include a site where a forest road is temporarily activated to allow access to the site.

See also: READY ACCESS, SILVICULTURE WORKERS

REQUIRED REST DAYS

See: REST PERIOD

RESIDENTIAL CARE WORKER

In Ontario, a person who is hired to supervise and care for children or developmentally disabled people in a house where the worker lives full-time.

RESIGNATION

A voluntary termination of employment by the employee. An employee may voluntarily choose to leave her employment for a variety of reasons. Possible reasons may include receiving a better job offer, an incompatible work relationship with the employee's superiors at work, job stagnation, a spouse or partner moving to a different location, or a return to school. If an employee chooses to resign, she will not be entitled to reasonable notice or payment in lieu of notice. As a result, it is a complete defence to a wrongful dismissal action if an employer is able to demonstrate that an employee resigned voluntarily.

Employment

There may be situations where it is unclear whether an employee has resigned or has been dismissed by an employer. Some of the factors that may demonstrate a resignation include:

- the employee intended to resign, and acted on that intention;
- the employee's decision to resign was voluntary; and
- the employee expressed an intention to resign, and acted in accordance with that intention.

Employers should request that employees tender their resignation in writing far enough in advance to allow the company to fill the position, and have the new employee trained by the departing employee before she leaves. In some provinces, employment standards legislation sets out minimum notice requirements for employees to inform employers about their intention to resign, although the amount of notice required varies by jurisdiction. See the chart in the definition of INDIVIDUAL TERMINATION for employee notice requirements across the country.

See also: CONSTRUCTIVE DISMISSAL, DISMISSAL, WRONGFUL DISMISSAL

REST PERIOD

Employees are entitled to a set amount of time off from work during each work week.

In the Maritimes, along with the federal jurisdiction, the Northwest Territories and Nunavut, an employee is entitled to one full day of rest in each seven day period, on Sunday if possible. British Columbia workers are entitled to 32 hours of rest per week. Manitoba provides for 24 hours off from work in each week, while Quebec requires an employee to receive 32 hours off work in every seven days. Ontario workers are entitled to 24 hours off from work in every work week, or 48 hours in every two week period. Saskatchewan provides for one day off in every seven days if the employee works 20 hours or more in a week. The Yukon allows for two full days of rest per week, with one on a Sunday, if possible. Alberta employees get one day off per week, two days off over two weeks, three days off over three weeks, or four days off over four weeks.

See also: WORK WEEK

RESTRICTIVE COVENANTS

See: NON-COMPETITION AGREEMENTS

R

S

SALARY

A fixed, periodic compensation paid for services performed. It is usually given as a yearly amount of money which is divided by the number of pay periods in the year. It may also be paid by the month, or on some other fixed period of time. Employees who earn a salary may be paid a fixed amount per period, regardless of the hours worked or production accomplished. Depending on the particular arrangement, some salaried employees may still be entitled to overtime pay.

See also: BENEFITS, BONUS, WAGES

SARS-RELATED EMERGENCY LEAVE

In Ontario, a temporary emergency leave without pay applying to employees affected by severe acute respiratory system (SARS). These special emergency leave provisions were set up as a result of an outbreak of SARS in Toronto and surrounding area, in the Spring of 2003.

See also: EMERGENCY LEAVE

SEASONAL BUSINESS

A business that suspends operations for a certain period every year, because of changing market demands characteristic of the business. Some jurisdictions exclude seasonal businesses from certain employment standards requirements, such as the hours of work provisions, given the seasonal aspect of their work.

See also: SEASONAL EMPLOYEES

SEASONAL EMPLOYEES

Individuals who work only part of the year for a seasonal business.

See also: SEASONAL BUSINESS

SEVERANCE PAY

"Severance pay" has a technical meaning and a common or colloquial meaning. Technically, severance pay is an amount distinct from notice, required by a statute to be paid by an employer on termination of an employee's employment. In its common or colloquial usage, severance pay means any amount of money paid to an employee because of termination of employment.

Only two jurisdictions specifically require statutory severance pay. In the federal jurisdiction, any employee who has been employed for one year or more is entitled to severance pay in the amount of the greater of two days' pay for each year of work, or five days' pay. In Ontario, severance is defined as a dismissal, including a constructive dismissal if the employee resigns within a reasonable period of time, a lay-off of 35 weeks or more in any period of 52 weeks, or a lay-off resulting from the end of an employer's business at a particular location. In that province, severance pay is required to be paid to employees with five years of service or more when 50 or more employees are terminated in a six month period or less as a result of the end of all or part of an employer's business, or the employer has a payroll in Ontario of $2.5 million or more. The amount of severance pay under Ontario legislation is one regular week's pay, multiplied by the sum of (a) the number of completed years of employment and (b) the number of completed months of employment not included in (a), divided by twelve, up to a maximum of 26 regular weeks' pay.

See also: REASONABLE NOTICE, TEMPORARY LAYOFFS, TERMINATION

SICK LEAVE

Absence from work as a result of illness or injury. Even though many jurisdictions do not specifically provide for sick leave, most employers have some form of sick leave plan in place for their workplace that provides for paid or unpaid sick leave. In those jurisdictions that specifically provide for sick leave, the law will set out the maximum time off allowed due to illness, and state that the employee's job will be protected during that time.

The federal jurisdiction provides for up to twelve weeks of sick leave after working for the company for three months. New Brunswick allows for five unpaid days off in each year, after the employer has worked 90 days for the employer. In Newfoundland and Labrador, an employee who has worked at least 30 days for the employer will be entitled to up to seven unpaid days leave for sickness, or family responsibilities. Quebec employees may take up to 26 weeks of sick leave after working for three months for the employer without being dismissed, suspended or transferred as a result of their sickness. In the Yukon, an employee may take one day without pay for every month employed by the employer, minus the number of days the employee has previously been absent due to illness or injury, up to a total of twelve days.

See also: EMERGENCY LEAVE, LEAVES OF ABSENCE

S

SILVICULTURE WORKERS

People who are employed in the forestry or silviculture industry. They are employed in reforestation work, including such things as clearing bush, cone picking, creek clearing, seed harvesting, applying herbicide, reclamation work, sheep herding, site preparation, stand sanitation, train building, fertilizing, girdling, planting, pruning, spacing or distributing trees, weeding, or supervision of any of these activities. These employees are often paid on a piece rate basis, meaning that they are paid per unit of production, regardless of the time worked.

See also: PORTAL-TO-PORTAL, READY ACCESS, REMOTE WORKSITE

SOCIAL INSURANCE NUMBER (SIN)

A unique nine-digit number that is assigned to all employees by the federal government. Every person who works in insurable or pensionable employment in Canada is required to have a SIN. An employer is required to keep the SIN of all of its employees on file, and this information is used for income tax and employment insurance purposes.

See also: PERSONNEL RECORDS

SPECIAL OCCASION LEAVE

In Quebec, an employee may be absent from work for one day, with pay, on their wedding day, or civil union day. Similarly, an employee is entitled to be absent from work without pay for the wedding or civil union of the employee's child, father, mother, sister, brother, or spouse's child.

See also: LEAVES OF ABSENCE

STATEMENT OF WAGES

At the end of each pay period, employers are required to give their employees a statement setting out the hours the employee is being paid for, the rate of pay, the amount and purpose of any deductions from the employee's pay, and the employee's net pay. Further information may be required in some jurisdictions, as set out in the chart below.

In British Columbia and Manitoba, if wage statements are the same from pay period to pay period, a new statement need not be given until a change occurs.

STATEMENT OF WAGES CHART

Jurisdiction	Information Recorded on Statement of Wages
Federal	period for which payment is made, number of hours worked, rate of wages, details of all deductions, actual sum being received by the employee
Alberta	regular and overtime hours of work, wage rate and overtime rate, earnings paid showing separately each component of the earnings for each pay period, deductions from earnings and the reason therefore, time off instead of overtime pay provided and taken, and the period of employment covered by the statement
British Columbia	name, address, hours worked, wage rate and basis, overtime wage rate and hours worked at this rate, any money, allowance or other payment the employee is entitled to, amount and purpose of each deduction, how wages are calculated if other than hourly or salaried, gross and net wages, how much money the employee has taken from the employee's time bank and how much remains
Manitoba	regular hours of work and overtime for which wages are being paid; wage rates; deductions and the reason for deductions; net wages
New Brunswick	dates of pay period, gross pay, deductions, net pay
Newfoundland & Labrador	gross wages, pay period, wage rate and hours worked, deductions, net wages
Nova Scotia	pay period, hours of work, wage rate, details of deductions, actual sum received by employee
Ontario	pay period, wage rate, gross wages (and manner calculated, if not provided elsewhere), particulars of deductions, amounts for room or board, net wages
Prince Edward Island	name and address of employer, name of employee, pay period, rate of wages, hours worked, gross wages, amount and purpose of each deduction, bonus, gratuity or living allowance, net wages

Employment

S

Jurisdiction	Information Recorded on Statement of Wages
Quebec	name of employer, name of employee, identification of occupation, date of payment and work period covered by payment, hours paid at the regular rate, hours being paid at overtime rate or hours off in lieu of overtime, nature and amount of bonuses, indemnities, allowances or commissions, wage rate, amount of wages before deductions, nature and amount of deductions, net wages paid to employee, information on gratuities where applicable
Saskatchewan	name of employee, period for which payment of wages is made, hours for which payment is made, rate of wages, category or class of employment, amount of total wages, any deductions from wages, actual amount of payment made
N.W.T./Nunavut	period for which payment is made, hours for which payment is made, rate of wages, details of deductions, actual sum received
Yukon	period for which payment is made, hours for which payment is made, rate of wages, details of deductions, actual sum received by employee

See also: HOURS OF WORK, PAY PERIOD

STATUTORY HOLIDAY

A paid day off work, legislated by the federal, provincial or territorial government, as they may apply to the particular employee, to enable people to celebrate days of national or regional significance. These days are called statutory holidays, public holidays, general holidays, special holidays, or paid holidays, depending on the province. On a holiday, employees are entitled to either rest from work while still receiving pay, or if they work, to receive premium pay for that work. Certain days are recognized nation-wide as holidays, such as New Year's Day, Good Friday, Labour Day and Christmas Day. Others are unique to a particular region, such as Family Day in Alberta, the National Holiday in Quebec, or National Aboriginal Day in the Northwest Territories.

STATUTORY HOLIDAYS CHART

	Fed.	Alta.[5]	B.C.	Man.	N.B.	Nfld. & Lab.	N.S.	Ont.[1]	P.E.I.	Que.[3]	Sask.	NWT[6]	NUN	Yukon[4]
New Year's Day	X	X	X	X	X	X	X	X	X	X	X	X	X	X
Good Friday	X	X	X	X	X	X	X	X	X	X	X	X	X	X
Victoria Day	X	X	X	X				X		X	X	X	X	X
Memorial Day						X								
Canada Day	X	X	X	X	X		X	X	X	X	X	X	X	X
1st Monday in August		X		X							X	X	X	
Labour Day	X	X	X	X	X	X	X	X	X	X	X	X	X	X
Thanksgiving Day	X	X	X	X				X		X	X	X	X	X
Remembrance Day	X	X	X	X^2		X	X^2				X	X	X	X
Christmas Day	X	X	X	X	X	X	X	X	X	X	X	X	X	X
Boxing Day	X							X						

[1] Ontario customarily observes an additional holiday not provided for by statute — Civic Holiday on the 1st Monday in August.

[2] In Manitoba, it is not provided that employees be paid for Remembrance Day if they are not required to work. In Nova Scotia if an employee is required to work, he or she shall be given a holiday with pay on another agreed upon day.

[3] In Quebec an additional National Holiday is observed on June 24.

[4] The Yukon Territory also observes Discovery Day, the third Monday in August.

[5] Alberta also observes Family Day on the third Monday of February.

[6] N.W.T. also observes National Aboriginal Day on June 21.

It should be noted that statutory holidays are governed by Employment Standards Acts and Regulations only. There are other holidays under separate legislation, or which have arisen out of common practice, that do not qualify as statutory holidays. For example, the Civic Holiday in Ontario is a day employers give employees off by tradition, but is not mandated by provincial or federal legislation. Other days are not strictly statutory holidays since they have their own Act to govern them, although they are treated similarly to statutory holidays. For example, Remembrance Day in Manitoba is governed by the *Remembrance Day Act.*

See also: CIVIC HOLIDAY, PREMIUM PAY

STUB PERIOD

In Ontario, the term "stub period" is often used to mean the period of time between the employee's start date and the beginning of the employer's vacation year. The employee's entitlement to vacation during this period of time is calculated as the ratio between the stub period and twelve months,

S

and the amount of vacation for the employee is the yearly entitlement for the employee multiplied by that ratio.

For example, if an employee began work on September 1, and the employer's vacation entitlement year was set at January 1, the stub period would run from September 1 to January 1 of the next year, and the ratio would be 4/12 months.

> *See also:* VACATION ENTITLEMENT YEAR

SUBSTRATUM DOCTRINE

When an employee is hired by an employer, a contract of employment is entered into between the two parties. Over time with the company, the employee may develop new skills, attain new positions, take on more responsibilities or have his salary increased. As a result, the contractual terms of the initial contract of employment may no longer be appropriate. In these situations the "substratum", or substance, of the initial contract of employment disappears, or has been so altered that the terms may no longer be valid. It may even occur that virtually all of the important terms of the agreement change, even though the initial contract of employment is not officially altered. This change in circumstances is characterized as the changed substratum doctrine.

This doctrine may be useful in wrongful dismissal situations. An employee who has signed a termination clause may not be held to it where his level of responsibility and status within an organization have increased substantially since he signed the initial contract containing the termination clause.

> *See also:* CONTRACT OF SERVICE, REASONABLE NOTICE, TERMINATION

SUNDAY OBSERVANCE

> *See:* DAYS OF REST

T

TEMPORARY LAYOFFS

A layoff that has not yet become permanent and is therefore not considered to be a termination. Due to changing business conditions an employer may want to let some employees go on a temporary basis, with the possibility of having them come back to work at a later date. If this period exceeds 13 to 20 weeks, depending on the jurisdiction, it will be considered a termination.

Situations where a company may consider layoffs include:

- a major downturn in the market for the company's product, resulting in a loss of sales and decreased production;

- declining markets regionally, nationally or internationally;

- uncompetitive production practices; or

- new, advanced plant technologies that may lessen the need for employees.

Every jurisdiction, except Prince Edward Island, has provisions dealing with temporary layoffs, specifying what a temporary layoff is, and at what point a layoff will be considered a termination. At common law, a temporary layoff may constitute a termination of employment resulting in a right to sue for wrongful dismissal.

See also: INDIVIDUAL TERMINATION, GROUP TERMINATION, TERMINATION

TERMINATION

The end of an employee's employment, which may be voluntary or involuntary. A voluntary termination of employment occurs when an employee chooses to leave a company, a sick leave turns into a long-term disability, an employee retires, an employee takes another job opportunity, or an employee dies. An involuntary termination is an end of the employment relationship that is initiated by the employer. Involuntary termination may be due to an employee's poor performance, a serious incident resulting in just cause, organizational restructuring, or the sale of the company. An employer may end the employment relationship with an employee at any time, either for cause, or with reasonable notice of the end of the relationship.

Employment standards legislation across the country provides minimum standards for termination, setting out the number of weeks of pay that employees who are dismissed should receive depending on their length of service with the employer. At common law, every employment contract is also deemed to include a provision allowing either the employer or the employee to terminate the employment contract upon providing reasonable notice of termination to the other party, unless the contract provides otherwise or there is just cause for termination. No official time periods have been legislated for reasonable notice beyond the minimum requirements, but over time courts have developed general guidelines. See

T

the REASONABLE NOTICE definition for a review of general factors a court will look at when determining notice.

For the statutory requirements dealing with termination, see INDIVIDUAL TERMINATION and GROUP TERMINATION.

> *See also:* GROUP TERMINATION, INDIVIDUAL TERMINATION, REASONABLE NOTICE.

TERMINATION CLAUSE

A term in a contract of employment between an employer and an employee setting out the terms and conditions for dismissing an employee from her job. According to general contract principles, a court will usually not interfere with the provisions that the parties to a contract have agreed to between themselves, and this includes the notice provisions of an employment contract. Without a termination clause, the common law reasonable notice requirements must be followed for non-union employees. It should be noted, though, that the employer and employee will not be allowed to create contract terms that are less than the reasonable notice requirements set out in the relevant employment standards legislation.

> *See also:* CONTRACT OF EMPLOYMENT

TIME BANK

In British Columbia, an employee may request that an employer credit overtime hours worked to a time bank, instead of paying overtime wages directly to the employee. If a time bank is set up, the employee may request at any time that the employer pay all, or part, of the overtime wages credited to the employee in the bank, or allow the employee to use the credited wages to take time off with pay. The employee may also request that the time bank be closed entirely. The employer is responsible for ensuring that all overtime wages in the time bank are paid out, or given as time off in lieu of overtime, within six months of the overtime being worked by the employee.

> *See also:* TIME OFF IN LIEU OF OVERTIME

TIME OFF IN LIEU OF OVERTIME

Time off work, earned because the employee previously worked overtime. It is an alternative to being paid overtime wages for the hours worked. The time off may be one hour off for each overtime hour worked, or one and a half hours off for each overtime hour worked.

The practice is specifically permitted in Alberta, British Columbia, Manitoba, Newfoundland and Labrador, Ontario, Quebec, and the Yukon.

See also: OVERTIME, PAY PERIOD, TIME BANK

V

VACATION

Employees are entitled to a certain number of days of paid time off from working. Vacations allow employees to have a break from work, which improves general employee well-being and productivity.

Under Employment Standards legislation, employees are typically entitled to two weeks of annual vacation time after they have completed one year of employment. Employers often increase an employee's vacation entitlement after an employee works for the employer for a certain number of years. In Saskatchewan, employees are entitled to three weeks of vacation time after one year of employment, while in Quebec employees can take up to three weeks of vacation time, although some of it may have to be unpaid.

The employee will be entitled to the greater of the amount of vacation provided pursuant to Employment Standards legislation or as provided for in the employment contract.

See also: COMMON ANNIVERSARY DATE, VACATION ENTITLEMENT, VACATION ENTITLEMENT YEAR, VACATION PAY YEAR, YEAR OF EMPLOYMENT

VACATION ENTITLEMENT

The amount of vacation time that an employee will be entitled to take in a year, whether under Employment Standards legislation or an employment contract. An employee's vacation entitlement will often depend on the number of continuous years of service the employee has worked for the employer.

See also: VACATION

VACATION ENTITLEMENT YEAR

In Ontario, a year of employment is defined to be a vacation entitlement year, for the purposes of determining an employee's entitlement to vacation.

V

The vacation entitlement year can be either alternative or standard. An alternative vacation entitlement year is defined to be a twelve month period beginning on a date chosen by the employer that is different than the date that the employee began working for the employer. A standard vacation entitlement year is defined to be a twelve month period starting on the day that the employee started working for the employer.

See also: COMMON ANNIVERSARY DATE, STUB PERIOD, VACATION, VACATION PAY YEAR, YEAR OF EMPLOYMENT

VACATION PAY

The amount an employee is entitled to be paid for their yearly vacation, which is calculated as a percentage of total gross earnings. Four per cent is the typical amount designated under Employment Standards legislation for vacation pay, although this varies across jurisdictions, and may be increased by the employer after a specified period of continuous employment. Gross earnings include wages and salary, and may also include commissions, overtime, vacation pay, banked time, severance, discretionary bonuses and room and board. Gross earnings usually do not include gratuities, gifts or travel allowances or expenses.

Generally, vacation pay must be paid prior to the start of the employee's vacation, although several provinces create exceptions to this requirement. If an employee is terminated before she has taken vacation, the employer must give the employee all outstanding vacation pay. Specific rules about payment deadlines are also provided in each jurisdiction.

It should be noted that the law treats vacation pay and entitlement to vacation as two distinct concepts. Vacation pay is based on gross annual earnings, while vacation entitlement is based on continuous length of service. Depending on the situation, the two will not necessarily match.

See also: VACATION, VACATION ENTITLEMENT, VACATION ENTITLEMENT YEAR, VACATION PAY YEAR

VACATION PAY YEAR

In New Brunswick, a year of employment is deemed to run from July 1 of one year, to the last day of June the next year. This is then used to determine an employee's vacation entitlement.

See also: COMMON ANNIVERSARY DATE, VACATION, VACATION ENTITLEMENT, VACATION ENTITLEMENT YEAR, VACATION PAY

VOTING AT ELECTIONS

An employee who qualifies to vote in a federal election is entitled to three consecutive hours, while the polls are open, in order to vote. If the hours of work interfere with this requirement, employees must be granted enough time off to make up three consecutive hours.

Each province has different rules about provincial elections. Generally speaking, the procedure is similar to federal elections, and the required number of hours to vote are between three to four consecutive hours.

Alberta, New Brunswick, Ontario, Quebec and the Yukon specifically allow time off to vote in municipal elections. In other jurisdictions, rules regarding time off from work would be found in municipal by-laws.

See also: LEAVES OF ABSENCE

W

WAGE RATE

See: RATE OF PAY

WAGES

Money paid to an employee for work or services.

Each jurisdiction has its own definition of what will be included when determining an employee's wages. It may or may not include vacation and holiday pay, or pay in lieu of vacation. As a general rule, tips and gratuities are not counted when calculating wages for purposes of Employment Standards legislation.

See also: BENEFITS, BONUS, SALARY

WALLACE DAMAGES

Damages paid to an employee for the employer's bad faith in the manner of dismissal, also known as bad faith damages. The behaviour of the employer in dismissing the employee may entitle the employee to a longer period of notice, according to the Supreme Court of Canada decision in *Wallace v. United Grain Growers Ltd.*, 97 CLLC ¶210-029. According to this decision, employers are required to act in good faith, and with fair dealing when they dismiss an employee. At the very least, employers should be candid, reasonable, honest and forthright with their employees, and should not act in a manner that is unfair, or in bad faith, by being untruthful, misleading or unduly insensitive. The Supreme Court of Canada decided that the notice period should be extended to compensate an employee when an employer has acted in bad faith in dismissing the employee.

In the case of *Wallace v. United Grain Growers Ltd.*, Wallace was recruited from a competitor company after 25 years of service to go to work for the United Grain Growers. He was top salesperson each year that he worked at United Grain Growers, until he was unexpectedly dismissed without explanation. When Wallace filed a wrongful dismissal action, United Grain Growers claimed that Wallace had been dismissed for cause, a position they maintained right up until the trial began. As a result of these actions, Wallace had emotional difficulties, and had a difficult time finding another job. The Supreme Court of Canada upheld a notice period of 24 months. The relevant factors for this long notice period included Wallace's age, his success with the company, the fact that he was seriously recruited to leave his last job, and his limited job prospects. Also, the 24 month notice period included the period of notice to compensate Wallace for the bad faith conduct by the employer in the manner in which he was fired.

> *See also:* AGGRAVATED DAMAGES, DAMAGES, MENTAL DISTRESS DAMAGES, PUNITIVE DAMAGES

WORK DAY

Time during which an employee works for the employer in one 24 hour period of time. Generally, an employee may not work more than eight hours in a day, and any time beyond that must be paid as overtime.

It should be noted that some provinces do not set maximum hours for a work day. Instead, they only set maximum hours of work for a week, for the purposes of calculating overtime. Newfoundland and Labrador and Quebec set the maximum hours at 40 per week, while Nova Scotia and Prince Edward Island set the maximum number of hours in a week at 48. New Brunswick has no limit on the number of hours that can be worked in a day, week or month, but employers are required to pay overtime after 44 hours of work in a week.

> *See also:* HOURS OF WORK, MEAL BREAK, OVERTIME, WORK WEEK

WORK WEEK

A period of seven consecutive days.

For Alberta, British Columbia, Saskatchewan, and the federal government, the week commences at midnight on Saturday. Elsewhere, the employer can begin their work week on any day, as long as their practice remains consistent.

> *See also:* AVERAGING AGREEMENTS, COMPRESSED WORK WEEK, HOURS OF WORK, WORK DAY

WORKING NOTICE

> *See:* PAYMENT IN LIEU OF NOTICE

WRONGFUL DISMISSAL

A dismissal without the required notice period.

Every non-union employment relationship is governed by a contract of employment between the employer and the employee, setting out basic requirements of the employment relationship. This contract, whether explicitly written down, or inferred by the court, sets out certain requirements, including how the relationship will end. A non-union contract of employment can be terminated at any point if there is JUST CAUSE. If there is no just cause for the ending of the employment relationship, it can still be ended by the employer as long as reasonable notice is provided. If the employee does not believe that she was terminated for just cause, or given reasonable notice of termination, then she may sue the employer, claiming wrongful dismissal. If the contract specifies the notice period, the REASONABLE NOTICE requirement is replaced by the contract's own notice requirement.

> *See also:* CONSTRUCTIVE DISMISSAL, DISMISSAL, JUST CAUSE, MITIGATION, REASONABLE NOTICE, RESIGNATION

WRONGFUL RESIGNATION

A resignation without the required notice.

When an employee wishes to leave a job, he must notify the employer, and indicate when he intends to leave. The employee must give reasonable notice of his last day, just as an employer is required to give reasonable notice when an employee is dismissed, unless there is just cause for the resignation. Although not very common, an employer can bring a wrongful

W

resignation claim against an employee who resigns without giving appropriate notice. In general, these actions are brought only against senior or very specialized employees. Similar factors to wrongful dismissal claims are used to determine what amount of notice is reasonable in a wrongful resignation claim, although the required notice period will be much shorter almost always. An employer must demonstrate that the resignation by the employee was voluntary, there was no cause for the resignation, there was no reasonable notice of the resignation, and the employer suffered a loss as a result of the lack of notice.

An employer who can demonstrate that an employee has wrongfully resigned will be able to recover losses that the employer suffered as a result of the lack of notice, including any costs associated with replacing the employee. Possible recoverable costs may include overtime worked by other employees, costs of advertising for a replacement, or the costs of hiring a new employee. This is subject to the employer's obligation to mitigate.

See also: REASONABLE NOTICE, WRONGFUL DISMISSAL

Y

YEAR OF EMPLOYMENT

Twelve consecutive months of continuous employment with the same employer.

This is usually used to determine an employee's vacation entitlement. Generally it begins on the day that the employee's employment begins, but in some jurisdictions an employer can set a common anniversary date for all employees. In New Brunswick, a vacation pay year runs from July 1 to the last day of June. In Quebec, a year of employment runs from May 1 to the last day of April. Ontario sets out specific rules for setting a vacation entitlement year.

See also: COMMON ANNIVERSARY DATE, VACATION ENTITLEMENT YEAR, VACATION PAY YEAR

YOUNG PERSON

Defined in Alberta as an employee who is 15 to 17 years of age. These individuals cannot work without someone with them who is 18 years of age or older. They also may not be employed in the province between the hours of 9 p.m. to 12:01 a.m. in certain fields, or otherwise between 12:01 a.m. and 6 a.m., without written consent.

In Prince Edward Island, a young person is someone who is under 16 years of age, the minimum age for the province. Employers may not hire a young person if the job is in the construction industry, or if the work is likely to be harmful to their health and safety, or to their moral or physical development. People under 16 years of age are also restricted from working between 11 p.m. and 7 a.m., or during school hours, and they may not work more than three hours on a school day, eight hours on a day other than a school day, or 40 hours in a week.

In the Northwest Territories and Nunavut, a young person is one who has not yet reached 17 years of age. Individuals under 17 years of age may not be hired in the construction industry, or if the work will be detrimental to the health, education or moral character of the young person, without specific consent. They are also not allowed to work between the hours of 11 p.m. and 6 a.m.

See also: ADOLESCENT, CHILD, MINIMUM AGE

LABOUR

A

ABSENTEEISM

Time away from work.

An excused, or "non-culpable", absence occurs when an employer permits an employee to be away from work for a legitimate business or personal reason. Employers are also required to accommodate absences that are related to an employee's disability, up to the point of undue hardship. Chronic absenteeism involves an employee who is habitually or frequently absent from work. Excessive absences from the workplace may require an employer to apply PROGRESSIVE DISCIPLINE, possibly leading to termination. Non-culpable absenteeism is usually treated as "innocent absenteeism" in a non-disciplinary manner.

> *See also:* AUTOMATIC QUIT

ACCREDITED EMPLOYERS' ORGANIZATION

A group of employers that is accredited by a labour relations board as the bargaining agent for a unit of employers.

> *See also:* DE-ACCREDITATION, EMPLOYERS' ORGANIZATION

A

AFFILIATED COMPANIES

Two or more business enterprises which are interdependent as the result of a parent-subsidiary relationship, having officers or employees in common, or for some other reason.

See also: SINGLE EMPLOYER STATUS

ALL-UNION AGREEMENT

A collective agreement in which the employer agrees to maintain a CLOSED SHOP.

See also: CLOSED SHOP

ALLIED PICKETING DOCTRINE

Under this doctrine, a union was permitted to picket at the premises of a company which had allied itself in some way with the primary employer. An allied employer may be a subsidiary company, a company with a common employer to the primary employer, or a company engaged in assisting the primary employer in carrying on their business during the labour dispute.

This doctrine has been used to determine where secondary picketing may be permitted at common law. See SECONDARY PICKETING for a full explanation of when and where secondary picketing is acceptable.

See also: PICKETING, SECONDARY PICKETING

ALLY

A person who acts in accordance with a common understanding to assist an employer in a lockout or in resisting a lawful strike. This may include a person who, for the benefit of the employer affected by a strike or lockout, performs work, or supplies goods or services that would normally be provided by the employer.

See also: LOCKOUT, PICKETING, STRIKE

ANTI-STRIKE BREAKING PROVISIONS

Provisions in labour relations legislation in some provinces that specifically disallow certain activities by employers during a lawful strike or lockout.

For example, in Alberta, no employers, employers' organizations, trade unions or employees may engage in dispute-related misconduct. This includes incitement, intimidation, coercion, undue influence, provocation, infiltration or any other conduct intended to prevent, interfere with or break-up a lawful strike or lockout. In British Columbia, employers may not use replacement workers during a strike or lockout. Both Manitoba and Ontario prevent employers from engaging in strike-related misconduct, or using professional strikebreakers. In Quebec, employers may not use another person to perform the duties of the employee who is on strike or locked out, or use employees who are on strike or locked out in another establishment. Employees in Quebec may continue working during a strike only if there is an agreement in place with the union, and only according to the terms of the agreement.

See also: LOCKOUT, REPLACEMENT WORKER, STRIKE

ANTI-UNION ANIMUS

An employer who is opposed to having a unionized workplace may demonstrate animosity toward a union, possibly involving speeches or actions directed at employees to attempt to turn them away from their union. These negative actions directed toward a union are also known as "bad faith" by an employer.

A union that believes an employer is acting in bad faith and is actively attempting to remove the union from a place of employment may bring an unfair labour practice complaint before a labour relations board. Actions that have been found to constitute anti-union animus by labour relations boards include the dismissal of a known union activist from his or her employment without reasonable cause for the termination being given, or the relocation of a plant to prevent it from becoming unionized.

See also: UNFAIR LABOUR PRACTICE

APPLICATION FOR CERTIFICATION

A request by a trade union to a labour relations board for designation as the bargaining agent for a specific group of employees that are considered appropriate for collective bargaining. The union is required to demonstrate that it has the support of a majority of the employees in the proposed bargaining unit of employees. In order for the union to be certified, some

Labour

A

provinces require a vote, while other provinces simply require that a certain percentage of employees sign cards to become a member of the union.

> See also: BARGAINING UNIT, CERTIFICATION, REPRESENTATION VOTE

APPRENTICE

A worker who is serving a special training period in preparation for certification as a skilled tradesperson. In some provinces, apprenticeship is regulated by statute, which governs the terms and conditions of apprenticeship for certain designated trades, such as electrician and automotive mechanic.

ARBITRATION

The procedure by which a board or a single person, known as an arbitrator, hears both sides of a controversy and issues a binding decision. The decision, or "award", is usually in writing.

In labour arbitration, the arbitrator takes his authority under the collective agreement. In private arbitration, the arbitrator takes authority from an arbitration agreement and the applicable arbitration statute, such as Ontario's *Arbitrations Act, 1991*. Arbitrators are often appointed by the parties themselves. Under special circumstances, labour arbitrators may be appointed by the Minister of Labour for the particular jurisdiction.

> See also: COMPULSORY ARBITRATION, EXPEDITED ARBITRATION, INTEREST ARBITRATION, RIGHTS ARBITRATION, VOLUNTARY ARBITRATION

ARBITRATION AWARD

The majority decision rendered by the arbitrator, or arbitration board, with respect to a dispute between the parties to the arbitration. The final decision of the arbitrator is binding on both parties to the dispute.

ARBITRATION BOARD

A group of individuals appointed or chosen to hear a case, or a group of cases, that is submitted for arbitration. Labour arbitration boards may be composed of a management representative, a trade union representative, and a neutral representative approved by both the employer and the union. The decision of a majority of the arbitration board will govern, although if the majority cannot agree, the decision of the chairperson may rule.

ARBITRATION CLAUSE

A clause included in an agreement stipulating that disputes arising during the term of the contract shall be settled by arbitration. With respect to labour relations, all jurisdictions in Canada have legislation in place requiring that an arbitration clause be included in all collective agreements.

ARBITRATOR

A third party who is chosen to hear a case, or a group of cases, that have been submitted for arbitration. The powers of an arbitrator granted by federal or provincial labour legislation often include the right to determine procedures, summon witnesses, determine whether a matter is actually arbitrable, compel witnesses to appear before the arbitrator, and assist the parties in resolving the dispute.

See also: ARBITRATION

AREA-WIDE BARGAINING

Collective bargaining that occurs between a union and all of the employers in a particular area for whose employees the union holds bargaining rights.

ASSOCIATION BARGAINING

See: MULTI-EMPLOYER BARGAINING

ASSOCIATION OF EMPLOYEES

The term used to describe a trade union in the province of Quebec. In the *Quebec Labour Code*, an association of employees is a group of employees formed to study, safeguard and develop the economic, social and educational interests of all of the members of the group, specifically through the negotiation and application of collective agreements.

In other provinces, an association of employees is a group that expresses employees' wishes to management. Its powers depend on whether or not it has bargaining rights under labour legislation.

See also: TRADE UNION

A

AUTOMATIC QUIT

Termination of an employee resulting from an absence without permission beyond a specified number of days. Many collective agreements have automatic quit clauses.

See also: ABSENTEEISM

AUTOMATIC RENEWAL

Extension of the operation of a collective agreement from one year to the next, in the absence of any notice of intent to modify or terminate the agreement. The automatic renewal can be provided for in the agreement itself.

AUTOMATION

A movement in the workplace toward using computers and other machines to perform work normally done by workers. The three main kinds of automated processes include:

- assembly-line automation, used in the automotive industry;

- computers, used in all modern offices; and

- utilizing electronic equipment as controls in manufacturing and processing, used in the refining industry.

See also: TECHNOLOGICAL CHANGE

B

BALLOT

The piece of paper used to cast a vote in a union election. A two-way ballot offers a choice between two contesting unions, while a yes-no ballot offers a choice between representation by a union, or no representation at all.

See also: ELECTION

BARGAINING AGENT

A trade union that acts as the exclusive representative of a group of employees with an employer, in respect of the employees' terms and conditions of employment.

> *See also:* COLLECTIVE AGREEMENT, COLLECTIVE BARGAINING, REPRESENTATIVE VOTE, TRADE UNION

BARGAINING HISTORY

The nature of the relationship that may have existed in the past between an employer and a particular union. This history is cited by labour relations boards when determining whether an action by one of the parties constitutes an unfair labour practice.

BARGAINING RIGHTS

The right of a trade union to represent workers in an appropriate bargaining unit. This right is created by certification by a labour relations board.

> *See also:* BARGAINING UNIT, CERTIFICATION, COLLECTIVE AGREEMENT, TRADE UNION

BARGAINING UNIT

A group of employees in a company, plant or industry that has been determined by a labour relations board or in a collective agreement to be the appropriate unit for collective bargaining. Depending on the legislative requirements in each jurisdiction, a bargaining unit is generally required to include two or more employees.

The main factors in determining whether a group of employees is an appropriate bargaining unit include the "community of interest" among employees, the nature of the work performed by the employees, organization and representation of the employees, as well as the desires, interests and interchangeability of the affected employees. For example, in a craft union an appropriate bargaining unit may include all members of a trade, such as all tool and die makers in a plant. In an industrial union, the bargaining unit may be composed of all production workers in a plant, or in all plants within a specific company in a certain geographic area.

> *See also:* COLLECTIVE BARGAINING, REPRESENTATION VOTE

B

BASE RATE

The lowest rate of hourly pay given to the lowest paid qualified job within a classification in a particular bargaining unit.

The **basic rate**, in contrast, is the straight-time rate of pay per hour, job or unit, excluding premiums, incentive bonuses, and other forms of remuneration.

BOYCOTT

An organized refusal by employees and/or their union to deal with their employer in order to gain advantages, or win concessions from the employer. A campaign by employees to discourage others from dealing with their employer could also be called a boycott.

Primary boycotts, which are a direct boycott by employees of their own employer, usually involve placing pressure on consumers or customers not to buy the goods of the employer who is directly involved in the dispute. Secondary boycotts often involve a refusal to deal with a neutral party in a labour dispute, in order to put pressure on the primary employer. Such boycotts are often accompanied by demands that the neutral employer bring pressure on the employer involved in the dispute to agree to the terms and conditions asserted by those who are boycotting. Production boycotts are simply another word for strikes brought by a group of employees against their employer.

See also: CONSUMER LEAFLETING, PICKETING, STRIKE

BUMPING

The exercise of seniority rights by workers, in order to displace junior employees when there are temporary layoffs or the discontinuance of a department within the company. For example, an employee who has worked for the company for 20 years who is being laid off may be able to use his seniority to bump an employee in a different job who has only a few years of job experience.

BY-LAWS

Specific provisions that supplement the charters or constitutions governing corporations, labour unions and other organizations. They are the corporation's, union's or organization's own internal rules for operation.

C

CERTIFIED BARGAINING AGENT

A union designated by a labour relations board as the exclusive bargaining agent for a group of employees.

See also: BARGAINING AGENT

CERTIFICATION

The official designation by a labour relations board of a trade union as the exclusive bargaining agent for employees in a particular bargaining unit, following an organizing campaign in which the union establishes that it has the requisite support among employees in the bargaining unit.

See also: APPLICATION FOR CERTIFICATION, BARGAINING UNIT, REPRESENTATION VOTE

CHECK-OFF

A system where union dues and fees are deducted by the employer from the employees' pay cheques and given directly to the union. A check-off assignment is a signed authorization from the employee permitting a voluntary check-off from the employee's wages. These authorizations can be either voluntary and revocable by the employee, or voluntary and irrevocable. In contrast, an automatic or compulsory check-off is one made without specific authorization by each employee. Under the RAND FORMULA, dues are deducted from both union members and non-members within the specific bargaining unit.

Every jurisdiction in Canada has legislation in place making it compulsory for the employer to comply with the check-off of union dues for all employees within a particular unit affected by a collective agreement, whether on the written authorization of the employee or in accordance with the terms of a collective agreement.

See also: RAND FORMULA, UNION DUES

CLOSED SHOP

A place of employment where the employer is obligated to hire and retain only employees who are members of the union. This is the strongest form of

Labour

union security clause, and it is often used in trades and industries where special crafts and skills are required. The union may use a hiring hall to provide the required number of workers to the employer, as necessary.

In a closed shop, there will usually be a clause in the collective agreement which binds the employer to hire only members of a specified union. A typical closed shop clause may read:

> The employer shall employ only members in good standing in the union. All employees shall remain members in good standing as a condition of employment.

> *See also:* ALL-UNION AGREEMENT, HIRING HALL, MAINTE-NANCE-OF-MEMBERSHIP, PREFERENTIAL HIRING, RAND FORMULA, UNION SECURITY CLAUSE, UNION SHOP

COLA CLAUSE

A provision in a collective agreement providing for payment of a cost of living allowance, based on increases in the Consumer Price Index as compiled by Statistics Canada during the length of the collective agreement, or based on another indicator of inflation. It is also known as a cost of living adjustment or allowance clause.

> *See also:* CONSUMER PRICE INDEX, COST OF LIVING

COLLECTIVE AGREEMENT

An agreement in writing between an employer and the union representing employees in the applicable bargaining unit, containing terms and conditions of employment including rates of pay, hours of work, and the rights or duties of the parties to the agreement. The agreement is ordinarily for a definite period, such as one, two, or three years, and usually not less than twelve months in duration. Amendments may be made to an agreement by mutual consent during the term of the agreement, in order to deal with any special or unique circumstances that may arise.

> *See also:* BARGAINING UNIT, TRADE UNION

COLLECTIVE AGREEMENT DECREES

The Quebec government may order that a collective agreement within the province, respecting any trade, industry, commerce or occupation, shall bind all the employees and professional employers within the province or in certain designated areas in the province, in accordance with the *Collective Agreement Decrees Act.*

COLLECTIVE BARGAINING

The process of negotiating the creation, revision or renewal of a collective agreement between an employer and a trade union. It is called "collective" bargaining because employees bargain together through the union, not individually.

> *See also:* COLLECTIVE AGREEMENT, COMPANY-WIDE BAR-GAINING, INDUSTRY-WIDE BARGAINING, MULTI-EMPLOYER BARGAINING, NEGOTIATION, TRADE UNION

COMMON-SITE PICKETING

Picketing directed at an employer that occurs at or near a site or place where other employers carry on business. In such a situation, the operations of the employers not directly involved in the dispute between the trade union and its employer may be disrupted by the picketing.

COMPANY-DOMINATED UNION

An employee organization, often within a single company, that is dominated or strongly influenced by management. Such unions were widespread in the 1920s and 1930s, but have since been made illegal by labour relations legislation across the country.

COMPANY-WIDE BARGAINING

Collective bargaining that takes place between a company with more than one plant or location, and one or more unions representing employees of a particular craft or skill. The terms and conditions arrived at are generally uniform throughout the company for the group of affected employees.

Labour

C

COMPULSORY ARBITRATION

Arbitration required by law. This type of arbitration is the usual process for settling disputes over the application or interpretation of a collective agreement.

> *See also:* ARBITRATION, EXPEDITED ARBITRATION, INTEREST ARBITRATION, RIGHTS ARBITRATION, VOLUNTARY ARBITRATION

CONCILIATION

The process by which an employer and a trade union who have reached an impasse in negotiations toward a collective agreement seek government assistance in resolving their dispute. Either party may apply to the government and a conciliation officer will be appointed. The officer will attempt to resolve the labour dispute through compromise or voluntary agreement. Unlike arbitration, the conciliator or conciliation officer does not bring in a binding award, and the parties are free to accept or reject her recommendation. Generally, conciliation is compulsory before a strike or lockout can occur.

> *See also:* ARBITRATION, MEDIATION

CONDONATION

Acquiescence by an employer of conduct by an employee which would otherwise be unacceptable, or illegal.

For example, an employer who does not discipline an employee for improper conduct as soon as the employer is aware of it may be deemed to have "condoned" that conduct, and the employer may be unable to discipline that same employee for a repetition of the conduct in the future. The theory is that condonation of conduct leads the employee to believe that it is acceptable.

CONSTRUCTION INDUSTRY

Businesses that are engaged in the construction, alteration, decoration, restoration or demolition of buildings, structures, roads, sewers, water or gas mains, pipe lines, tunnels, bridges, canals, dams or other works.

Most provinces have specific legislative provisions dealing with labour relations in the construction industry. The exceptions are the federal government and Manitoba, which have no legislation dealing with the construction industry, and British Columbia, which repealed its construction industry legislation in 2001.

CONSUMER LEAFLETING

The handing out of pamphlets or leaflets containing information about an employer, and its practices. Leafleting often occurs in an attempt by employees to persuade members of the public to take a certain course of action with respect to the employer, through informed disclosure. For example, unionized employees who are engaged in a dispute with their employer may hand out pamphlets informing consumers about products made by non-union employees, in order to persuade consumers not to buy those products. Leafleting is often used in conjunction with picketing, or strikes by employees.

While in many cases leafleting will occur at the site where the primary employer has its offices, there may also be situations where leafleting occurs at a neutral third party location. In general, leafleting at such sites may be permitted as long as:

- The message conveyed by the leaflet is accurate, not defamatory or unlawful, and does not encourage people to commit unlawful acts;

- The leaflet clearly states that the dispute is only with the primary employer;

- The manner in which the leafleting is conducted is not coercive, intimidating or unlawful;

- The leafleting does not keep people from entering or exiting the place where the leafleting is occurring; and

- It does not prevent employees of neutral sites from working, or interfere with suppliers trying to get to the neutral site.

See also: BOYCOTT, PICKETING, SECONDARY PICKETING

CONSUMER PRICE INDEX

A statistic released monthly by Statistics Canada which follows changes in retail prices of selected consumer items in major Canadian cities. The index and its monthly fluctuations are often used to calculate the COLA payments

C

(Cost of Living allowance) in collective agreements. Strictly, it is not a COST OF LIVING index, although it is often described as such.

See also: COLA CLAUSE, COST OF LIVING

CONTRACTING OUT

The practice of an employer where work is assigned to workers outside of the company, instead of being given to employees of the company. In the unionized context, many collective agreements contain a provision prohibiting contracting out of bargaining unit work.

COOLING-OFF PERIOD

A period of time required by federal or provincial legislation following legal notice of a pending labour dispute, during which time there cannot be a strike or a lockout. Generally, it results from the unsatisfactory conclusion of compulsory conciliation attempts, and wages and conditions of work are usually frozen under the conditions set by the previous collective agreement. During this period of time, every effort is made to settle the dispute between the parties.

CO-OPERATION CLAUSE

A clause within a collective agreement, sometimes also called a harmony pledge, in which the employer and the union agree to co-operate on some specific issue.

COST OF LIVING

The relationship of the retail cost of consumer goods and services to the purchasing power of wages.

See also: COLA CLAUSE, CONSUMER PRICE INDEX

COUNCIL OF TRADE UNIONS

Any association of trade unions, including an allied council, a trades council, or a joint-board. A labour relations board may certify a council of trade unions as an appropriate bargaining agent for a unit of employees.

See also: TRADE UNION

COUNTER-PETITION

A document containing signatures of employees who support a trade union, filed by the union in response to a petition filed by employees who do not want to be represented by a trade union.

See also: DECERTIFICATION, PETITION

CRAFT UNION

A trade union that limits its members to a particular craft, for example, carpentry. Today, most craft unions have broadened their jurisdiction to include many occupations and skills that are not closely related to the originally designated craft.

D

DE-ACCREDITATION

In British Columbia, when an accredited employers' organization is in place, one of the employers named in an accreditation may apply to that province's Labour Relations Board to be removed from the list of names included in the accredited organization.

See also: ACCREDITED EMPLOYERS' ORGANIZATION

DECERTIFICATION

Termination of the exclusive bargaining rights of a trade union in respect of a unit of employees. Any employee within the bargaining unit may apply to the labour relations board for decertification, although labour relations legislation in each jurisdiction put restrictions on when and how a decertification application may be made.

See also: CERTIFICATION

DUTY OF FAIR REPRESENTATION

Labour relations legislation across the country, as well as common law principles, impose a duty on trade unions, or people who are acting on behalf of trade unions, to fairly represent employees who are members of the bargaining unit, with respect to their rights under the applicable collec-

Labour

D

tive agreement. Employees who claim that a trade union has not represented them fairly can bring a complaint before the applicable labour relations board.

There are several typical situations in which a union may find itself in conflict with the interests of one or more of its members, or where an individual member of the union may feel he has been treated unfairly by the representative trade union. First, the union may have favoured one set of interests over another when bargaining. Second, the union may determine that a particular employee's grievance is without merit, or that it is in conflict with other interests that the union wants to protect. Third, the union may not give sufficient attention to an individual employee's concerns, making it difficult for the person to resolve his grievance. Finally, a union may unjustly refuse to deal with an individual's concerns. As a result, a union is required to exercise its discretion in good faith, objectively and honestly when dealing with the negotiation and administration of collective agreements, or grievances brought forward by its members.

DUTY TO BARGAIN IN GOOD FAITH

Once notice to bargain has been given by a trade union or an employer, both parties are required to bargain in good faith, making every reasonable effort to negotiate and enter into a collective agreement.

This duty is an essential element of collective bargaining, since it would be difficult to conclude a collective agreement without cooperation between the employer and the union. During negotiations, both parties are required to listen to the other side's point of view, disclose any relevant information to the other party, and refrain from bad faith, or surface bargaining. Surface bargaining occurs where a party to the negotiations is completely unwilling to negotiate with the other party or to work together to create a collective agreement for the parties. For example, a party engaged in surface bargaining may put forth unreasonable demands, and then refuse to waver from this position or consider any alternatives.

See also: COLLECTIVE AGREEMENT, COLLECTIVE BARGAINING, TRADE UNION

E

ELECTION

In representation proceedings under labour relations law, an election is a vote of employees by ballot to indicate whether or not they wish to be represented by a union. In the case of two or more contending union organizations, it is used to determine which one has majority support. Any disputes over the organization of the election, or its results, may be resolved by application to the applicable labour relations board.

Union elections are held within a union to determine officials who will be responsible for making the crucial decisions about union policy and day-to-day operations. Procedures surrounding these elections, such as their frequency, the requirements for nominations, and the voting process, are determined by the union constitution and by-laws. If there is a dispute over the interpretation of the requirements of the constitution, or an allegation that the election requirements and procedures in the constitution have not been respected, in general an application may only be made to a court, not a labour relations board, and the court will apply the constitution in accordance with general contract law principles.

See also: BALLOT, REPRESENTATION VOTE

EMPLOYEE

A person employed to do work who is entitled to wages for the labour or services performed. An employee has the right to belong to a trade union, participate in its lawful activities, and bargain collectively with his or her employer through a bargaining agent.

The term employee is defined in labour relations legislation in each jurisdiction, setting out people who are excluded from the definition, including persons employed in a professional capacity, or who exercise managerial functions. Professionals may be defined to include medical doctors, dentists, architects, engineers or lawyers.

See also: EMPLOYER

EMPLOYER

A person or firm who has control over the employment of workers and the payment of their wages. An employer may voluntarily bargain collectively

E

with a recognized trade union acting on behalf of employees, or a specific group of employees.

See also: COLLECTIVE BARGAINING, EMPLOYEE, TRADE UNION

EMPLOYERS' ORGANIZATION

A group of employers formed for the purpose of regulating relations between employers and employees. It includes an accredited employers' organization.

See also: ACCREDITED EMPLOYERS' ORGANIZATION

EXCLUSIVE BARGAINING RIGHT

The right of a union, designated as the bargaining representative for employees in a bargaining unit, to bargain collectively on behalf of all employees in the unit.

See also: BARGAINING UNIT

EXPEDITED ARBITRATION

A process of arbitration by which the parties to a collective agreement may refer any dispute arising from the interpretation, application, administration or alleged violation of the agreement to a single arbitrator.

An application for expedited arbitration may only occur after the expiration of a certain number of days from the date at which the grievance was first brought to the attention of the other party, as set out in legislation, or once the grievance procedure under the collective agreement has been exhausted.

See also: ARBITRATION, COMPULSORY ARBITRATION, INTEREST ARBITRATION, RIGHTS ARBITRATION, VOLUNTARY ARBITRATION

F

FEDERAL JURISDICTION

The federal parliament, as a result of the *Constitution Act, 1867*, has legislative authority over employment and labour relations in certain federally-regulated industries. These industries include air transportation, broadcasting, telecommunications, banks, pipelines, railways, interprovincial highway transportation, shipping, and grain elevators. Generally, all other employment organizations fall within provincial jurisdiction.

FINAL OFFER VOTING

A required vote by employees in a bargaining unit as to whether to accept or reject the last offer put forward by the employer in collective agreement negotiations.

Under the *Canada Labour Code*, where notice to bargain collectively has been given and the Minister believes that it is in the public interest that the employees in the affected bargaining unit have the opportunity to accept or reject the last offer given by the employer to the trade union, the Minister may order a vote to be held. If a majority of the employees accept the employer's last offer, the parties are bound by that offer as part of their collective agreement, and any lawful lockout or strike immediately ends.

See also: LAST OFFER VOTING

FIRST COLLECTIVE AGREEMENT

Once a trade union has been appointed as the sole bargaining agent for a group of employees, the union and the employer will begin negotiations to create the first collective agreement between the parties.

This is often a difficult task, as it is the first time that the parties are entering into negotiations with each other, and it may occur directly after a long and bitter fight for certification by the union. As a result, most jurisdictions have legislation in place to provide assistance to parties who are unable to conclude a first collective agreement. In some jurisdictions a mediator may be appointed, while in other jurisdictions a labour relations board or "interest arbitrator" may be appointed to review the dispute between the parties, and settle the terms of the agreement. Strikes and lockouts may be prohibited during the negotiation process, and any existing statutory freeze of wages or working conditions already in place may be continued.

See also: COLLECTIVE AGREEMENT, STATUTORY FREEZE PERIOD

Labour

F

FOREMAN

A supervisory employee who is usually classified as part of management. A working foreman or leadhand is one who regularly performs production work or other work unrelated to supervisory duties, likely does not have any disciplinary authority over employees he supervises, and may be a member of the bargaining unit.

FREEDOM OF ASSOCIATION

The *Canadian Charter of Rights and Freedoms* provides that everyone has the protected right to freedom of association (section 2(*d*)). This right includes the freedom to join with others in lawful, common pursuits and to establish and maintain organizations and associations, such as trade unions.

G

GOOD FAITH BARGAINING

See: DUTY TO BARGAIN IN GOOD FAITH

GRIEVANCE

Any disagreement respecting the interpretation, application, administration or alleged violation of a collective agreement. It may also be a complaint relating to the conduct of an employer or union. It can be brought by a union or employer, but is usually brought by a union. The method for dealing with individual grievances is set out in the applicable collective agreement, allowing for a series of steps that ultimately result in the dispute being taken to arbitration.

H

HIRING HALL

An office from which a union fills requests by employers for workers by referring workers to employers. A central hiring hall is a central place where union workers gather for referral to seasonal or casual jobs. A joint hiring hall is sponsored by employers as well as a union. A preferential hiring hall is a hiring hall where union members get first referral to union jobs.

See also: CLOSED SHOP

I

ILLEGAL STRIKE

A strike called in violation of the applicable law. Strikes are generally illegal when they occur during the term of a collective agreement, when they occur before conciliation procedures have been complied with, or when they begin while certification proceedings are under way.

See also: STRIKE

INCUMBENT UNION

A union holding the bargaining rights for employees in a bargaining unit.

INDUSTRIAL RELATIONS

A broad term denoting relations between unions, unions and management, management and government, unions and government, or employers and employees with respect to the workplace.

INDUSTRY-WIDE AGREEMENT

A collective agreement covering all employers and employees in a particular industry.

INDUSTRY-WIDE BARGAINING

Collective bargaining of terms and conditions of employment for an entire industry. This type of collective bargaining often occurs in the construction industry.

INJUNCTION

A court order restraining a party from committing a particular action, or directing a party to take a particular action. Because the injunction is

Labour

I

included in a court order, the court has the power to hold parties that disobey the injunction in contempt of court.

An *ex parte* injunction is one where the application for an injunction is made without the presence of the party who will be affected by the proposed injunction.

Examples of injunctions include labour injunctions preventing picketing employees from blocking access to or from a property, or injunctions against former employees preventing them from soliciting clients of the former employer.

INTEREST ARBITRATION

An arbitration process by which parties unable to agree upon a collective agreement have the terms of the collective agreement decided by an arbitrator or board of arbitration.

> *See also:* ARBITRATION, COMPULSORY ARBITRATION, EXPEDITED ARBITRATION, RIGHTS ARBITRATION, VOLUNTARY ARBITRATION

INTERIM AGREEMENT

A collective agreement setting out conditions only for the period from the end of one agreement to the completion of negotiations of the next collective agreement.

INTERIM CERTIFICATION

In certain circumstances, particularly where an employer and a trade union have been engaged in a long dispute over what the proposed bargaining unit of employees should look like, a labour relations board may choose to certify the union as the bargaining agent for a unit of employees on an interim basis, pending a final determination of the definition of the bargaining unit. This may arise, for example, in situations where the employer and the union are unable to agree over whether a particular position within the proposed bargaining unit is an excluded management position. With an interim certification order, the union and the employer can begin collective bargaining, even though the exact structure of the bargaining unit has not been finalized. Once the bargaining unit has been determined, the labour relations board can then issue a final certification order.

Manitoba legislation contains specific provisions allowing the Labour Relations Board to award interim certification.

See also: CERTIFICATION

INTERPRETATION BULLETINS

Explanatory releases issued by an administrative agency, such as a labour relations board, in order to set out what it believes to be the meaning of a particular law. These bulletins are useful for employers and trade unions who appear before these administrative bodies.

J

JOB ACTION

Collective action taken by employees on the job in order to compel an employer to agree to certain terms and conditions of employment. It may consist of actions such as work slow-downs or refusal to work overtime.

See also: BOYCOTT, CONSUMER LEAFLETING, PICKETING, STRIKE, WORK TO RULE

JOB CLASSIFICATION

A category of jobs or a job title at a particular workplace. Often collective agreements list various job classifications and their applicable wage rates.

JOB CLASSIFICATION SYSTEM

A job rating system using an analysis of the requirements of the work. The system is designed to create a hierarchy of jobs based on such factors as skill, responsibility or experience, time and effort. The system is used to determine the value of each job in relation to other jobs in the workplace, or to arrive at a system of wage rates for different jobs or classes of jobs.

JOB DESCRIPTION

A description of the duties of a particular job, reporting relationship, working conditions, the degree of responsibility, and qualifications required for the job.

Labour

J

JOB SECURITY

A worker's sense of having continuous employment because she has special skills, seniority, or protection provided in a collective agreement. The term is also used to describe the protection, in almost all collective agreements, against discharge except where the employer has just cause.

JUDICIAL REVIEW

A review by a court of a decision of an administrative tribunal or body. The court may uphold the decision, amend it, overturn it, or send it back to the tribunal for further review. Examples are court reviews of decisions of a labour arbitrator or labour relations board.

Arbitration and labour relations board decisions are given a high level of deference by courts of law, because of their special knowledge and skill in the areas of labour and employment law. Arbitrators have exclusive jurisdiction to deal with all disputes that arise out of a collective agreement between an employer and a union. Parties may challenge the arbitration decision by asking for a court review on the basis of one of three possible errors: an error of jurisdiction, an error of fact, or an error of law. But, a court will generally defer to the arbitrator based on their level of expertise in the area in question, the existence of a clause that limits or removes the possibility of judicial review, known as a "privative clause", and the nature of the question under review. Jurisdiction questions will likely be scrutinized more closely by a court than questions of fact or questions of interpretation of a collective agreement or labour legislation, where the arbitrator has special knowledge and skill.

See also: JURISDICTION

JURISDICTION

The authority of an administrative tribunal or court to hear and decide the merits of a case or issue. In general, courts will not interfere with decisions of labour relations boards or labour arbitrators if the decision was within the jurisdiction of the board or arbitrator.

See also: JUDICIAL REVIEW

JURISDICTIONAL DISPUTE

Also known as an inter-union dispute, a jurisdictional dispute is a conflict between two or more unions as to which one's members are entitled to perform a certain type of work. Most jurisdictional disputes occur in the construction industry. It may also include a dispute between an employer and one or more trade unions over the assignment of work.

L

LABOUR DISPUTE

A controversy concerning terms or conditions of employment between an employer and an employee, group of employees, or trade union. In general, it involves a dispute between employees or their union, and the employer.

LABOUR ORGANIZATION

See: TRADE UNION

LABOUR RELATIONS

A term used to denote all matters that may arise out of an employer-employee relationship where employees are unionized. Specifically, labour relations deals with COLLECTIVE BARGAINING between employers and trade unions representing a group of employees.

All ten provinces, along with the federal government, have legislation dealing with labour relations. The main labour relations legislation in Canada includes:

❏ Federal: *Canada Labour Code*, R.S.C. 1985, c. L-2

❏ Alberta: *Labour Relations Code*, R.S.A. 2000, c. L-1

❏ British Columbia: *Labour Relations Code*, R.S.B.C. 1996, c. 244

❏ Manitoba: *Labour Relations Act*, S.M. 1987, c. L10

❏ New Brunswick: *Industrial Relations Act*, R.S.N.B. 1973, c. I-4

❏ Newfoundland and Labrador: *Labour Relations Act*, R.S.N. 1990, c. L-1

❏ Nova Scotia: *Trade Union Act*, R.S.N.S. 1989, c. 475

❏ Ontario: *Labour Relations Act, 1995*, S.O. 1995, c. 1

❏ Prince Edward Island: *Labour Act*, R.S.P.E.I. 1988, c. L-1

Labour

L

❑ Quebec: *Labour Code*, R.S.Q. 1977, c. C-27

❑ Saskatchewan: *The Trade Union Act*, R.S.S. 1978, c. T-17

LABOUR RELATIONS BOARD

A board, provided for under labour relations legislation, responsible for hearing and adjudicating disputes under labour relations legislation, including disputes relating to certification or decertification of trade unions, conduct of representation votes, complaints of bad faith in collective bargaining or unfair labour practices, and unfair representation complaints by employees against unions. Some labour relations boards also have authority over disputes under various other statutes. Each jurisdiction has its own labour relations board:

- **Canada Industrial Relations Board** — a chairperson, at least one vice-chairperson, and not more than six other full-time members;

- **Alberta Labour Relations Board** — any number of members, with one member designated chair, while others may be designated vice-chairs;

- **British Columbia Labour Relations Board** — a chair, vice-chairs and an equal number of employer and employee representatives;

- **Manitoba Labour Board** — a chairperson, one or more vice-chairpersons, and an equal number of employee and employer representatives;

- **New Brunswick Labour and Employment Board** — a chair and one or more vice-chairs, as well as an equal number of employer and employee representatives;

- **Newfoundland & Labrador Labour Relations Board** — a chairperson and one or more vice-chairpersons, along with two employer representatives, and two employee representatives;

- **Nova Scotia Labour Relations Board** — two employer representatives, two union representatives, and an independent chairperson;

- **Ontario Labour Relations Board** — a chair, one or more vice-chairs, and an equal number of representatives of employers and employees;

- **Prince Edward Island Labour Relations Board** — one chairperson, one or more vice-chairpersons, and as many members as the Lieutenant Governor in Council determines;

- **Quebec Labour Relations Commission** — a president, two vice-presidents, commissioners and members;

- **Saskatchewan Labour Relations Board** — equal numbers of employers and organized employees, with a chairperson and two vice-chairpersons.

LAST OFFER VOTING

In British Columbia, before the commencement of a strike or lockout, an employer may ask that a vote be taken of the employees in the bargaining unit, to determine whether they accept or reject the employer's last offer in respect of all matters remaining in dispute between the parties. A trade union bargaining with an employers' organization may also request a final offer vote of member employers. No more than one vote by either party may be taken with respect to the same dispute, and if the voting results are in favour of accepting the final offer, a collective agreement is formed.

If, during a strike or lockout, the British Columbia Minister of Labour considers it to be in the public interest, the Minister may direct that the union or the employers' organization conduct a last offer vote.

See also: FINAL OFFER VOTING

LEAFLETING

See: CONSUMER LEAFLETING

LOCAL UNION

The basic unit of labour organization formed in a particular plant or locality. The members participate directly in the affairs of their local, including the election of officers, financial and other business matters, relations between their organization and employers, and the payment of dues to the union. Local unions may be independent, autonomous units, or they may be affiliated with a national or international union, in which case they will usually have a number — e.g. Canadian Auto Workers Union, Local 999.

LOCKOUT

The closing by an employer of a place of employment, a suspension of work, or a refusal by an employer to continue to provide work to a number of employees, in order to compel the employees to agree to certain terms and

L

conditions of employment, or to refrain from exercising their existing rights and privileges.

See also: STRIKE, WORK STOPPAGE

LOCKOUT VOTE

When two or more employers are involved in the same dispute with employees in the same bargaining unit, a vote may be held among all the affected employers before a decision is made to lock out the employees.

M

MAINTENANCE OF MEMBERSHIP

A union security system under which an employee is not required to join a union, but employees who are already members and those who voluntarily join the union are required to remain members in good standing as a condition of employment. An "escape period" of seven to fifteen days, allowing members to resign from the union after the signing of the contract, is often included in a maintenance of membership clause. A slightly stronger maintenance of membership clause may require that all new employees become and remain union members, while all employees who are members at the time of a new collective agreement are required to retain their membership.

These clauses ensure that a majority of the workers in the unit support the union, unless an expansion in the work force occurs and the new workers fail to join the union. The inclusion of an "escape period" will increase the vulnerability of the union to a loss of membership, while requiring all new employees to become union members likely will result in a reduction in non-union members over time. An example of a representative maintenance of membership clause may read:

> All employees who on [date] are members of the Union in good standing in accordance with its constitution and by-laws, and all employees who become members after that date shall, as a condition of employment, maintain their membership in the union in good standing for the duration of the collective agreement in which this provision is incorporated.

See also: CLOSED SHOP, MODIFIED UNION SHOP, PREFEREN-TIAL HIRING, UNION SECURITY CLAUSE, UNION SHOP

MAJORITY REPRESENTATIVE

A union that is designated as the bargaining agent by a majority of the employees in a bargaining unit. In an election in which a REPRESENTA-TION VOTE is cast, a union may be selected by a majority of employees voting, although not necessarily by a majority of those employees within the unit.

MANAGEMENT RIGHTS

The body of rights relating to an employer's operations that do not require discussion with or concurrence by the union, or are not subject to collective bargaining. Such rights may include matters relating to hiring, production, manufacturing and sales. Many collective agreements include a management rights clause setting out or limiting these rights.

MEDIATION

A process of settling disputes, including labour disputes, whereby the disputing parties use a third party, called a mediator, to actively assist the parties in resolving outstanding issues between them. A mediator is normally a private individual chosen by the parties. A number of labour relations statutes permit arbitrators to "change hats" and act as a mediator where requested to do so by the parties.

Mediation is non-binding, conducted without prejudice and usually parties share the cost of the mediation. If mediation leads to an agreement, the agreement is then binding on the parties.

> *See also:* ARBITRATION, CONCILIATION, MEDIATION-ARBI-TRATION, PREVENTATIVE MEDIATION

MEDIATION-ARBITRATION

Using this process of settling labour disputes, the parties first attempt to settle their dispute by mediation, with the assistance of a mediator-arbitrator. If the parties are unable to settle their dispute using mediation, the mediator-arbitrator will then determine the grievance by arbitration. In other cases, mediation can occur after arbitration has already begun.

This process is also known as Med-Arb.

> *See also:* ARBITRATION, MEDIATION

M

MEMBERSHIP

With respect to trade unions, membership is the status of being a member in a trade union. A member is a person who has applied to be part of the trade union, and who has paid to the union an amount for initiation fees or monthly dues. In certification applications, proof of membership is required in order to establish the necessary percentage of support for the union.

MERGER OF BARGAINING AGENTS

If two or more trade unions merge or amalgamate, the new trade union becomes a successor union, which may be deemed to have acquired the rights, privileges, and duties of the predecessor union or unions.

See also: SUCCESSOR RIGHTS, SUCCESSOR UNION

MODIFIED UNION SHOP

An establishment in which the employer and the union have agreed that all current members of the union, and those who join later, must remain union members if they wish to retain their jobs. Joining the union may be compulsory with respect to new employees under a modified union shop. Workers who did not belong to the union at the time of the original agreement are not compelled to join the union. A maintenance of membership clause in a collective agreement results in a modified union shop.

See also: MAINTENANCE OF MEMBERSHIP CLAUSE, UNION SHOP

MULTI-EMPLOYER BARGAINING

Multi-employer bargaining, or association bargaining, is collective bargaining between a union and a group or association of employers.

N

NEGOTIATION

Discussions between labour and management representatives in an effort to conclude a collective agreement, or resolve an issue that arises between the parties during the term of a collective agreement. The parties to the negotiation are called negotiators or negotiating parties.

NOTICE TO BARGAIN

Written notice, given either by a certified trade union or by the employer whose employees are represented by the trade union, to the other party of the intention to bargain with a view to concluding a collective agreement. Once notice to bargain has been served, a failure by the other party to meet and bargain in good faith may lead to complaints of unfair labour practices. Failure of a trade union to serve notice to bargain on an employer once the union has been certified as the bargaining agent for a unit of employees may result in an application to a labour relations board for the termination of its bargaining rights.

> *See also:* COLLECTIVE AGREEMENT, DUTY TO BARGAIN IN GOOD FAITH

NO-UNION VOTE

In a representation vote, a choice on the ballot indicating that the employee does not wish to be represented by any trade union or council of trade unions listed on the ballot.

O

OPEN SEASON

A period of time during which trade unions other than the one who negotiated the current collective agreement may apply for certification, or where employees may apply for DECERTIFICATION of the existing trade union as their representative. Generally, it is defined in labour legislation to occur around the period where a current collective agreement is about to expire.

OPEN SHOP

A workplace where union membership is not required as a condition of securing or retaining employment.

> *See also:* CLOSED SHOP, MAINTENANCE-OF-MEMBERSHIP, PREFERENTIAL HIRING, RAND FORMULA, UNION SECURITY CLAUSE, UNION SHOP

O

P

PENSION PLAN

An arrangement to provide definite sums of money for payment to employees following retirement. They are governed by pension benefits legislation. Some examples of pension plans include:

- **Career-earnings plan**: employee accumulates each year a unit of pension equal to a percentage of earnings;

- **Contributory plan**: financed by both the employer and the employees;

- **Defined-benefit plan**: the size of the monthly retirement pension is fixed according to a benefit formula and varies with the employee's length of service, wage level, or both;

- **Final-earnings plan**: pension is based on the length of service and average earnings for a stated period just before retirement;

- **Flat-rate plan**: pays a given amount to all eligible employees regardless of wage level or years of service;

- **Funded plans**: paid from an accumulated fund, such as an insured plan where the actual pension payments are made by the insurance company;

- **Defined Contribution** or **Money-purchase plan**: employer contributes a certain amount of money each year and allocates it among covered employees, the pension of each being determined by the annuity which may be purchased on the retirement date by the total amount of money credited to his account;

- **Non-contributory plan**: pension is financed solely by the employer;

- **Pay-as-you-go plan**: employer pays benefits and operating costs from current earnings, rather than from a fund, contrary to pension benefits legislation in many jurisdictions which require advance funding of pensions;

- **Uniform-benefit plan**: provides a flat amount of pension to the employee after she fulfils certain age and service requirements; and

- **Unilateral plans**: initiated, financed and operated solely by management or a union, apart from collective bargaining.

PETITION

A form containing signatures of employees indicating a lack of support for a trade union. A petition may be filed as evidence before a labour relations board to demonstrate support for a decertification application by employees.

See also: COUNTER-PETITION, DECERTIFICATION

PICKET LINE

A collection of workers, known as pickets, who patrol a place of business dispensing information to the public, or to other workers. This may include information about the existence of a labour dispute, a union's desire to represent the employees, working conditions for non-union employees, or an attempt to persuade and influence employees to not enter the premises or do business with the employer.

See also: PICKETING

PICKETING

An organized effort by people, often carrying placards, in a public place at, or close to, an employer's place of business. Picketing activity can range from one or two people carrying placards, to large numbers of people standing outside the employer's business causing difficulties for people who wish to enter or exit the premises. Picketing may even extend to consumer boycotts and political demonstrations. Picketers convey information to the public through the use of handbills, arm bands, placards, sandwich boards or sound trucks, and the information may include such things as setting out the issues in a labour dispute, attempting to persuade workers to join a strike or join the union, or discouraging customers from buying or using the employer's goods or services. Picketing usually occurs at the employer's place of business, although it potentially can occur at other premises that may or may not be related in some way to the employer. A broad range of activity will constitute picketing, and it is seen as one of the most effective forms of expression available to unions in order to pressure employers in labour relations disputes.

The main purposes of picketing include: conveying information about a labour dispute in order to gain support for its cause from other workers,

P

clients of the employer, or the general public; and placing economic and social pressure on the employer, its suppliers, and customers.

> *See also:* ALLIED PICKETING DOCTRINE, ALLY, BOYCOTT, CONSUMER LEAFLETING, PICKET LINE, PRIMARY PICK-ETING, SECONDARY PICKETING

PLACE OF EMPLOYMENT

Any site or place where an employer operates or does any thing forming part of the operation of the business, as well as any place where an employee of the employer carries on the business of the employer.

PREFERENTIAL HIRING

A system of hiring employees where the employer agrees to hire only union members as long as they are available. If no union members are available, however, then non-union workers may be employed and these non-union members are not required to join the union. Frequently, a qualification is added to a preferential hiring clause that, in the event of layoffs, all non-union employees be laid off first.

The general effect of a preferential hiring agreement is that it encourages union membership and prevents, as far as possible, the employment of non-union workers. A preferential hiring clause may read:

> In hiring new persons, management agrees to give preference to a person or persons who are members of [a specified] Union, provided that person or persons have the ability to do the work to be performed at the normal speed, quality and cost. All new employees shall be on probation for thirty (30) days. When it becomes necessary for the company to reduce the force in a department, employees who are not affiliated with the Union, or whose membership has for any reason lapsed, shall be laid off before there are any other lay-offs, provided, however, that the Union member retained can do the work at approximately the same cost and quality. Where there is no choice in relation to the work performed or Union membership, strict seniority will prevail.

> *See also:* CLOSED SHOP, MAINTENANCE-OF-MEMBERSHIP, UNION SECURITY CLAUSE, UNION SHOP

PRE-HEARING VOTE

Upon an application for certification, a trade union may request that a pre-hearing representation vote be taken, prior to a determination by the labour relations board of the appropriate bargaining unit. In order for the pre-hearing vote to take place, the trade union must demonstrate that it has sufficient support for the application.

PREVENTATIVE MEDIATION

Mediation by a neutral third party during the closed period of a collective agreement to assist in resolving contentious problems before they reach the bargaining table.

See also: MEDIATION

PRIMARY PICKETING

Picketing that occurs at the place of business of the employer of the picketing employees.

See also: PICKETING, SECONDARY PICKETING

PROFESSIONAL STRIKEBREAKER

A person who is not involved in the labour dispute, whose primary purpose is to prevent, obstruct, interfere with, restrain or disrupt the exercise of any right in anticipation of or during a lawful strike. Some Canadian labour relations statutes prohibit the use of professional strikebreakers.

See also: REPLACEMENT WORKER, SCAB, STRIKEBREAKER

PROJECT AGREEMENT

In the construction industry in Ontario, employers and construction unions can negotiate specific agreements on terms and conditions of employment for major industrial projects within the industrial, commercial and institutional sector, which are separate from province-wide construction agreements. Non-construction work may be included in these agreements, and more than one project may be included.

P

PROVINCE-WIDE AGREEMENT

Within the industrial, commercial and institutional sector of the construction industry, a collective agreement between an employer's association and an employee bargaining agent which is binding upon all unions affiliated with the employee bargaining agent, and upon all employers under the employer's association with whom the union holds bargaining rights for their employees.

See also: CONSTRUCTION INDUSTRY, PROJECT AGREEMENT, RESIDENTIAL CONSTRUCTION INDUSTRY BARGAINING

R

RAND FORMULA

In 1946, Mr. Justice Rand was appointed an arbitrator in a dispute between the Ford Motor Company in Windsor, Ontario, and the International Union, United Automobile, Aircraft and Agricultural Implement Workers of America. In his decision resolving this matter, Rand developed the Rand Formula as a new form of union security. This formula provides for an employer to deduct union dues from all employees in a bargaining unit, whether or not they are members of the union. Since all workers in a bargaining unit benefit from a union-negotiated contract, the Rand formula stipulates that all employees should pay union dues as a condition of continuing employment, even if they decide not to join the union as members.

All jurisdictions have legislation in place requiring the check-off of union dues, either in accordance with a collective agreement, or an employee assignment authorizing the employer to deduct union dues from his or her pay.

See also: CHECK-OFF, UNION DUES

RATIFICATION VOTE

Formal approval of terms negotiated in a collective agreement by vote of the affected union members, as well as employers or employer associations. The ratification validates the agreement entered into between the employer and the union, on behalf of all employees in the bargaining unit.

RECOGNITION

Employer acceptance of a union as the exclusive bargaining representative for the employees in a bargaining unit.

REFUSAL TO BARGAIN

Refusal by an employer or union to negotiate a collective agreement or part thereof with the other party.

See also: COLLECTIVE BARGAINING

REINSTATEMENT

Re-employment of an employee by reason of an agreement, or an order of an arbitrator, an arbitration panel or a labour relations board directing an employer to re-employ a dismissed, suspended, demoted or transferred employee to his former job. For example, an employer may be required by an arbitration award to reinstate an employee who was dismissed without just cause.

Also, when a strike or lockout ends, any employee who was affected by the dispute is generally entitled to be reinstated in employment in preference to any replacement workers hired to do their work during the strike or lockout.

See also: ARBITRATION AWARD, LOCKOUT, REPLACEMENT WORKERS, STRIKE

RELATED EMPLOYER

See: SINGLE EMPLOYER STATUS

RELIGIOUS OBJECTION

In an agreement with a union security clause, some employees may be exempt from joining the union or from paying union dues, based on their religious beliefs. If compulsory dues check-off is in place, labour relations legislation may require that an employer remit the dues that are deducted from the employee's wages to be given to a charity agreed upon by the employee and the union, instead of being given to the union.

See also: UNION SECURITY, UNION SECURITY CLAUSE

R

REPLACEMENT WORKER

A worker who is hired to do the work of an employee who is on strike or locked out. Questions often arise about the rights of replacement workers to work, and to vote, compared to the rights of the striking employees that they replace.

For example, the use of replacement workers is specifically prohibited in British Columbia's *Labour Relations Act*. According to that Act, employers may not utilize the services of someone who (a) is hired after the earlier of the date notice to start collective bargaining is given and the date bargaining actually begins; (b) ordinarily works at another of the employer's places of business; (c) is transferred after the earlier of the notice to bargain and the start of bargaining to the location where the strike or lockout is occurring; or (d) is employed by the employer, in order to perform the work of an employee who is locked out or on strike.

See also: SCAB, STRIKEBREAKER

REPRESENTATION VOTE

A vote ordered by a labour relations board to determine whether employees in an appropriate bargaining unit wish to have a particular union represent them as their bargaining agent.

See also: BARGAINING AGENT, BARGAINING UNIT

RESIDENTIAL CONSTRUCTION INDUSTRY BARGAINING

In Ontario, there are special provisions in the *Labour Relations Act* dealing with the residential construction industry in certain areas of the province.

The affected areas in Ontario include the residential construction sectors of the City of Toronto, the Regional Municipalities of Halton, Peel, York and Durham, and the County of Simcoe. Under these provisions, all new and renewed collective agreements are deemed to be three years long, and all expire at the same time. The affected parties may only engage in strikes or lockouts at specific periods, and parties may jointly agree to refer issues relating to the collective agreement to arbitration. The Director of Labour Management Services in the province is also required to convene a meeting at least twice a year, where representatives of employers or employers' organizations and trade unions or councils of trade unions can meet to discuss collective bargaining and labour relations issues in this specialized industry.

See also: CONSTRUCTION INDUSTRY

RETROACTIVE PAY

Delayed payment of part of the wages earned during a particular period, where the delay is caused by negotiated wage increases dating back earlier than the date they were agreed upon.

RIGHT OF ASSOCIATION

See: FREEDOM OF ASSOCIATION

RIGHTS ARBITRATION

An arbitration process where the parties to a collective agreement submit their differences arising from the interpretation, application, administration or alleged violation of the agreement to an arbitrator or board of arbitration. The arbitration process replaces the right to strike or lockout during the term of the collective agreement.

See also: ARBITRATION, COMPULSORY ARBITRATION, EXPE-DITED ARBITRATION, INTEREST ARBITRATION, VOLUN-TARY ARBITRATION

S

SCAB

A pejorative term for a worker who refuses to join his or her co-workers in a strike. Sometimes, this term is also applied to members of a non-striking union who pass through a striking union's picket line in order to get to their work.

See also: REPLACEMENT WORKER, STRIKEBREAKER

SECONDARY PICKETING

Picketing that occurs at a place other than the business premises of the employer. Secondary picketing, like primary picketing, will likely be allowed unless the picketers engage in behaviour that is illegal.

Historically, the right to picket at secondary locations was limited. Unions have the right to freely express their views on the conditions of their employment, and to provide information to the public about their situation. But

S

this right to freedom of expression may come in conflict with the rights of innocent third parties to engage in economic activity completely separate from the particular labour dispute at issue. Some courts found that any secondary picketing was not allowed at all, while other courts expanded the definition of primary picketing to include locations that were not necessarily the primary workplace of the employees, companies with the same parent company as the company at issue, or companies who had *allied* themselves with the initial employer. Allied companies could include employers who were assisting the employer being picketed in carrying on business during the labour dispute. Currently, in the absence of any legislative restrictions, secondary picketing may be found to be acceptable at almost any secondary location, unless the picketers are engaged in illegal behaviour.

See also: ALLIED PICKETING DOCTRINE, COMMON-SITE PICKETING, PICKETING, PRIMARY PICKETING

SENIORITY

Length of an employee's service with a particular company. Seniority may provide preference or precedence in position for an employee over other employees in a similar situation. Employees with the greatest seniority are generally granted preference with respect to layoffs, and are often given certain advantages with respect to promotion, and the selection of vacation days. Specifically, in an unionized environment, job seniority may require that the worker with the most years of service with the company will be the first to be considered for a promotion within a range of jobs subject to seniority, and will be the last chosen to be laid off. This proceeds down the line to the newest employee with the least amount of seniority with the company.

See also: BUMPING

SHIFT

The work period of a group of employees in a company that has different groups working different periods of time during the same day.

For example, a company may have a shift running from 8 a.m. to 4 p.m., a shift from 4 p.m. to 12 a.m., and a shift from 12 a.m. to 8 a.m.

See also: SPLIT SHIFT, SWING SHIFT

SHOP STEWARD

See: UNION STEWARD

SINGLE EMPLOYER STATUS

A labour relations board may declare that two or more employers operating associated or related businesses, undertakings or other activities having common control or direction are a single employer. The declaration of single employer status will only be granted to preserve existing bargaining rights, and not to expand or create new bargaining rights, as an alternative to the normal certification process.

See also: AFFILIATED COMPANIES

SPLIT SHIFT

A division of an employee's daily working time into two or more working periods, in order to meet peak needs of the employer. As a result, there will be a break of several hours between shifts for an employee.

See also: SHIFT, SWING SHIFT

STATUTORY FREEZE PERIOD

Many jurisdictions have legislative provisions that prohibit an employer from altering employment conditions, such as hours of work or wage increases, when either an APPLICATION FOR CERTIFICATION has been filed, or NOTICE TO BARGAIN has been given by the trade union. This statutory freeze period requires the employer to carry on business as usual, as if the certification application or notice to bargain had not been made.

STRIKE

A cessation of work, a refusal to work or to continue work, a slow down, or other concerted activity by employees in combination or in accordance with a common understanding in order to compel an employer to agree to specific terms or conditions of employment. Strikes are usually seen by trade unions as a last resort, when collective bargaining and all other means have failed to obtain the demands of the employees from the employer. Except in very specific cases, strikes are legal only when a collective agreement is not in force.

There are many different types of strikes, including:

- **Economic strike**: a strike to force changes in wages, hours, or other working conditions;

Labour

S

- **Illegal strike**: a strike during the term of operation of a collective agreement, or prohibited by labour relations legislation;

- **Industry-wide strike**: a strike by all the organized workers in a particular industry;

- **Jurisdictional strike**: a strike resulting from a jurisdictional dispute between two unions;

- **Recognition strike**: a strike to compel acknowledgement of a union by management as the bargaining agent for a group of workers;

- **Rotating or hit-and-run strike**: a strike organized as a series of surprise short-term work stoppages at various locations in a firm or industry, so that only part of the employees stop work at any given time;

- **Secondary strike**: a strike called against one employer with a view to influencing or furthering a strike by employees of another employer;

- **Sympathetic strike**: a concerted work stoppage by workers not directly involved in a labour dispute, as an attempt to demonstrate labour solidarity and to exert indirect pressure on the other employee's management; or

- **Wildcat, outlaw, or unauthorized strike**: a strike that is launched without the consent of union officials, and which violates the collective agreement, or a strike by a minority of the workers in a plant or bargaining unit; such a strike is usually a reaction to a specific problem in the workplace, rather than a planned action.

See also: LOCKOUT, WORK STOPPAGE

STRIKE VOTE

A vote conducted among employees in the bargaining unit on the question of whether or not the employees should go out on strike.

STRIKEBREAKER

A worker who is hired during a strike primarily for the purpose of defeating a strike, or who continues to work during a strike. By performing the job duties of the people on strike, they may weaken or break the strike.

See also: PROFESSIONAL STRIKEBREAKER, REPLACEMENT WORKER, SCAB

SUBCONTRACTOR

A company or business who performs for another company or business part of the work which the latter has contracted to do.

SUCCESSOR EMPLOYER

An employer who purchases a business and thereby becomes bound to a collective agreement. Where an employer who is bound by, or is a party to, a collective agreement with a trade union sells the business, the person to whom the business has been sold is bound by the collective agreement as if the new employer had been a party to it from the beginning, until the Board otherwise declares.

SUCCESSOR RIGHTS

The rights, privileges, and duties of a union or employer that continue to apply following a merger, sale, amalgamation, or transfer of jurisdiction of a company.

See also: MERGER OF BARGAINING AGENTS

SUCCESSOR UNION

A union that succeeds another by reason of a merger, amalgamation or transfer of jurisdiction. The new union then acquires the rights, privileges and duties of the predecessor union.

SWING SHIFT

A shift that overlaps other shifts. Sometimes, people who work swing shifts are assigned special tasks such as maintenance, while at other times they may be used as a relief shift for regular shift employees.

See also: SHIFT, SPLIT SHIFT

T

TECHNOLOGICAL CHANGE

An introduction by the employer of a change in equipment, material, or manner of carrying on the work, undertaking or business of the employer.

This includes the introduction of labour-saving machinery, or new production techniques. Such change may result in manpower reductions, also known as technological unemployment. As a result, depending on the language in the collective agreement, the collective agreement between the trade union and the employer may be reopened to negotiation once the employer announces a substantial technological change in the workplace.

See also: AUTOMATION

TORT

A wrongful act, occurring outside of any contractual agreement, where the injured party may bring a legal action for damages in order to compensate her for her injuries.

TRADE UNION

An organization that represents employees in their relations with their employers. An organization will not be considered a union if it is dominated or controlled by an employer or an employer's group. There is usually a written constitution, rules or by-laws for the organization, setting out the objects, purposes, and conditions of membership. Finances for the organization are obtained through dues paid by the employees as a condition of membership in the union.

In many cases, a trade union organized around either craft or industry lines has a national or central office which determines policy for the union as a whole, administers the union's finances, maintains affiliations with outside bodies such as Labour Federations, ensures harmonious relations between the various branches of the union, and provides legal, financial and public relations expertise to the various branches. They usually hold regular conventions of delegates from each of their local unions, where general policy for the organization is set and at which officers are elected. It is at the branch, or local level that unions carry out their day-to-day work of conducting membership drives, negotiating collective agreements, and processing grievances.

See also: INCUMBENT UNION

TRIBUNAL

A body created by legislation which exercises various limited functions of a judicial nature, although its members are not judges. The tribunal must apply the law, and arrive at decisions while observing the principles of natural justice. A LABOUR RELATIONS BOARD is an example of a tribunal.

U

UNFAIR LABOUR PRACTICE

A practice on the part of either union or management that violates provisions of applicable labour relations law. Activities by employers or unions that are considered "unfair" include acts of intimidation, coercion, interference, discrimination, or a failure to bargain in good faith.

> *See also:* ANTI-UNION ANIMUS, DUTY OF FAIR REPRESENTATION, DUTY TO BARGAIN IN GOOD FAITH, GOOD FAITH BARGAINING

UNION

> *See:* TRADE UNION

UNION ACTIVITY

Any activity related to a union. The term generally refers to activities that have as their object the organization of workers and the carrying out of union objectives.

UNION DUES

Periodic payments by union members of money to a union to provide financial support.

> *See also:* CHECK-OFF, RAND FORMULA

UNION OFFICERS

Members of the union who are elected to make decisions about union policy and day-to-day operations of the union. The responsibilities of a union officer are outlined by the union constitution and by-laws.

Labour

U

UNION SECURITY

The security that a union has in its relationship with its members.

Threats to union security may result from anti-union activities by employers, active competition from other unions, or lack of internal support from the workers within the union. Certain anti-union activities are prohibited by legislation across Canada, which define and prohibit unfair labour practices by employers. Competition between unions is regulated by statute through provisions for legal recognition of unions as exclusive bargaining agents. As a result, lack of internal support is the most serious threat to union security. Initially, a union will go through the process of certification, where a labour relations board designates a particular union as the sole bargaining agent for all employees within a particular bargaining unit. Once certified, the union has the exclusive right to bargain collectively with the employer on behalf of the employees within the unit. At this point, unions may secure support from their members by having a union security clause.

UNION SECURITY CLAUSE

A provision in a collective agreement that fixes the position of the union to represent employees, and the relationship of the union to the workers and their jobs. Some examples of union security clauses include CLOSED SHOP, UNION SHOP, PREFERENTIAL HIRING and MAINTENANCE-OF-MEMBERSHIP clauses. The RAND FORMULA is also a form of union security.

UNION SHOP

A form of union security where every worker covered by the collective agreement must become and remain a member of the union. In a union shop, the employer is able to hire non-union workers, but all employees are required to become union members as a condition of employment. This is one of the most popular forms of union security clauses. A typical union shop clause may provide that:

> All employees in the bargaining unit must become and remain members in good standing of the Union within thirty (30) days of the signing of the agreement as a condition of employment. All new employees shall become members in good standing of the Union within thirty (30) days of employ-

ment and remain in good standing as a condition of employment.

> *See also:* CLOSED SHOP, MAINTENANCE-OF-MEMBERSHIP, PREFERENTIAL HIRING, UNION SECURITY CLAUSE

UNION STEWARD

Person elected to represent workers in a particular local union, shop or department. She may be responsible for collecting dues, soliciting for new members, announcing meetings to other employees, and receiving, investigating and dealing with grievances brought by union members.

UNIT

> *See:* BARGAINING UNIT

V

VOLUNTARY ARBITRATION

The parties to a collective agreement may agree to resolve a dispute arising outside the collective agreement by submitting to arbitration, even though they are not required by law to submit that dispute to arbitration.

> *See also:* ARBITRATION, COMPULSORY ARBITRATION, EXPEDITED ARBITRATION, INTEREST ARBITRATION, RIGHTS ARBITRATION

VOLUNTARY RECOGNITION

An employer and a trade union may agree that the employer shall recognize the trade union as the exclusive bargaining agent for the employees in a defined bargaining unit. As a result, no formal certification process is required.

> *See also:* BARGAINING UNIT, CERTIFICATION, REPRESENTATION VOTE

Labour

V

W

WORK STOPPAGE

Any cessation of normal business operations resulting from a strike or lockout. Every collective agreement must contain a provision for the settlement of disputes without a work stoppage during the term of a collective agreement.

See also: LOCKOUT, STRIKE

WORK TO RULE

A practice where workers obey to the letter all laws and rules pertaining to their work, thereby effecting a slowdown. The practice also frequently involves a refusal to perform duties which, though related, are not explicitly included in the job description. It is a technique used by a union or group of employees to compel an employer to agree to desired terms or conditions of employment.

See also: JOB ACTION, STRIKE

Z

ZIPPER CLAUSE

A provision in a collective agreement that may not be renegotiated by the parties to the collective agreement while the provision is still in force. It must be expressly stipulated as such in the collective agreement. The zipper clause is intended to prevent the employer or the union from demanding renewed negotiations during the life of the agreement.

HUMAN RIGHTS

A

ACCOMMODATION

Efforts to assist employees to deal with, or overcome, the discriminatory effects of a workplace rule, practice or barrier that has an adverse effect on employees identified by a particular ground of discrimination, such as disability. The concept of accommodation recognizes that jobs may be performed effectively in a variety of ways, and that equal treatment is not the same thing as identical treatment. Practically speaking, it involves an exemption from, or an adjustment to, general policies and facilities for an individual with particular needs or requirements at work.

Human rights laws in all jurisdictions across Canada require employers to provide reasonable accommodation to employees. The accommodation process is an individualized process that requires careful consideration of the individual person and her needs. Accommodation may occur at any stage of the employment relationship, such as during the selection process, in the terms and conditions of employment, or how the job is performed. It is most often associated with persons with disabilities. For example, an employer may provide a ramp for a person in a wheelchair, or modify an employee's job duties to accord with her specific needs. Accommodation may also encompass women who bear a disproportionate burden of child-care responsibilities being granted flexible working hours, or allowing persons with religious beliefs that prevent them from working on certain days to

123

change their shift schedules. Unions and employees also have a duty to assist with accommodation.

See also: BONA *FIDE* OCCUPATIONAL REQUIREMENT, DIS-CRIMINATION, DUTY TO ACCOMMODATE, UNDUE HARD-SHIP

ADVERSE EFFECT DISCRIMINATION

A practice, policy or rule that appears to be neutral on its face, but inadvertently has a discriminatory effect on a particular individual or group. In a case where adverse effect discrimination can be shown, the policy or standard can remain in place, but the individual or group of affected employees may be required to be accommodated by the employer, unless the employer can demonstrate that there is a rational connection between the job and the specific requirement, and that any further accommodation would result in undue hardship for the employer.

Adverse effect discrimination is also known as indirect discrimination.

See also: DIRECT DISCRIMINATION, DISCRIMINATION, SYSTEMIC DISCRIMINATION

AFFIRMATIVE ACTION

Action designed to prevent, eliminate or reduce disadvantages that are or are likely to be suffered by a group of individuals, when the disadvantages are based on or are related to the race, national ╱ ethnic origin, colour, religion, age, sex, marital status, or physical ╱ mental handicap of members of that group. It is often aimed at improving employment opportunities with respect to the affected group.

AFFIRMATIVE ACTION PLAN

A written program to actively eliminate employment standards and practices that tend to discriminate on the grounds of race, creed, sex, or national origin.

See also: AFFIRMATIVE ACTION

AGE DISCRIMINATION

An individual who has been refused employment or continued employment on the basis of age, or during the course of employment has been treated adversely in relation to another employee because of his age, may be found to have been discriminated against on the basis of age.

 The federal government, Manitoba, Nova Scotia, Prince Edward Island, Quebec, Northwest Territories, Nunavut and Yukon do not provide a minimum and maximum age limit in their human rights legislation. In Alberta age is defined as 18 years and older; in New Brunswick it is 19 years and older; in British Columbia and Newfoundland and Labrador age is limited to 19-65 years; while in Ontario and Saskatchewan it is limited to 18-65 years. Given these age limits, some policies or practices may not be discriminatory, even though they differentiate on the basis of age. An example would be mandatory retirement practices in Ontario or Saskatchewan, where an employee is required to retire once he reaches a pre-set age, normally 65 years or older. Mandatory retirement policies in some jurisdictions have been found to be acceptable in various court challenges under the *Charter,* even though they distinguish on the basis of age. It should be noted that some jurisdictions have eliminated, or are planning to eliminate, mandatory retirement policies entirely.

 See also: RETIREMENT

ALCOHOLISM

Addiction to alcohol. It is a chronic disease characterized by an inability to control drinking. Alcoholism is considered a disability under human rights legislation. An employer may be required to accommodate an employee suffering from alcoholism if the disease prevents the employee from performing her job, from attending work regularly, or otherwise being unable to meet the obligations of her job. Such accommodation may include offering counseling services, or providing access to treatment facilities.

 See also: DISABILITY, DRUG DEPENDENCE, MENTAL DISABILITY, PHYSICAL DISABILITY

ANALYSIS OF WORKFORCE

Under employment equity legislation, an employer may be required to look at its workforce in order to determine what percentage of its employees fall within the four targeted groups: women, Aboriginal peoples, visible minorities and persons with disabilities.

In Quebec, public, municipal, educational, health and social services bodies and institutions that employ 100 or more employees are required to con-

Human Rights

A

duct an analysis of their workforce to determine how many persons they employ that belong to the target groups. The analysis must indicate the number of members in each target group, the proportion represented by each target group in each type of occupation, the relevant recruitment area for the public body, and the required skills and experience necessary for each type of occupation.

See also: DESIGNATED GROUPS, EMPLOYMENT EQUITY

ANCESTRY

See: RACE

B

BOARD OF INQUIRY

See: HUMAN RIGHTS TRIBUNAL

BONA FIDE OCCUPATIONAL REQUIREMENT

An employment limitation that might otherwise be discriminatory under human rights legislation that is related in an objective sense to the performance of the employment concerned in that it is reasonably necessary to ensure the efficient and economical performance of the job without endangering the employee, other employees and the public. It must be imposed honestly and in good faith by the employer, and not for ulterior reasons aimed at defeating prohibitions against discrimination.

An employer may justify a workplace standard as a *bona fide* occupational requirement by establishing three things:

- The employer adopted the standard for a purpose rationally connected to the performance of the job;

- The employer adopted the particular standard in an honest and good faith belief that it was necessary to the fulfillment of that legitimate work-related purpose; and

• The standard is reasonably necessary to the accomplishment of the legitimate work related purpose.

See also: ACCOMMODATION, DISCRIMINATION, DUTY TO ACCOMMODATE, UNDUE HARDSHIP

C

CHARTER

The *Canadian Charter of Rights and Freedoms*, R.S.C. 1985 (Appendix II) (Constitution Act 1982, Part I of Schedule B to the Canada Act, 1982, c.11) sets out fundamental rights and freedoms for all Canadians. It is divided into six sections: Fundamental Freedoms, Democratic Rights, Mobility Rights, Legal Rights, Equality Rights and Language Rights.

The Charter only applies to relations between individuals and the government, specifically Parliament, provincial legislatures, and federal and provincial government. It does not apply to relations between private individuals, such as relations between non-government employers and employees. Human rights codes and the common law regulate these relationships, although it should be noted that all legislation must conform to the Charter.

CHILDBIRTH

See: SEX

COLOUR

See: RACE

CONTRACTOR'S PROGRAM

Under the Federal Contractors Program, federal contractors who employ 100 or more persons, and who wish to bid on goods or services contracts for the federal government worth $200,000 or more, must achieve and maintain a fair and representative workforce. The requirements under the program are similar to those required under federal employment equity legislation, although the program is neither legislated nor mandatory except for persons who wish to do business with the federal government.

Human Rights

C

The Quebec government also has a contract compliance program that is similar to the federal program. The Quebec compliance program applies to both contractors and subcontractors who have more than 100 employees and who bid on government grants or contracts worth at least $100,000.

See also: EMPLOYMENT EQUITY

CREED

Many human rights statutes prohibit discrimination because of "creed". The term creed has been interpreted to be essentially equivalent to RELIGION or religious beliefs.

CRIMINAL CONVICTION

Some jurisdictions prohibit an employer from discriminating against employees because they have been convicted of a criminal offence. In some jurisdictions employers may discriminate against employees convicted of a criminal offence unless the employee has been pardoned. In other jurisdictions, discrimination is permitted only where the conviction is related to the employment or intended employment.

To determine if an offence is unrelated to particular employment, relevant factors are the employer's ability to carry on its business safely, the connection or relationship between the offence and the workplace, details of the offence, circumstances surrounding the charge, extenuating circumstances, length of time between the conviction and the employment decision, employee's employment history, employee's age at the time of the offence, and rehabilitation efforts.

D

DESIGNATED GROUPS

For the purposes of employment equity, the four designated groups are women, aboriginal peoples, persons with disabilities and members of visible minorities. These groups historically have faced higher rates of unemployment, underemployment and employment discrimination in the workforce.

See also: EMPLOYMENT EQUITY

DIRECT DISCRIMINATION

Practices, policies or rules which are discriminatory on their face. For example, a requirement that only males may apply for a position as a fire fighter would be viewed as direct discrimination against women. Such a policy, practice or rule will automatically be struck down, unless an employer can demonstrate that the standard is a *bona fide* occupational requirement for the job, and that it cannot accommodate the needs of female employees.

> *See also:* ADVERSE EFFECT DISCRIMINATION, DISCRIMINATION, SYSTEMIC DISCRIMINATION

DISABILITY

A condition which impairs a person's ability to carry out the requirements of daily life. It includes any previous or existing mental or physical disability, including a dependence on alcohol or drugs. Discrimination on the basis of a disability constitutes a human rights violation.

> *See also:* ALCOHOLISM, DRUG DEPENDENCE, MENTAL DISABILITY, PHYSICAL DISABILITY

DISCRIMINATION

Unequal treatment of persons, whether through hiring or employment rules, or through variation of the conditions of employment. Discrimination because of a personal or group characteristic such as sex, age, marital status, race, or creed is illegal under human rights legislation.

In all parts of Canada, discrimination in employment on the grounds of race, colour, religion or creed, age, sex, marital status, mental or physical disability is prohibited. In most parts of the country, discrimination is also prohibited with respect to national or ethnic origin, place of origin, family status, ancestry, and sexual orientation. In some parts of the country, discrimination in employment is prohibited based on criminal conviction, political beliefs, language, social origin or conditions, or place of residence.

> *See also:* ADVERSE EFFECT DISCRIMINATION, DIRECT DISCRIMINATION, SYSTEMIC DISCRIMINATION

Human Rights

D

DIVERSITY PROGRAM

A non-legislated version of employment equity, that focuses broadly on creating an inclusive, welcoming workplace for people of all backgrounds.

　　See also: EMPLOYMENT EQUITY

DRUG DEPENDENCE

Chemical dependence on a drug or use of a drug for purposes for which it was not medically intended, resulting in the compulsive use of a substance despite possibly severe negative consequences. Drug dependence has been recognized as a form of disability, so an employer may be required to accommodate an employee suffering from drug dependence if the disease prevents the employee from performing his job, or from attending work regularly, or otherwise being unable to meet the obligations of his job.

　　See also: ALCOHOLISM, DISABILITY, MENTAL DISABILITY, PHYSICAL DISABILITY

DUTY TO ACCOMMODATE

Employers and unions are required to make every reasonable effort, short of undue hardship, to accommodate an employee falling under a protected ground of discrimination in the relevant human rights legislation. Accommodating employees in the workplace is a duty under all human rights laws across Canada. Based on caselaw, employers will often have a duty to accommodate even where this duty is not explicitly stated in the human rights legislation governing the employer.

Once an employee has demonstrated that he has been discriminated against in the workplace, an employer must show that the discriminatory standard is a *bona fide* occupational requirement for the job, and that the employee cannot be accommodated up to the point of undue hardship.

　　See also: ACCOMMODATION, *BONA FIDE* OCCUPATIONAL REQUIREMENT, DISCRIMINATION, UNDUE HARDSHIP

E

EMPLOYMENT EQUITY

A process of achieving the removal of all barriers to equal participation and treatment of employees, so that the internal composition of the workplace mirrors the makeup of the population from which the organization recruits. Women, members of visible minorities, persons with disabilities, and Aboriginal people face special barriers to equal access and treatment in employment. Under employment equity, employers must take proactive steps to identify their internal barriers to equality and remove them, by developing and implementing a detailed employment equity plan.

The federal government and Quebec are the only two jurisdictions in Canada with legislation in place dealing with employment equity in specific workplaces.

See also: ANALYSIS OF WORKFORCE, CONTRACTOR'S PROGRAM, DESIGNATED GROUPS, DIVERSITY PROGRAM, EMPLOYMENT SYSTEMS REVIEW

EMPLOYMENT SYSTEMS REVIEW

Employers covered by the federal *Employment Equity Act* are required to conduct a review of their employment systems, policies and practices, in order to identify employment barriers against persons in designated groups that result from those systems, policies and practices.

The systems reviewed should include those for

- recruiting, selecting and hiring employees;
- promotion and the movement of employees between occupational groups;
- training and development;
- termination of employment, including dismissals, resignations and retirement; and
- accommodation of the special needs of members of the designated groups.

See also: DESIGNATED GROUPS, EMPLOYMENT EQUITY

EQUAL PAY FOR EQUAL WORK

The principle that wage rates should be based on the job, rather than upon the sex, race, or any other personal characteristic of the worker, or upon other factors not related to his ability to perform. As a result, male and female employees should be paid the same wage for doing identical work. Legislation requiring equal pay for equal work exists in every province in

Human Rights

E

Canada either under human rights legislation, or provincial employment standards legislation.

See also: EQUAL PAY FOR SIMILAR OR SUBSTANTIALLY SIMILAR WORK, EQUAL PAY FOR WORK OF EQUAL VALUE, PAY EQUITY

EQUAL PAY FOR SIMILAR OR SUBSTANTIALLY SIMILAR WORK

This principle applies to situations where male and female employees may have different job titles, but perform substantially the same work. In determining whether work is the same or substantially the same, one must determine whether the work in question requires the same skill, effort, responsibility and working conditions. It has been used, for example, to compare nurses' aides to orderlies, and male janitor positions to female cleaner positions. Legislation requiring equal pay for substantially similar work exists in every jurisdiction in Canada, and equal pay complaints may be filed under human rights or employment standards legislation, depending on the jurisdiction.

See also: EQUAL PAY FOR EQUAL WORK, EQUAL PAY FOR WORK OF EQUAL VALUE, PAY EQUITY

EQUAL PAY FOR WORK OF EQUAL VALUE

The principle that wages should be based on the value of the work performed. Value of work is determined by a structured process, called job evaluation. Job characteristics such as skill, effort, responsibility and working conditions are given weighted values and employees performing work having similar total weighted value are paid equal wages without regard to type of work performed or differences in job descriptions.

The federal jurisdiction and Yukon's public sector have legislation requiring equal pay for work of equal value.

See also: EQUAL PAY FOR EQUAL WORK, EQUAL PAY FOR SIMILAR OR SUBSTANTIALLY SIMILAR WORK, PAY EQUITY

ETHNIC ORIGIN

See: RACE

F

FAIR EMPLOYMENT PRACTICES

The practice of employers or unions of offering workers equal employment opportunities regardless of race, national or ethnic origin, colour, religion, age, sex, marital status, handicap, or other characteristics.

FAIR WAGES

Defined by the federal *Fair Wages and Hours of Labour Act* as wages generally accepted as current for competent workmen in the district in which the work is being performed for the character or class of work in which such workmen are respectively engaged; but that in all cases such wages as are fair and reasonable.

FAMILY STATUS

The status of being in a parent-child relationship. It may also be defined as the status of being related to another person by blood, marriage or adoption. A child may include a son, daughter, stepson, stepdaughter, or an adopted child, while a parent may include a father, mother, stepfather, stepmother, or adoptive parent.

See also: MARITAL STATUS

FEDERAL CONTRACTOR'S PROGRAM

See: CONTRACTOR'S PROGRAM

FEMALE-DOMINATED CLASS

For the purposes of pay equity legislation, a job class within a work establishment or a bargaining unit in which a significant percentage of the members, usually 60 per cent or more, are female. It may also include a job class within a work establishment or a bargaining unit that is determined to be female, based on historical incumbency or gender stereotype.

See also: MALE-DOMINATED CLASS

Human Rights

F

FLEXIBLE WORK WEEK

See: FLEXTIME

FLEXTIME

A system providing workers with some freedom in deciding when they start and finish work, subject to the requirement that they are present during certain core hours, and fulfill a minimum attendance requirement each day. It is a variation, but not a reduction, in working hours that is intended to provide better time planning for employees and for the flow of work.

See also: WORK–LIFE BALANCE

FRINGE BENEFITS

Non-wage benefits, or premium payments and services provided by an employer to an employee in addition to regular wages and salaries. They include such things as paid vacations, pensions, health and welfare provisions, life insurance, hospitalization insurance, car allowance, fitness club membership, and other benefits.

See also: WORK–LIFE BALANCE

G

GENDER

See: SEX

GENDER WAGE GAP

The difference between the wages of female-dominated job classes within an employer organization and the wages of equally valued male-dominated job classes by a pay equity study, based on skill, effort, responsibility and working conditions.

See also: FEMALE-DOMINATED CLASS, MALE-DOMINATED CLASS, VALUE OF A JOB

GENDER PREDOMINANCE

A categorization of work in terms of whether it is performed predominantly by women or predominantly by men. In determining gender predominance for a particular job class within an organization, an employer must look at what percentage of employees within the class are male or female, the historical gender dominance for that job class, and any gender stereotypes for the work involved.

See also: FEMALE-DOMINATED CLASS, MALE-DOMINATED CLASS

GREEN-CIRCLED RATE

A wage rate that is lower than a wage rate that has been newly established as the result of a pay equity plan or a job evaluation plan.

See also: RED-CIRCLED RATE

H

HARASSMENT

Engaging in a course of vexatious comment or conduct that is known or ought reasonably to be known to be unwelcome. In the workplace, employees have the right to be free from harassment by the employer, employer's agent or other employees related to prohibited grounds of discrimination such as age, race, national or ethnic origin, colour, religion, sex, marital status, family status, and physical or mental disability.

A course of vexatious comment or conduct means that there is an observable pattern of behaviour, such as verbal comments or statements, actions, gestures, or physical contact. In determining whether such conduct is unwelcome, the issue is whether a reasonable person would realize that the conduct was unwelcome to the person complaining. So, even if the person who is engaging in harassing conduct believes that he "didn't mean anything" by his conduct, the complainant may be experiencing fear, stress, and other consequences as a result of the conduct.

Examples of comments or conduct that may be considered to be harassment include:

- Verbal abuse, threats or intimidation;

- Unwelcome remarks, jokes, comments, or innuendos about a person's gender, age, marital status, ethnic or national origin, religion, appearance, or any other area prohibited by a jurisdiction's human rights legislation;

- Displaying pornographic, racist, or other offensive or derogatory pictures;

- Practical jokes or other jokes which cause awkwardness or embarrassment;

- Unwelcome invitations or requests, whether indirect or explicit, or intimidation;

- Leering or other gestures;

- Unnecessary physical contact such as patting, pinching, touching or punching; or

- Physical assault, including sexual assault.

See also: RACIAL HARASSMENT, SEXUAL HARASSMENT

HUMAN RIGHTS

Rights protected under human rights legislation. They include the right to equal treatment in employment without discrimination on the basis of race, colour, national or ethnic origin, creed, sex, sexual orientation, age, marital status, disability, and other factors.

Every jurisdiction in Canada has human rights legislation in place prohibiting discriminatory practices in employment by employers, trade unions, employer or employee associations and employment agencies. Most human rights statutes also prohibit discrimination in the provision of services and in accommodation of premises. The main human rights legislation in Canada includes:

❏ Federal: *Canadian Human Rights Act,* R.S.C. 1985, c. H-6

❏ Alberta: *Human Rights, Citizenship and Multiculturalism Act,* R.S.A. 2000, C. H-14

❏ British Columbia: *Human Rights Code,* R.S.B.C. 1996, c. 210

❏ Manitoba: *Human Rights Code,* C.C.S.M. c. H175

❏ New Brunswick: *Human Rights Act,* R.S.N.B. 1973, c. H-11

❏ Newfoundland and Labrador: *Human Rights Code,* R.S.N. 1990, c. H-14

❏ Nova Scotia: *Human Rights Act,* R.S.N.S. 1989, c. 214

❑ Ontario: *Human Rights Code*, R.S.O. 1990, c. H.19

❑ Prince Edward Island: *Human Rights Act*, R.S.P.E.I. 1988, c. H-12

❑ Quebec: *Charter of Human Rights and Freedoms*, R.S.Q. 1977, c. C-12

❑ Saskatchewan: *Saskatchewan Human Rights Code*, S.S. 1979, c. S-24.1

❑ Northwest Territories and Nunavut: *Fair Practices Act*, R.S.N.W.T. 1988, c. F-2

❑ Yukon: *Human Rights Act*, S.Y.T. 1987, c. 3

HUMAN RIGHTS COMMISSION

All jurisdictions in Canada, except for British Columbia, have a human rights commission in place. In general, the role of the Commission is to administer the relevant human rights legislation, which may include investigating complaints of discrimination, referring complaints to the tribunal, education, research, and creating programs to help reduce or eliminate disadvantage for the groups covered under the legislation. The relevant human rights commissions in Canada include:

- **Canadian Human Rights Commission** — a Chief Commissioner and a Deputy Chief Commissioner, along with three to six full- or part-time members;

- **Alberta Human Rights and Citizenship Commission** — appointed members, with one being appointed chief commissioner;

- **Manitoba Human Rights Commission** — ten members, with one designated as the chairperson;

- **New Brunswick Human Rights Commission** — three or more members with one designated as chairperson;

- **Newfoundland and Labrador Human Rights Commission** — three or more appointed members, one of whom is the chairman;

- **Nova Scotia Human Rights Commission** — between three and twelve members, with one designated as the Chair of the Commission;

- **Ontario Human Rights Commission** — at least seven members, with one appointed chairman;

Human Rights

H

- **Prince Edward Island Human Rights Commission** — between three and nine members, with one designated as chair;

- **Quebec Commission des droits de la personne** — fifteen members, including the president and two vice-presidents;

- **Saskatchewan Human Rights Commission** — at least three members, with one designated Chief Commission, and one designated Deputy Chief Commissioner;

- **Yukon Human Rights Commission** — between three to five members.

HUMAN RIGHTS TRIBUNAL

A tribunal provided for under human rights legislation that is responsible for hearing and adjudicating inquiries into alleged cases of discrimination. In some jurisdictions, such as in New Brunswick, Newfoundland and Labrador, and Nova Scotia, these same functions are performed by Boards of Inquiry.

In most jurisdictions, complaints are brought before the tribunal or board by the appropriate human rights commission. Complaints may be heard by a single tribunal member, or by a panel of members. In British Columbia there is no commission, so the Human Rights Tribunal is responsible for processing, investigating, mediating and adjudicating all disputes.

I

INDIRECT DISCRIMINATION

See: ADVERSE EFFECT DISCRIMINATION

J

JOB CLASS

A class of positions within an organization that have similar duties and responsibilities, similar qualifications, filled by similar recruiting procedures, and the same compensation schedule, salary grade or range of salary rates. A job class may consist of a single position, or a single person doing a job within an organization. Once all of the classes within a company are determined, an employer can determine the gender predominance of each class, for the purposes of pay equity.

See also: GENDER PREDOMINANCE, PAY EQUITY

JOB-TO-JOB COMPARISON

A method of comparing male and female job classes for the purposes of determining pay equity within an organization. It is the most common type of job comparison, and in it each female job class is compared with a male job class of equal or comparable value.

See also: PAY EQUITY, PROPORTIONAL VALUE COMPARISON, PROXY COMPARISON, WAGE LINE COMPARISON

L

LANGUAGE

A prohibited ground of discrimination in Quebec, under its *Charter of Human Rights and Freedoms*.

LIE DETECTOR TEST

An analysis, examination, interrogation or test taken or performed by means of or in conjunction with a device, instrument or machine, whether mechanical, electrical, electromagnetic, electronic or otherwise, and that is taken or performed for the purpose of assessing or purporting to assess the credibility of a person.

New Brunswick and Ontario employment standards legislation provide employees with the right not to take a lie detector test.

M

MALE-DOMINATED CLASS

A job class within a work establishment or bargaining unit in which a significant percentage of the members are male. Generally, at least 60 per cent or more of the members are required to be male to be considered a

M

male-dominated class. Also, a job class may be determined to be male-dominated based on historical incumbency or gender stereotypes.

See also: FEMALE-DOMINATED CLASS

MARITAL STATUS

Includes the status of being engaged to be married, married, separated, divorced, widowed, or single. Marital status includes common-law relationships.

Discrimination on the basis of marital status is not allowed in any jurisdiction in Canada. Except in Saskatchewan, where it is specifically excluded by legislation, it can also include discrimination based on the fact that the employee is married to a particular person, rather than simply because of her status as a married person. For example, an employee who is fired because her spouse is suing her employer may attempt to claim discrimination on the basis of marital status.

See also: FAMILY STATUS

MENTAL DISABILITY

Any mental disorder, developmental disorder or learning disorder, regardless of its cause or duration. A number of mental conditions have been considered a disability for which accommodation by an employer will be required, including perceived mental disabilities. Specifically, depression, learning disabilities, and mental illness have been found to constitute mental disabilities, while alcohol and drug addictions have been found to be both a physical and a mental disability. Any rule, practice or procedure that treats an employee differently on the basis of his mental disability may constitute prohibited discrimination.

See also: ALCOHOLISM, DISABILITY, DRUG DEPENDENCE, MENTAL DISORDER, PHYSICAL DISABILITY

MENTAL DISORDER

A disorder of thought, perception, feeling or behaviour that impairs a person's judgment, capacity to recognize reality, ability to associate with others, or ability to meet the ordinary demands of life.

See also: MENTAL DISABILITY

N

NATIONAL ORIGIN

See: RACE

O

OBESITY

A condition where a person is significantly overweight. In some jurisdictions, obesity that can be shown to have been caused by a bodily injury, birth defect or illness may qualify as a physical disability, and therefore an obese person may be protected from discrimination because of his condition of obesity.

See also: DISABILITY, PHYSICAL DISABILITY

P

PAY EQUITY

An area of law requiring that employers pay employees in "female" jobs equally to employees in "male" jobs of the same value. Unlike equal pay provisions, that require an individual to file a complaint, pay equity is based on the assumption that wage discrimination against women is endemic to the economy and requires a broad and systemic remedy. Pay equity legislation does not simply prohibit wage discrimination, but places positive obligations on employers to look over their pay equity practices and ensure that they are in compliance.

Pay equity is a complicated process and is governed by the relevant legislation. The basic components of all pay equity processes, though, include:

1. Identify the unit for which the pay equity plan will be developed;

2. Identify the job classes for comparison purposes;

3. Identify female and male job classes;

4. Assess the value of jobs using a gender-neutral system;

Human Rights

P

5. Compare male and female job classes, using various methods of comparison (job-to-job approach, wage-line approach or proxy comparisons, for example);

6. Identify where compensation adjustments are required, or where there are disparities in compensation that violate pay equity legislation;

7. Develop a pay equity plan setting out how the differences in compensation will be remedied; and

8. Make compensation adjustments, often over a period of years.

Within each jurisdiction that deals with pay equity, some limits may be placed on which employers are affected by pay equity legislation. In the public sector, pay equity is legislatively mandated in Manitoba, New Brunswick, Newfoundland and Labrador, Nova Scotia, Ontario, Prince Edward Island, Quebec, and the federal jurisdiction. In the private sector, only the federal jurisdiction, Ontario and Quebec have passed legislation requiring employers to implement pay equity. The federal legislation differs from Ontario and Quebec in that it is complaints-based.

See also: JOB-TO-JOB COMPARISON, PROPORTIONAL VALUE COMPARISON, PROXY COMPARISON, WAGE LINE COMPARISON

PAY EQUITY PLAN

A plan setting out how differences in compensation that violate pay equity legislation will be remedied. Generally, a pay equity plan should contain:

- a description of the unit for which the pay equity plan has been developed;

- an identification of all of the job classes which formed the basis of comparisons, including which were female and which were male;

- a description of the gender neutral system used to evaluate job classes;

- where more than one method of comparison was permissible, the method of comparison used for each job class;

- the results of the comparisons;

- an identification of those job classes where permissible differences in compensation exited;

- for those job classes where differences in comparison exist which are not permissible, a description of how the compensation will be adjusted to achieve pay equity; and,

- a schedule for the payout of compensation adjustments.

PHYSICAL DISABILITY

Any degree of physical impairment, infirmity, malformation or disfigurement caused by bodily injury, birth defect or illness. Any rule, practice or procedure that treats an employee differently on the basis of his physical disability may constitute prohibited discrimination under human rights legislation. A wide range of physical conditions have been considered disabilities, for which accommodation by an employer will be required. Some examples of physical ailments that are physical disabilities include, but are not limited to: amputation, asthma, back problems, diabetes, epilepsy, hearing impairment, heart conditions, HIV and AIDS, lack of physical coordination, paralysis, physical reliance on a guide dog or wheelchair, speech impediment, or visual impairment. Alcohol and drug addictions have been found to be both a physical and a mental disability, while in certain circumstances obesity has been found to be a physical disability.

> *See also:* ALCOHOLISM, DISABILITY, DRUG DEPENDENCE, MENTAL DISABILITY, OBESITY

PLACE OF ORIGIN

> *See:* RACE

POLITICAL BELIEF

A belief in the tenets of a political party, demonstrated by membership in the party, contributions to the party, or open and active participation in the affairs of the party. Political belief is a prohibited ground of discrimination in a number of jurisdictions, including British Columbia, Manitoba, Newfoundland and Labrador, Prince Edward Island, Quebec and the Yukon.

PREGNANCY

> *See:* SEX

Human Rights

P

PROPORTIONAL VALUE COMPARISON

A method of job comparison that is set out in the Ontario *Pay Equity Act*. It is used to determine pay equity within an organization when an employer has female job classes with no appropriate male comparators under the job-to-job system. The proportional value method of comparison requires employers to look at the relationship between the value of the work performed and the pay received by male job classes, and apply the same relationship to setting the appropriate pay for female job classes.

> *See also:* PAY EQUITY, PROXY COMPARISON, WAGE LINE COMPARISON

PROXY COMPARISON

Under the Ontario *Pay Equity Act*, the proxy method of job comparison is only available to Ontario public sector employers where it has been determined that pay equity cannot be achieved through either job-to-job or proportional value comparisons. The proxy method of job comparison allows female job classes in public sector workplaces to be compared with similar job classes that have achieved pay equity in another public sector establishment. Employers in the broader public sector who may take advantage of the proxy comparison method, called SEEKING ORGANIZATIONS, include female predominant sectors such as homecare, nursing homes, corrections, childcare, and others.

> *See also:* PAY EQUITY, PROPORTIONAL VALUE COMPARISON, SEEKING ORGANIZATION, WAGE LINE COMPARISON

Q

QUALITY OF WORKING LIFE PROGRAM

A process designed to assist employers, unions and employees in implementing joint problem-solving approaches to improve the quality of working life within organizations, in the interests of improved labour-management relations, organizational effectiveness and employee work satisfaction.

> *See also:* WORK–LIFE BALANCE

R

RACE

A person's racial identity. Any rule, practice, procedure, action or inaction on the part of an employer that denies employment, or differentiates between employees based on race may constitute prohibited discrimination. A complaint of race discrimination will likely also include discrimination on the basis of colour, national or ethnic origin, or possibly ancestry. All jurisdictions in Canada prohibit discrimination on the basis of race.

RACIAL HARASSMENT

Harassment that occurs when a person engages in a vexatious course of action or makes comments that refer to or emphasize the race or race-related characteristics of an individual. It is prohibited under human rights legislation. The comment or conduct does not have to be directed at an individual employee to constitute racial harassment. Racial jokes, cartoons or comments, as well as the display of racist, derogatory or offensive pictures, graffiti or materials not directed at specific individuals may still constitute harassment. Harassment may also occur when the comment or conduct is motivated by a person's race, even if the harasser does not specifically refer to a person's race. For example, if an individual is consistently treated less favourably than others, and is the subject of practical jokes or derogatory slurs, it could be said that the behaviour was racially motivated even if no specific references to race are made.

Some examples of racial harassment include:

- offensive comments, slurs or insults;

- unwelcome remarks, jokes, innuendoes or taunting;

- displaying caricatures or other types of drawing or graphic materials;

- racially motivated physical assaults; or

- negative evaluations without appropriate basis.

See also: HARASSMENT, SEXUAL HARASSMENT

Human Rights

R

RED-CIRCLED RATE

A wage rate that is higher than a wage rate that has been newly established as a result of a pay equity plan or a job evaluation plan. Differences in pay rates between male- and female-dominated job classes may be permitted if the differences are based on red-circling.

See also: GREEN-CIRCLED RATE

RELIGION

A system of beliefs generally based on the existence of a deity. An employee is entitled to be free from discrimination on the basis of religion. Religion generally refers to a professed system and confession of faith, including both beliefs and observances or worship. Some religions that have been recognized by human rights tribunals include: Seventh Day Adventist, Baptist, Roman Catholic, Sikh, Worldwide Church of God, Jewish, Bahaism, Buddhist, Church of Scientology, Hindu, Islam, Jain Society of Toronto, Native Peoples (spiritual observances), Wicca, and Zoroastrian. Generally, religion will not include secular, moral or ethical beliefs or political convictions.

Religious discrimination will often occur as adverse effect discrimination, where a neutral rule that is applicable to all employees has the unintended effect of discriminating against employees who practice a certain religion. For example, a rule that all employees work on Saturday seems fair, but does not consider those employees whose religion prevents them from working on Saturday as it is considered a day of religious observance.

See also: CREED

RETIREMENT

A permanent withdrawal from the labour force.

There are a number of different types of retirement practices:

- **Delayed retirement** means that an employee retires after the normal retirement date, usually with the consent or at the request of the employer;

- **Disability retirement** is withdrawal before the normal retirement age because of physical incapacity;

- **Early retirement** is withdrawal before the normal retirement date; and

- **Mandatory retirement** is the requirement that employees retire on reaching a specified age.

  See also: AGE DISCRIMINATION

S

SEEKING ORGANIZATION

An employer in Ontario who has applied to the Pay Equity Commission to use a proxy method of comparison. These employers, who must be part of the broader public sector in Ontario, are in female predominant sectors of the workforce, such as homecare, nursing homes, corrections, childcare, and others. The proxy method of comparing jobs allows organizations that cannot use job-to-job or proportional value comparisons to still do pay equity. It allows an organization to find male comparators for its female jobs in an outside organization.

See also: PAY EQUITY, PROXY COMPARISON

SEX

The character of being male or female. It is a prohibited ground of discrimination that typically forms one of the biggest areas of complaints for employees and employers. Any rule, practice, procedure, action or inaction on the part of an employer that demonstrates a preference for, or provides a benefit for, one sex over another may constitute prohibited discrimination on the basis of sex.

Sex discrimination includes discrimination on the basis of pregnancy and child birth, where a woman may be refused a position, or be terminated as a result of her pregnancy or pregnancy-related leave.

SEXUAL HARASSMENT

Any conduct, comment, gesture or contact that is of a sexual nature, or that might on reasonable grounds be perceived as being of a sexual nature by a particular employee, and that is likely to cause offence or humiliation to an employee. It includes repeated sexual remarks or physical contact that is degrading, as well as threats or reprisals against a person who rejected a sexual advance.

Human Rights

S

Some examples of sexual harassment include:

- verbal abuse or threats;

- unwelcome remarks, jokes, innuendoes or taunting;

- displaying pornographic or other offensive or derogatory pictures;

- practical jokes causing awkwardness or embarrassment;

- unwelcome invitations or requests, whether indirect or explicit, or intimidation;

- leering or other gestures;

- unnecessary physical contact such as touching, patting, pinching or punching; or

- physical assault.

See also: HARASSMENT, RACIAL HARASSMENT, SEXUAL SOLICITATION

SEXUAL ORIENTATION

A person's orientation towards sexual relationships with persons of the opposite sex or same sex. Employees who are involved in a same-sex relationship are entitled to the same treatment in all respects of employment policies as opposite sex partners. Otherwise, discrimination on the basis of sexual orientation, or same-sex partnership status, will be found. Employers are not required to provide benefits to their employees, but if they do they will be required to treat same-sex employees and their partners equally to people with opposite sex partners.

It should be noted that Alberta does not specifically include sexual orientation as a prohibited ground of discrimination, but the Supreme Court of Canada has "read in" sexual orientation to the Alberta human rights legislation.

SEXUAL SOLICITATION

Sexual advances or invitations. Human rights legislation generally prohibits sexual solicitation by a person in a position of authority over an employee.

See also: SEXUAL HARASSMENT

SOCIAL CONDITIONS

A prohibited ground of discrimination under the Quebec *Charter of Human Rights and Freedoms*. It may include the right of each person, for himself and his family, to financial assistance and social measures provided by law in order to ensure an acceptable standard of living, as well as the right of every employee to fair and reasonable working conditions, having regard to the health, safety and physical well-being of the employee.

SOURCE OF INCOME

Individuals may legally derive their income from a number of places, including employment earnings, insurance, pensions, investments, government support programs such as social assistance, Worker's Compensation, Canada Pension Plan, along with many other possibilities. Some jurisdictions include source of income as a prohibited ground of discrimination in their human rights legislation. These jurisdictions include Manitoba, Nova Scotia, Prince Edward Island, Saskatchewan and Yukon.

SUBSTANTIALLY SIMILAR WORK

See: EQUAL PAY FOR SIMILAR OR SUBSTANTIALLY SIMILAR WORK

SYSTEMIC DISCRIMINATION

Discrimination that is widespread or traditionally inherent in a particular organization or context. For example, a male-dominated company may be alleged to engage in systemic discrimination against women.

See also: ADVERSE EFFECT DISCRIMINATION, DIRECT DISCRIMINATION, DISCRIMINATION

Human Rights

T

TELECOMMUTING

A work arrangement in which employees work at any time or place that allows them to accomplish their work in an effective and efficient manner, often by use of data transmission by telephone or cable. Usually, telecommuters will work from their home, although this is not necessarily the case.

T

Telecommuting provides a number of benefits for employers, including reduced costs in office space, improved productivity, enhanced worker recruitment and retention, reduced absenteeism and improved job satisfaction and morale. Not all companies, or positions, are appropriate for telecommuting. Some factors to consider include:

- The ability to monitor the employee's work;

- The nature of the job — administrative, professional, computer-based and communications jobs are often appropriate;

- The nature of the organization — information-based organizations are more appropriate than industrially-based;

- The nature of the employee — some workers may suffer from boredom, career concerns, family stress, or isolation;

- The situation of the employer — not enough office space, relocation costs, low morale, or high absenteeism may lead an employer to consider telecommuting;

- The organizational culture — should be proactive, open, committed to new ways of operating, and be able to maintain links between staff, functions and time; and

- Costs — tools, training, and processes necessary to alternative work arrangements.

See also: WORK-LIFE BALANCE

U

UNDUE HARDSHIP

An employer has a duty to accommodate an employee's disability (or religion, etc) up to the point of undue hardship. It is difficult to set out a test for undue hardship that will be appropriate in every situation, since each situation is unique. Each individual employee will require different forms and levels of accommodation, while each employer will be in a different situation in terms of their resources and ability to provide appropriate accommodation.

The possibility of performing the affected job in different ways while still accomplishing the employer's legitimate work-related purpose should be considered. Also, the skills, capabilities and potential contributions of the individual claimant and others like him must be respected as much as possible. Some factors that have been considered in assessing undue hardship include:

- costs of accommodation measure (generally seen as the most important factor in assessing undue hardship);

- disruption of operations;

- health and safety;

- major disruption of a collective agreement;

- size of employer's operations;

- problems of employee moral; and

- interchangeability of workforce and facilities.

See also: ACCOMMODATION, *BONA FIDE* OCCUPATIONAL REQUIREMENT, DISCRIMINATION, DUTY TO ACCOMMODATE

V

VALUE OF A JOB

Under pay equity legislation, employers are required to value jobs within the company, for the purposes of comparing jobs that are female-dominated and those that are male-dominated. The four key criteria used to assess the value of a job are:

- Skill: including intellectual and physical qualifications acquired by experience, training, education or natural ability. The methods by which skills are acquired may not be considered, though;

- Effort: including both physical and intellectual effort;

- Responsibility: for technical, financial or human resources positions;

- Working conditions: including both the physical and psychological conditions, such as noise, temperature, isolation, physical danger, health hazards, and stress.

Human Rights

V

VICARIOUS LIABILITY

Liability for the wrongful acts of another, even though the person being held responsible may not have done anything wrong. It is sometimes called "no fault" liability.

Vicarious liability often arises in situations where employers may be held vicariously liable for damages or harm caused by their employees. For example, an employer who operates a day care centre may be required to pay compensation to a child who had been sexually assaulted by an employee, even if the employer was unaware of the assault and could not have prevented it.

W

WAGE LINE COMPARISON

A method of job comparison for the purposes of pay equity, in which the wages for job classes are compared indirectly, by comparing female job classes with the earning curve of all predominantly male job classes.

See also: PAY EQUITY, PROPORTIONAL COMPARISON, PROXY COMPARISON

WORK-LIFE BALANCE

The balance between the demands of a person's work and her family or home life. Many employees in today's workforce face a conflict between their work responsibilities and family or other life commitments. Work-life conflicts are on the increase because of the changing nature of the workforce, the workplace, and the family model. The workplace is becoming more demanding, with workers facing ever-increasing productivity expectations. New technologies, such as e-mail, voice-mail, laptop computers and pagers have made it harder and harder for workers to truly get away from the office. At the same time, the traditional family structure, in which one partner had full-time responsibility for domestic concerns, such as childcare and household chores, while the other partner concentrated on his career, is less prevalent in society. Dual-income families are now the norm, rather than the exception. This work/life conflict shows up for employees as:

- Increased workload and hours of work;

- More stress;

- Declining physical and mental health;
- Increased absenteeism;
- Lower job satisfaction; and
- Lower commitment to employers.

Employers can assist employees in balancing their work and family lives by providing flexibility in hours of work, work options and leaves; providing childcare support; and, by showing understanding, compassion and sensitivity.

See also: FLEXTIME, FRINGE BENEFITS, QUALITY OF WORKING LIFE PROGRAM, TELECOMMUTING

Human Rights

W

HEALTH & SAFETY

A

ACCIDENT

An unexpected mishap or event, often resulting in injury to a worker. For the purposes of workers' compensation legislation, an accident must arise out of and occur in the course of employment in order for an employee injured in the accident to qualify for compensation.

ACCIDENT FUND

Under workers' compensation legislation, assessments are levied upon employers and gathered into a common fund, out of which benefits are paid to workers who are injured on the job.

C

CANADIAN CENTRE FOR OCCUPATIONAL HEALTH AND SAFETY (CCOHS)

An independently administered federal Crown corporation which provides a free information service about occupational health and safety. According to its mission statement, the CCOHS aims to be the Canadian Centre of Excellence for work-related injury and illness prevention initiatives and

Health & Safety

occupational health and safety information. To promote health and safety in the Canadian workplace, the CCOHS facilitates consultation and cooperation among jurisdictions and between labour and management, assists in the development and maintenance of policies and programs, and serves as a national centre for information relating to occupational health and safety.

Further information on the CCOHS is available on their Web site at **http://www.ccohs.ca/**.

COMPENSABLE INJURY

An injury for which the injured worker is entitled to benefits under workers' compensation legislation

> *See also:* PRE-EXISTING CONDITION

CONTROLLED PRODUCT

A hazardous material, product or substance as classified by WHMIS, and subject to WHMIS. Suppliers of controlled products within Canada are required to provide employers with information on the hazards, as well as the ingredients of the controlled products, through cautionary labels and material safety data sheets.

> *See also:* HAZARDOUS MATERIAL, MATERIAL SAFETY DATA SHEETS, WHMIS

D

DESIGNATED SUBSTANCE

A biological, chemical or physical agent, or combination of such agents, to which the exposure of an employee is prohibited, regulated, limited, restricted, or controlled. Such a designation is restricted to substances known to be particularly hazardous. For example, Ontario health and safety legislation has set out the following designated substances: acrylonitrile, arsenic, asbestos, benzene, coke oven emissions, ethylene oxide, isocyanates, lead, mercury, silica, and vinyl chloride.

DUE DILIGENCE

Actions taken that are prudent in the circumstances and that a person would reasonably be expected to do under particular circumstances. In the context of occupational health and safety legislation, due diligence means taking all reasonable precautions in order to prevent injuries or accidents in the workplace.

E

EMPLOYER DUTIES

Under health and safety legislation, an employer is under a positive duty to ensure the health and safety of its employees by preventing accidents and injury to health that arise out of, are linked with, or occur in the course of employment. Occupational health and safety legislation sets out in detail employer and employee requirements in an attempt to ensure the health and safety of employees at work.

Employers should take all reasonable measures to protect their workers' safety, comply with the legislation, and ensure that their workers do the same. This positive duty on employers includes cooperating with employees, providing training and instruction, ensuring competence, instituting health and safety programs, and inspecting the premises on a regular basis. A breach of a duty under health and safety legislation can result in charges, fines and possibly imprisonment.

See also: WORKERS' DUTIES

H

HAZARD INFORMATION

Information on the proper and safe use, storage and handling of a controlled product, including information relating to its toxicological properties.

See also: CONTROLLED PRODUCT

HAZARD SYMBOL

Any visible indication displayed on a controlled product or container to show the nature of the product's hazard.

See also: CONTROLLED PRODUCT

Health & Safety

H

HAZARDOUS AGENT

See: HAZARDOUS MATERIAL

HAZARDOUS MATERIAL

Any prohibited, restricted or controlled product subject to WHMIS. Under WHMIS, there are six classes of hazardous materials:

- compressed gases;

- flammable and combustible materials;

- oxidizing materials;

- poisonous and infectious materials;

- corrosive materials; and

- dangerously reactive materials.

There are nine categories of materials that are excluded from WHMIS regulation, because other legislative schemes deal with these substances, although they may eventually be added to WHMIS. They include:

- explosives;

- cosmetics, drugs, food or devices;

- pest control products (pesticides, herbicides, insecticides)

- radioactive materials;

- consumer restricted products;

- wood and products made of wood;

- tobacco and products made of tobacco;

- manufactured articles; and

- hazardous waste.

See also: CONTROLLED PRODUCT, MATERIAL SAFETY DATA SHEET, WHMIS

HAZARDOUS OCCUPATIONS

Jobs which are classified as dangerous by provincial or federal laws, and in which employment of minors is restricted or forbidden. Federal legislation provides workers with the right to refuse work that is considered hazardous to health or safety.

HEALTH AND SAFETY COMMITTEE

A committee composed of workers and management, set up for the purpose of promoting a greater concern for improvement of safety and health in the workplace. In most jurisdictions these committees are called joint health and safety committees, and are required by legislation where the employer employs more than a certain number of employees at a workplace.

See also: JOINT HEALTH AND SAFETY COMMITTEE

HEALTH AND SAFETY REPRESENTATIVES

In some smaller workplaces, instead of organizing a joint health and safety committee, health and safety representatives may be appointed to be a liaison between the employer and their coworkers. The representative is responsible for inspecting the workplace, identifying workplace hazards, making recommendation to the employer, investigating work refusals, and investigating serious accidents. Health and safety representatives are required in some jurisdictions for smaller employers.

See also: JOINT HEALTH AND SAFETY COMMITTEE

I

INDUSTRIAL HEALTH

A branch of public health which concerns itself with the health and well-being of workers. A body of rules and practices have evolved with the object of eliminating hazards and industrial fatigue in the work environment.

J

JOINT HEALTH AND SAFETY COMMITTEE

A work place committee composed of representatives of workers and management whose duties relate to the initiation and maintenance of a safe and healthy work place. Established by the relevant health and safety legislation in each jurisdiction, the committee may be mandatory, or discretionary.

J

Health & Safety

Representatives of the committee meet on a regular basis to deal with health and safety issues in the workplace by: identifying potential health and safety problems and bringing them to the employer's attention; receiving, considering and disposing of worker complaints relating to health and safety in the workplace; establishing educational programs; participating in health and safety-related inquiries and investigations; and accessing government and employer reports and information on behalf of employees.

See also: HEALTH AND SAFETY COMMITTEE, HEALTH AND SAFETY REPRESENTATIVES

M

MATERIAL SAFETY DATA SHEET

A document required by WHMIS on which specified information regarding a controlled product is disclosed. The data sheet sets out what the hazards of the product are, how to use the product safely, what to expect if recommendations are not followed, what to do if accidents occur, how to recognize symptoms of overexposure, and what to do if such incidents occur. The sheets are more comprehensive than a supplier or workplace label, and they are sent by the supplier to the employer with every new controlled product they buy. A data sheet may not be more than three years old, and an employer must have one for each product it produces.

There are nine categories of information that a supplier must provide on a material safety data sheet:

1. Hazardous Ingredients: chemical names, percentages, and acute toxicity data for the individual components;

2. Preparation Information: who is responsible for preparation and date of preparation of the data sheet;

3. Product Information: product identifiers (name), manufacturer and suppliers' names, addresses and emergency phone numbers;

4. Physical Data: physical and chemical properties;

5. Fire or Explosion Hazard: conditions under which product may catch fire or explode;

6. Reactivity Data: information on the chemical instability of a product and the substances it may react with;

7. Toxicological Properties: health effects;

8. Preventative Measures: protective equipment, how to safely use, handle, store, dispose of and transport controlled products; and

9. First Aid Measures: instructions for immediate treatment of personal injury as a result of exposure to the controlled product.

See also: CONTROLLED PRODUCT, HAZARDOUS MATERIAL, WHMIS

O

OCCUPATIONAL DISEASE

A disease that is caused by the condition of a work site. For example, coal miners may develop black lung, or a nurse may be infected with HIV from a contaminated needle. Some jurisdictions in Canada have legislation that lists occupational diseases and industries or processes that are connected with those diseases.

OCCUPATIONAL EXPOSURE LIMITS (OELs)

For airborne contaminants, a safe limit below which no ill health effects will result from exposure. There are three types of OELs:

1. Time-weighted average exposure limits (TWAEL) — average of the concentration of an airborne contaminant to which an employee may be exposed daily in an 8-hour day or a 40-hour week without harmful health effects;

2. Short-term exposure limits (STEL) — maximum concentration of an airborne contaminant to which an employee may be exposed in any period of up to 15 minutes; only four exposures per workday are permitted at such maximum levels, there must be a 60 minute interval between exposures, and the TWAEL for the workday cannot be exceeded;

3. Ceiling exposure limit (C or CEL) — maximum concentration of an airborne contaminant to which one may be exposed at any time.

Health & Safety

R

Note: dust, fumes, mists and aerosols are measured in milligrams of material per cubic meter of air (mg/m³), while gases, vapours and smoke are measured in parts per million of air (ppm) or in mg/m³.

See also: THRESHOLD LIMIT VALUES

P

PHYSICAL AGENTS

Sources of energy that may cause injury or disease, such as noise, vibration, radiation, and extremes in temperature or pressure.

PRE-EXISTING CONDITION

In workers' compensation law, a mental or physical condition that existed prior to the compensable injury, such as diabetes, or arthritis. Generally, an employee will not be entitled to benefits for disability resulting solely from the effects of his or her pre-existing condition, although if the pre-existing condition causes no disability, but reacts with some occupational factor to produce a disability, the employee will generally be entitled to be compensated for the entire disability.

See also: COMPENSABLE INJURY

R

RIGHT TO REFUSE UNSAFE WORK

A statutory right of workers to refuse to perform work which they have reasonable cause to believe would constitute an imminent danger to the health or safety of themselves or other workers. The worker must inform his employer or supervisor immediately of the unsafe work, and an investigation must be conducted. The employee may not be suspended, fired or docked pay for refusing unsafe work, although the employee must first have reasonable cause to believe that the work is dangerous.

See also: WORKERS' RIGHTS

T

THRESHOLD LIMIT VALUES (TLVs)

Restrictions on the exposure of workers to hazardous chemical substances in the workplace. They are set by the American Conference of Governmental Industrial Hygienists at levels that are generally believed will not cause adverse health effects in most adult workers, even with repeated daily exposure. TLVs form the basis for most occupational health and safety laws set by the provinces and territories, and they are based on animal and human exposure studies. TLVs have been adopted into Occupational Exposure Limits (OELs) in many jurisdictions in Canada.

The three types of TLVs are:

1. Threshold Limit Value - Time-Weighted Average (TLV-TWA) — time-weighted average concentration for a normal 8-hour work day or a 40-hour work week to which nearly all workers may be repeatedly exposed without adverse effect;

2. Threshold Limit Value - Short-term Exposure Limit (TLV-STEL) — maximum concentration to which an employee can be exposed for a period up to 15 minutes continuously without suffering adverse effects, provided exposure does not occur more than four times per day at intervals of not less than 60 minutes, and provided the TLV-TWA is not exceeded;

3. Threshold Limit Value - Ceiling (TLV-C) — concentration of exposure that should not be exceeded even instantaneously.

See also: OCCUPATIONAL EXPOSURE LIMITS

TOXIC SUBSTANCES

A chemical or biological agent that, when inhaled, ingested or absorbed into the body in an excessive dose, is an irritant, allergen, asphyxiant, poison, carcinogen, mutagen, or teratogen. Therefore, it is a substance that has a harmful health effect that may vary in severity. These substances are also commonly termed hazardous substances, hazardous materials, or hazardous agents.

See also: HAZARDOUS MATERIAL

Health & Safety

T

W

WHMIS

Workplace Hazardous Materials Information System (WHMIS) is a nation-wide program that is designed to protect workers and employers by providing them with specific health and safety information about hazardous materials used or produced in the workplace. The objective of the program is to ensure that employers and employees have the information that they need to work safely with controlled products by means of product labels, material safety data sheets and worker education and training programs.

See also: CONTROLLED PRODUCT, HAZARDOUS MATERIALS, MATERIAL SAFETY DATA SHEET

WORK INJURIES FREQUENCY RATE

A ratio calculated as:

$$\frac{\text{Number of disabling injuries}}{\text{Number of person-hours worked}} \times 1{,}000{,}000$$

WORK INJURIES SEVERITY RATE

A ratio calculated as:

$$\frac{\text{Days lost}}{\text{Number of person-hours worked}} \times 1{,}000{,}000$$

WORKER EDUCATION AND TRAINING PROGRAM

Certain employers must develop, implement and maintain a hazardous products education and training program for their employees. Employees are required to be educated and trained if they: store, handle, use or dispose of a controlled product; supervise or manage employees who do the above; or work near a controlled product such that the employee could be at risk during normal storage, handling, use or disposal of the product, during maintenance operations or in emergencies such as an accidental leak or spill. The program must be developed and implemented by the employer in consultation with the applicable health and safety committee. The employer should review the information and training provided to employees with the health and safety committee at least once a year, or more frequently if new conditions arise.

See also: CONTROLLED PRODUCT, JOINT HEALTH AND SAFETY COMMITTEE

WORKERS' COMPENSATION

A disability insurance system that protects both employers and employees against the impact of work-related injuries. It compensates injured workers for lost income, health care and other costs related to an injury sustained on the job, and also protects employers from being sued in the courts by workers for workplace injuries. Benefits are paid out of a fund, and each province has its own workers' compensation legislation:

❑ Federal: *Government Employees' Compensation Act,* R.S. 1985, c. G-5

❑ Alberta: *Workers' Compensation Act,* R.S.A. 2000, c. W-15

❑ British Columbia: *Workers Compensation Act,* R.S.B.C. 1996, c. 492

❑ Manitoba: *The Workers Compensation Act,* R.S.M. 1987, c. W200

❑ New Brunswick: *Workers' Compensation Act,* R.S.N.B. 1973, c. W-13

❑ Newfoundland and Labrador: *Workplace Health, Safety and Compensation Act,* R.S.N.L. 1990, c. W-11

❑ Nova Scotia: *Workers' Compensation Act,* S.N.S. 1994-95, c. 10

❑ Ontario: *Workplace Safety and Insurance Act, 1997,* S.O. 1997, c. 16

❑ Prince Edward Island: *Workers' Compensation Act,* S.P.E.I. 1994, c. W-7.1

❑ Quebec: *Act Respecting Industrial Accidents and Occupational Diseases,* R.S.Q., c. A-3.001

❑ Saskatchewan: *The Workers' Compensation Act, 1979,* S.S. 1979, c. W-17.1

❑ Northwest Territories and Nunavut: *Workers' Compensation Act,* R.S.N.W.T. 1988, c. W-6

Health & Safety

W

❏ Yukon: *Workers' Compensation Act*, S.Y. 1992, c. 16

See also: ACCIDENT, ACCIDENT FUND, WORKERS' COMPEN-
SATION BOARD

WORKERS' COMPENSATION BOARD

A workplace accident insurance system established in each province, that
gives workers who suffer workplace injuries health care benefits, financial
assistance and vocational rehabilitation. All of the benefits and services that
are provided by the boards are paid for by participating employers, through
assessments.

See also: WORKERS' COMPENSATION

WORKERS' DUTIES

All workers must comply with safety requirements, as set out in the applicable occupational health and safety legislation, in order to protect themselves and others in the workplace. The required duties include: taking
reasonable care to protect the health and safety of himself and his co-
workers; using personal protection and safety equipment as required; following safe work procedures; reporting any injury or illness immediately;
reporting unsafe acts and unsafe conditions; and participating in joint health
and safety committees. Under most statutes, workers can be charged with
safety violations, and if convicted, be subject to a fine and/or imprisonment.

See also: EMPLOYER DUTIES, WORKERS' RIGHTS

WORKERS' RIGHTS

All workers have three fundamental rights under occupational health and
safety legislation:

- Right to know or to be informed about known or foreseeable hazards
  in the workplace;

- Right to refuse dangerous work if they have reasonable cause to
  believe that a situation constitutes a danger to themselves or another
  worker; and

- Right to participate in identifying and resolving job-related safety and
  health problems.

See also: EMPLOYER DUTIES, RIGHT TO REFUSE UNSAFE
WORK, WORKERS' DUTIES

TOPICAL INDEX